BEYOND BRIEF COUNSELING AND THERAPY

AN INTEGRATIVE APPROACH

Second Edition

JACK H. PRESBURY

LENNIS G. ECHTERLING

J. EDSON MCKEE

All of James Madison University

PEARSON

Merrill
Prentice Hall

Upper Saddle River, New Jersey
Columbus, Ohio

Library of Congress Cataloging-in-Publication Data

Presbury, Jack H.
  Beyond brief counseling and therapy : an integrative approach / Jack H.
Presbury, Lennis G. Echterling, J. Edson McKee. — 2nd ed.
    p. ; cm.
  Rev. ed. of: Ideas and tools for brief counseling. c2002.
  Includes bibliographical references and index.
  ISBN 0-13-230092-3
  1. Brief psychotherapy. 2. Short-term counseling. I. Echterling, Lennis
G., 1948- II. McKee, J. Edson. III. Presbury, Jack H. Ideas and tools for brief counseling. IV. Title.
  [DNLM: 1. Psychotherapy, Brief—methods. 2. Emotions. 3. Narration. 4.
Professional-Patient Relations. WM 420.5.P5 P928b 2008]
  RC480.55.P72 2008
  616.89'14—dc22

                                                    2007015265

Vice President and Executive Publisher:
  Jeffery W. Johnston
Publisher: Kevin M. Davis
Editor: Meredith D. Fossel
Senior Editorial Assistant: Kathleen S. Burk
Project Manager: Mary Harlan
Production Coordination: Pine Tree Composition, Inc.

Design Coordinator: Diane C. Lorenzo
Cover Design: Jeff Vanik
Cover Image: Jupiter Images
Production Manager: Susan W. Hannahs
Director of Marketing: David Gesell
Marketing Manager: Autumn Purdy
Marketing Coordinator: Brian Mounts

The previous edition of this text was published under the title *Ideas and Tools for Brief Counseling.*

This book was set in Berkeley by Laserwords Private Limited, Chennai. It was printed and bound by
R. R. Donnelley & Sons Company. The cover was printed by R. R. Donnelley & Sons Company.

Pearson Education Ltd.
Pearson Education Singapore Pte. Ltd.
Pearson Education Canada, Ltd.
Pearson Education–Japan

Pearson Education Australia Pty. Limited
Pearson Education North Asia Ltd.
Pearson Educación de Mexico, S.A. de C.V.
Pearson Education Malaysia Pte. Ltd.

10 9 8 7 6 5 4 3 2 1
ISBN-13: 978-0-13-230092-6
ISBN-10:   0-13-230092-3

This book is dedicated to our families—
our wives, our children, and our students
in the Brief and Crisis Counseling classes.

PREFACE

Many second editions of books simply involve updating the literature, adding more recent innovations in the field, and discarding material that is no longer relevant. However, we have made dramatic changes in this second edition of our brief counseling text. In fact, we have changed the title to reflect these major revisions, additions, and exciting developments in the field.

In 2005, Lewis stated that there were approximately fifty brief models of counseling and psychotherapy existing in the literature. Gross and Capuzzi (2007) characterized the movement toward brief approaches as "a major player in today's counseling and therapy marketplace" (p. 25). In light of this movement, you may wonder why we have selected as our main title *Beyond Brief Counseling and Therapy*. It is because "brief" is no longer, in our estimation, the main focus of the work. If one adopts an attitude of working efficiently and deliberately with clients, places the emphasis on client strengths, and sets goals for the future, then the work will proceed briefly. In other words, "brief" is a by-product of this attitude.

In the 1980s and 1990s, brief counseling approaches challenged the generally accepted assumption that counseling and therapy must be lengthy in order to bring about any significant and lasting personal change. Today, the belief that working briefly can create effective and life-changing outcomes for many clients is becoming generally accepted. However, concepts such as the relationship, empathy, meaning, and the eliciting of emotions seem to have faded due to the prevailing focus on problem solution. Furthermore, the trend toward "manualized" approaches to counseling based on empirical research has appeared to turn the counselor–client relationship into an inflexible algorithm of counselor interventions. With this movement, the uniqueness of each individual client is sometimes overlooked. Many of the crucial insights regarding the counseling relationship that have been developed over the past 100 years appear to have become the "baby tossed out with the bathwater." We believe that the time is right to go beyond manualized models, to seek an integrative approach to brief counseling and therapy, to recapture the facilitative aspects of the relationship, and to re-humanize the process. In fact, many of today's interveners are beginning to reinvent intervention. They appear to be creating a synthesis of newer brief approaches with the effective common factors of therapy that have been developed over many years.

The subtitle we have selected is *An Integrative Approach*. The techniques offered in this book spring mostly from narrative and brief counseling, but they are presented as useful only if you pay close attention to your relationship with the client. This important idea was earlier articulated by Carl Rogers as the therapeutic set of "core conditions" (Prochaska & Norcross, 2007). As most research shows, it is the way you collaborate with your client that does the work. Although we have drawn heavily from a postmodern view, we did not want to abandon the rich discoveries that counselors and therapists have made during the profession's first century. Although most books on brief counseling and therapy emphasize their differences from traditional approaches, we offer a bridge between the past and the future. The postmodern era challenges us to reconsider our beliefs and to do something different than we have done before. Taking up this challenge, in this volume we attempt to go *Beyond Brief Counseling and Therapy*.

Chapter 1, "Foundations of Brief Counseling: The Fly Bottle," offers the rationale for using a brief approach to counseling. Many practitioners in the helping professions are questioning the old notions of the mechanistic and medical models that view clients as defective machines or as pathological protoplasm. These counselors are now attempting to understand the process of change itself and are trying to find ways to tap the natural resources that clients possess. These new approaches to helping are vindicating older humanistic notions of potential and growth.

Chapter 2, "The Centrality of the Counseling Relationship: No Magic Tricks," points out that any technique will fail unless you have established a relationship with your client. In this chapter, we discuss the various common factors that have been found by many researchers to be indispensable to the counseling process. Such research inevitably leads back to Carl Rogers, who articulated the core conditions for a successful counseling relationship. We discuss the concepts of empathy and acknowledgment, as well as the "LUV Triangle"—listening, understanding, and validating the client's perspective. We also describe Bill O'Hanlon's technique, "Carl Rogers with a Twist," which is a way of adding possibility statements to our reflections of client concerns.

Chapter 3, "Empathy and Caring," is the heart, not only of this book but also of any successful counseling relationship. In fact, empathy and caring are the heart of what makes us human. We discuss the recent neurological research that demonstrates how people are hardwired to be empathic beings. We also explore how empathy involves both cognitive and emotional features. The techniques you practice in this chapter are relevant to all counseling, and they include communicating empathically with clients, using your self as a therapeutic tool, and using reverse empathy to promote your client's sense of resolve.

Chapter 4, "Helping Clients Frame Goals: The Pull of the Future," suggests that it is teleology—not etiology—that is the main concern of successful counselors. You start your counseling work with a view to the future, rather than to the past. One of the most effective counseling activities is helping clients to frame their goals. Goals serve as beacons that can guide your counseling work. In this chapter, we discuss how to develop well-formed goals and how to ascertain whether your counseling relationship is one in which your client is complaining, visiting, engaging fully, or participating involuntarily. We also describe how to use the tools of finding exceptions and scaling techniques.

Chapter 5, "Facilitating and Perturbing Change: Counseling and Chaos," is based on the fundamental point that change is always happening. As a change agent, you are facilitating this change process by helping clients to alter their perceptions, revise their representations, and expand their openness to possibilities. People are complex systems—living systems that are adaptive and self-organizing. Instead of falling apart, complex adaptive systems reorganize themselves and grow. When they are perturbed, they experience brief periods of chaos, but then put themselves back together in a new way in the process of emergence. The specific tools you will be practicing in this chapter are helping your clients to reframe their concerns, offering techniques that help people to reorganize their thinking, and presenting counterintuitive interventions that perturb clients and encourage them to think differently.

Chapter 6, "Constructivist Counseling: Invented and Imposed Realities," offers alternate ways of looking at reality through social constructionism and constructivism. Social constructions are the worldviews, expectations, and stereotypes that culture imposes on individual members. Constructivism is the belief that one's personal reality is invented, rather than discovered. One assumption of constructivism is that one can never fully know another person's reality from an objective stance. Only by encountering a client in an authentic relationship can you gain an empathic knowledge of that person's experiential world. Your goal in counseling is not to get clients to become more realistic, but to help them reconstruct the way they are representing themselves and their world. One of the important tools for deconstructing a client's negative story—and co-constructing a better one—is your use of the question. In this chapter, we offer you suggestions on how to use questions effectively and discuss some questions you should avoid. The "miracle question" technique is a way of inviting the client to construct a detailed scene in which the client has resolved the major concerns of his or her life. Each of these techniques is discussed in this chapter, as well as how to encourage, rather than praise or reinforce, client behaviors.

Chapter 7, "Narrative Counseling: Clients' Lives as Stories," focuses on the notion that humans are the only species who are storytellers. Moreover, metaphors are not just narrative tools for poets and artists: Clients use them as they portray their concerns, and counselors use them to communicate empathy and promote reframing. Clients come to counselors with stories that are outdated, tragic, and rigidified. As a result, these clients experience their lives as repetitive, negative, and unchangeable. Your task as a counselor is to help your client create a new and therapeutic narrative.

Building on the two previous chapters, Chapter 8, "Meaningful Stories, Meaningful Lives," offers ideas and tools for helping your clients transform their experiences into something meaningful that promotes successful change. No matter what concerns or problems your clients bring to you, the problems are always rooted in the implicit philosophy of life that your clients have adopted. Therefore, one of the fundamental points of this chapter is that your clients, as meaning makers, are not passive victims of their troubling circumstances. Instead, they are on an active quest to seek meaning as they attempt to find a resolution to their concerns.

Chapter 9, "Brains, Emotions, Thoughts, and Counseling: Cool Reason and Hot-Wiring," discusses the importance of managing emotional arousal in clients. A common misconception is that emotions are messy contaminants to effective problem solving. In fact, discoveries in neuroscience are revealing that emotions are essential to good thinking. Other research has shown that, when you are counseling, you are influencing a brain in ways that lead to actual neurological changes. In this chapter, you will also learn how to manage your client's emotional arousal by the use of immediacies and gentle interpretations.

As a counselor, you will regularly deal with people in critical circumstances. Even if your community agency, mental health center, school, or private practice does not emphasize emergency services, you will find yourself frequently performing some form of crisis counseling. Therefore, Chapter 10, "Counseling People in Crisis: Promoting Resilience and Resolution," describes how you can adapt brief counseling techniques to crisis situations. The particular strategies discussed include reaching out with LUV, finding the survivor, helping the survivor take heart, and helping the survivor to begin moving on toward a successful resolution. The goal of crisis counseling is to help victims become survivors who can go on to become thrivers in their lives.

Chapter 11, "The Reflecting Team, Consulting Break, and Offering Suggestions," presents strategies for the latter portion of the counseling session. We describe the reflecting team, a technique involving other counselors in your work. We also discuss the distinction between suggestions and advice. Advice is when you "just tell 'em," but suggestions are more subtle and tailored to your client's style. Finally, we include guidelines for offering successful suggestions.

In Chapter 12, "The 'Brief Attitudes' and Consolidating Change," we review the fundamental attitudes of successful brief counseling. Brief counseling is not just a set of techniques to be applied to a problem. Rather, it is an attitude about the nature of reality, people's resilience, the process of change, and the importance of every therapy session. In this chapter, we describe how you can capitalize on positive momentum once you have completed the initial session with your client. We discuss techniques for deciding when to terminate with clients, as well as rituals for consolidating changes that the client has made. Clients sometimes have misgivings at the termination of counseling, so we suggest some ways of dealing with these.

In Chapter 13, "Humanistic Counseling and Working With Involuntary Clients," we present an integration of brief and humanistic perspectives and practices. We propose that brief counseling can have "depth" results that reach all the way into the self of the client. Also, we discuss in greater detail the challenges presented by the involuntary client. We offer hints on helping this person to become engaged more fully in the counseling process and suggestions for dealing with the referring third party.

Finally, in Chapter 14, "Other Brief Approaches and Theory as a Tool," we explore the exciting developments toward integrative approaches to counseling and therapy and speculate on future practices. We discuss specific brief approaches, such as motivational interviewing, brief Gestalt therapy, time-limited existential therapy, brief psychodynamic therapy, brief behavior therapy, and brief cognitive-behavioral therapy. We end this chapter by emphasizing theory as a practical tool in your counseling and therapy work. To help you begin the task of developing your personal theory of counseling, we suggest that five main approaches to helping are emphasized by the existing theories.

By understanding the ideas and using the tools of brief counseling, you can increase your success as a counselor. In addition to reading this book, we encourage you to attend workshops and presentations on this approach to helping people. We have found attending workshops with Bill O'Hanlon, Michelle Weiner Davis, Donald Meichenbaum, Scott Miller, and others to be inspiring and important in our own development as counselors. Many of the people mentioned in this book are actively involved in training. Seek them out. Obviously, reading this book can only be one step in your professional growth as a counselor. We wish you much success in your journey.

ACKNOWLEDGMENTS

Many people have supported and assisted us in writing this book. Our graduate students conscientiously read early drafts, enthusiastically gave us detailed feedback, and diplomatically presented helpful suggestions. We are especially indebted to David Yost for his help with this manuscript. Our colleagues generously offered both their clinical expertise and personal encouragement. We also appreciate the conscientious work of the reviewers for this edition. Their careful attention to detail and suggestions for improvements were a tremendous help. We are grateful for the expertise they brought to this endeavor as both practitioners and educators. Thanks to Margaret Herrick, Kutztown University of Pennsylvania; Nicholas Mazza, Florida State University; Timothy C. Thomason, Northern Arizona University; and Riley H. Venable, Texas Southern University. We gratefully acknowledge their countless contributions and constant encouragement.

Our families were tireless in their support and forbearance. In particular, we thank Barbara McKee, Lin Presbury, and Mary Lou Wylie, our constant companions on our life journeys. With intuitive artistry and determined persistence, they have tolerated our writing projects, nurtured us through our troubled times, and reminded us of the beauty and joy that exist beyond brief counseling and therapy.

BRIEF CONTENTS

CONTENTS

NOTE: Every effort has been made to provide accurate and current Internet information in this book. However, the Internet and information posted on it are constantly changing, so it is inevitable that some of the Internet addresses listed in this textbook will change.

CHAPTER 1

Foundations of Brief Counseling
The Fly Bottle

"[My aim] is to shew the fly the way out of the fly bottle"
Ludwig Wittgenstein

CHAPTER GOALS

The goals of this chapter are to help you understand the following fundamental ideas and use these tools:

- Counselors who understand theory are likely to be more flexible, creative, and effective in their use of techniques.
- Brief counseling has become an integrated approach, borrowing from many theories and techniques.
- The focus of brief counseling also has evolved. At first, it was on the cause of a problem, then on how it was maintained, and then on its solution. Now the focus is on facilitating the resolution of a client's concern.
- No matter what brief counseling techniques you may use, you need to follow some essential guidelines.
- Actively using the tools in this book will help you gain a greater experiential understanding of the brief counseling concepts and develop skills in performing brief techniques.

STORY

In this book, we want to underscore the place of narrative in successful brief therapy. We see our task with clients as one of helping them to find their voices and tell their stories in ways that lead to healing, growing, and achieving goals. So, in keeping with this emphasis on narrative, we have decided to tell the story of this book's creation.

Like most stories, this one begins with some foreshadowing of things to come. As therapists and counselor educators, we had grappled with the challenges and frustrations of managed care, heard the many calls for brief interventions, and felt tempted by the appeal of promising new therapeutic approaches. We also were intrigued by the possibility that the counseling profession was on the verge of a major paradigm shift.

At the same time, we had serious doubts and concerns. Over the years, we had developed a healthy skepticism about therapeutic fads, which seemed to pop up far too frequently in the counseling field. After observing this cycle—initially unrealistic promises, rumblings of misgivings, disappointing findings, and the ultimate discarding of the approach—take place time and time again, we came to assume that, if the claims for a counseling technique sounded too good to be true, they probably were.

In addition to these doubts, we also had concerns that these techniques might sabotage the counselor's ability to be authentic, warm, and accepting—the foundation, as we saw it, of any effective counseling. To us, many of the brief therapy strategies smacked of manipulation and seemed almost Machiavellian in their emphasis on maneuvering clients and orchestrating change. Nevertheless, in spite of our strong ambivalence, we decided to pursue our interest in brief counseling.

Early in our investigation, we attended a workshop on solution-focused brief therapy. After becoming quite excited by this way of working with clients, we asked the workshop presenter a question about the theory behind the techniques she was presenting. Her reply was startling, "We don't care how this works. We just know that it does." As we discussed her answer among ourselves, we came to the humbling realization that our own behaviors reflected a similarly cavalier attitude regarding theory. We became troubled by our sense of sloppy thinking as we had continued to add techniques, willy-nilly, without considering the implications of these strategies on our fundamental assumptions about people and change. We began looking for some ideas that could inspire and inform our tools—rather than tools that would mold our ideas or, worse yet, muddy our thinking.

As we reflected on how the counseling and psychotherapy profession had changed over the years, we recalled reading *On Becoming a Person* (1961) and *Client-Centered Therapy* (1951) in graduate school. At the time, we wondered how we would ever learn to be the kind of therapist Carl Rogers described and seemed to personify. We were fortunate that many of our mentors, professors, and supervisors were skilled therapists, but their expertise seemed dauntingly beyond our reach. They appeared to be guided by an inner peace or set of principles that allowed them to be approachable and unpretentious. Even though they often ventured into new and threatening territory, they had an air of confidence—even serenity—about themselves as they engaged with clients—by caring, not by giving answers. They had a way of being intensely interested in people, tuning into the rich themes of their stories, and communicating a profound faith in the ability of clients to change, grow, and heal. They were patient and accepting and did not feel compelled to comment just to fill the silence. When they did talk, almost everything sounded profound. We listened, learned, and discovered, in our encounters with them, that we actually knew more than we thought we knew about the therapeutic process.

Then, decades after our own graduate training, we found ourselves in another period of doubt, turmoil, confusion, and self-examination regarding our identities as practitioners and trainers. Will we be able to use—and teach—brief techniques and still be true to ourselves? Are those lessons about the importance of the relationship, core dimensions, and common factors in therapy that we learned years ago still valuable to the counseling trainees of today?

After months of reading the philosophical and counseling literature, thinking about these concepts, talking (and arguing!) with one another, counseling clients, and training counselors, we agreed that our answer is an enthusiastic "yes!" Our hope is that reading this book will enlighten, assist, and encourage as much change for you as writing it did for us.

REFLECTING QUESTIONS

1. What are your own reactions to our story?
2. How does our initial ambivalence regarding the idea of brief therapy compare to your reaction?
3. At this time, what is your vision of yourself in the future as a brief therapist?

OVERVIEW

Our Goals

Since we emphasize throughout this book the fundamental centrality of goals in all effective interventions, we want to begin the book with a statement of our own goals. First, we wanted to create a book that is well grounded in theory. Many books on brief therapy emphasize the practice of techniques without a serious consideration of the ideas, concepts, and philosophical assumptions that offer a foundation and a meaningful framework for these strategies. Of course, we want intervention strategies that are useful and effective, but these techniques ultimately must be based on a supporting theory if our interventions are to make any sense to us. Our aim is to strike a balance between ideas and tools by providing a rationale for the various interventions, and by offering you opportunities to experience these ideas through activities and practice. It is our belief that theory without application is only a meaningless light show, and that technique without a guiding theory is merely a shot in the dark.

Our second goal was to produce a book that is truly integrative. While some other books on brief approaches emphasize their differences from traditional counseling and therapy, we wanted a book that offers a bridge between the past and the future. The postmodern era challenges us to reconsider our beliefs and to do something different than we have done before. It does not require, however, that we abandon the rich discoveries counselors and therapists have made during the profession's first century. We also bring to our discussion the exciting breakthroughs in neuroscience research that deepen our understanding of such concepts as empathy, personal change, and achieving resolution. Finally, in the spirit of integration, we draw upon a variety of current theoretical perspectives, including, for example, cognitive-behavioral, existential, humanistic, and systemic.

Our third goal was to highlight the issue of culture. In this book, we will be using the term *culture* to mean more than ethnicity or race. We also include gender, age, sexual orientation, physical ability, social class, religion, and spirituality as cultural issues involved in offering brief counseling. Most theorists and practitioners of brief counseling approaches have not emphasized the importance of taking a multicultural point of view in working with clients. However, we believe that the concepts and techniques resonate quite well with respect to different worldviews, appreciation of the strengths and resources of diverse cultures, and recognition of the impact of oppression.

The recent research is now lending support for the efficacy of brief approaches in different cultures. For example, in one study in China, researchers found that solution-focused brief therapy, combined with paroxetine, demonstrated significant efficacy in treating clients suffering from obsessive-compulsive disorder, as compared to a randomly assigned control group of clients who received medication only (Fang-Ru, Shuang-Luo, & Wen-Feng, 2005). A brief approach also was helpful in promoting family harmony among East Asian elders, who valued filial piety, and their younger family members, who grew up in the United States and did not share their elders' expectations (Lee & Mjelde-Mossey, 2004). In addressing the cultural dissonance, family counselors used such strategies as incorporating multiple worldviews, collaborating with each family member, using cultural strengths and resources, and employing face-saving techniques.

If we respect each one of our clients as an individual with a unique culture, we must then remain humble about what we can know of his or her world prior to our first meeting. Most versions of brief counseling demand that the counselor approach the client as a "nonexpert" who must inquire in order to grasp the client's unique world. With these three goals in mind—theoretical grounding, the integration of various counseling approaches, and an appreciation for multicultural perspectives—we embarked on this project.

IDEAS

A Rationale for Theory

> "I came to theory because I was hurting."
> —*bell hooks*

Steve de Shazer (1991) maintained that precisely how the therapy works is something we can never know: "One can only know that it does work. . . . Make up your own explanation; it is as good or better than mine" (pp. xvii–xviii). At de Shazer's invitation, we shall attempt in this book to delve more deeply into an explanation that will place this type of work in a theoretical context and that will explain how the techniques achieve their impact.

While technicians without a theory are groping in the dark, it is also true that counselors should not let grand theories become the driving force in their work with clients. It is most important to remain open to what is happening in your relationship with a client, whether it fits the theory or not. As Bill O'Hanlon (1995) said, "It's OK to have a theory, so long as the theory doesn't have you."

Many members of the counseling profession—students, practitioners, and educators— seem to place little value in theory. When you enter a professional counselor's office, you will likely find plenty of books about counseling techniques, professional issues, and client problems on the shelves but rarely more than a couple of books on theory. When you attend a professional counseling conference, you will notice that the program also reflects this bias. The program is packed with presentations and workshops on counseling strategies, practice concerns, and policy issues. However, it is rare to find a session that deals only with ideas, concepts, or theories. You may see yourself as sharing this attitude. After all, you are studying this field because you want to do *counseling*, not *theorizing*. Like someone who fast-forwards a DVD to "the good parts" of a movie, you may find yourself skipping the theory portion of a book to find "the good stuff," the actual counseling techniques. Or, you may consider reading a theory section to be such a tedious chore that you endure it only in the hope that it will pay off in the form of a powerful counseling method.

Our experience as counselors has taught us two fundamental lessons that run counter to this prevailing attitude about the place of theory in our therapeutic work. The first lesson is that we are all theorists, and the second is that there is no fundamental gap between theory and action. As Immanuel Kant (in Kolb, 1984) put it, "Thoughts without content are empty; intuitions without concepts are blind" (p. 106).

You will find a lot of theory in this book. We make this statement not as a warning but as an invitation, because we truly believe that the theory offers you new and exciting ideas with important implications for counseling. This theory explains the changing view of how things in the world function and how change itself takes place. Our science and art are entering a new paradigm that calls for innovation and a fresh view of the world. As the authors of this book, we hope that, as you gain a better understanding of the ideas that are behind the tools of brief counseling, you will know not only why you do what you do but also how to decide what to do next. In other words, engaging in theory helps you with your counseling, and engaging in counseling helps you with your theory.

Our View of the Brief Approach

Ludwig Wittgenstein once said that his aim in doing philosophy was to shew the fly the way out of the fly bottle. In Vienna, in Wittgenstein's time, people trapped flies by putting some honey in a vinegar bottle. The fly would smell the honey crawl into the bottle, and either remain stuck in the honey or fly in circles until it died. "To 'shew the fly the way out of the fly bottle' was not to *solve* . . . problems, but to *dissolve* them" (Palmer, 1994, pp. 329–330).

While recent approaches to brief counseling and therapy have come to focus on solutions rather than problems, the authors of this book prefer *resolution* as the end goal. The concept of resolution reflects the focus of brief therapy on helping clients achieve a better outcome—a *positive resolution*—in the future. Often, people's concerns do dissolve and reach resolution without their having "solved" anything. The counselor's goal is to assist clients toward resolution of the fundamental issues they face in life—not merely to find solutions to their problems. As Gilligan (1997) put it, you can assume that a client is "stuck in a narrow understanding of, or limited connection to, his or her potentiality. Identifying resources and activating them are seen as central to helping the client" (p. 6).

When you work with clients, you have certain options as to how you view them. You could, for example, see them as defective, ignorant, or ill. Many traditional psychotherapists have adopted these views. In contrast, the ideas and tools described in this book are founded on the assumption that people are inherently healthy and that they are capable of dissolving their own "stuckness."

Instead of viewing problems as fundamental flaws in people's character or biology, you can view such dilemmas metaphorically as being stuck in the fly bottle. The events and circumstances leading your clients to this fly bottle may have been unavoidable and even traumatic. However, their current sense of hopelessness and stagnation is a fly bottle that they themselves have constructed. If the constraints of the bottle are removed, their concerns will dissolve into a sense of resolve. You do not need to fix their wings or teach them how to fly. If you can help them find their way out of their stuckness, they will fly free on their own and achieve resolution.

Integrative Theory and Practice

When you began your training, you may have been dismayed at the multitude of theoretical approaches you found in your counseling and therapy texts. In fact, Prochaska and Norcross (2007) placed the most recent number of distinct theoretical approaches to counseling and psychotherapy at 400. Perhaps even more daunting, these approaches seemed to differ so markedly in philosophy, personality theory, and technique. Ultimately, you may have felt discouraged that some of these various "orthodoxies" claimed to be irreconcilable with any other approach. The implicit message was that one must choose a single theory and become a disciple of that approach. If you are an existentialist, you can't be a behaviorist; if you are psychodynamic, you can't be a cognitive-behaviorist. Worse yet, if you subscribe to the tenets of brief therapy, you can't be anything else! In spite of this situation, there exists a recent and promising movement toward integrative theory and practice.

What does it mean to say that an approach to counseling and therapy is "integrative"? It means that, in spite of the continuing competitive nature of the various theoretical approaches, you can take an open and flexible stance that is meta-theoretical, a position that rises above partisan adherence to any particular theory or technique. Rather than entering into the dispute as to which theory is best, an integrative meta-theory accepts that each has its place and recognizes that borrowing from several approaches is not heresy.

Neimeyer and Stewart (2000) characterized this position as "postmodern." A postmodern philosophy does not assume that there exists a fixed truth, but that clients are themselves theorists who come with a construction of what is real and true for them. "Constructivist therapists not only attend to the meanings that their patients give to their own problems but also help them see problems as meaningful options that have outlived their usefulness" (Sharf, 2004, p. 17). As with the integrative approach, constructivist counselors do not adhere to a single doctrinaire theory. Instead, they are committed to understanding the client's worldview from a phenomenological perspective—in other words, from the inside out. Furthermore, counselors who work from an integrative standpoint use ideas from any orthodox approach that fits the client's experience and the issue needing work: "Thus, they have more resources at their disposal than when they use a single theory" (Sharf, 2004, p. 570).

Despite the fact that mental health professionals have, for half a century, been attempting to break down the barriers that separate the various theories of counseling and psychotherapy, progress continues to be slow. The primary obstacles to integration have been turf issues and other political considerations. One major turning point was the publication of the "Dodo Bird Verdict" by Luborsky and his colleagues (2002). As a result of their meta-analysis of outcome studies, these authors found no significant difference in the effectiveness of the various theoretical approaches to psychotherapy. The term "Dodo Bird Verdict" comes from an early chapter of Lewis Carroll's *Alice in Wonderland* in which several animals have a race. At the end of the race, they all clamor to claim a prize.

> . . . the Dodo suddenly called out, "The race is over!" and they all crowded round it, panting, and asking, "But who has won?"
>
> This question the Dodo could not answer without a great deal of thought, and it stood for a long time with one finger pressed upon its forehead (the position in which you usually see Shakespeare, in the pictures of him), while the rest waited in silence. At last the Dodo said, "*Everybody* has won, and *all* must have prizes."

This race to determine which therapy is best has repeatedly ended in disappointing ties. "After nearly 50 years of research, we are only partially able to specify which type of treatment is best for which type of client with which type of problem" (Prochaska & Norcross, 2007, p. 528).

Instead of seeking an integration of the dizzying array of competing theories and techniques, some therapists have declared themselves "eclectic." However, many have criticized this attempt at rapprochement as mere "theory smushing" or a "throw everything at them but the kitchen sink" model. For example, Prochaska and Norcross (2007) pointed out that many clinicians perceived eclecticism as a disorganized and indecisive strategy. At its worst, eclecticism is "haphazardly picking techniques without any overall theoretical rationale . . . [T]he practitioner, lacking in knowledge and skill . . . grabs for anything that seems to work" (Corey, 2005, pp. 463–464). Such a hodgepodge approach is no better than operating from a narrow dogmatic orthodoxy.

Another attempt to achieve uniformity in the field of counseling is *evidence-based practice* (EBP). Prochaska and Norcross (2007) characterized this movement as "an international juggernaut racing to achieve accountability in all forms of health care" (p. 544). The idea of EBP has tremendous appeal, but defining just what constitutes evidence turns out to be problematic. For example, this search for empirically supported outcomes considers client satisfaction an unreliable criterion. Consequently, the client's phenomenological experience is typically ignored.

Instead, the aim of EBP is the creation of treatment manuals for specific disorders. These protocols provide detailed instructions and guidelines, offer handout materials, and describe the sequence of interventions that the therapist should implement (Sharf, 2004). The notion of treatment manuals, the reliance on controlled outcome research, the focus on specific disorders, and the effort to validate specific treatment methods have all recently come under attack (Prochaska & Norcross, 2007). Criticisms include that EBPs minimize the importance of the therapeutic relationship, suggest that all therapists are equally skilled, and ignore the complexity of the individual client's worldview (Norcross, Beutler, & Levant, 2005).

One productive step toward integration took place in 1983 with the formation of the Society for the Exploration of Psychotherapy Integration. The society promoted a formal movement toward complementary approaches and against the "dogma eat dogma" situation that had existed in the field (Norcross & Goldfried, 2005). Since then, the notion of integrating aspects of various theories has been gaining respectability.

In contrast to the EBP movement's focus on techniques and procedures, the APA Division of Psychotherapy's Task Force on Empirically Supported Therapy Relationships published a review focusing on the therapist's contribution to the therapy relationship (Prochaska & Norcross, 2007). Their conclusions stand in marked contrast to the EBP approach. They asserted that it is the quality of the relationship that contributes to positive outcomes in therapy, regardless of the type of treatment. Furthermore, extensive research already has demonstrated that relationship characteristics such as therapeutic alliance, empathy, collaboration, and goal consensus are effective. Other elements that are probably effective include the therapist's degree of positive regard, congruence, self-disclosure, and feedback.

Obviously, the above findings of the APA Task Force emphasized the personhood of the therapist over the therapist's technique. Who you are and how well you can engage with your clients are better predictors of a successful outcome with your clients than any protocol, algorithm, or manual. In this book, we have constructed an approach to brief counseling that is aligned with the APA Task Force's findings. In future chapters, you will find ideas and tools that are drawn from many psychotherapeutic approaches.

An Integrative Hierarchy of Counseling Approaches

We human beings are incredibly complex creatures. Our brains, with their 100 billion neurons, each of which has over a thousand connections, contain *more interconnections than there are particles in the universe* (Kurzweil, 1999). The recent explosion of discoveries in neuroscience is casting light on many previously unknown aspects of our remarkable brains. In this book, we offer some of these insights as they apply to counseling. But people are all much more than their neural synapses, behaviors, emotions, or thoughts. They live at different levels of existence, as do their problems and concerns.

We have designed a hierarchical model, which includes eight interacting levels of human existence, to illustrate how all the approaches to counseling are related, though separate. (see Figure 1-1). We offer this model to demonstrate one way that the various theories of counseling and psychotherapy can be reconciled. To label this a hierarchical model does not imply that one level is superior to others but merely indicates what assumption is being made in support of the intervention.

Neural The fundamental assumption of counseling theories at this level is that the human condition can be reduced to the level of the brain/body. When the neural processes are functioning normally, they operate largely outside of our conscious awareness. These constant and vital functions include maintaining body temperature, regulating blood-sugar level, producing neurotransmitters, and encoding memories.

The Fundamental Assumption Is . . .	The Essential Problem Is . . .	The Possible Interventions Include . . .
SYSTEMIC		
We become sick when we adjust to a sick system.	Dysfunctional families and other systems.	Family therapy, advocacy, institutional change.
EXISTENTIAL		
We need to live courageously or we will become alienated.	Failure to confront the basic human condition.	Authentically encountering another, seeking meaning.
HUMANISTIC		
We have "being needs" as well as "deficiency needs."	Denial of aspects of self not accepted by others.	Unconditional positive regard, encouraging self-acceptance.
COGNITIVE		
Beliefs about events create emotions.	Irrational and unrealistic thinking.	Disputation of beliefs, analysis of self-talk.
PSYCHODYNAMIC		
Our early experiences can make us weak or rigid.	Fixation caused by trauma or poor caregiving.	Analysis, catharsis, interpretation.
SOCIAL LEARNING		
We learn by example.	Mistaken attitudes and behaviors based on bad models.	Assertion training, appropriate modeling.
BEHAVIORAL		
We are reactive mechanisms.	Too much or too little behavior in a context.	Behavior modification, systematic desensitization.
NEURAL		
Everything happens at the brain/body level.	Dysfunction of neurons or neural networks.	Medication, psychosurgery, altering brain by counseling.

FIGURE 1-1 An integrative hierarchy model of counseling approaches.

Often, it is only when processes fail to work properly that they come into our awareness as negative moods, unmet needs, or dysfunctional behaviors. Problems are due to the dysfunction of neurons, neural networks, or neurotransmitters. Therefore, interventions include such methods as medications, psychosurgery, and psychological interventions that alter brain processes.

Behavioral The basic assumption of theories that focus on the behavioral level of human existence is that people are reactive mechanisms. By attending carefully to only what we can observe—the actions of other humans—we do not need to invoke the concept of a "mind" as the cause of a particular reaction. Associations create behavioral responses. An innocuous stimulus can become a feared stimulus by immediate pairing with a noxious stimulus. Behaviors can be strengthened by reward.

Fundamentally, at this level all problems that plague the human condition can be characterized as either too much or too little behavior in a particular context. Consequently, counselors and therapists work to change behaviors through such interventions as systematic desensitization, exposure, and behavior modification.

Social learning A practitioner relying on social learning theory assumes that human beings, one of the most social of species, are taught how to deal with the challenges of life by following the example of others. Because people are so interdependent and connected to others, they do not need to be rewarded directly to change their attitudes or behaviors. Reinforcement can be vicarious; people can learn from watching models being rewarded for their actions. From a social learning point of view, thinking is a mechanical process; no consciousness is required to be a successful and adaptive learner.

Most of the problems that people experience in life are the result of mistaken attitudes and behavioral dispositions that they learned from bad models. Therefore, counseling and therapeutic interventions involve corrective instructional training, such as stress inoculation training, exposure to positive models, assertion training, and reattribution.

Psychodynamic Psychodynamically oriented therapists operate under the assumption that early life experiences can create personal vulnerabilities and interpersonal rigidity throughout one's adult life. As a result of traumas or lack of appropriate nurturance, children acquire defenses that stifle their creativity or cause physical symptoms. Even if they escape these early dysfunctional relationships, people may continue to displace their distorted attitudes onto others. Counselors and therapists often encounter this transference in their work with clients. From this psychodynamic perspective, the important mental processes are automatic and largely unconscious.

All chronic, deep-seated personal problems are the result of the fixation of libidinal energy. Therefore, therapeutic interventions make the unconscious conscious through analysis of resistance and transference, interpretation, insight, and catharsis. When clients achieve insight and have a corrective emotional experience in therapy, then they can develop a new prototype for relationships.

Cognitive As the Roman Philosopher Epictitus said, it is not what happens to us that determines how we feel, but it is our beliefs about the event that create emotions. From a cognitive perspective, our irrational thoughts and unrealistic beliefs distort the way we interpret events and conceive of ourselves. Such warped thinking and inadequate representations of reality can sabotage our self-esteem, relationships, and problem-solving abilities.

At the cognitive level, therapists offer a variety of interventions, including analysis of self-talk, disputation of beliefs through the use of Socratic methods, and challenging people to become scientific about their beliefs.

Humanistic A counselor subscribing to a humanistic perspective recognizes that people have requirements, or "being needs," that are higher than the basic necessities of food, clothing, and shelter. If people are nurtured, they can develop toward self-actualization. Because we need to be loved and approved of, all of us have been raised under conditions of worth, which has caused us to deny aspects of ourselves.

Problems occur when we turn ourselves into the person that others wish for us to be and lose the sense of our true self. Humanistic interventions involve providing an environment of unconditional positive regard, eliciting experiences of the denied aspects of self, and promoting greater self-acceptance.

Existential   The fundamental challenge at this level of the human experience is confronting our own mortality. We realize that we will die, that life may be meaningless, and that we must choose our behaviors and be responsible for our choices while keeping in mind that we are ultimately alone. As a result, we develop lifestyles and personal philosophies that are either courageous or alienating.

The existential problem that many people bring to counseling is that they have adopted "sell-out" strategies in order not to face their human condition. Overwhelmed by their mortality, they have denied the inevitability of their death, have made Faustian bargains to gain immortality, or have distracted themselves by a compulsive but fruitless pursuit of happiness.

Existential counseling takes place within an authentic encounter in which both counselor and client journey through their "dark night of the soul" together. Confronting their human condition, both client and counselor become more open to what it means to be human.

Systemic   People are systems who live within systems. If the system is sick—and we adjust to it—we will be sick, too. The way in which people experience themselves has much to do with the roles they play within a system. The most influential and formative system is a person's family of origin. Each family member takes on a personality that is able to play the role assigned in the family.

Problems naturally arise when the family or the system in which one finds oneself is dysfunctional. The individual then adopts dysfunctional interactions that carry into adulthood. Therefore, the focus of therapeutic interventions is less on what caused the present difficulty and more on what currently maintains it. There are many approaches to systemic therapy, but the central notion is to free the individual from the tyranny of the family of origin and the habitual roles one plays.

Our attempt at designing this shorthand for the various psychotherapies would, no doubt, draw criticism from those who subscribe to any one of these particular approaches. It is not possible to fully capture the essence of each theory and practice in such a brief sketch, and our treatment is by no means comprehensive. We are simply trying to show that working at one level does not mean that a counselor has to subscribe exclusively to that type of approach. As with the Dodo Bird's verdict, all these approaches work (and all must have prizes), depending on your client's concerns and goals.

It should be possible, therefore, to combine theories and practices within a comprehensive and integrated approach to counseling and therapy without taking a piecemeal, "eclectic" stance. Your own approach to working briefly with clients can be an integrated one, and while you may borrow from many levels of theory and technique, you do not have to do so haphazardly. You can incorporate the interventions that seem to work best, and that are drawn from both the "common factors" approach and postmodern ideas about the change process.

A Brief History of Brief Counseling

In order to understand how the ideas and tools contained in this book have evolved, we will trace for you the roots of the brief counseling movement. This is by no means meant to be an exhaustive history, but, in the spirit of being brief, we will give you the high points that have brought us to the present.

Since the end of World War II, there have been significant changes in thinking about pathology versus health, catharsis versus encouragement, problems versus resolutions, and looking toward the future versus digging into the past. Some of these newer notions may, at first, seem counterintuitive to you and difficult to accept, while others will appear to be just good common sense.

The cybernetics connection   In 1948, Norbert Wiener coined the term *cybernetics*, which he took from the Greek *kybernetes*, meaning steersman. A cybernetic system involves a purposeful, self-organizing entity that is heading toward a goal. While people have often been characterized in psychology as simply passive reactors to their environment, the idea of purpose and goal-directness began to cast human striving as teleological: working toward a desired state. The central idea of cybernetics is the feedback loop, by which a system receives the information necessary to self-correct in its effort to either maintain a steady state or to move toward a goal (Nichols & Schwartz, 2006).

Gregory Bateson was enthralled with the cybernetics idea and began to translate the concepts of engineering and mathematics into the language of the behavioral sciences (Becvar & Becvar, 2003). In 1949, the psychiatrist Jurgen Ruesch invited him to join in a study of human communication in psychotherapy. Before that time, Bateson had not been especially attracted to psychotherapy, having already achieved fame as a cultural anthropologist along with his former wife, Margaret Mead. Bateson interviewed many psychiatrists in order to understand the communication processes that took place in a psychotherapy session, but he found their explanations to be filled with jargon and abstruse ideas. So Bateson turned to the work of Norbert Wiener and attempted to bring psychoanalytic processes under the heading of cybernetics.

In 1952, Bateson received a large grant to study communication. He needed good researchers to help carry out the project, so the first person he hired was John H. Weakland, who was one of his former students. The next person was Jay Haley, then a graduate student at Stanford who was studying fictional films. Haley recalled, "I went over to talk to Gregory about it, to get an advisor. We had a big argument and he hired me on the project" (Lipset, 1980, p. 200). Later, Bateson hired Don Jackson to serve as psychiatric consultant on the project. Jackson was a psychiatrist of a different stripe, having studied under Harry Stack Sullivan, who introduced him to the idea that all mental disturbances were relational in nature (Teyber, 2006).

Sometime later, Don Jackson began to establish an institute in Palo Alto. It became known as the Mental Research Institute (MRI) and attracted a number of creative participants, including Virginia Satir and Paul Watzlawick. Weakland and Haley acknowledged their indebtedness to Bateson as their teacher and guide, but they also drifted away from his research program and into MRI (Prochaska & Norcross, 2007).

The MRI influence　In 1967, Watzlawick, Beavin, and Jackson published *Pragmatics of Human Communication*. In this seminal work, they analyzed human communication and laid the groundwork for subsequent theorizing in brief therapy. Also during that year, the Brief Therapy Center was opened at MRI when Paul Watzlawick joined Arthur Bodin, Richard Fisch, and John Weakland in the investigation of communication patterns in human relationships (Weakland & Fisch, 1992). Weakland and Jay Haley jointly initiated visits to Phoenix to discuss hypnosis with Milton Erickson. Fisch was trained as a psychiatrist in the Sullivanian tradition, rather than the Freudian paradigm. He later took some training at MRI and found himself influenced by their approach. He was especially attracted to the ideas of Jay Haley. When he learned that Haley had gotten his inspiration as a result of his training with Erickson, Fisch attended a couple of workshops with Erickson.

The most significant work performed at MRI, which has also been called the Palo Alto Group, was the emphasis on communication and change in psychotherapy, which was distinctively different from the personality and pathology emphasis in the prevailing psychiatric and psychological communities. The question they asked was not about etiology—the historical cause of the client's problem—but, rather, what elements of human communication contribute to change.

Then, in 1974, Watzlawick, Weakland, and Fisch published *Change: Principles of Problem Formulation and Problem Resolution*. In this volume, they drew upon the principles outlined in *Pragmatics* and offered a model for brief therapy based upon their view of how specific types of communication can be employed to interrupt problem patterns. Rather than search for *causes* of dysfunctional communication patterns, the MRI group thought it more productive to understand what might be *maintaining* the problem and how to interrupt it.

Earlier, Haley (1973) had stated that psychotherapy should be strategic; counselors must be intentional in their approach: "Strategic therapy is not a particular approach or theory but a name for those types of therapy where the therapist takes responsibility for directly influencing people" (p. 17).

In this passage, Haley displayed the influence of cybernetics on his thinking. Therapy should be purposeful and directed toward a goal, making corrections according to whether the therapy is on course. A strategic approach would keep the goal in mind and do what is necessary to arrive at that goal.

Milton Erickson: The practical therapist　In his teens, Milton Erickson contracted polio, which left him paralyzed from the neck down. Later, when he had recovered the use of the upper part of his body, with legs still paralyzed, he embarked alone upon a 1,000-mile canoe trip with only a few dollars in his pocket. At the beginning of the journey, he could neither walk nor carry his canoe. Upon his return, he could swim a mile and he could walk. Perhaps this experience, more than any other, shaped his belief that one cannot dwell on the past or on what doesn't work but, rather, must find a way to overcome difficulties through ordeal. This became the guiding philosophy of his therapy.

Jay Haley first traveled to Arizona to meet with Erickson in 1953 (Bloom, 1997). Through many hours of recorded conversations and editing of numerous papers written by Erickson, Haley was able to extract and systematize the major ideas behind the work that Erickson called "common-sense therapy." After two decades of collaboration with

Erickson, Haley established his own approach to therapy. He labeled Erickson's therapy "uncommon" (Haley, 1973) and his own approach "strategic."

Haley interested many other therapists in Erickson's way of working. A number of ambassadors from MRI made regular pilgrimages to Erickson's small home in Phoenix, and Erickson's ideas, which seemed to dovetail nicely with Gregory Bateson's, became the foundation for modern brief therapy. Fisch (1982) described some of Erickson's innovative techniques. For example, when starting a session with a client, Erickson would not ask for a lengthy history or encourage the client to express feelings. He refrained from interpreting a client's resistance and actually used the resistance to the client's benefit. "He simply did not waste time arguing with patients, focusing instead on the task the patient was to perform to resolve his problem" (Fisch, 1982, p. 159).

"Erickson's First Law," as de Shazer (1982) later called it, was "As long as they are going to resist, you ought to encourage them to resist" (pp. 10–11). Whether giving direct instructions to a client or seemingly capitulating to the client's resistance, Erickson continued to have an impact on the client's behavior. While this may have seemed devious and manipulative to some, Erickson's motive for such behaviors was to influence the client to change for the better.

Milton Erickson's contributions to conceptualizing trance as an everyday experience, together with his lifelong attitude of looking for possibilities rather than pathologies, have significantly impacted the field of brief therapy. Erickson died in 1980, about the time when his ideas were beginning to take hold, but his influence continues to be deep and powerful.

Steve de Shazer and the BTC   John Weakland and his colleagues established the Brief Therapy Center (BTC) when they began to suspect that what clients do to maintain their problems is much more important than what has caused the problems. With this notion, the BTC group began to formulate what they called a "brief" model of therapeutic intervention. Problem identification was the crucial first step in order to establish what was maintaining it. Fisch and Schlanger (1999) stated that some of their cases had not turned out well because of "our jumping too quickly into suggesting some action to clients . . . and our not recognizing or eliciting clients' position or frame of reference regarding their problem" (pp. 147–148).

Steve de Shazer described his therapeutic lineage as proceeding directly from the work of Erickson, Haley, Bateson, Watzlawick, and others of the MRI and the BTC. While living in the Palo Alto area, de Shazer became a close friend of John Weakland and, as a result of their many discussions, was influenced by the brief therapy approach (de Shazer, personal communication, 1998). According to Weakland and Fisch (1992), de Shazer was associated with the people at MRI from 1972, when he took a workshop there.

The difference between the MRI approach and the ideas that de Shazer later adopted was his focus on solutions. In contrast to Weakland and Fisch, De Shazer was not concerned with what maintained problems but, rather, what solutions could be found to these problems.

Later, working with a small group of creative family therapists, de Shazer helped to found the Brief Family Therapy Center (BFTC) in Milwaukee, with the idea that the

Center would be a place for both service and research into the efficacy of their methods. The Center became a Mecca for young psychotherapists who wished to be trained in nontraditional approaches to therapy.

Another important insight of de Shazer was that a solution may not bear much resemblance to the problem itself (de Shazer, 1991). He believed that our time with clients is best spent looking for "exceptions" to the litany of frustrations the client brings. As the counselor shifts the client's narrative from complaint to solution, the process of therapy then involves creating workable goals, which we explore in Chapter 4.

The work of the people at BFTC, with their emphasis on solutions rather than problems, has greatly influenced the practice of brief counseling. O'Hanlon and Weiner-Davis (1989) referred to this group of people as "the team that made Milwaukee famous," after an advertising slogan for a brand of beer. Today, de Shazer's legacy is still in the process of evolution, and it has proliferated into a number of variants with many different names. Hoyt (1994) attempted to capture the essence of the approach by referring to it as "competency-based future-oriented therapy." As solution-focused brief therapy continues to evolve, it will be its genotype that endures, no matter what form its phenotype may take.

Beyond technique and brief counseling   One of the core members of the Brief Family Therapy Center, Eve Lipchik, dreamed up various innovative methods of solution-focused brief therapy. In time, she became concerned that people were viewing this form of therapy as nothing more than a set of techniques and a series of prescribed questions.

In her book *Beyond Technique in Solution-Focused Therapy*, Lipchik (2002) stated that the originators of the solution-focused approach had assumed that those who were learning how to do counseling in this way were already good at establishing a therapeutic relationship with their clients. She was deeply troubled to discover that this assumption proved not to be the case.

Furthermore, Lipchik found that attendees of her workshops quickly grew bored and restless with theoretical explanations that were the grounding for this type of work. They seemed to want to know how to do it without knowing how to think about it. Finally, Lipchik discovered that those who considered solution-focused brief therapy to be a minimalist approach to intervention were thinking of it as simply a crafty manipulation of language. She felt that all such attitudes miss the point.

Lipchik considered it essential to marry theory and practice, relationship with technique, and to shift her approach to therapy away from the formulaic and mechanical. One move she made in this effort was to eliminate the word *brief* from the way she referred to her work. According to Lipchik, the term "brief" may create a false assumption regarding this approach. She saw "brief" as a byproduct of this way of working with clients rather than its focus: "[B]revity will be the result of the best-fitting interaction for a particular client, not speedy application of technique" (2002, p. 18).

As we see it, the term "brief" is an attitude that brings about an intention to work as efficiently as possible in order not to waste the client's time and money. "Brief" does not imply a quick fix, nor the ignoring of important aspects of the client's concerns. We can work with the issues that clients bring without "going sightseeing." This means that we stick to what the client is presenting and avoid following down our notions of "underlying pathology" or the so-called "real cause."

Borrowing concepts from Harry Stack Sullivan and reworking those of solution-focused brief therapy, Lipchik articulated a new set of assumptions that are compatible with our own. These assumptions include the centrality of a collaborative relationship, the uniqueness of each client, and the value of emotions in counseling. Such concepts reflect the recent and exciting developments in the brief counseling field.

EXPERIENCING THIS IDEA

Have you ever wondered how the computer can scan and make sense out of those universal price codes that are now on every single product that we buy? To help you learn about finding a resolution, we have a challenge for you. You have one minute to resolve the puzzle in the problem presented in Figure 1-2.

Success Strategies

Perhaps you were immediately able to resolve the problem in Figure 1-2, but most people are not successful at first and become frustrated with this task. Below are some reminders to help you recall the success strategies that you have used before to deal with similar riddles and problems. You can read each of the success strategies below and then return to the figure to apply it. As you know from your own past experiences, sometimes you can resolve a confusing situation without actually knowing how you do it, so we encourage you to try one even if it does not make sense.

• **Rely on your strengths.** Many of your successes in life have been due to taking full advantage of your own competencies, instead of trying to be something that you are not. In dealing with the problem above, however, you might first have tried to mimic a computer by counting the dark lines and dots in order to break the binary code or find the algorithm. Instead of acting like a computer, take another minute to rely on your reading skills to discover the answer. If you have not been successful yet, then go on to read the next paragraph.

• **Seek a resolution by taking a different point of view.** If you have not yet found the answer, then you may want to remind yourself that many realizations have appeared to you in the past when you have taken a different perspective. In the case of the bar code problem, you may have assumed that the best way to view the figure is in the way

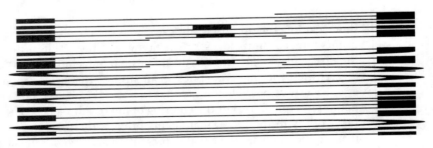

FIGURE 1-2   Universal price code.

that we have presented it to you. Instead, you may want to rotate the book sideways 90 degrees to the left and see how your perception of the figure changes. After using this additional strategy for another minute, you may want to go on to the next paragraph.

• **Do something different.** In your life, there certainly have been times when you have successfully overcome confusing situations by making a simple change in what you were doing. In this case, you may be looking at the page the way that you look at any typical page: straight ahead, 12 to 18 inches away, and with both eyes open. Instead, you may want to bring the page nearer, close one eye, hold the book sideways, and alter the angle of the page by tilting it slowly until it is lying almost perpendicular to your eye.

• **Seeing the goal can help you achieve it.** As you look back on your life, you may have found that one of the best ways to succeed is to clearly see the goal. In the case of this problem, the answer you are seeking is, in fact, the phrase *THE RESOLUTION*. Now that you see the goal, see if you can successfully find "the resolution" in the figure.

REFLECTING QUESTIONS

1. What were your first reactions to the problem?
2. What would your reaction be if we had only reflected on your feelings or suggested that you talk about other times when you have felt confused?
3. How did you find the answer?

Implications of These Ideas for the Counselor

Based on these innovative ideas, we offer below essential guidelines you need to follow, no matter what techniques or interventions you may offer in counseling.

• **Honor every client as unique.** Any time you begin to think you have the answer to your client's problems because you have worked with similar issues or because a solution works for you personally, you need to remind yourself that your client is a unique person. Treat all of your clients as matchless, appreciate each as irreplaceable, and remain curious about their one-of-a-kind, distinctive lives.

One of the authors of this book (J.E.M.) advises his students to always approach their clients with the "I'm not from around here" attitude. This stance maintains a belief in the individuality of all clients and respects the fact that they are the experts on their own lives. You may be the expert on how to create the conditions for change, but this expertise cannot extend to knowing the client's experience.

• **Always look for the survivor, not the victim.** Clients have undiscovered talents, overlooked strengths, untapped resources, and unrealized potential to resolve the challenges that face them. Most of your effort as a counselor is helping clients to realize their own talents, strengths, and resources. If you remain curious about how people have survived the negative events in their lives, you begin to hear about their resilience and their assets.

The "positive psychology" movement, initiated by Seligman (2000) and others, has suggested that instead of focusing on client suffering, we search for client resilience. This idea is, in fact, a return to "themes [that] were advanced by humanistic psychologists in the 1960s and 1970s" (Prochaska & Norcross, 2007, p. 553).

Obviously, if you enter into a counseling relationship looking for pathology, you will likely find what you seek. If you ask about your clients' suffering, then suffering is what your clients will focus on. If you fail to look for strength in your clients, your clients will fail to find it in themselves. But when you see strength exhibited by a client—and the client has not yet acknowledged this strength—refrain from immediately pointing it out. Instead, ask your client, "How did you get yourself to do that?" Ask, but don't tell. Remember, you are not from around here!

Lipchik (2002) stated that the purpose of therapy is to help clients "recover something in themselves (self-respect, love, legitimacy) as well as in others" (p. 15). Your job as a counselor is not to take over their lives and tell them what to do to relieve their pain. This approach would only disempower them and diminish their self-confidence. The fact that your clients have been able, for the most part, to deal with life's everyday demands and to survive in a sometimes hostile environment is *prima facie* evidence that they are resourceful people.

You may recall the children's story of Dumbo, who had lost his mother and was ostracized by his social group. His "real" name was Jumbo, Jr., but he had come to accept the term "Dumbo" as an apt description of his inadequate personality and limited capability. He felt discouraged and alone until a little mouse suggested that by holding a magic feather in his trunk, he would be able to fly. And he did! But of course, he finally found that he could fly even when he had lost the feather. We counselors are attempting to offer our clients a temporary prosthetic feather until they realize their own latent abilities and strengths, and can fly on their own.

Your client may be coming to you feeling discouraged and overwhelmed by what seems to be an endless barrage of disappointments, frustrations, losses, complications, and crises. Keep in mind that no client is a passive, pathetic, and clueless victim of circumstances. Somehow, some way, your client has been able to persevere enough to survive. So, you recognize the hardships your client has endured, but you are curious about how your client has been able to survive (Echterling, Presbury, & McKee, 2005).

Your clients' concerns can sometimes feel overwhelming to you, too. However, if you maintain the attitude of looking for strengths, you can avoid being sucked into their misery. You must seek exceptions to the problem-saturated narrative they bring, times when they have risen above the ordeals of living. To be sure, you are not asking them to look on the bright side. Instead, you are working to juxtapose, or create a balance, between their truly negative feelings of injury and vulnerability and their latent sense of resilience and resolve.

• **Accept that your client may be hesitant, but never resistant**. For many years, counselors and therapists have thought that breaking down the resistance of their clients was an essential first step of change. However, instead of portraying resistance as a personal flaw in your client, you can recognize it as a consequence of your relationship. A client may be resistant with one therapist and not with another. Rather than dismissing the client's reluctant attitude as something existing within his or her "bag of skin," you can look for resistance in the interaction between yourself and the client. Then you can explore ways of encountering your client so that the counseling experience becomes a catalyst for change.

Sometimes, clients will stick to their old patterns of behaving because their lives feel otherwise so chaotic; they adopt a "better the devil you know than the devil you don't" attitude. Even though the clients understand that their repeated behaviors are counterproductive, they feel that at least they are well rehearsed and familiar. Clients are not resisting change so much as fearing it (Cowan & Presbury, 2000). Furthermore, when you see what looks like resistance, this means your clients are telling you that you have not yet been able to convince them that change will not hurt more than old wounds. You have "sided" too quickly with the notion of change.

• **Only clients can truly change themselves—you can't just tell 'em**! Logic, advice, and reasonable arguments do not create lasting or significant change. Instead, when clients seem immovable, your first task as a counselor is to communicate an empathic understanding of the client's feelings. When clients believe that you truly understand them, they begin to feel that it is safe for them to attempt change.

You can facilitate positive change within clients by creating the proper conditions, but you cannot make it happen. Change is the client's job, not yours. It would be exceedingly grandiose of you to believe that by some magic intervention, instruction, or incantation you can transform a client, Pygmalion-like, into a fully functioning and happy human being. You can't, but they can.

• **Seek to have an effect—don't search for the cause**. In the medical profession, the prevailing notion is that manifest symptoms are indicators of some underlying cause that must be diagnosed and fixed. Searching for causes is not only a failed strategy in counseling, but it is inefficient as well. The question that must be asked is where the client wishes to go from here.

Unfortunately, most clients have been raised in the tradition of modern science. They believe that to know the origins of their agony will produce the clue to changing their lives for the better. Your challenge is to help them accept the idea that new behavior patterns can eclipse the old. Specifically, as Lipchik suggested, you might ask, "If you could solve your problem without having to know why you have it, would that be okay?"

• **Help your clients find resolutions, not define problems**. In fact, achieving a sense of resolution may not have anything to do with a particular problem. Our counseling students often find this statement vexing until they realize the way in which they have resolved many of their own concerns in the past. For example, it has been said that "time heals all wounds." While this statement is not precisely true, it is the case that memories of pain and trauma are, over time, reduced due to the accumulation of new, positive, and perhaps even joyful memories.

Psychologists call this phenomenon "retroactive inhibition"; it is an extinction process by which new thoughts eclipse old ones (Dobbs, 2006). Merely searching for solutions to the client's stated problems can seriously constrain your progress in counseling. Fundamentally, life concerns are not solved, but resolved. For this and other reasons, we have chosen to call our approach *resolution-focused brief counseling and crisis intervention*. Resolutions are not logical. They cannot be rationally brought about. And they do not necessarily have much to do with the "problem" as stated by the client.

When people's painful issues begin instead to dissolve, they simultaneously experience problems as becoming resolved and themselves as becoming more resolute.

• **Value emotions—they can move your clients toward resolution.** When people resolve a concern, they feel a sense of satisfaction and peace. They also feel confident, even courageous, as they become resolute in coping with whatever comes up in the future. Existentialists call this "the courage to be."

The earlier brief approaches of the Mental Research Institute and the solution-focused models were based on cognitive-behavioral procedures, so these theorists "eschewed talk about feelings . . . [but] clients' emotions are as much a subject of therapy [as] their thoughts and behaviors" (Lipchik, 2002, p. 20). These brief therapists considered that language was a collaboration of thought and action, and that altering the client's story was sufficient to change their emotional accompaniment.

However, there has been much recent work in neuroscience on the nature of emotions and their important contribution to good thinking. Managing emotions in the counseling session is a crucial part of working efficiently and effectively with clients. Remember—there's no motion without emotion.

• **Recognize that change is the one constant in life.** Most theories of counseling and therapy have held to the Newtonian Laws of Motion. For example, the idea that "objects at rest tend to stay at rest" leads to the belief that, when clients are stuck in a problem configuration, they must be somehow motivated to move and change. In addition, the idea that "for every force, there is an equal and opposite counterforce" suggests that if the client's concerns are significant, the therapist then needs to muster heroic counterforces in order to get the client to quit resisting a change. But Newton's Laws were made for "dead rocks" and other nonliving objects, not for living systems that are always changing. People change, often imperceptibly, and it is our job to attempt to help clients see that they are not irrevocably stuck or immovable. You can count on change.

Related to this guideline is the idea that even a small change can bring about dramatic consequences, a concept that is quite consistent with the new sciences of chaos and complexity. It is the Butterfly Effect. So, if your client's circumstances seem so stagnant that even you begin to feel hopeless, remind yourself that change is always happening. In fact, engaging with your client in an authentic relationship automatically changes the context. You can then invite the client to envision some action, no matter how trivial or insignificant it may first appear, that would make a difference.

"Hope," Emily Dickinson said, "is that thing with feathers." Feathers have so little substance that they seem inconsequential, but they enable a bird to rise above and transcend its earthbound conditions. Making a minor change for the better can restore hope, give someone a sense of greater control, and gather momentum for transformation.

• **You can't change the past, so work to change the future.** Many clients believe that insight into the origins of their difficulties will be sufficient to resolve them. They may use counseling to ferret out memories of long-lost hurts, disappointments in love, or failures of their parents that may have started their concerns.

This model works perfectly well for a malfunctioning car. Say, for example, your engine seems to be missing as you drive along. You might surmise that the cause of this problem lies in the fuel system or the electrical system. Investigation on the basis of these hypotheses might lead you to discover that you have a clogged fuel filter or a broken spark plug. You replace either filter or plug, and your problem is solved. Discovering the problem and fixing it has improved your future experience with the car.

But this automobile metaphor is a false analogy for complex human concerns. Not only can you not replace the parts in a person's memory, you wouldn't know where to look for them in the first place. What you can do is help your client work toward building a new future that renders the past less powerful.

An important thing to remember is that, while your automobile is complicated, it is not complex. Complex systems work quite differently than those that are merely complicated. We complex humans can survive difficulties and even find that we have grown from having gone through them. We do more than survive; we thrive (Echterling, Presbury, & McKee, 2005).

Our counseling students sometimes speak ironically of "AFGOs" as salvaging something good from a negative experience and learning something valuable as a result. In the poetic language of our students, an *AFGO* is "Another Fucking Growth Opportunity." In other words, we despair when the negative event happens, but we can take useful lessons from it. There are positive exceptions to even the worst experiences. The maxim that "nothing is ever all bad" can help you aid your clients toward retrieving the times when as children they experienced joy, despite the fact that they were truly mistreated. As it is sometimes said, "It's never too late to have a happy childhood."

TOOLS

We have designed this book to provide you with plenty of opportunities to become skilled in using the tools of brief therapy. We strongly believe that the format and style of a book should have a working symmetry with the therapeutic approach it presents. You will notice that, since we emphasize that every intervention should be goal oriented, we begin each chapter with a statement of the chapter's goals. Because we promote a narrative perspective in counseling, we include in each chapter a story that portrays the concepts. Many books open with a number of chapters that focus entirely on theory and do not deal with practice until the ending chapters. Consistent with our belief that theory and practice are intertwined, all of our chapters include both ideas and tools.

We invite you to engage with us actively as you read our book by doing more than merely underlining sentences or highlighting words. Instead, we encourage you to make the most of this book in the following ways.

• **Collaborate with us on this book.** Rather than just reading "Ideas and Tools for Brief Therapy," we would like for you to join us as a coauthor in creating a *personalized* book that is custom-designed for you. For example, we encourage you to jot down in the margins your reactions to what we say, outline the material in your own way, critically evaluate our arguments, and even pose some of your own reasoning. You may want to keep a journal of your own epiphanies ("aha experiences"), creative observations, personal growth experiences, and possible therapeutic applications. By the time you finish reading this book, it will become a truly collaborative venture that adds an important chapter in your own life narrative.

• **Get involved in the stories.** As we said earlier, we find the idea of narrative to be an exciting recent development in counseling theory. In each chapter, we tell stories from our own personal and professional experiences. These are not neat and tidy scenarios with two-dimensional characters who simplistically personify the concepts. Rather than skimming through these stories looking for "the point," we suggest that you read for meaning as you would a short story, poem, or biography. Throughout each chapter, you will be returning to the story in order to gain a deeper understanding of the ideas portrayed in the story and to practice the tools of brief counseling.

• **Participate in *all* the activities.** There are five types of activities. The first activity that you encountered in this book was *Reflecting Questions* at the end of the story. *Experiencing This Idea*, the second type, provides opportunities to gain a deeper awareness of the concepts. *Listening in on a Session* is the third kind of activity you will find in this book and provides you with an opportunity to hear brief therapy in action. *Using This Tool*, the fourth type, offers chances for you to begin practicing the skills of brief counseling. The final activity you will encounter is at the end of every chapter—the *Segue*, or transition activity.

REFLECTING QUESTIONS

This activity invites you to explore some of your thoughts and reactions regarding the chapter's story and other activities. We realize that it is tempting to answer these questions quickly and then immediately move on to the next section of the chapter. However, we strongly encourage you to write down your reflections. The very act of writing—of putting your observations and reflections into words on paper—can not only help you to articulate your ideas but also encourage you to explore the nuances and intricacies of your reactions.

EXPERIENCING THIS IDEA

Each of these activities includes an activity that involves you in using an idea in several possible ways: to gain a richer understanding of the chapter story you read earlier, to expand your own self-awareness, or to increase your insight into the change process. These activities can help you to really "get" the concept and "burn in" the idea by using it in meaningful ways. For example, earlier in this chapter we gave you a problem and asked you to resolve it. At the start, we tried to mislead you by mentioning computers and universal price codes. Then we invited you to recall your own past success experiences and apply those strategies to this problem. This experience has important parallels with that of a client trying to achieve resolution. As you can see, we are challenging you to become an active participant in this process.

LISTENING IN ON A SESSION

These activities offer you an opportunity to hear how a brief therapist can work with the people whose stories you read at the beginning of the chapters. As you read these dialogues, keep in mind that they are not scripts or "magic words" to memorize. Instead, remind yourself that this is *one* therapist's way of using brief therapy strategies with a particular client. Instead of passively reading through the dialogues, we invite you to place your personal mark on them by reviewing the process, reflecting on the dynamics, using your own words, and proposing your own interventions.

USING THIS TOOL

These structured activities for practicing the techniques of brief therapy include designing intervention strategies for the characters you met in the chapter story, applying these approaches to your own experiences, or practicing these techniques with others. For example, in each of the remaining chapters, we ask you to join with two colleagues to form a small practice group. One of you volunteers to be a client seeking counseling to address a particular concern. Another volunteers to serve as the brief counselor who uses the tool presented in the chapter. Finally, the third person serves as the recorder who observes the activity, leads the feedback discussion, and reports the group's experience to other colleagues.

Remember the "wax on, wax off" drills from the movie *The Karate Kid*? Conscientiously doing those drills helped the protagonist to build a foundation for successfully performing martial arts. It is the same for successfully learning brief counseling. There is no better way to gain these skills than through practice. It is only by performing these techniques again and again that they can become second nature to you as a brief counselor.

SEGUE

The purpose of this activity is to get you in the right mood or the appropriate frame of mind for the concepts and techniques that you will be learning in the next chapter. By taking some time to experience these segues, you can gain a sense of the cohesion and interconnectedness of the ideas and tools presented throughout this book.

A Guarantee

Few guarantees can be offered in the counseling profession, but we can confidently guarantee that, the more active you are in reading this book and participating in these activities, the more knowledge and skills you will gain.

SUMMARY

Counselors are now attempting to understand the process of change itself and are trying to find ways to tap the natural resources that clients possess. They are also integrating a variety of theoretical perspectives to help them conceptualize their clients in ways that promote effective and time-efficient counseling. In any successful counseling experience, your client is actively engaged in the process of discovery and change. As you read this book, we invite you to be just as active and involved. The consequences will be your own discoveries and changes.

SEGUE TO CHAPTER 2

You cannot rely on techniques alone to do counseling. Any successful intervention is based on the relationship. Think about the times when you made important breakthroughs in your own life, and identify one person who helped you. What was there about this relationship that facilitated this change?

Resource

Brief Family Therapy Center
PO Box 13736
Milwaukee, WI 53213
briefftc@aol.com
414-302-0650
www.brief-therapy.org

The Brief Family Therapy Center is the first agency to develop solution-focused brief therapy concepts and techniques. Founded by Steve de Shazer in 1978, the Center has been a clearinghouse for books, videos, audiotapes, training, and consultation opportunities.

CHAPTER 2

The Centrality of the Counseling Relationship

No Magic Tricks

"My humanity is bound up in yours,
for we can only be human together."
Desmond Tutu

"we are so both and oneful
night cannot be so sky
sky cannot be so sunful
i am through you so i"
e. e. cummings

CHAPTER GOALS

Reading and experiencing the ideas in this chapter will help you to understand these important concepts:

- As a counselor, you do not have a bag of magic tricks. Instead, you have a tool kit, and you practice your craft by forming a helping relationship and using basic tools of change.
- Power and expertise always remain with the client.

Reading about and practicing the tools in this chapter will help you to develop these valuable skills:

- Listening, understanding, and validating to connect therapeutically with clients.
- Deconstructing clients' self-defeating portrayals of themselves and their problems.

STORY

Bhavana bursts into the school counselor's office right after her second-period English class ends. She tells the secretary that she has an emergency and needs to talk to her counselor NOW! As luck would have it, the counselor has just finished a session with another student, and Bhavana only has to wait a couple of minutes. After she invites Bhavana into her office, the counselor asks what is troubling her. Red-faced and misty-eyed, Bhavana takes a deep breath, and angry words pour forth from her like lava from a volcano.

"I can't take it! I'm always getting myself into these messes!" Bhavana tearfully exclaims. "Yesterday afternoon, Todd, he's my boyfriend, borrowed my car and he was supposed to pick me up at 4:30 because my group was meeting at the library to work on our final project for English class. I waited and waited, but . . . like . . . no Todd. I called his house and one of his housemates said that he was drinking beer with a bunch of guys from his fraternity. Well, that really pissed me off and I started freaking out because 50 percent of our final grade is based on our group project and my group hates me anyway and Todd picks today to be the frat boy. He's so immature and selfish! Just like a man to let you down right when you count on him to come through for you."

Bhavana pauses and looks at the counselor expectantly, waits a moment or two, and goes on to sadly confess, "I'm such a loser! I always end up with guys that treat me like dirt. I think I take after my mother, because she's unlucky with men, too."

She hangs down her head, looks out the window, and appears to be stuck.

REFLECTING QUESTIONS

1. If you were the counselor, how would you respond to Bhavana's statement?
2. What does Bhavana want from you?
3. How is she portraying herself in her story?

OVERVIEW

In this book we will offer you many therapeutic tools and techniques that may seem as though they might work like magic. We do not wish to imply this. There is no magic in counseling techniques. Furthermore, any technique will fail unless you have established a relationship with your client. In this chapter we discuss the various "common factors" that have been found by many researchers to be indispensable to the counseling process. Such research always leads back to Carl Rogers, who articulated the core conditions for a successful counseling relationship.

In this chapter we discuss the concepts of attending to and acknowledging client stories and what we call the LUV triangle: indicating that you are actively *Listening,* communicating empathic *Understanding,* and authentically *Validating* the client's perspective. We also describe Bill O'Hanlon's idea, which he called "Carl Rogers with a Twist." This technique is a way of beginning to add possibility statements to our reflections of client concerns. As clients start to inform you of the problems in their lives, you subtly deconstruct the clients' stories of stagnation and hopelessness by relabeling unproductive descriptions and creatively misunderstanding some self-defeating aspects of the stories.

No matter what techniques you use, keep in mind that any time clients revert to problem-saturated talk, you must then return to acknowledging their complaints. Take care not to get ahead of the client. If you do, all the fancy techniques found in brief approaches to counseling will be of no use.

IDEAS

A Riddle

Here is a riddle for you. Read the following, and try to answer the question, What am I? Spend some time seeking a solution before reading the paragraph below the riddle, which ends with the answer.

> I'm not in earth, nor the sun, nor the moon.
> You may search all the sky—I'm not there.
> In the morning and evening—though not at noon,
> You may plainly perceive me, for like a balloon,
> I am suspended in air.
> Though disease may possess me, and sickness and pain,
> I am never in sorrow nor gloom;
> Though in wit and wisdom I equally reign.
> I am the heart of all sin and have long lived in vain;
> Yet I ne'er shall be found in the tomb.
>
> (Lord Byron's "Enigma," in Oltmanns & Emery, 1998, p. 40)

Before we tell you the answer, we want to emphasize that, once you know the answer, the one that was there all along, you can never *not* know the answer. What clients learn and discover in counseling is like this. Once clients discover the answers to the dilemmas they face, they can never *not* know these answers. Presuming that the answer to a client's concerns is *within the client* is the most basic tenet in the brief resolution approach to counseling. Well, the answer to the above riddle is the letter *I*. Did you see it? Now you do, and you cannot *not* see it.

Answers to human concerns are usually hidden in what people already know. Like the embedded *I* in Lord Byron's "Enigma," the answer becomes obvious once you have discovered a new way to look at the problem. Answers are often quite simple, as well. Perhaps you have seen a magician perform a magic trick that to you seemed quite impossible at the time, and then later, when the secret to the trick was exposed, you thought, Why didn't I see it before?! Magicians are masters at keeping your focus on one thing while they, with a little slight of hand, do something else.

In a way, people are like this when it comes to their concerns. They stay focused on the negative feelings and the accompanying stuckness while, at the same time, they ignore possible alternative ways of looking at their lives. You could say that they have hidden the rabbit in the hat and forgotten that it is there. And when they finally do realize where it is and pull the rabbit out of the hat, it looks for all the world like a magic trick!

The techniques of brief counseling are not magic. They are not mysterious or secret, and they do not reflect some hidden, special, and spontaneous power within the helper. In other words, as a brief counselor, you do not have a bag of magic tricks. Instead, you have certain ideas and understandings, some fundamental values regarding the dignity of clients, and a tool kit to influence and encourage them to heal, change, and grow. You practice your craft by forming a helping relationship and using basic tools of change. These basic tools, or common factors of effective helping, include the "core conditions" of listening and empathizing. Without communicating to your clients that you are sincerely interested in them and willing to do your best at understanding their situation, they will not invite you to help. To paraphrase Scott Miller, you must be invited into the house before you start rearranging the furniture.

EXPERIENCING THIS IDEA

Think about a time in your life when you have made important discoveries. These discoveries may have been how you thought about yourself, your attitudes about life, or your place in the world. Now pick one person who influenced you the most as you went through the process of making these changes, someone who was there for you during this time of change. Recall your experiences with this person.

REFLECTING QUESTIONS

1. How did this person influence you?
2. What was it about this person's manner, apart from specific words or actions, that you found helpful?

Magic Tricks and Miracles

In 1997, Gale Miller published a book on brief therapy under the misleading title *Becoming Miracle Workers*. The name would seem to imply that, when one learns the tools of brief therapy, one can then do magic and that the tools themselves might hold miraculous powers to change clients and help them out of their misery. It certainly is an appealing idea!

Moore and Gillette (1990), drawing on masculine Jungian archetypes, describe the magician as someone who knows something others do not. People come to him with their questions, pains, and concerns in hopes of a cure. The magician, whether priest or counselor, is viewed by those who seek his advice as someone who can peer into issues that are not revealed to ordinary people. "He is a seer and a prophet in the sense of not only predicting the future but also of seeing deeply" (p. 99).

Without doubt, many men and women in the helping professions have sought to assume the role of miracle worker or magician with their clients. Conventional wisdom has suggested that counselors should be trained to the point of possessing knowledge far superior to that of their clients, so that when dispensing sage advice they can both capture the client's awe and offer correct information. This belief is the root metaphor of the medical model.

But you have to face facts. You are neither seer nor sage. Although you may continually strive to master the knowledge and skills of the counseling profession, you will never attain magical powers over your clients or become the expert on their issues. Power and expertise always remain in the client's domain. Most practitioners of brief therapy suggest that, instead of adopting the position of a guru or expert with your clients, you must instead assume a position of ignorance, of not knowing. By taking on the stance of "I'm not from around here," which we mentioned in Chapter 1, you cannot assume the position of spectator of the client's world, but rather you must "be with" the client in his or her world. In the postmodern view of science, "the pure scientist's traditional posture of *Theoros,* or spectator, can no longer be maintained: we are always—and inescapably—participants or agents as well" (Toulmin, 1982, p. 255).

Whatever the client may think or do can no longer be considered to simply reside within the client's "bag of skin." On the contrary, what the client may think or do when he or she is with you is a *function* of being with you. Whether you like it or not, you participate in—or co-construct—clients' stories as they tell them. You are in relationship with the client and the client's world. With this in mind, you must always do the best you can to establish and maintain a respectful therapeutic or working relationship with your client. If there is any magic in counseling, it is in the relationship that you develop with the client. Without the richness of the relationship, any tools you may attempt to use will be mere incantations cast to the wind.

Common Factors

As you read in Chapter 1, years of research have found that counseling is effective, but no particular model appears to be greatly superior to any other (Prochaska & Norcross, 2007). These results brought about a search for "common factors," or those curative elements that are shared across theoretical schools regardless of their stated aims. In order to reduce the chaos and make sense of these various therapies, Kleinke (1994) surveyed authors who had identified common factors in psychotherapy that appear to be shared, no matter what the ostensible focus of each approach might be. Regardless of the differences in their approaches to counseling and psychotherapy, all the theorists that Kleinke surveyed regarding common factors agreed that it is the caring relationship that establishes the foundation for effective work. In such a safe and trusting environment, clients can take risks trying new ways of thinking and acting and can understand their thoughts and actions from a different perspective (Goldfried, 1980).

Fred Duhl, a well-known family therapist, dressed up in hip waders and fishing gear when he addressed a convention of therapists in order to make the following point: "The ways of the fish are more important than the tools of the fisherman" (Young, 1992, p. 32). No techniques can work if you do not first have a working relationship with your client. You might say that the relationship is what "hooks" the client into collaborating with you as a counselor. Furthermore, each client will respond to the techniques you are offering in a different way. Just as an expert fisherman allows the fish to run, rest, and "resist," all the while keeping a tender touch on the line so as to know when to reel the fish in, so does the sensitive counselor remain tuned to the client's moods and moves. This tentative, yet totally involved, attitude on the part of the counselor will do as much to help the client as any technique we can suggest in this book.

A Caveat: Listen to Your Clients

Active Listening
Reflective Listening

Imagine our surprise when we picked up the July/August 1997 issue of *The Family Therapy Networker* and read that three of the well-known exponents of solution-focused brief therapy had made the discovery that listening to clients is more important than flashy technique! Our surprise was that *they* were so surprised by this realization. In their article entitled "Stepping Off the Throne," Barry Duncan, along with Mark Hubble and Scott Miller, stated, "[W]hen faced with a seeming choice between technique and relationship, a therapist is often better off focusing on relationship" (1997, p. 28). This insight came to these authors as a result of their "impossible cases" study. This study was an attempt to show that the techniques of solution-focused brief therapy could be applied to all sorts of client problems and diagnoses. After absorbing the techniques of Weakland, de Shazer, Erickson, and others, Duncan, Hubble, and Miller wanted to show that the techniques of these master therapists were useful with the most difficult cases with which other approaches had failed.

As a result of their outreach efforts, Duncan, Hubble, and Miller were referred some "nightmare clients" by a local psychodynamically trained psychiatrist, whom they are now sure was seeking revenge. Ironically, although this trio of therapists eventually was able to report some success with these clients, this success apparently had little to do with their technical skills. What mattered was not the "technical wizardry" of the therapists or the particular therapeutic approach. Their success was credited more to the attitude they brought the therapeutic effort. What these therapists found was that success "is far more heavily influenced by what the clients bring into the room and the relationship that is created there" (Duncan et al., 1997, p. 24).

Realizing what they had lost in their haste to fix their clients and blinded by their "theoretical arrogance," these therapists decided to eschew their therapeutic tactics and, instead, listen to what the clients were saying to them. Duncan reported that he spoke fewer than 15 sentences in one successful session. "I used no genograms, marital contracting, head tapping, guided imagery, miracle questions, finger waving, trance suggestions, enigmatic Ericksonian prescriptions, lies, manipulations or gurulike pronouncements" (Duncan et al., 1997, p. 26). Instead, the therapy team "dethroned" themselves as therapeutic experts and began to listen to what clients made of their own situations, what theories the clients had, and how the clients thought that their problems might be solved.

Heeding the advice of the philosopher Pascal, who wrote that people are more persuaded by reasons that they themselves have discovered than by those from the minds of others, the team began to refrain from intervening too soon. Instead, they began listening more and inviting more participation on the part of their clients. They were encouraged both by the positive results in their sessions and by research that suggests "that positive change is correlated with how much clients—but not therapists—say" (p. 26). Specifically, a meta-analysis of over 1,000 process-outcome studies (Bergin & Garfield, 1994) concluded that the most important determinant in successful outcomes was the quality of the client's participation. As a result, the team went back to the drawing board for a rationale that supported what they were learning from their "impossible" clients. "The work led us in two apparently divergent directions—into a hard-boiled examination of outcome literature and into a rereading of Carl Rogers" (Duncan et al., 1997, p. 26).

Rogers Rediscovered

It is not unusual for a person-centered therapist to attend a workshop or conference where people are speaking with great enthusiasm about a new theory or technique that has been developed in their field, only to realize that it is right out of a Carl Rogers book! Often, without credit to Rogers, the new approach has been given a new name and declared a new discovery—much like Columbus "discovering" America in spite of the fact that people were already living there. Rogers's ideas have become so pervasive that their influence is felt in nearly all of the newer forms of therapy (Presbury, McKee, & Echterling, 2007). What initially had seemed to be his simplistic, overly optimistic, and naive ideas are now appreciated for their "profound beauty and importance" (Kahn, 1991, p. 35). The notion of the importance of carefully listening to clients is a topic that pervades all of Rogers's writing, but perhaps no passage is more poignant than the following:

> One thing I have come to look upon as almost universal is that when a person realizes he has been deeply heard, there is a moistness in his eyes. I think in some real sense he is weeping for joy. It is as though he were saying, "Thank God, *somebody* heard me. Someone knows what it's like to be me." In such moments I have had the fantasy of a prisoner in a dungeon, tapping out day after day a Morse code message, "Does anybody hear me?" And finally one day he hears some faint tappings which spell out "Yes." By that one simple response he is released from his loneliness, he has become a human being again. There are many, many people living in private dungeons today, people who give no evidence of it whatever on the outside, where you have to listen very sharply to hear the faint messages from the dungeon. (Rogers, 1969, p. 224)

Multicultural reconsideration of Rogers   For years, one of the major criticisms of Rogers was that his ideas reflected only western, White, middle-class values (Sharf, 2004). For example, some have warned that his preoccupation with self-actualization is not universal, and may indeed prove detrimental should counselors promote this value in certain cultures (Prochaska & Norcross, 2007).

Certainly, Western culture has come to value the separateness and autonomy of the individual over interdependence and connectedness. However, most critics of Rogers have not appreciated his emphasis on empathically understanding clients and responding to their diverse worldviews with respect and positive regard. Rogers cautioned that the ultimate reality resides in the phenomenal world of the client. Consequently, his ideas challenge us to not simply tolerate this phenomenological diversity but to celebrate it.

More recently, other practitioners have recommended Rogers's approach as a valuable perspective in cross-cultural situations. For example, Spangenberg (2003) promoted person-centered counseling in South Africa. Citing Rogers's remarkable group work in South Africa and compatibilities with traditional African healing practices, Spangenberg proposed that the person-centered approach overcomes many of the obstacles that block authentic communication between people from different cultures.

Counselors have used a person-centered approach successfully with impoverished children and adolescents in Brazil (Freire, Koller, & Piason, 2005). Although these clients faced profound hardships, including poverty, neglect, abuse and abandonment, they responded well to interventions. The practitioners concluded that this approach is effective in promoting resilience, even under extraordinarily adverse conditions. Person-centered counseling is also effective with sexual-minority adolescents (Lemoire & Chen, 2005). This approach offers therapeutic conditions that counteract the stigmatization that sexual-minority adolescents face.

Rogers and brief counseling   Although Kahn (1991) did not see Rogers's methods as sufficient for a complete therapy, he considered their relationship aspects to be indispensable. He wrote that, no matter what theory we hold dear or how we view the human mind, "there is much to be learned by paying careful attention to Rogers's advice about the relationship between therapist and client" (pp. 35–36).

Walter and Peller are solution-focused brief therapists who have placed little emphasis on building a trusting relationship with a client. They presume that trust simply exists. However, in spite of their lack of emphasis on the Rogerian approach, they specifically cite the basic techniques of Rogers as important to maintaining a working relationship in which the client feels supported and understood. Among these techniques are "reflective listening and empathic listening, the restating what the client said, with the same affect and tone. . . . [This remains essential to communicating] initial support of the client's position" (1992, pp. 42–43).

In addition, solution-focused brief therapists O'Hanlon and Beadle (1994) described a therapeutic technique called "Carl Rogers with a Twist" in their book describing their therapeutic approach called "possibility therapy." Following Rogers, they communicate acceptance of their clients. However, "then we add a little twist. We communicate, 'where you are now is a valid place to be, AND you can change'" (p. 15).

Though they cite Rogers in naming their technique, O'Hanlon and Beadle see what they do as an intervention, rather than an attempt to listen to the client with the intent of encouraging him or her to further explore a concern. The "Rogers" part of the technique is employed as an acknowledgment of the client's concern, but they also add the important possibility statements that are implied in what the client says. In fact, Carl Rogers himself used the technique of "Carl Rogers with a twist" on the famous "Gloria" videos (Rogers, 1965).

Duncan, Hubble, and Miller (1997) have taken the advice of Rogers more to heart and now place more emphasis on carefully attending to the client and establishing that crucial bond between therapist and client. They have come to believe that extreme care must be taken to ensure a high-quality relationship after reports from their clients that simple courtesy and confirmation of the clients' position had been experienced as very powerful. Initially, they thought of such behaviors as "foreplay," a way to woo the client into doing the real work of therapy. However, their reading of Carl Rogers convinced them of the importance of the core conditions of empathy, warmth, genuineness, and acceptance:

> Now, we realized that the relationship was, in fact, the therapy. . . . [C]lients are far more likely to consider these "core variables" responsible for their improvement than theories and flashy technique. (Duncan et al., 1997, p. 29)

By 1997, the "impossible case" project of Duncan, Hubble, and Miller was 10 years old, and they regarded the project as generally successful. But the project's greatest success proved to be in the reorientation of the therapists. The therapy team members reported that now, when they train and supervise others, "we encourage them, above all, to listen and to notice the effect of their words on their clients. . . . [W]e emphasize the factors that are common to all good therapy" (Duncan et al., 1997, p. 33).

Lipchik (2002) pointed out that there is a major difference between hearing and listening. In a way, this distinction is like the difference between sensation and perception. We do not perceive everything that we sense in the world, but we rather focus on what is important to us. Likewise, a good counselor becomes exquisitely attuned to aspects of what is heard that are most important. In other words, said Lipchik, counselors listen selectively: "What we hear is everything our client tells us. . . . We do not ignore anything we hear, but at the same time, we only respond to what is potentially useful for the client" (p. 44). Learning to carefully listen, rather than merely hear what your client is saying, is a skill that you will need to perfect over time.

A dyed-in-the-wool person-centered therapist might criticize the realizations of these solution-focused therapists as nothing but "old wine in new bottles," but we don't believe Carl Rogers would object. It was never his wish to create a person-centered movement. Rather, Rogers hoped to influence the behavior of therapists in relationship to their clients. Nevertheless, the results of the "impossible case" project and the words of Duncan, Hubble, Miller, and others have vindicated the faith Rogers placed in the therapeutic relationship.

Acknowledgment and Therapeutic Distance

Becvar, Canfield, and Becvar (1997) spoke of the counselor's attitude as one of "beneficence," a term that "dates back at least 2,500 years to the time of Hippocrates in classical Greece. . . ." (p. 57). They considered this stance to be the primary moral imperative for the helping professions. *Beneficence* means engaging in acts of kindness and doing no harm (Becvar & Becvar, 2006). Merely doing no harm, however, could imply mere acts of passive observation, acts of charity, or acts of sympathy. As a counselor, you are required to do much more than this. You must engage with your client—you must seek to enter the client's world and understand it from his or her frame of reference.

Such engagement does not mean simply being kind. Instead, you must "be with" the client. This admonition is central to the notion of a therapeutic relationship and is considered scripture among humanists—so much so as to have had its utterance now seem almost cliché and trite. *Being with* conveys the idea that a counselor must not only be totally focused on the client but communicate a deep concern for the client's plight.

While you attempt to enter the client's world, still you must strive to achieve the proper therapeutic distance from the client's concerns. Optimal therapeutic distance means that you maintain a boundary between client and yourself—albeit a permeable boundary. Some have called this a "detached concern." This separation not only preserves you in the relationship, but serves as a model for the client as well. Clients often come to counseling having been submerged by their concerns and feeling overwhelmed by their emotions. To focus inordinately on pain and confusion only causes the client to sink deeper into discouragement.

By maintaining a proper *therapeutic distance* (a term we prefer to *detached concern*), you avoid exacerbating the client's problems. Furthermore, when working in the brief resolution mode, you invite the client to move away from the pain and problem into a more hopeful realm, seeking to find the survivor in the victim. While the difference between a "therapeutic alliance" in the psychodynamic sense and a "working alliance" is not completely clear in the counseling literature, we would assert that a working alliance is intended to be somewhat less intimate and of shorter duration. If this connection works well, aspects of the relationship such as client dependence, transference, and difficulty with termination may be minimized.

The optimal balance between intimacy and detachment is always dependent on the mutually agreed-upon contract between you and the client. This contract, however, is largely implicit and is always in flux. Some days the client can tolerate more distance and at other times will demand more intimacy. Your best clue is that when attempts are made to influence the client's movement toward a goal, and the client returns to "problem-saturated talk," then this is a signal that you must move a bit closer and reacknowledge the client's concerns.

Acknowledgment can be communicated without highlighting the client's negative mood. DeJong and Berg (1998) suggested that, rather than highlighting the client's pain and discouragement in the present, you might say, "Things have been pretty discouraging for you." (Notice that this statement places concerns in the past tense.) Then you immediately proceed to look for client behaviors that have transcended the negative situation. The difference between DeJong and Berg's preferred responses and the ones they consider less useful is that you are suggesting that the client's emotions are situational, relational, and time limited.

Portraying emotions in these ways has profound implications for how clients view their concerns and themselves. *Situational* concerns do not require that clients get "personality transplants." Rather, they are about events that have taken place that can be remedied or overcome. Such negative events are not chronic aspects of the client's character. In order to convey this, you might say, "So, there have been some situations that seem to have knocked you for a loop at times." *Relational* concerns imply a contribution on the part of someone else and that the problem exists between at least two people, not within one person. This may relieve the client of some feelings of crushing responsibility: "It sounds like when you have been with him, these feelings have overwhelmed you, but in other relationships you feel pretty confident." Finally, the *time-limited* connotation of the acknowledgment suggests that the problem will not last forever: "These issues have preoccupied your thoughts for a while, and it seems you are now working hard to get past this troubled time." You can suggest that the client's problem is time limited without resorting to hackneyed and obviously empty reassurances, such as, "This is just a phase you're going through."

If you have been trained to probe and uncover deeper feelings so that the client might get in touch with "repressed" or disavowed emotions, you may find the above notions of acknowledgment a bit lightweight. Perhaps they are. But whether you have offered an adequate acknowledgment or not depends on the client. You must remain sensitive to the client's nonverbal communication and to whether the client seems willing to move toward resolution talk. O'Hanlon and Beadle (1994) suggested that clients will send a message if they do not feel sufficiently understood as a result of your acknowledgment. At such times, more acknowledgment is required. Empathy is, after all, the extent to which clients believe they are understood—not the extent to which you believe *you* understand.

O'Hanlon and Beadle (1994) used the metaphor of the sport of curling, in which the participants use brooms to sweep a path for a stone sliding along the ice, to explain how carefully you must move the client toward solutions. A curler sweeps immediately in front of the stone, and so the counselor must sweep directly in front of the client by opening up possibilities. The curler must pay close attention to where the stone is and less to where it should go. "Translated into therapy-land, that means we'd better pay more attention to where clients actually are than to our theory about where they should be" (p. 11).

Unless the client experiences your empathy—your accurate understanding of his or her world—you will not receive an invitation to help. Unless that invitation is received, clients will appear to resist your best attempts to assist them. You cannot say that the client is noncompliant in such a situation. It is more likely that you have not yet convinced the client that you truly understand. To restate a line from the movie *Cool Hand Luke,* "What we have here is failure to communicate." Communicating empathy is your job, and the communication is never complete until the client gets it.

Implications of These Ideas for the Counselor

The ideas concerning the centrality of relationship in any productive encounter have important implications for your day-to-day work with clients:

• No matter how well informed you become about people and counseling in general, the individual client *always* remains the expert on his or her own experience.

• Whatever the client does in the counseling session is a function of being *with* you. You and the client are both participants in the co-construction of the client's story.

• The most important aspect of successful counseling is the *relationship*. This means that you must attempt to communicate to the client that you care, that the client can trust you, and that you will do your best to listen and understand. Without this as the basis of your work, the counseling is likely to go nowhere.

Counselors must carefully listen to what clients have to say, so you must somehow communicate to the client that he or she has been heard. But this does not mean that you encourage clients to further explore all the nuances of their pain. The notion of "Carl Rogers with a Twist" implies that you also seek to add a possibility statement to your acknowledgment.

• It is important to communicate empathic *understanding* to your clients, while at the same time maintaining a therapeutic distance. This means that you do not allow yourself to be overwhelmed by the client's pain.

• Any time you are attempting to lead the client away from a focus on the concern and the client returns to "problem-saturated talk," this is your signal to *return to acknowledging* the client's current version of the story.

• Before you attempt to engineer a change in the client's story, make sure you have been *invited* to do so. Any time your client resists, this means you have been "dis-invited." Go back to acknowledging.

TOOLS

Establishing the Counseling Relationship

When you begin a counseling relationship, there are two fundamental tasks that you must perform: *attend to* and *acknowledge* the client. According to Webster's New World Dictionary of the American Language (1968), *attend* means to give heed to, be mindful of, minister to, or serve. *Acknowledge* means to recognize as having authority or worth and accept as being true or having value.

Attending and *acknowledging* are terms that sum up well the behavior of the successful counselor in the beginning stages of counseling. However, even though they are well-defined terms that convey the proper attitude, they do not immediately imply precise, concrete behaviors. We might come closer by stating that there is a triad of behaviors that you must show in order to convince your client that you are, indeed, attending and acknowledging. We call this the "LUV Triangle" (see Figure 2-1). In the LUV Triangle, you display behaviors that convey to the client that you are *listening, understanding,* and *validating* the client's view of things. Similarly, Scott Miller (1996) used the acronym *LAV* to describe these behaviors (Listen, Acknowledge, Validate). However, his terms are not all at the same level of abstraction. Acknowledging includes listening and validating,

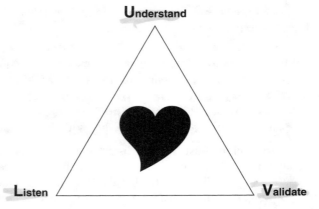

FIGURE 2-1 The LUV Triangle.

and the foundation of your attending and acknowledging process is your empathic understanding. (Besides, we think that "LUV Triangle" is a catchier mnemonic device.) Finally, keep in mind that for you to listen and understand will not be useful for the client unless you also communicate that you are doing so; validation means that you accept the client's story or worldview but not necessarily all aspects of the client's behavior.

Even with the use of these more concrete terms, it is probably still not completely clear to you what you are actually doing. So, let us describe what the precise behaviors are that would be called for at the beginning of a counseling relationship. The most important aspect of these behaviors is that the client must perceive that you are attempting to establish the LUV Triangle. In other words, you must successfully communicate these conditions to the client. It is one thing to intend to send a certain message, and quite another for the message to be received as planned. Communication includes both a sender and a receiver. Check to make sure your client receives your communication and that you are accurately receiving the client's intended message. This point cannot be overstated.

What do you need to do in order to show your commitment to *listen* to the client? According to Egan (2007), it helps to perform the following behaviors.

- Face the client with an engaged, inviting manner.
- Adopt an open, nonthreatening posture.
- Lean toward the client.
- Maintain good eye contact.
- Keep a sense of poise, and refrain from fidgeting.

How will the client know that you *understand* what is being said? There are a variety of specific strategies that you can use to communicate your understanding:

- Repeat or paraphrase what the client has said.
- Check your understanding by saying what you think the client means and asking for verification.
- Nonverbally match your client's mood and the pace or rhythm of his or her communication.
- Use words, phrases, and expressions that are similar to the client's.

Be particularly alert for the metaphors that the client uses to portray the problem and those that imply what the client hopes to change. Here is an example of what we mean by this:

Client: I feel like I am back-sliding.

Counselor: As you feel yourself on this slippery slope, you seem to be hoping to grab onto something solid to stop this slide.

At this stage, you stay with the content that the client is giving you, without probing or going beyond the facts that are offered. You do not need to know more than the client spontaneously offers about the pain and trouble. Clients will produce this problem-saturated talk on their own until they are convinced that you "get it." The LUV Triangle is your vehicle for communicating that you do.

Finally, what can you do in order to convey your willingness to *validate* the client? There are a number of simple behaviors you can use to communicate that you support and affirm the client:

- Nod affirmatively as the client speaks.
- Smile warmly, and offer minimal encouragers ("um-hmm," "I see," "yes, go on").
- Refrain from conveying skepticism, doubt, or the desire to debate with the client.

Of course, you should not ask questions that may indicate you are repudiating the client's presentation of his or her experiences or behave in any way that suggests you are devaluing the client. Instead, by validating, you are indicating in every way you can your openness and willingness to believe what the client is telling you.

"Carl Rogers with a Twist"

We find that most people misunderstand Carl Rogers and his way of working with clients. Ask the average counselor, and he or she will say that the essence of Rogers's work was the "um-hmm" and the "I hear you saying . . ." phrases. They understand his approach only superficially and think it is simply being a kind, friendly, accepting person—an attitude sometimes pejoratively known as "Little Bo Peep psychology"—you know—"Leave them alone and they'll come home. . . ." Others, even farther off base, think it is the "How does that make you feel?" question. Unfortunately, Rogers originally termed his approach "nondirective," and many people took this to mean you do nothing as a counselor but listen and smile.

However, a close analysis of Rogers's work reveals an extremely subtle maneuvering strategy that influenced clients to center the conversation on themselves and to begin to realize their personal power. Although we think the term *empowering* implies misplaced action (meaning that one does not empower someone else), if any set of techniques qualifies as helping someone to become empowered, it is Carl Rogers's way of counseling.

O'Hanlon and Beadle (1994) have said that what Rogers did was *acknowledge* the client, and that the focus of the acknowledgment was not so much on the client's feelings as the client's meanings. If the client hears meanings coming back from you that match his or her own, the client feels understood. While many would call this understanding "merely cognitive," it seems to do the job. O'Hanlon and Beadle's notion of "Carl Rogers with a Twist" (which sounds more like a cocktail than a technique) involves doing three tasks simultaneously as you acknowledge the client:

- Feed back the meaning of the client's complaint.
- Place that complaint in language of the past tense.
- Replace client language of "stuckness" or despair with language of possibility.

For example, instead of saying to the client, "You *are experiencing* a lot of *depression* about your *inability* to resolve this situation," you might say, "You *have gone through* some times when you *have* felt *really down* because you have *not yet* found a way to resolve this situation."

O'Hanlon insisted that we must "watch our language" with clients, and that the use of subtly different feedback—while retaining the client's meaning—can change the way the client views the situation. In the above example, substituting "you have gone through" (past tense) for "you are experiencing" (present tense), and "really down" (a normalizing phrase) for "depression" (a diagnosis), and "not yet" (implying that it's a matter of time) for "inability" (a personal flaw or helplessness), all serve to reframe the situation. You convey the important message, in so many words, that the client has been having reasonable reactions to a situation that has existed in the past but that will be resolved. In this way, you are offering the client a more positive and hopeful view without disputing the version of his or her story. But it is important that you do not minimize the client's concern during this process by saying something like, "Those things are all in the past, and your reaction was normal. I know you are strong enough to get through this." Such a statement implies you know more about the client's experience and capability than the client does.

Past-tense phrasing   You can characterize these negative emotions as taking place in the past by using a variety of phrases. For example, you might say, "For a long time you have felt . . . ," or "You didn't seem to be able to shake the feeling of. . . ." Placing these emotions within a circumscribed time period suggests that these feelings or perceptions were influenced by situations that may have changed.

You could say, "When that happened, you felt . . . ," or "Because he didn't seem to be paying attention to you, you believed . . . ," or "When she would do that, you thought that it meant. . . ." You can even suggest that this feeling or perception may be different now by saying, for example, "Until now, it has seemed to you that. . . ."

Possibility Statement

Dropping in some suggestions of the possibility of a future resolution is an excellent way of planting the seeds of change. Your reflections may begin with statements such as, "*So far,* you have not seemed to be able to . . . ," or "You have *not yet* been able to accomplish this." Other possibility phrases include, "You *haven't quite* mastered the skill of . . . ," or "When this happens again, *you're wondering how* you will handle it differently," or "You're thinking that it might be difficult, but you still *really want* to do it." These possibility statements must be inspired by either what the client has explicitly said or what is implied by the client's affect; otherwise, you run the risk of getting too far ahead of the client's story. Furthermore, if the client seems to balk or reject your addition of a possibility statement, you can respond by saying, "You looked just then like I didn't get that quite right. How would you say it instead?"

Another less obvious aspect to this form of feedback is that a reframe is automatically built into it. When clients tell you how things are going or what kind of person they take themselves to be, the opportunity for you to normalize the situation is present. For example, a "loser" is someone who, despite many setbacks, keeps on trying; a "lazy" person is someone who must think about a job for a while before starting it; and a "control freak" is someone who has wonderful attention to detail and works for the best outcome.

In addition, you can rephrase client assertions about "the way things are" into more tentative terms. Instead of colluding with the client's absolute pronouncements about reality, you can accept the client's declaration as a point of view or "*one way* to look at it." For example, you can preface your acknowledgments with such phrases as, "So, in your *opinion* . . . ," or "The *way you see* it . . . ," or "It *seems* to you that. . . ." Each of these statements suggests that it is the person's *perception,* rather than reality itself, that is being considered here.

You get the idea: When clients use damning phrases to characterize themselves or statements that portray themselves as helpless in their situation, you can modify and loosen the client's construction of self and world by feeding back more positive terms as if the client had used those words in the first place. This technique is not, however, an attempt to argue the client out of his or her version of the story. Remember: You are validating that version. But you are also substituting the labels the client places on self and opening up the restrictive aspects of the story. By taking care to communicate your respect, you can successfully carry out this process without coming across as the stern teacher correcting the client on improper word usage. Getting comfortable using "Carl Rogers with a Twist" is something that takes practice. Don't expect yourself to get good at it right away. We think that you will find this a useful technique for simultaneously acknowledging the client's complaint, while at the same time beginning to deconstruct it.

LISTENING IN ON A SESSION

Review the story at the beginning of the chapter. A resolution-focused counselor might engage with Bhavana in ways that promote the relationship by using the LUV Triangle and "Carl Rogers with a Twist."

Bhavana: (After her litany of complaints about the recent events, Bhavana pauses, looks at the counselor expectantly, and waits a moment or two.)

"I'm such a loser! I always end up with guys that treat me like dirt. I think I take after my mother because she's unlucky with men, too."

Counselor: (She looks directly at Bhavana and speaks in a calm but concerned tone of voice. The counselor decides to invite Bhavana in deconstructing her story.)

"You've been having to deal with so many problems with Todd lately that you are wondering what it might be like to be treated well by a guy."

Bhavana: (Her voice starts to quiver and her eyes fill with tears as she continues, pausing often to wipe her eyes and blow her nose with a tissue from the box the counselor keeps by the client's chair.)

"I really wish I knew . . . anyway, Todd finally showed up about 6:00 and tells me he had a flat tire. I screamed and yelled at him for making me late and not calling. Then I got into this huge fight with him and called him a stupid asshole. He just looked at me and walked away. I can't believe what a complete bitch I am! By the time I got to the library, it was closed. I was going to call somebody in my group last night to explain everything, but I was so embarrassed about screwing things up that I just couldn't do it. So now my group thinks I blew off my part of the project."

Counselor: (Since Bhavana has returned to problem-saturated talk, the counselor returns to the LUV Triangle by indicating understanding, nodding her head affirmatively, and speaking empathically, while adding a twist at the end.)

"So it must have felt like the whole world has been against you since yesterday afternoon. It looked to you like Todd let you down. Then you thought your group may have gotten the wrong idea about you, too. You've been feeling really upset, and now you've come here to find a way out."

Bhavana: (Her voice becomes softer and takes on a sad quality. The tears begin again, and her demeanor and tone of voice suggest that Bhavana sees herself as helpless.)

"Yeah! It's like I'm in really deep water and I can't even see the shore."

Counselor: (Softly and leaning forward.)

"Yeah, you've felt that you've been in way over your head lately, and now you're looking for a place to come ashore."

REFLECTING QUESTIONS

1. Point out the verbal and nonverbal examples of the LUV Triangle in the above interaction.
2. Identify the "twists" that the counselor offered.
3. Write another possible LUV Triangle statement or "Rogers with a Twist" response to Bhavana's last comment.

USING THIS TOOL

Join with two colleagues to form a group of three members. One of you volunteers to be a client by sharing a situation in which you feel stuck. Another volunteers to help by using the "Carl Rogers with a Twist" technique. In other words, feed back the meaning of the client's words, but use the past tense in acknowledging complaints, and use the present and future tense to suggest possibilities of successes. Finally, the third person serves as the recorder who observes the activity and leads the feedback discussion.

You Need Two Things

We believe that the use of this technique can be a crucial turning point in the therapeutic relationship. This is the first time that the counselor becomes *intentionally* influential in attempting to deconstruct, or free the client from, a restrictive story. Because this technique is so fundamental to becoming an effective brief counselor, you need to do two things.

First, practice this technique until it feels as natural to you as the LUV skills. Second, take time in your group to talk about your reactions to being both compassionate and influencing, genuine and intentional, heartfelt and goal oriented.

Deconstructing Client Complaints

When clients begin to give descriptions of their concerns, they believe that what they offer is a recollection of the facts of their lives. In other words, they are simply describing events happening in the real world that impact their lives and that these are objective, immutable happenings. You will find in the literature of many brief approaches that the way clients talk about problems in their lives is referred to as "problem-saturated" talk or the client's "complaint." On first reading, you may think these terms are disrespectful or a trivialization of the client's pain, but the words are really meant to remind us that "the map is not the territory." No matter how faithful the client believes he or she is to the facts of the matter, in the constructivist view there really are no facts of the matter.

Client descriptions of their problems are their interpretations of the facts. These descriptions are loaded with personal meaning for the client, and it is usually this meaning—and not the facts themselves—that causes the client to suffer. The ancient philosopher Epictetus is often quoted as saying that it is not what has happened to us that causes us pain but, rather, what we have made of what has happened. We are victims of the meaning we assign to events. Milton Erickson said that his clients came with problems they couldn't solve, so he gave them problems they could solve. This means that problems can be deconstructed—changed into other problems that seem less discouraging. In other words, problems are negotiable. Your task is to renegotiate the client's complaint so that it is looser, more workable, and offers a way out.

We hasten to point out, however, that this does not mean that you attempt to turn problems into nonproblems. You are not trying to talk the client out of the problem or minimize it in the way that a parent or well-meaning friends might have done. We all can recall examples of those attempts: "You think you've got problems?! You should think of the starving people in Africa," or "In a year, you'll laugh about this," or "So what if you missed this one—there are plenty more fish in the sea." If you can vaguely recall any of these responses to your complaints, you also realize that they are utterly useless! When you attempt to deconstruct complaints, you are not trying to get clients to "look on the bright side." You are subtly offering another interpretation of the complaint that may throw the problem into a more workable frame.

Everyone's world is a constructed world. That is, the way we see things and what we view as facts are filtered through our representations and our meanings. When you attempt to deconstruct a client's world, you are not simply trying to get the client to see things your way. Rather, you are perturbing the schemas that the client has constructed. This approach is not the disputation therapy that is sometimes seen in the "cognitive" techniques. Deconstruction is quite different than *disputation*. In the latter approach, the counselor actively exposes and corrects the client's irrational, self-defeating thinking. Albert Ellis, who never minced words, asserted that irrational beliefs "can be elicited and demolished by any scientist worth his or her salt, and the rational-emotive therapist is exactly that: an exposing and nonsense-annihilating scientist" (Gelso & Fretz, 1992, p. 250). Pretty strong stuff!

Instead of viewing clients as faulty in their thinking, a therapist can validate, rather than dispute, client perspectives. You are not trying to talk the client out of his or her assumptions and into yours. However, by attempting to loosen the client's rigid categories and self-defeating assumptions, you hope to send these constructions into disarray so that the client can rebuild, or reconstruct, a world with more possibilities. In that sense, the client becomes empowered to meet the world head-on and with less trepidation. The client's new assumptions and constructions will be built upon the same "facts" but will offer a new way of seeing these "facts."

A client may construct a story that is self-defeating by using dead-end, all-or-nothing, irrefutable, and insoluble complaints that express certain emotions, but also sabotage a search for resolution. Below are some of the most common stagnating portrayals that clients are likely to use. With each of them, we offer some suggestions for deconstruction. Please keep in mind that these suggestions, and all such suggestions in this book, are meant to be examples rather than rigid prescriptions for your counseling behavior. You can use your own creativity in deconstructing client complaints, and you must also pay careful attention to how the client responds. Remember the axiom coined by the solution-focused therapists: If your intervention doesn't work, do something different.

• **The client's complaint is couched as** *universal*. In other words, it is "always" or "never" happening.

To deconstruct this portrayal, you can respond by describing the circumstances as possibly *episodic* or *situational*. For example, you might say, "So you've been going through some really hard times recently, and it seems that this problem has been happening nearly all the time."

• **The client's portrayal is the** *absolute truth* **or "***reality***."** The client implies that his or her interpretation is the only valid representation of the events.

The basic deconstructing strategy is to respond to these assertions as *perceptions,* the client's interpretation of the facts. In this case, you may be prefacing your responses with, "So it has seemed to you that . . . ," "The way it has looked to you is . . . ," "In your eyes . . . ," or "From your perspective . . ."

• **The client heavily relies on a** *label* **or** *diagnosis* **to characterize self and others.** The client, for example, announces, "I am an enabler," "My daughter is an anorectic," or "My son has a conduct disorder."

Here, you attempt to deconstruct by describing the specific behaviors that relate to the diagnosis, or relabel the behaviors. For example, you may respond to the self-described "enabler" by saying, "So many times when he has wanted money for alcohol, you have let yourself give it to him, and then you have lied to his employer about his being 'sick.'" To the parent who labels a daughter as "anorectic," you might answer, "So let me check this out. Your daughter has not been eating enough, and she has become so thin that it's endangering her health?" And with the parent who diagnoses a child with "a conduct disorder," you might respond, "So your son seems to be someone who has questioned authority an awful lot."

The purpose of deconstructing stories that rely on such diagnostic characterizations of people is that behaviors are much easier to change than labels.

• **The client gives a litany of problems.** The client presents a long list of concerns, complaints, and grievances.

Focusing on one concern that seems the most workable or most urgent to the client is a good deconstructive method. You may say, for example, "Wow! It sounds like it's just been one thing after another for you. I can understand how you have felt so overwhelmed. If you could choose only one concern to start with, which would you pick?"

- **The client portrays himself or herself as a *passive victim*.** The client claims helplessness in the face of the concern.

As appealing as motivational speakers may occasionally sound, deconstructing a client's self-portrayal as a victim requires more than an inspirational slogan or challenge. Instead, you can offer a deconstructive strategy by externalizing the problem. For example, you might say, "So nearly every time that refrigerator has beckoned to you, you have found yourself listening to that Siren song," or "When that old depression monster began to whisper in your ear and tried to get you down, you decided to give in."

Please note that you should present such an externalization of the problem not to control the client's behaviors, moods, and thoughts, but rather merely attempt to *influence* the client. In other words, you would not say to yourself, "The devil made me do it," but "The devil whispered in my ear and told me to do it." We will describe the technique of "externalization" in greater detail in a later chapter.

- **The client speaks in *pejoratives* by making negative statements about self or others.** Working to deconstruct this portrayal involves responding to the pejoratives in a neutral manner, normalizing them, and *separating the behaviors from the labels*. For example, you might say to a client, "So, you have been seeing yourself as 'overly dependent' because you like to rely on your mother for things you realize that you could do for yourself."

- **The client's rendition of the situation is *vague* and unclear.** The deconstruction process could include engaging with the client to *clarify* the circumstances without probing the feeling level. In other words, you can encourage the client to "video talk" it (O'Hanlon & Beadle, 1994). For example, you might say, "I would like to be really clear on how this has been for you. I guess I'm kind of a visual person. Pretend that we are watching a video of what you are describing and you are the guide telling me what I'm seeing. What would be happening?"

- **The client's concern is stated in the *present tense*.** He or she may be saying, for example, ". . . and so now I'm so fed up with my life, there's no choice but to kill myself."

Your deconstructing strategy here is to place the problem in the *past tense* and offer the current conclusion as only one of a number of menu options. Responding to the above client statement, you might empathically engage in the deconstruction process by saying, "So far, you've felt like nothing has worked, and, as you sorted out your options, the one that came up first as a possibility was suicide because you haven't yet found a way to overcome this problem."

- **The client's complaint is characterized as a *state*.** In other words, the concern is presented as something that is fixed and unchangeable, and the client feels "locked in."

One promising deconstruction approach with such a characterization is to turn it into a *process*—an ongoing dynamic that is subject to change. For example, you might say to a client, "Yeah, you've really had some tough times getting launched from your family, and you have sometimes wondered whether your autonomy is worth all that effort." Another possible response is reflecting, "It just seems so hard to get through all this rehearsal for being a grownup," or "Sometimes it has looked like you'd have to choose between being adult and being in your family, but what you really want is to find that place where you have both."

> • **The client speaks of the situation as *global*.** The concern is seen as something that happens across all situations.

When a client portrays the problem as global, your best deconstructive strategy is to *contextualize* the problem. This technique involves creatively misunderstanding a statement so that the client will name an exception. For example, you might speculate, "So I guess even when you're in church or at work, you still have found yourself acting that same way." Or you may wonder, "I guess when you were at Disney World riding the Tower of Terror, these thoughts were still going through your mind."

LISTENING IN ON A SESSION

Let's go back to this chapter's story and continue with the dialogue between Bhavana and her school counselor.

Bhavana: "I guess that I got myself to come here because I can see that my whole life is impossibly screwed up."

Counselor: "Well, with all the frustrations that have piled on since yesterday, it sure has seemed to you like these things have been happening all your life."

Bhavana: "Yeah . . . and if I weren't such a loser, I wouldn't have been in this mess to begin with."

Counselor: (Softly and leaning forward)
"Let me check something out with you, Bhavana. When you've been talking about yourself as a 'loser,' it sounds like you think that you made a mistake about choosing Todd as your boyfriend and you have been blaming yourself since then."

Bhavana: (Reflecting)
"Yeah, but Todd's not such a bad guy. I just don't think I can depend on him to be there for me even when he makes a promise. Now with everything else that's happening, I don't know what to do."

Counselor: "It looks like since yesterday, it's just felt like it was one disappointment after another for you, Bhavana. With all that has happened, everything must have seemed really discouraging."

REFLECTING QUESTIONS

1. In what ways has the counselor encouraged the client in the deconstruction process?
2. How has the counselor used the LUV Triangle in this interaction?
3. How might you respond to Bhavana's comments?

USING THIS TOOL

Realizing that you would not try to deconstruct every single stagnating portrayal a client offers, choose just five of the many that are embedded in this chapter's story, and offer a deconstructing statement for each.

Stagnating Portrayals: *Deconstructing Statement:*

1.

2.

3.

4.

5.

An Important Reminder

Establishing a counseling relationship in which your clients feel as though you have listened, understood, and validated their story can be a challenge. When you add the attempt to deconstruct the client's story in order to give it more possibilities, you will find yourself walking a tightrope. Turning to the LUV Triangle will never fail to help you keep that balance. You can always go back to communicating to the client that you are listening, understanding, and validating.

The Rule is This: Any time you attempt to create change in your clients by using one of the influencing techniques in this book, and your client appears reluctant to latch on to your attempt, this means you must return to the LUV Triangle.

   As you add "Carl Rogers with a Twist" or any other deconstruction technique, you must constantly be sensitive to the reaction you are getting. If the client is hesitant, this is a message to you that you have forgotten to attend to and acknowledge the pain he or she is experiencing and that you have run too far ahead. After you have returned to LUV for a while and the client seems once more to feel sufficiently understood, try again to begin adding possibility statements to your feedback and subtly deconstructing the client's complaint. Your client will let you know if he or she is ready to go with you toward resolution.

USING THIS TOOL

Return to your small groups of three. One of you elaborates on your previous client presentation by adding dead-end, all-or-nothing, irrefutable, and insoluble portrayals of your concerns. Another volunteers to help by using any of the suggested strategies for deconstructing client traps. Finally, the third person serves as the recorder who observes the activity, leads the feedback discussion, and reports the group's experience to the class.

SUMMARY

The techniques of brief counseling are not magic. They are not mysterious or secret, and they do not reflect some hidden, special, and spontaneous power within the helper. In other words, a brief counselor does not have a bag of magic tricks. Instead, you have tool kits, and you practice your craft by forming a helping relationship and using basic tools of change. These basic tools for effective helping include using the LUV Triangle and "Rogers with a Twist."

SEGUE TO CHAPTER 3

Think about a time when you felt in tune with someone. Perhaps you were dancing with somebody who predicted your every move. Maybe you were singing a duet, sharing a joke, or recalling a story together. Whatever the experience, you felt in sync with this person—finishing each other's sentences and reading each other's minds. How did this experience affect you? Once you have considered your answer, start the next chapter.

Resource

The Association for the Development of the Person-Centered Approach (ADPCA)
www.adpca.org

ADPCA is an international organization that sponsors an annual conference and disseminates information about other person-centered activities and organizations throughout the world. It publishes a newsletter, a journal, and an annual membership directory.

CHAPTER 3

Empathy and Caring

This above all: to thine own self be true,
And it must follow, as the night the day,
Thou canst then be false to any man.
William Shakespeare

CHAPTER GOALS

Reading and experiencing the ideas in this chapter will help you to understand these important concepts:

- We are hardwired to be empathic beings.
- Empathy involves both cognitive and emotional features.
- Caring is an essential element of a collaborative counseling relationship.

Reading about and practicing the tools in this chapter will help you to develop these valuable skills:

- Communicating empathically with clients.
- Using your self as a therapeutic tool.
- Using reverse empathy to promote your client's sense of resolve.

STORY

He had planned to spend his Saturday morning cleaning the roof gutters, a chore that would typically take only a couple of hours. Carus had done it every September for nearly four decades, and, although he complained about the tedious and messy job, he took pride in personally taking care of his house. Besides, carrying out this annual autumn ritual somehow connected him to the passing of another season.

Carus couldn't remember exactly when he began to fall. One moment, he was standing on a ladder rung, preparing to step onto the roof. The next instant, like an ice cube scuttering along a countertop, the ladder began to careen across the asphalt driveway. When Carus felt the sudden, jolting loss of support under him, his first reaction was annoyance—as if the ladder were a defiant and willful child who was playing a foolish prank.

But then Carus was falling, and, as everything began to play out in slow motion, he felt neither fear nor shock. Instead, with nothing to grab, he gave himself over to the wrenching, malevolent pull of gravity. He calmly rotated his body to its left side, covered his head, and braced for the inescapable impact eight feet below.

As his body slammed into the asphalt, Carus had this odd sense of detachment. In the brief moment before he lost consciousness, he heard what seemed like the snapping of brittle, dry sticks, but curiously the sounds came from inside of him. Immediately, there was also a grating, crunching sound in his left cheekbone as his face collided with the harsh, gritty surface of the driveway. When his chest caved in on itself, everything went black. Carus later learned that he had fractured three bones on the left side of his face and three ribs. He had multiple contusions, and his left lung had collapsed.

Lying in the hospital room for the next three days, Carus breathed shallowly because sharp, biting sensations pierced his ribs with each intake of air. He reassured himself that the pain would go away eventually. What troubled him deeply, though, was his belief that family and most other people—strangers, friends, colleagues, even ones who had known him a long time—now looked at him differently.

They now considered him to be someone who was no longer able to do any mildly challenging physical task without doing harm to himself. In their eyes, it was as if he had impulsively decided to run with the bulls at Pamplona or fly off to Mexico to dive off the cliffs at Acapulco.

Sure, he felt embarrassed about his accident, but he also felt like there was some other malicious force lurking nearby, just outside of his consciousness—something much more threatening than gravity.

REFLECTING QUESTIONS

1. What were your reactions as you read the account of the fall and the injuries that Carus suffered?
2. What are some of the unstated emotions that Carus has been experiencing as a result of this accident?
3. If you were his counselor, what might you say to Carus?

OVERVIEW

To say that counseling is an "interpersonal process" may, at first, seem so obvious as to be not worth stating at all. But closer examination of this statement reveals that for two "persons" to be engaged in a truly meaningful process together, they must be willing to drop their roles, set aside their defenses, and encounter each other authentically. Such an encounter is neither easy nor automatic—you have to work toward this achievement with your clients.

The client comes to the first counseling session as a person in need of help, but is initially cautious, sometimes circumspect, and hoping to preserve his or her dignity by whatever means possible. So, the client offers a *persona,* a false front, and not the true person he or she is. Likewise, the counselor presents as someone who is calm, educated, skillful, and capable of helping. While the counselor may indeed possess these attributes, the personhood—the real self of the counselor—is not at first apparent in the interaction.

What needs to happen in order to turn this situation into a true interpersonal process? These two people must develop a relationship in which they are able to drop enough of their façades to create a closer bond of mutual understanding. In other words, there must be an authentic, empathic, and caring connection between them.

Perhaps no one did more to legitimize the place of empathy in the counseling process than Carl Rogers (Presbury, McKee, & Echterling, 2007). Rogers insisted on several "necessary and sufficient" core conditions for a successful therapeutic relationship. Included in these conditions was the notion that the counselor must experience an empathic understanding of the client's frame of reference and then communicate this experience to the client (Corey, 2005). The ability to communicate this empathy is an essential counseling skill.

IDEAS

The Empathic Connection

Because *empathy* is such a common word today, you may be surprised to learn that it did not exist until the late nineteenth century (Modell, 2003). The German psychologist Theodor Lipps used the word to mean projecting the self into an object of perception. Empathic ability is our capacity to project our own experience into the mind of the other person "as if" we were that person.

There has been a recent resurgence of studies exploring empathy. One intriguing conclusion of this research is that we use our bodies "as a template that enables us to feel our way into the other's experience" (Modell, 2003, p. 187). We can feel ourselves "walking in the other's shoes" so that we experience what it is like to be this person. This is empathy.

Empathic Accuracy

We presume that the many people who populate our world have experiences similar to our own. But we do not have direct access to the subjective experience of others as we do to our own. Philosophers call this "the problem of other minds." Realizing this problem, the question we must ask ourselves is how it is possible to understand and relate to others as well as we do?

According to Ickes (1997), empathic ability is a biologically inherited predisposition to intuitively connect with others. This "wired-in" interpersonal aptitude has evolved over the eons and is the result of our being social animals. However, you must practice to refine this innate capacity.

Empathy comprises both our emotional and our cognitive abilities to sense and appraise the current condition of another person. Cognitive scientists call this "dual processing" (Stanovich, 2004). Lazarus (1991) described these two modes of appraisal: One is "automatic, involuntary, and unconscious," and the other is "time-consuming, deliberate, volitional, and conscious" (p. 188). The first mode of appraisal emerges as an intuition or feeling (it is sometimes referred to as emotional contagion), while the second is a kind of reasoning often described as role taking or perspective taking. Combining these modes of empathic appraisal makes for an accurate understanding of others.

Empathy Research

Most counselors, as well as many researchers, have emphasized the emotional component of empathy. For example, Watt (2005) argued that the term *empathy* should be used only to refer to intuiting the emotional state of another person. He pointed out that the term *empathy* and its closest synonym *compassion* both denote "suffering with another person." He went on to state that the three components of empathy are "(1) feeling what someone is feeling; (2) knowing what someone is feeling; (3) having some intent to mitigate their suffering" (p. 188).

Empathy arises from an inborn, natural attachment to members of our species and a "universal mammalian phenomenon of nurturance and maternal care" (Watt, 2005, p. 188). One intriguing line of research that supports this claim is the study of prairie voles. Another exciting development is the discovery of "mirror neurons" in the brain.

Loving prairie voles, heartless montane voles   Voles are mouselike creatures that live in the western part of the United States. They exist in two major varieties that behave quite differently when it comes to attachment. Prairie voles are incredibly loving, devoted and committed mates and parents. Even when a partner dies, these voles rarely seek a new mate. They are social creatures who occasionally raise their offspring together with other couples, and they display great concern should one of their children stray from the nest.

Montane voles, on the other hand, are negligent parents, promiscuous mates, and generally "heartless" creatures. They live in solitary burrows and abandon their young soon after they are born. Montane voles have little interest in social contact, except for sexual encounters.

Recent studies of these creatures have revealed a difference in a single gene that encodes a hormone receptor in the vole's brain, accounting for these dramatic differences. The loving prairie vole possesses the receptor for oxytocin, but the callous montane vole does not. Researchers studying the effects of oxytocin on the brain have nicknamed it "the cuddle chemical" or "love potion number 9." In humans, oxytocin induces labor in pregnant women and, after the birth of the child, promotes lactation, bonding, and nurturing behavior.

Researchers have conjectured that this hormone is responsible for healthy interpersonal relationships in humans. Our attachment to others, our desire to mate and nurture children, and our ability to interact on a social level may be greatly influenced by how much oxytocin is available in our brains. You know from casual observation that some people feel strong empathy and attachment to their fellow humans, while others are far less connected. Like prairie voles and montane voles, humans differ enormously in their capacity for empathizing with others. Perhaps your choice to be involved in a helping profession came about as a result of having greater amounts of oxytocin receptors in your brain than, say, an average stockbroker.

Mirror, mirror on the neural network   In a 2005 article, the well-known neuroscientist V. S. Ramachandran offered a bold claim. He predicted that "mirror neurons will do for psychology what DNA did for biology; they will provide a unifying framework and help explain a host of mental abilities" (p. 1). In fact, the development of these neurons in our brains was possibly responsible for the great leap forward in human evolution—what Ramachandran called the "big bang" of evolution. Approximately 50,000 years ago, the human brain reached its present size, and coincidental with this biological achievement came our newly acquired ability to "read minds"—to understand what might be going on in the minds of others (Dobbs, 2006). This skill is associated with the development of mirror neurons in the brain, and with these neurons the early humans began to imitate each other and to create a shared culture.

What are mirror neurons? Shortly before 1996, three neuroscientists at the University of Parma were attaching electrodes to the premotor cortex of monkeys to study brain activity in voluntary motor movements. When these monkeys reached for a raisin, this area of the brain would light up. Later, an amazing event took place. The "eureka moment" came when one of the scientists walked into the room where a monkey was and casually reached out and picked up a raisin. As the monkey observed the scientist's action, its premotor neurons began to fire in a way identical to when the monkey had actually picked up a raisin (Dobbs, 2006). Researchers began to refer to these neurons as "monkey see, monkey do" neurons. They also found that the monkey's neurons would fire even when it heard the experimenters doing something it had previously experienced, such as tearing a piece of paper.

Subsequent research with humans revealed that these same neural circuits exist in all of us, enabling us to imitate the actions of others and understand what they mean. Moreover, when we humans hear someone describe an action such as "hand grasps ball," our mirror neurons light up. In other words, not only do these neurons fire when we see or hear the behavior of people, they are triggered when others use language to describe their internal states and actions.

In a *New York Times* article entitled "Cells That Read Minds," Sandra Blakeslee (2006) offered more research indicating that mirror neurons are responsible for our ability to empathize with our fellow creatures. These neurons allow us to grasp the minds of others, not by conceptual reasoning but through direct simulation of their internal states, and we do this by feeling rather than by thinking.

Scientists now believe that mirror neurons are responsible for the evolution of culture and the pleasure we derive from viewing art, sports, and even erotica. Mirror neurons have been cited as the reason for a counselor's ability to understand and empathize with clients. Studies have shown that those who rank high on measures of empathy have particularly active mirror neurons.

Making Sense of Other People

One problem with assuming that empathic ability is wholly innate—either you have it or you don't—is that, if this were true, then empathy could not be learned or taught. But we do know that people's ability to make sense of others increases with experience. In our own work as counselor trainers, we find that people can be taught to improve their skills in making sense of others. To the extent that empathic ability arises from "perspective taking," this ability can be refined. However, it may be that the talent for catching other people's experience through "emotional contagion" comes as original equipment in beginning counselors.

Emotional Intelligence

Since the introduction of Goleman's (1995) original book on *Emotional Intelligence,* the notion that people vary along a dimension of the ability to use emotions effectively has gained popularity (Blume, 2006; Kemper, 2000; Salovey, Bedell, Detweiler, & Mayer, 2000). Blume (2006) identified four major categories of emotional intelligence that are important in social relationships: emotional expression, facilitation, interpretation, and regulation. For the sake of simplicity, we have adapted and distilled the findings of Salovey and his colleagues (2000) into skills having to do with the understanding of self and others (for the comprehensive list, see Blume, 2006, p. 230, table 7.2).

"Self skills" include the abilities to

- recognize emotion in one's own physical and psychological states;
- experience congruence between what one feels and what one expresses;
- use emotions in problem solving and creative efforts;
- remain open to one's own emotions, whether pleasant or unpleasant;
- monitor and reflect on one's own emotional states; and
- manage emotions in situations that call for lower emotional expression.

When interacting with others, an emotionally intelligent person can

- identify emotion in other people;
- recognize incongruence between their statements and their emotional state;
- understand how different emotions are related;
- understand how certain events give rise to particular emotions;
- interpret complex and conflicting emotions; and
- manage emotions in others.

Goleman (1995, 2005) asserted that emotional intelligence is more important to one's success in life than intellectual or academic intelligence, and that one's "EQ" can be raised with training. Offering a cautionary note, Blume (2006) countered that, although emotional intelligence is certainly important, there is no convincing evidence, as of yet, that these skills could be significantly improved.

Nevertheless, a major part of the training for counselors and psychotherapists is involved in the attempt to increase such skills. Personal counseling is often recommended for trainees in order to help them become more sensitive to their own emotional states.

We recommend personal counseling for our students as an important training element, and we subscribe to the notion that you don't have to be sick to get better (Echterling, Presbury, & McKee, 2005; Staton et al., 2007). In addition, practicing these skills with clients in actual supervised counseling sessions offers the opportunity to refine one's understanding of emotional states in others.

EXPERIENCING THIS IDEA

With two other people, go over the above lists of emotional intelligence pertaining to self and others. Discuss which of these items still present a challenge for you, and devise a plan to increase your emotional intelligence. Ask for feedback from the other two members about ways that you could improve your interactions with others.

Caring

In 1980, Carl Rogers (quoted in Schmidt, 2002) offered the following opinion: "It is impossible to accurately sense the perceptual world of another person unless you value that person and his or her world—unless you, in some sense, care" (p. 39). Of course, because you have chosen to be a member of the helping profession, it is obvious that you care about people. Caring stirs you to reach out to a client, tune into his or her concerns, and engage in the intense work of helping this person toward a successful resolution of these concerns. Caring is a crucial aspect of your emotional intelligence. "It is the core—the heart, if you will—of the helping process" (p. 1).

However, in order for this process to take place, your caring must be intentional. Intentionality is the control people exert over the purpose or direction of their lives (Schmidt, 2002). Applied to the helping relationship, intentionality means that you must have a strategy, a way of attaining the outcomes your clients wish to achieve. You must create the circumstances in which this realization can take place.

Some counselors still claim to be "nondirective" in their approach to their work with clients. As we previously stated, such a declaration is usually founded on a misconception of the term that Carl Rogers originally used to describe his approach. They believe that Rogers meant that the counselor is passive, possessing no plan and remaining unintentional as to where the relationship must go. Patterson and Hidore (1997) suggested that changing the term *nondirective* to *noncontrolling* might clear up this misconception.

In contrast to those nondirective therapists who believe that caring is necessary and sufficient for success, many brief approaches to therapy overlook the fact that caring is essential to the counseling success. For example, the index of the comprehensive *Handbook of Solution-Focused Therapy* (O'Connell & Palmer, 2003) does not include words such as *caring, empathy,* or *warmth.* In some circles, such counselor–client relationship elements are seen as unnecessary or even counterproductive. For example, from the perspective of rational emotive behavior therapy, an effective therapist does not have to be warm or emotionally empathic (Prochaska & Norcross, 2007). As De Jong and Berg (1998) put it, "We believe that empathy, like any other skill, can be overemphasized. We definitely do not recommend that you use the type of empathy that is sentimental or that tends to amplify negative feelings" (p. 37).

However, some authors have expressed concern regarding the overemphasis of brief therapists on techniques and their neglect of aspects of a caring relationship (e.g., Lipchik, 2002). Mearns and Thorne (2000) worried that brief approaches to therapy may succumb to the dominant zeitgeist that demands "a cautious, carefully circumscribed form of therapy where the key criteria are the achievement of prescribed goals, proven cost-effectiveness and predictable therapist behaviour. . . . Within such a straightjacket it is perhaps possible to go through the motions . . . [but lose] the relational depth which demands the therapist's investment as a person" (p. 212).

Techniques alone may make for successful outcomes in auto repair, accounting, or even some helping professions. However, technique without caring will doom counseling to failure. For this reason, we do not list our techniques in this book as a manualized and formulaic approach to helping. Instead, we attempt to place them all in the context of a caring, empathic relationship.

Therapy without any clear intention or purpose may, on rare occasions, be successful (Schmidt, 2002). However, this reminds us of that old saying, "Sometimes, even a blind squirrel finds an acorn." At its worst, an unintentional relationship is haphazard and ineffective. As Schmidt put it, "a relationship that wanders aimlessly without moving in a positive and beneficial direction can hardly be called 'helping'" (p. 29).

But what about caring? Can you intentionally care? Isn't caring something you either feel or you don't? We are not speaking of a romantic form of love when we use this term. Instead, like *agape,* caring is a feeling of attachment or closeness to another person. Hundreds of writers over the centuries have attempted to make sense of this form of caring, including Plato, Saint Paul, and C. S. Lewis. The term *agape* comes from the Greek and Christian writers who interpreted it as an unconditional, self-sacrificing, volitional, and thoughtful love. The eighteenth-century economist Adam Smith used the phrase "fellow feeling" to capture this emotional bonding with other humans. The psychologist John Bowlby (1969/1982) called it "attachment." When we intentionally focus on the other person with what Rogers (1980) called "unconditional positive regard," a caring relationship is inevitable.

EXPERIENCING THIS IDEA

Take a photograph of someone who cares for you and take a close look. As you gaze over this person's features, notice in particular the eyes, the smile, and the expression on his or her face. How has this person shown to you that he or she cares for you? Reflect on how this caring has made an impact on your life. What emotions does this image evoke in you?

Implications of These Ideas for the Counselor

These ideas have noteworthy implications for the centrality of empathy in our work as counselors.

• **Counselor, empathize with thyself.** If you are a counselor early in your career, you may think that there will be a time when you have reached a plateau of mastery where you will not need to struggle to improve at this work. However, we are always guilty of not being good enough for our clients. Despite this seemingly gloomy outlook, there certainly will be a time in your professional development when you have your feet under you well enough to be comfortable knowing you must always strive to be better.

Part of being empathic is being empathic with yourself and cutting yourself some slack. While acknowledging that you need to strive to be better, you must simultaneously allow yourself to be where you are in your professional development. Early in their careers, most counselors worry about their performance, and this concern interferes with their effectiveness. It's a paradox. They try so hard to be good at counseling that they diminish their natural ability. They cannot always hear or fully assimilate what the client is telling them because they are "trying too hard to be helpful, to win approval from a supervisor, to prove their own adequacy to themselves, to be liked by the client . . . [or] wondering how best to phrase what they are going to say next" (Teyber, 2006, p. 79).

We find that counselors in training and those who are early in their careers "put too many chips into the game." In other words, they have based their entire sense of competency and self-esteem solely on whether their clients improve.

Remember that you are in a collaborative relationship with your client, and, as far as we know, no one ever succeeded in unilaterally changing another person for the better. No matter how many rabbits you pull out of the hat, if your client is not inclined to change, it won't happen. Counseling is a lonely business. If you need for someone to say, "Great job!" then part of your work will be to achieve a better sense of intrinsic evaluation—to arrive at the place where you know you have done your best and given all you can—and that has to be enough.

- **You've got to show them that you care.** There are two major skills associated with the effective use of empathy: the first is *perceiving,* and the second *communicating* (Welfel & Patterson, 2005). In other words, being open to the client's experience and simply allowing your mirror neurons to pick it up is not sufficient. The LUV Triangle is effective only if your clients experience you as *truly* listening, understanding, and validating. You can empathically experience your clients' feelings and their predicament, but unless they know that you are experiencing at this level, your empathy amounts to (as one of our grandfathers used to put it) "no more than a fart in a windstorm."

But when your client feels that you care and senses that your empathy goes deeper than merely attending to the story, he or she becomes more willing to self-disclose and self-explore. At this point in the relationship, it matters little which technique you use, so long as you continue to empathically, and authentically, interact. As we often tell our students, "You can say just about anything to clients, if they know you love them." This "LUV" cements the bond between you and your client without placing the client under any obligation to reciprocate.

- **Empathize, don't sympathize.** We have found that many new counselors find client suffering to be infectious. Sometimes, these counselors overidentify with their clients' pain, and walk away from an intense session feeling as if they were poisoned by the agony and despair that they have witnessed (Staton et al., 2007). Such a response is sympathy, rather than compassion or empathy. We encourage our counselors in training to find a therapeutic distance from their clients' anguish so that they will not be overwhelmed by the encounter.

The notion of empathy is very confusing to beginning counselors. They often think it means becoming so close to the client that the counselor takes on or absorbs the client's pain. They may regard doing less than this as not caring enough. But too much caring of this sort is good for neither the client nor the counselor. Counselors sometimes find it difficult to maintain this optimal distance between being too removed from the client and being too close.

As we mentioned in Chapter 2, there is an art to achieving the optimal distance in counseling relationships. Here, we focus on the issue of emotional contagion. Although the relationship in counseling is an intimate one, a certain degree of detachment is necessary. The counselor must remain concerned while being objective: "Those who err on the side of closeness burn up with the emotions. . . . Those who err on the side of detachment become calloused to the pain of people" (Becvar, Canfield, & Becvar, 1997, pp. 55–56). Somewhere between is the optimal therapeutic distance.

• **Own your professional power.** If you are a new counselor, you may find yourself feeling intimidated by the fact that clients now see you as an important resource in their lives (Teyber, 2006). You may be reluctant to exert your professional power by engaging wholeheartedly in the therapeutic process. At other times, you may fear you possess too much power. You may even be afraid that a single mistaken comment will cause irreparable damage to your client. These concerns serve to reduce the impact you might otherwise be able to have on your client.

On your way to developing "good enough" mastery of your counseling skills, you are likely to pass through the phase of your professional development known as the "imposter phenomenon" (Harvey & Katz, 1985). You originally chose to become a counselor because you believed that you had "the right stuff." You were a good listener, you cared about others, and you were empathically drawn to helping when you saw people in trouble. But when you began to take classes and you realized that there was a standard that counselors must meet, which initially seemed beyond your grasp, perhaps your first reaction was to hide your lack of competence.

As you reflect on those feelings of insecurity and inadequacy that you experienced at the beginning of your counselor training program, you might remember that you tended to secretly believe that you were a fraud, and that sooner or later you would be found out and excommunicated from the ranks. There was a lot more to becoming a counselor than you had realized, and you were not certain that you had what it takes. Perhaps those professors who accepted you into their program had made a serious mistake!

This doubt does not go away when one gets out of graduate school. There will be times during your career when you find you have sunk into your role, your self-efficacy has diminished, and you seem to have lost the sense of what you are trying to do with clients. This feeling is accompanied by the confusing notion that you are fumbling in the dark, and you will likely then be overcome by a sense of shame. It's an occupational hazard.

The antidote is simple: Talk to someone. You always will need a consultant with whom you can be honest or a counselor who will help you sort out your confusion at times. According to Jourard (1971), "Honesty can literally be a health insurance policy" (p. 133). Self-disclosure is the remedy for shame. Ironically, when you present yourself to others as you truly are, you will find yourself becoming more accepting of yourself. As a result, you can be more open and accepting of your clients.

• **Train yourself for greater empathy.** According to Prochaska and Norcross (2003), "Training in empathy—or rather experiencing and witnessing empathy—will come about only in authentic, I–Thou relationships, including experiential groups and personal therapy" (p. 158). We do not train counselors in our program using role-playing exercises. It is not possible for two people in a role-play situation to be in an authentic relationship, and while the counselor-in-training might learn to reflect feelings, he or she cannot experience true advanced empathy for the client, because the client is playing a role. This is not an I–Thou connection between two human beings; it is a simulation.

Egan (2007) suggested that overly cognitive, nonsystematic training programs, run by individuals who themselves lack basic helping skills, can be a devastating combination. Luckily, there are few such programs in our profession. You need to take responsibility for enhancing your empathic skills by connecting to supervisors who can also serve as inspiring models. As someone who has entered a counselor training program, you likely have good emotional intelligence about people, but you may not fully realize that you possess it. In fact, you may not place much value on this ability because the GRE does not have an "EQ" score, and you may assume that everyone else has it, too (Young, 2005).

You are the most important therapeutic tool that you have, so value yourself as an instrument that needs attention and care. Bringing your authentic and transparent self to the counseling relationship is often the catalyst for successful change. When there is no need for second-guessing or wondering about you as a person, your client is more likely to embark with you on the uncertain journey of therapy. So use yourself as an instrument, and dedicate yourself over your lifetime to maintaining a vivid sense of who you are. Successful therapists "do not hide behind the façade of the professional role" (Young, 2005, p. 19).

To be sure, becoming a counselor or psychotherapist is a lifelong process. The years of experience that the three authors of this book have (combined) number nearly 100. Over time, we have learned much from our clients and our colleagues, from our readings, from our students, and from living life. In spite of having what are obviously many years under our belts, we are still learning and still working to keep ourselves open to new experiences. This process includes constant tune-ups of our "instruments."

TOOLS

Empathy as Technique

Arthur Deikman (1982), a medical doctor, pointed out that there is a significant difference in the type of encounter that a doctor and patient experience together versus the intersubjective experience of counselor and client. The physician "applies scientific techniques in an impersonal way," while the counselor engages with the client in a mode of "participatory knowing" (p. 29). The objective stance of the physician exists in marked contrast to the emotional communication that takes place between the subjective awareness of client and counselor. When you communicate emotionally with your client, you are engaging in a heart-to-heart encounter that is an intermingling of subjective awareness and emotions. At a visceral level, you experience what your client is feeling. This "subjectivity, the essence of art, is antithetical to rational science" (Deikman, 1982, pp. 30–31).

As we suggested earlier, if you were to seek help from your mechanic or accountant, you would not require more than a cordial relationship. But counseling is an emotionally laden situation. People come seeking personal support for concerns that are central to their lives. They expect a more intense and authentic connection with a counselor. Furthermore, the strength of this connection portends the success of the work.

In Chapter 2, we outlined the behaviors for the LUV Triangle. When you successfully communicate that you have listened, understood, and validated the client, you are establishing a working relationship. The client can then believe that you are committed to being helpful, will not be judgmental, and will not demean the client's feelings. The LUV interaction is a crucial beginning. However, it is also necessary to engage the client's emotions, so that the relationship becomes more than a mere utilitarian exchange. This level of relationship can take place only when you allow yourself to care and empathize with clients.

Caring and the Collaborative Relationship

Adopting the perspective of the other person produces empathic concern. Davis (1994) asserted that both affective empathy and perspective taking must be present in the observer for the full empathic response. This combination of cognitive/affective appraisal can produce empathic accuracy "which helps span, at least temporarily, the perpetual gulf which lies between individual social actors" (p. 221).

The ability to read others and to take their perspective, together with a high level of empathic reactivity, increases tolerance and decreases aggression (Feshbach, 1978). In other words, when we feel a strong sense of empathy toward another person, we accept that person as he or she is. Self-acceptance is the key to increased tolerance of others and a more open stance in your relationships. Empathy is your birthright. Refine it so that you can use it as a tool for understanding what is happening to both your client and yourself moment to moment in the counseling relationship.

The working alliance, alternately known as the *therapeutic alliance,* the *holding environment, joining,* or *presence,* is positively correlated with successful outcomes in counseling and psychotherapy (Teyber, 2006). The term that Teyber prefers is "collaborative relationship," because it emphasizes the nonhierarchical quality of the counselor–client connection and suggests that both participants are responsible for the work.

As with empathy, the foundation of a collaborative relationship does not rest on technique but on your genuine expressions of respect, caring, warmth, and concern for your client. Clients may not be able to define exactly what they mean by respect and warmth, but they seem to know these qualities when they see them. You can communicate your personal warmth and respect for your clients by keeping your posture open, wearing a calm smile, and making sure that your body language is congruent with the content of your words (Ivey & Ivey, 2007). "Congruence," Carl Rogers said, "is the opposite of presenting a façade. . . . To be transparent to the client, to have nothing of one's experience in the relationship which is hidden . . . this is, I believe, basic to effective psychotherapy (in Jourard, 1971, p. 147).

If you are able to convey your congruence, empathy, and caring, together with communicating LUV, then you have created the conditions that are essential for a collaborative relationship. And, if you can effectively set this initial tone, then you are also easing your client's sense of distress and shame (Teyber, 2006).

Communicating Empathy

The attending and acknowledging skills we discussed in Chapter 2 as LUV are similar to what Young (2005) called the "Nonjudgmental Listening Cycle." In this cycle, he included such techniques as open questions, minimal encouragers, paraphrases, summaries, and reflection of feelings.

Carl Rogers, who had initiated the idea of "reflection of feelings," eventually became dissatisfied with the idea that a therapist should learn to reflect feelings as a display of accurate empathy. In fact, Rogers (1987) revealed, "I even *wince* at the phrase reflection of feeling. It does not describe what I am trying to do when I work with a client" (p. 39, emphasis in original). His concern was that reflection was being taught to counselors in training as an intellectual technique. He worried that this behavior could become a sterile exercise and fall short of the complex interpersonal experience he had in mind when he first wrote about reflection as a technique. It is possible for a counselor to reflect a client's feelings based only on the words without a full empathic appreciation for what it means to be expressing these feelings. As a song once stated, "It ain't no good unless you feel it."

You Are Your Instrument (Self as Technique)

As you work on enhancing your empathic skills, it is helpful for you to keep in mind that not all empathy is equal. Empathic communications vary in their accuracy, depth, and impact. For example, *primary empathy* is conveying an understanding of the client's stated major themes and concerns. Advanced empathy, on the other hand, is a deeper level of understanding that invites clients to delve into issues that had been outside of their awareness (Gladding, 2007). *Advanced accurate empathy* goes beyond the contents of a client's words and reaches for what may be suggested, implied, overlooked, and—until now—undiscovered. It is really "getting it" as if you were living your client's life. Such empathy is much more than mere technique. As Young (2005) put it, "an accurate [empathic] reflection of feelings has the almost magical power to deepen the relationship between client and counselor. Nothing transmits nonjudgmental understanding more completely" (p. 137).

Be the artful dancer   Counseling is, in part, an artistic endeavor. In some art forms, it is easy to see a distinction between the artist and the artistic behavior. For example, Picasso would pick up a brush, dab it in a chosen color of paint, and apply it to the canvas. The brush—the instrument—is an extension of the artist but not the artist himself. On the other hand, when the famous dancer Isadora Duncan created her art, she *was* the art. As the poet William Butler Yeats put it, "You can't tell the dancer from the dance." This observation applies to counseling: "You can't tell the counselor from the counseling." You are your instrument.

LISTENING IN ON A SESSION

Review the story at the beginning of the chapter. A resolution-focused counselor could communicate empathy with Carus in the following way.

Carus: (With a sense of urgency, he pours out his story during the first 10 minutes of the session. He winces and shifts in the chair as if he is in even more pain as he recalls his accident and the reactions of others.)

" . . . I was lucky though: just a couple of broken ribs and facial fractures. That pain will go away eventually, but what troubles me most is that I feel I gotta prove to myself, and everyone else, that I'm still capable, strong—for my age—and coordinated, not some pitiful inept, bumbling *meshuganah!*"

(Carus sighs, shaking his head from side-to-side.)

"I know, I know. I should have checked the ladder or I should have had someone hold it, but I didn't. And I'm reminded of my carelessness every time I look in the mirror or try to take a deep breath."

(A long silence ensues as Carus gazes down, deep in his thoughts, shakes his head again, and sighs.)

Counselor: "Wow, that came pouring out of you like the dam had burst and for the first time, too. That's a lot of painful stuff to keep all bottled up inside with no one to share it with."

Carus: "Well, I guess I had to find someone who deserved to hear it."

Counselor: "I'm sorry, I'm not with you."

Carus: "You're my second counselor. See I . . . happened to mention to my wife that I was feeling kind of depressed. I really just wanted to talk to her about it but she panicked and got me an appointment with a psychiatrist. He was 'strictly business' and after I refused to take the medication, I quit him and decided to try you."

Counselor: (She begins to offer a reflection.)

"So, you feel like we're connecting and . . . "

Carus: (He quickly interrupts.)

"Yeah, I know we are. I can tell because of this weird thing that happened while I was in the hospital. It's kind of a long story—you sure you want to hear it?"

Counselor: "As the old story goes, I'm all ears."

Carus: "About 20 years ago we . . . I mean, some of the guys at work and a couple of the fellas in the neighborhood and I . . . started playing poker about once a month at my house. As we get older the membership changes, a couple of them have moved, two of the regulars have died, and another guy has gotten too old to play."

(Carus's voice wavers, he wipes a tear from his eye, and blows his nose with a tissue from the counselor's box.)

"Damn, I haven't thought about those guys in a long time; I guess I really miss them . . . Anyway, about a year ago, this bright young MD joined us and we all took a liking to him and so he's a regular now. The day of the accident, I wake up in the emergency room and he's dressing my wounds and making calls to specialists on a Saturday and getting them to come to check me out . . . He wasn't even on call that day. Things were kind of a blur and I suppose I was in shock, but one thing did stick with me and that was the look of genuine concern on his face. Sure, he was cool, calm and collected as the old saying goes, but I don't think you can fake what's in your heart. I knew I was going to get good care and was going to be all right."

Counselor: "That must have been a tremendous relief! To find your friend there taking charge, and I can tell by the way your voice sounded just now that his being there with you in that compassionate way meant a lot to you. Maybe even something that you were surprised to see in him."

Carus: (With more energy)

"Yeah, I guess lying there in that hospital bed for three days really had an effect on me. Well, I became hyperaware of the doctors, nurses, aides, and technicians of all sorts—who probably meant well, but to paraphrase Teddy Roosevelt, they meant well, feebly. Now don't get me wrong, I think all of them were well qualified. And they weren't hostile or mean-spirited in any way. It's just that I didn't feel like they really cared about me. They were above the fray and didn't get involved emotionally or personally with me or my troubles. I was just the trauma case in room 327. The longer I stayed, the more I began to resent things like their phony cheerfulness. 'Don't you know that it's too dangerous to be up on ladders at your age?' But what was worse was the doctor who was reading my chart and didn't even remember me from the day before. He even plopped his fat ass right down on my bed without asking. He didn't even look at me as he talked. He had the bedside manner of a groundhog."

Counselor: "If I'm reading you right it must have taken a lot of will power not to go off on them because just listening to your description, I'm getting a cold feeling in my stomach. I can't imagine how you managed to be civil."

Carus: "Well, I wasn't exactly charming, but at least I didn't tell anybody off like I wanted to. I almost said, 'In case you've forgotten, the modern version of the Hippocratic oath stresses that physicians are supposed to have warmth, sympathy, and understanding and be humble. I guess you must have missed that lecture.' Anyway, after my failed attempt at counseling or therapy or whatever you want to call it, I woke up one morning with a realization. I thought I was angry but then as I lay there with it, I realized that I felt cheated and kind of sad, the same way I did in the hospital. In my physical rehab and psychiatric appointments I was being asked to do all the work with no say so and if I did ask a question, they'd get defensive and fend me off with medical jargon. I decided right then and there that I'm not about to bare my soul to someone unless it's close to the way that Michael was with me that Saturday in the emergency room."

Counselor: "That was a really moving story and I must say that after what you've been through a lot of people wouldn't have given us counselors and therapists a second and third chance like you did. I feel honored that you are saying you saw something in me that gave you the confidence that we could work together."

Reflecting Questions

1.   In what ways did the counselor use empathy as a technique?
2.   How did the counselor use self as an instrument in this session?
3.   What reactions did you have as you read about Carus's experience?

USING THIS TOOL

Form a small group of three. Take turns sharing an experience that evoked some strong emotions in you. As one shares for about 5 minutes, another person responds with empathy and caring. The third person observes and leads the feedback discussion. Once you have processed this encounter, move on until each of you have taken all three roles.

Positive Emotions

The study of human emotions, for the most part, has been a study of negative feelings (Echterling, Presbury, & McKee, 2005). If you type "anxiety" as your subject heading in the database PsycInfo, you will find thousands and thousands of studies. Change the topic to "anger," and again you will have an overwhelming number of hits. Try "depression" and you will have similarly impressive results. However, if you submit "courage," "compassion," or "joy," you will find only a handful of studies. Even comprehensive models of basic affective states contain far more negative than positive emotions (Fernandez-Ballesteros, 2003).

Recently, both researchers and practitioners in counseling and psychology have begun to turn their attention to positive emotions (e.g., Frederickson, 2002; Larsen, Hemenover, Norris, & Cacioppo, 2003; Watson, 2002). They see positive emotions as a frontier of uncharted territory that holds vast potential for improving lives (Haidt, 2003). Current studies have examined a wide range of positive feelings that have rarely been mentioned in the psychological literature. However, clients usually come to counseling because they are feeling *bad*. They are compelled to talk about what is *wrong* in their lives and are looking for some way to *fix* it (Ivey & Ivey, 2007). While we must acknowledge their concerns in a way that lets them know that we understand, our real purpose is to help them begin to focus on what is *right* with their lives and what does not need to be *fixed*.

Recent research has demonstrated that people undergoing times of loss and adversity actually experience positive as well as painful emotions (Larsen et al., 2003).

Positive psychology, which is an emphasis on strength-based approaches to counseling and psychotherapy, is becoming a major new force in the field (Pedersen & Seligman, 2004; Snyder & Lopez, 2002). As Seligman (2002) put it, "We've become too preoccupied with repairing damage when our focus should be on building strength and resilience" (p. 1).

Frederickson (2002) stated that when they are experiencing positive emotions "people transform themselves, becoming more creative, knowledgeable, resilient, socially integrated, and healthy individuals" (p. 123). There is even evidence from neuroscience that adds support to Frederickson's ideas. PET scans of the brain reveal that when people are experiencing positive emotions there is more activation in their left frontal lobes, while negative emotions are accompanied by more activation in the right frontal area (Davidson, 1993).

LISTENING IN ON A SESSION

Review the story at the beginning of the chapter and the earlier segment. A resolution-focused counselor could communicate advanced empathy with Carus in the following way.

Counselor: "Carus, I wanted to back up a minute and check something out with you. You sounded really sad a minute ago when you were talking about the guys that were no longer in your poker group."

Carus: "Yeah, I don't know where that came from. I know I was talking about Michael being at the hospital but I don't see any connection to the accident with Stan, Ricardo, and Mac."

(His voice trails away, then silence.)

"They kind of fell by the wayside . . . That's an odd thing for me to say about these old friends—falling by the wayside. The truth of the matter is two of them died and one guy just got too old to play. No, I don't think I'm really *sad* about them. I mean I was sad at their funerals and it was sad to see Ricardo's skills diminish over time and he couldn't play any more. I thought I was over the grief or sadness or whatever . . . Aren't there stages for that? Shouldn't I be over it by now?"

Counselor: "Well, I know this might sound evasive but it may depend on the person. Maybe the sadness isn't about your friends but about something else."

Carus: "I'm not sure what you mean? Like what else?"

Counselor: "Well, I was struck by a couple of things that you said earlier and maybe there's a connection somehow to that elusive feeling that's been troubling you that has so many sides to it—anger, sadness, a sense of regret and also a specter of malice or ill will that you described as lurking about somehow."

Carus: "Yeah, that's true. It's like the accident has dredged up some stuff that maybe I've been not dealing with or paying attention to that I should be."

Counselor: "And just now you said your friends had *fallen by the wayside* . . ."

Carus: (Interrupting)

"Hmmm, my *falling* was an accident but their *falling* was different . . . I guess maybe my choice of words *might* mean something I must admit. I did think about dying as I was falling. Also, when I was recovering, I felt kind of feeble and over the hill, useless, like I'd lost my confidence, not just in my ability to be on a ladder anymore but to do anything the least bit dangerous. It's been a month since the accident, but it took me three tries to use a new saber saw in my workshop that I bought right before the accident. I was shaking so hard that I thought I'd suffered neurological damage."

(Long pause, barely audible)

"So, I guess, deep down . . . Oh man, this is hard!"

(The counselor waits patiently without interrupting, leaning forward slightly more with a calm look of expectation.)

"I guess I've just lost my nerve."

Counselor: "That's a pretty scary thing for somebody like you who's used to taking risks to suddenly be faced with that thought. Life itself seems to be more dangerous than before, and more lonely."

Carus: (There are tears in his eyes as he looks at the counselor.)

"You know, it's all I can do to handle getting old and slow. And losing my friends really broke my heart, but I don't think I'll be able to face losing my nerve—I just can't."

Reverse Empathy: Entraining Emotions

Normally, when we think of empathy, we consider it to be tuning into the client's concerns and negative emotions. But we can also empathize with a client's strengths, successes, hopes, and positive emotions, too. Furthermore, when you read about empathy, it is always the counselor who is the one possessing a high level of empathic ability, while any consideration of empathy on the part of the client is usually ignored.

However, accurate empathy, in which the counselor attempts to understand and communicate this understanding to the client, is only one side of the story—clients have empathy, too. Appreciating the empathy that clients bring to counseling offers you another therapeutic opportunity. By creating an empathic resonance in clients, you can elevate their emotional arousal and set the stage for a reframe or a shift in focus. Before considering the process involved, let's take another look at empathy and its neurological substrate.

The roots of empathy can be traced to infancy (Goleman, 1995, 2005). Shortly after birth, infants will display sympathetic crying when they hear one of their nursery-mates cry. This reaction is the precursor to empathy. By their first birthday, children seem to understand that another crying child's distress is not their own, but they still express concern and an urgent confusion as to what to do. Later, a more mature empathy begins to form. Some people appear to become highly sensitized to other people in this way, while others are less so. For example, a study of brain-injured patients with lesions between the amygdala and the association area of the visual cortex revealed their inability to understand the emotional aspects of messages from others. "A sarcastic 'Thanks,' a grateful 'Thanks,' and an angry 'Thanks' all had the same neutral meaning for them" (Goleman, 1995, p. 102).

By contrast, Goleman pointed to a study by Levenson and Ruef (1992) on empathy between married partners. The couples in the study were videotaped, and their physiological responses monitored, while discussing a distressing aspect of their marriage. Each person then reviewed the videotape separately and reported what he or she was feeling at each moment. Finally, still hooked up to biofeedback equipment, the participants viewed the videotape once more and were asked to describe their partners' moment-to-moment feelings. Remarkably, as they focused on their spouses, the most empathically accurate persons displayed physiological reactions that mimicked those of their partners (and this was before we knew of mirror neurons). The biofeedback patterns of the least empathic persons merely repeated their own original reactions during the discussion. Empathy, then, is the ability to become emotionally aroused and resonate with the person you are encountering. It can be an emotional contagion in which you reciprocally transmit and catch moods from each other.

Obviously, when two people are in the ecstasy of romantic love, they each empathically affect and "infect" the other with their emotional sensitivity and communication. Furthermore, it turns out that when any two people are in contact the more expressive person is the one who sets the emotional tone of the encounter. "The person who has the more forceful expressivity—or the most *power*—is typically the one whose emotions entrain the other" (p. 117, emphasis added). This means that, by increasing your emotional communication, you can get the other person to feel what you are feeling.

Client narratives usually contain the potential for two valences: problem-saturated talk and resolution talk. Initially, when clients are speaking of their concerns, you acknowledge with LUV and empathy. But later, when the time seems right for such an intervention, you can attempt to get clients talking about positive events while you "entrain" their emotions and connect them to their resolution stories.

The rule is this: When clients are talking about their pain, your communication of empathy should be at a minimum level of intensity. However, when the conversation switches to resolution talk, your communication should be of a "more forceful expressivity" as mentioned above. In return, you can expect that the client will become more emotional and connect this feeling to the language of the moment. In other words, when you display more energy and interest in their successes, you activate their empathic connection to these successes as well.

Your hope is that by getting excited about client successes, they will become excited, too. You can then "drag and drop" that arousal from problem-saturated talk to resolution talk. Since all memories are constructed memories, your aim is to reduce the focus on discouraging or despairing memories and juxtapose these with memories of successes that will form new versions of events. By becoming excited and emotionally aroused when the client is talking about success, you entrain this same enthusiasm in the client. But, as you attempt to arouse the person, you must be careful not to over-arouse. As Le Doux (1996/1998) advised, "You need to have just the right level of activation to perform optimally" (p. 289). Your enthusiasm must also be genuine. Any feigned interest in a client's success will be sensed as disingenuous. If you are a counselor who is more interested in positive emotions than in those of discouragement and despair, then you are the right person for this work.

LISTENING IN ON A SESSION

Review the story at the beginning of the chapter and the two previous segments. A resolution-focused counselor could foster reverse empathy in the following way.

Carus: (With some sense of grudging pride, he shares a recent experience.)
"Well, I was able to talk with one of my friends this week and tell him that I felt insulted when he said I was getting a little too old to be climbing ladders. Amazingly, he was calm and responsive and the conversation went well."

Counselor: "Wow! You overcame your fear that bringing it up would make things even worse and you got the situation to turn out well. How did you summon the courage to do that?"

Carus: (Now showing increased energy)
"Well, I just decided it was worth the risk and I didn't want to live with all that tension and resentment in our relationship."

Counselor: "You know, as you were saying that, I somehow had a really good feeling that this might mean your courage for living in general is increasing, as crazy as that sounds."

Carus: (Displaying still more enthusiasm)
"Now that you mention it, I feel that, too!"

USING THIS TOOL

Return to your small groups of three. Each person takes a turn of sharing some concern that stirs up some feelings of discouragement. As the listener, offer LUV and empathy, but explore for exceptions to this concern. When you find something positive, express your feelings with energy and enthusiasm. The third person takes the role of observer. After you have processed this exchange, then continue until each of you has had these experiences.

SUMMARY

Empathy, the cognitive ability to see other people's perspectives and the emotional capacity to have a sense of their feelings, is a hardwired trait that has contributed to our survival as a species. The quality of your empathy with a client is the most important factor in your potential for success. Moreover, caring is an essential element of any collaborative counseling relationship. In this chapter, you practiced several skills involving empathy, including communicating empathically with clients, using your self as a therapeutic tool, and using reverse empathy to promote your client's sense of resolve.

SEGUE TO CHAPTER 4

Think about a time when you were aspiring to achieve something important. How did thinking about this future possibility affect how you were presently acting? After reflecting on your answer, begin reading this next chapter.

Resource

Solution Focused Brief Therapy Association
www.sfbta.org

The purpose of the association is to hold an annual conference in North America for Solution Focused Brief Practitioners to exchange ideas, learn new stuff, and, in general, have a fun time together. Those who attend a conference will be considered members of the SFBTA for that year.

CHAPTER 4

Helping Clients Frame Goals

The Pull of the Future

"The future is made of the same stuff as the present."

Simone Weil

CHAPTER GOALS

Reading and experiencing the ideas in this chapter will help you understand the following concepts:

- Your focus is on teleology and teleonomy, not etiology. The future is now. Helping clients to frame goals for the future also changes their current way of viewing themselves and the world.
- Clients can be *visiting, complaining, engaging fully,* or *presenting involuntarily* in their counseling relationship with you.

Reading and practicing the tools in this chapter will help you develop three fundamental brief counseling skills:

- Inviting clients to set goals.
- Finding the gaps in the client's story that are the exceptions to the problem.
- Using scaling techniques to help clients recognize that resolution is not an all-or-nothing proposition, to envision their goals with greater detail and vividness, and assess their progress in achieving these goals.

STORY

"This is NOT how I want to be living my life," Jamelle muttered as she sat in her car, caught in the 45-minute traffic jam, gritting her teeth and gripping the steering wheel. With a vague sense of dread, she concluded that, if anything, she would be squandering her life even more when she finally did make it to work.

Like every other day at her management trainee job, she would endure hours sitting in her Dilbert-like cubicle and performing meaningless tasks. She never knew why she was doing the assignments that mysteriously appeared on her computer screen. Nobody could satisfactorily explain to her the purpose of the chores she completed at her computer. On those rare occasions when she did bring up a question or offer a suggestion to one of her supervisors, she was worried that she was being seen as either dim-witted or naive—in either case, definitely not management material. The only certainty at work was that she always felt behind the other trainees.

But work was not the only place where she felt inadequate and behind, like a student who arrives both unprepared and late for a test or a birthday present that's both cheap and belated. "Who am I kidding?" Jamelle thought. "I'm just as messed up and clueless in my personal life." All her friends were either sprinting ahead on fast-track career paths, happily pairing off in intimate relationships, or having babies—and some were even successfully managing to do all the above. While they were moving forward with their lives, Jamelle was bouncing around like a pinball from one trivial point to another, careening along without any real sense of direction or purpose.

One particularly frantic day, all the management trainees had to attend an intensive workshop on new federal regulations. The red-faced, clenched-jawed workshop leader was like a drill instructor, using the Socratic method of questioning as an attack weapon rather than a learning tool. The expressions on the faces of everyone else seemed to range from gaunt apprehension to grim determination as they struggled with the challenging questions and frantically took notes on the complex material.

Jamelle was certain that her face had that frozen, "deer in the headlights" look. Like a threatened animal, she certainly felt that same sickening sense of paralysis. In fact, she was so panicked and flustered that, although her neighbors had several pages of notes by the end of the workshop, her pen had barely moved. After the others filed out of the room, Jamelle remained to jot down as much of the material as she could remember and left feeling relieved that the workshop leader had not targeted her for interrogation. After lunch, the trainees were all scheduled to meet with someone in the company's Employee Assistance Program, and so Jamelle found herself sitting in a comfortable chair facing a counselor.

REFLECTING QUESTIONS

1. What do you see as the primary issue that Jamelle faces?
2. If you were Jamelle's counselor, how would you help her to address this primary issue?

OVERVIEW

One of the assumptions of the medical model is that knowing the etiology, or cause, of a client's current symptoms is ultimately necessary in order to find a cure. Because etiology always exists prior to symptoms, taking a client's history has been the traditional beginning of the counseling process. However, in brief counseling, you start your counseling work with a view to the future, rather than to the past. Strange as it may seem, it is possible for something that has not yet happened to cause a change in someone's present condition. In fact, hope and a sense of purpose—both essential parts of any successful life—are actually rooted in the future. When people act now to realize an anticipated possibility, their future is causing their present. This idea, first articulated by Aristotle, is known as teleology, or final cause.

If the future actually played out in a manner that is strictly teleological, then we would always know with a great deal of certainty what is going to happen. Human life, however, is more often lived "teleonomically"— that is, we know the general direction of our lives, but we are not certain about the specific circumstances of our future (Mahoney, 1995). Although they are neither definite nor inevitable, goals help us to maintain purpose and hope in our lives.

One of the most important activities in which you can engage with clients is seeking to understand, and helping to frame, their goals. Once articulated, goals serve as teleonomic guides for the direction of the counseling work. In this chapter, we discuss how to develop well-formed goals with a client and how to ascertain whether your counselor–client relationship is that of a "customer," "complainant," "visitor," or "involuntary." Third parties, people who refer clients to you, often have goals that are not the same as those of the client. We offer suggestions for framing the referral and working to align third-party goals with client goals. Finally, we describe how to use the tools of finding exceptions and how to employ scaling techniques.

IDEAS

A Brief History of the Past and Future

When someone asks us to explain why we behave in a certain way, we often point to our *past* and offer a *cause* as the answer. We may say something like, "I've always done it that way," or "That's the way I learned it." In other words, we see past events as causing our current behaviors. This "past causes the present" assumption is common in most people's thinking.

When clients come to you for counseling, they often want you to discover what's causing the troubling experiences and behaviors that are vexing them. They have the idea that some past trauma, habit, character deficit, or unexamined experience is holding them prisoner to their discouraging ways of thinking, feeling, and acting. These clients want to know the *etiology* of their current situations. Etiology is the deterministic notion that is the stock-in-trade of most traditional scientific thought. In this view, all events are caused, and the causes always precede, or come before, the effects. When health care practitioners seek a diagnosis, they are looking for the origin or cause—the etiology—that has led to the current symptoms.

But is it possible that behaviors in the present could be caused by the future rather than the past? At first glance, this idea sounds a bit preposterous, doesn't it? Nevertheless, recognizing how the future can cause the present offers a valuable perspective for you as a counselor. Taking this point of view, your goal is to help clients construct a future image that will change their current ways of thinking, feeling, and acting and set them on a hopeful trajectory toward the future.

Decades ago, Martin Seligman (1974) developed the theory of "learned helplessness," the notion that when an organism—be it rat or human—exhausts all its known strategies to get to a goal, it finally gives up. People who feel helpless to escape their current situation come to believe that their behaviors have no purpose. Their cognitive maps lead nowhere. As a result, they often grow discouraged, experience depression, and see little use in trying to alter their circumstances. Ultimately, they lose hope. The hopeless person is afraid of wanting something, because such a desire will only increase the pain. The discouraged person eventually comes to a place where the only thing that is desired is freedom from the pain. This attitude leads clients to frame their goals for counseling as wanting to make something go away. Your task is to assist your client in formulating a goal that is the presence, rather than the absence, of something and to help the client toward feeling hopeful about achieving this goal.

Happily, Martin Seligman was not content to leave us with the morbid legacy of learned helplessness. In 1978, he began to modify his theory by adding the notions of expectations and attributions. He saw changing expectations—visions of the future—as the key to ridding people of helplessness (Kirsch, 1990). Life involves inevitable disappointments, frustrations, and setbacks. When people attribute these events to failures in their personal characters and permanent flaws in their personalities, they expect nothing but helplessness in the future. But if they believe that temporary external causes are to blame for these events, then they are less likely to develop learned helplessness or depression. In other words, instead of seeing themselves as losers because they have suffered setbacks, clients could come to see that, in spite of past difficulties, they still have the resilience and resolve to make future events turn out differently. In his 1991 book *Learned Optimism,* Seligman stated the following:

> Life inflicts the same setbacks and tragedies on the optimist as on the pessimist, but the optimist weathers them better. . . . Even when things go well . . . the pessimist . . . is haunted by forebodings of catastrophe. (p. 207)

In a still later book, Seligman (2002) extolled the virtues of happiness as an antidote to helplessness. The shift from focusing on client helplessness and despair to optimism and happiness was complete. Nobody can truly predict what the future will bring. But we humans always anticipate its outcomes, and we hope for a good result. Unlike rats, people construct complex images of the future. Our futures can be optimistic or pessimistic, based on our attributions. If we see ourselves as capable, resourceful, and full of resolve, we will likely view the future optimistically. If we see the world as hospitable and offering opportunity, we can face uncertainty and occasional setbacks with a steadfast attitude. As the counselor, you try to help tip the balance of clients' expectations toward an optimistic future; a future filled with possibility is, in turn, the cause of a resolute and hopeful present.

Toward an Uncertain Future

Alfred Adler was originally a colleague of Freud, until they parted company over the sexual theory (Day, 2004). Adler stated that our basic striving was for superiority. However, by this term, he did not mean that we want to dominate others but that we wish to surpass ourselves and overcome our current condition (Prochaska & Norcross, 2007). Every person is a prophet: We proceed by predicting how events will turn out. Therefore, we are not so much impelled by our instincts or by our history as we are compelled by our goals in life and our predictions of the future.

Each of us creates an ideal self that represents the person we wish to become, and we establish a "life style" (Adler coined this now popular term) based on our "fictional finalism." By fictional finalism, Adler meant that we live now in light of where we expect to end up, even though we cannot know for sure. Adler stated that our future is far more causative of our current moods and behaviors than is our past. Of course, the future we envision is not necessarily the future we will ultimately have. It is fictional in the sense that it is metaphorical—the story we tell ourselves about where we are going. It is our mythic quest, our journey into the relative unknown.

Pudmenzky (2004) identified three types of "end-attaining" activity: teleomatic processes, which are *end-resulting;* teleological processes, which are *goal-seeking;* and teleonomic processes, which are *end-directed.* These are useful distinctions for understanding the process of setting goals for the future.

Teleomatic processes are those studied by physicists in which an *end result* is reached due to physical laws that govern the behavior of matter and energy. Gravity is an example of teleomatic process. Its end states are realized without any purpose or control. A falling rock or Newton's apple reaching its destination are examples of teleomatic processes. Discouraged clients will often imagine themselves to be caught up in such processes, as helpless victims of any wind that blows. They have lost their sense of direction and their internal motivation. They are, in their minds, at the mercy of physical forces. Your mission is to help them reclaim their power over the environment.

Teleological processes have definite goal states "in mind" and possess the necessary resources and methods for achieving the goal. They are like a smart missile that flies unerringly to a target. There are two major steps you will follow in your work with clients that mimic teleology: First, you attempt to help clients crystallize a goal and envision the route to that goal. After that, you work to establish in the client's mind the fact that he or she possesses the necessary resources for attaining that desired outcome. However, you must be careful to elicit, or draw out, these overlooked resources that the client already possesses, rather than attempting to convince the client from your point of view that he or she has what it takes.

Finally, teleonomic processes are those that engage in *end-directed* behavior because of the operation of an internal program (Mayr, 1982; O'Grady & Brooks, 1988). They are directed toward some end but should not be regarded as inevitably leading to that exact end. When a client is asked to name a goal, it becomes a fictional finalism. Such a goal has a direction, but is only a path toward the desired end. For this reason, while you treat the client's goal as if it is teleological, you know that life goals are really teleonomic. You use goal statements to provide a direction rather than to attain a specific outcome.

Be on the lookout for a change in the goal. Often, the first thing the client claims to desire will give way to another more important goal. Because you know that no one can precisely predict where he or she will end up in the future, you can remain flexible as you go though the process of establishing goals with your clients. Goals are a tool for focusing your work with the client toward the future and specifying steps along the path.

Overcoming Blocks to a Hopeful Future

Your clients who feel dispirited and discouraged are often trapped in a paradoxical state: they desire a change in their situation, but they also may fear change. As they contemplate going into an uncertain future, they will tend to cling to familiar practices, even if they are painful. Somehow, you must help them tip the balance (Young, 2005), so that they allow themselves to relinquish the relative security of the present, however unsatisfactory, and take up that uncertain path to the goal they seek. Tipping the balance is not simply a situation in which one weighs the pros and cons of an issue and makes a decision. You must stay with clients and hear their stories until a clear path toward a goal emerges for them. If you encourage clients to continue this exploration, they will likely open up to new possibilities and become ripe for change.

Remember that no matter how well you believe that you are empathically "walking in their shoes," you have never actually been over your clients' terrain. It is important that your client—and not you—determines the goals in counseling. Mahoney (1995) criticized some counselors as attempting to sell maps of the road ahead: "They claim to be well traveled and to know the best route for traveling to the destinations sought by their clients. They are, in a sense, travel agents" (p. 391).

Unlike Mahoney's travel agents, to be truly helpful you must journey with the client, offering compassion and comfort, respecting the client's need to rest, and assuring the client's safety and well-being. It is at these times when your humanity is much more important than your techniques. But simply resting will not necessarily help the client to construct a new image of the future. While you take your cues from the client as to how to proceed moment to moment, you must at the same time remain strategic, deliberate, and mindful of the need for the client to establish a goal and travel in the direction of that goal.

Implications of These Ideas for the Counselor

These ideas about teleonomy have important implications for your work with clients:

- You are not attempting to find the past causes of the client's present concerns. Instead, you are interested in establishing what the client desires for the future.
- The client will often indicate a desire for the present situation to go away. You must then help the client find a goal that involves the presence of something they desire.
- People who are discouraged or depressed have lost a sense of purpose and control of their lives. Coming to believe that they can get to a better place will help restore their feeling of hope and resolve.
- People live their lives according to a "fictional finalism." Where they think they will end up creates either an optimistic or a pessimistic mood. In this sense, the future causes the present.

- We are not so concerned with whether the stated goal will be accomplished as we are that the client continues to move forward in a hopeful manner.
- Clients are always wavering between changing and trying to stay the same. Your job as a counselor is to tip the balance in favor of change.
- The client's job is to establish the goal for counseling. It is your job to make sure the goal is well formed.

TOOLS

Inviting Clients to Set Goals

Beginning your goal-setting work with clients involves the simple step of asking them what they hope to achieve by coming to counseling. The initial goal statements that clients offer in response to your question, according to Sklare (1997), are likely to fall into one of four categories: positive, negative, harmful, or "I don't know." Each of these responses presents different challenges to your efforts to help clients develop well-formed goals.

Positive goals, the first category, are those in which the client articulates a desire for something that will change the situation for the better. However, the client's initial goal statements are often phrased in vague terms, such as "to be happy," "to have better self-esteem," "to get along with others," or "to have better communication." Your challenge is that none of these statements is a goal for which you can really contract. If you do, you have agreed to a trip bound for "Never-NeverLand," because such goals are simply too abstract and nebulous. You must "boil down" such a goal to something specific.

Negative goals, Sklare's second type, are those in which the client wishes something to go away. This goal statement, which is the most common initial response of clients, involves the absence of a problematic condition or situation. Examples are statements such as, "I want my parents to get off my case," or "To be less depressed," or "People wouldn't reject me." These goals either rely on other people changing their behavior or imply that the clients themselves will have little or no personal control over the outcome. You need to help the goal become the presence—not the absence—of something. It is best to seek clients' vision of positive goals rather than to ask what they are willing to do. Prematurely asking for specific behaviors puts pressure on the client. Either the client does not know what behaviors will lead to a goal, or if the client does know, he or she may be unwilling to attempt such behaviors.

Your best response to goal statements that are the absence of something is to ask "instead" or "difference" questions. "When your parents get off your case, how will your life be different?" "When you climb out of that depression, what different feelings will you be noticing?" "When you find yourself not feeling rejected, how will you feel instead?"

Not infrequently, clients will offer a goal that falls under the third category: harmful. *Harmful goal* statements involve wishes for outcomes that either put the client at unnecessary risk or sabotage future opportunities for personal fulfillment. For example, it's not unusual to hear adolescent clients wishing to drop out of school, have a baby, hurt someone, or run away from home. Such statements may entice you into debating the merits of these goals, cautioning clients regarding potential hazards, or skirting the issue of goals entirely. The challenge you face is how to engage in the counseling process with such clients without supporting goals that you believe to be harmful to them or others. You can ask the hypothetical, "If you were to do that, what would it do for you?" or you might say something like, "I get the impression that if you were to do that, your hope is that something in your situation would get better. I wonder what that would be." (Note: If the client's goal continues to be harmful to self or others, you must become a manager of the situation, as well as a counselor, and take action to avoid a tragic outcome.)

When clients offer the fourth type of response—"*I don't know*"—to your request for a goal statement, they are signaling that they are not yet invested enough to begin the work of changing. Such clients may be in counseling involuntarily, referred by a third party who wishes them to change in ways the clients do not desire. In other situations, these clients may be just so discouraged that they cannot seem to muster the energy necessary to become involved in the goal-setting process. Clients who are in crisis often cannot see any options for change in their situation (James & Gilliland, 2005). They are so overwhelmed by recent events that they cannot clearly contemplate the future. Your work with such clients is to "find the survivor in the victim" (Echterling, Presbury, & McKee, 2005). This approach will be discussed in more detail in Chapter 13. As the old adage goes, "You can lead a horse to water, but you can't make it drink." Your challenge is to see if you can discover your clients' tastes well enough to get them to "swallow" the notion of working with you toward a resolution of their situation.

You might say something like, "I get the feeling that you are not yet ready to think of a goal for our work together. Let's talk more about what brought you here." You need to go back to acknowledging the client's concerns with LUV and wait for another opportunity to seek a goal.

Well-Formed Goals

Once a client has started to envision the future, you then will be helping to crystallize an initially amorphous goal statement so that it is explicit, specific, realistic, and valued by the client—in other words, a well-formed goal (De Jong & Berg, 2002). Well-formed goals must also be concrete and not too ambitious (doable) and represent some small difference (baby steps). (Remember: The best way to eat an elephant is one bite at a time!) By creating such a goal, clients gain a sense of direction and hope, become more motivated and involved in counseling, and increase their momentum towards therapeutic outcomes. You can help clients formulate successful goals by following a few simple principles described below.

Help create positive goals   The first, and most fundamental, principle is to encourage your clients to state their goals in the positive, describing what they will be doing or thinking rather than what they will not. Never accept a contract to work toward the absence of something.

For example, you can ask what the client will be doing when the negative condition is no longer present. A client may say, "My goal for counseling is that I'd like to stop having these rage reactions." In response to this statement, you could ask, "What will you be doing when you are no longer having these reactions?" Another strategy for redirecting a negative goal into a positive one is to use terms that encourage clients to see possible alternatives and choices. As mentioned above, beginning your questions with phrases such as "when you are no longer," "in place of," and "rather than" invites your clients to begin thinking outside the box of a negative goal statement (Sklare, 1997).

Sometimes it is helpful to ask "the circular question": what others will be noticing or saying about the client when the goal is achieved. This question adds the interpersonal dimension to the client's view of the world and helps to make his or her situation a bit more objective. An example of this circular questioning is, "When you have changed so that your parents are no longer on your case, how will they be seeing you differently? What will your parents say that they have noticed about you that allows them to ease up on you?"

Dig for goals in problem-saturated talk   Working with clients whose initial goal statements seem harmful can be particularly challenging. The first thing you must realize is that such goal statements represent a yearning for thwarted, but unstated, positive goals. The goal to drop out of school may represent a frustrated desire to succeed or to maintain self-esteem. For a teenage girl, the desire to have a baby is often the result of feeling unloved and wanting to have someone give her unconditional positive regard. (Of course, we all know that expecting this from a baby is certainly misguided.) The desire to injure someone is often the result of wanting respect and not getting it or the urge to even a score. Finally, the desire to run away from home may reflect seeking more autonomy or a safer environment.

Your job in these situations is, not only to dig for the positive goal beneath the surface of a harmful goal statement, but also to acknowledge the client's discouragement. People do not move from a discouraged position to a hopeful one without first feeling that someone has understood their pain. You can acknowledge the client's level of frustration without focusing on it, and you can also, at the same time, slip in a possibility statement. This is where O'Hanlon and Beadle's "Carl Rogers with a Twist" comes in. You could say, for example, "Wow! It sounds like you have been trying everything you know to get better grades and were even sometimes thinking about giving up, because you haven't yet hit upon a way to do better in school."

Finding a workable goal that exists beneath the initial goal statement is always difficult. This is where your skill as a counselor comes in. In this book, we can offer suggestions, but they are only guidelines that point out what you must do: find out what the client wants and to have him or her state it in useful terms. While it is unnecessary, and unwise, to probe for additional problem-saturated descriptions, it is okay to search for goals and exceptions (the times when the problem is not happening). The point here is that you need to find what the client will be a customer for and have it stated as a goal that will not be harmful. Remember the rule: If your client will not cooperate with your attempts to move the session forward, then you probably have not acknowledged enough—go back to LUV.

Help create action goals   The third principle for forming goals is that you are more likely to develop an effective goal if you avoid nouns, diagnoses, or static words and instead use action words ending in *-ing*. If, for example, a parent says, "Our goal for counseling is to treat Johnny's conduct disorder," you might ask, "How will Johnny be different when he is *doing* more of what you expect of him?" or "When you are no longer worry*ing* about that problem, what will you be think*ing* about instead?"

If your clients reply simply, "I don't know," to your request for a goal, you might be able to nudge them toward a positive goal statement by inviting them to guess. For example, Sklare (1997) offered such counselor responses as, "If you did know . . . ," "If you did have an idea . . . ," "If you could figure it out . . . ," and "If it weren't beyond you . . . " (p. 27). These are possible leads that might set aside the client's reluctance and arrive at a hypothetical goal. By asking the hypothetical *if*, you relieve your client of any obligation for knowing the answer. Instead, you offer an invitation to speculate on a possibility. "In some cases, persistent repetition of *if* questions may be needed to ascertain the reasons the client is in the counselor's office" (Sklare, 1997, p. 26). Sometimes, what is produced is a problem statement instead of a goal statement: "The teacher says I have a bad attitude," or "They say I don't fit into society," or "The judge says I'm mental." In any case, such statements can begin a process that might eventually arrive at a well-formed goal.

You might follow each of these statements with something like, "If the teacher doesn't like your attitude, what would she say you were doing if you had a better attitude?" or "How would you be behaving if people thought you did fit into society?" or "So the judge doesn't believe you are thinking straight? How could you convince him that you are okay?"

If any of the above queries produces a goal statement for the referring party, you can then follow up by asking, "What part of what they want is something that you want, too?" or "How does that fit for you?" Well-formed goals must be the client's—and not the counselor's or the referring third party's—goals.

Be presumptive as you help clients envision change   The fourth principle of effective goal setting is to be presumptive, rather than subjunctive. Word all your statements and questions in ways that suggest that positive change is not only possible but also inevitable. Questions that ask "if" are okay for using hypotheticals when the goal is vague or harmful. You would not, for example, want to say, "*When* you do get pregnant . . . " or "*When* you finally run away from home. . . ." But when referring to positive goals, it is useful for you to presume that they are inevitable.

Using presumptive questions and statements implies that the current situation is temporary, and that it will obviously change—for the better. For example, rather than asking, "*If* the situation were to change in the way you wish, how *would* you be feeling about Johnny?" you would phrase the question, "*When* the situation changes for the better, how *will* you be feeling about Johnny?" This distinction between expecting change and wishing for change is an important and subtle use of language that can force the client to speak in terms of differences and possibilities.

Keep it simple   Finally, your client is much more likely to develop an achievable goal if you keep it simple. As stated above, make sure the client's aspirations are concrete, focused, and doable. One common complication is a goal that a client offers but nevertheless believes it to be out of reach. With such a seemingly unattainable goal, you can explore what smaller "on track" goal would be a successive approximation to the larger goal. For example, you can ask, "So, when you are already on track to being an outgoing and sociable person, what's the first thing you will be doing differently?" The goal should either be behavioral (a change in doing) or meaningful (a change in viewing). A workable goal cannot be "pie in the sky." (For readers who do not recognize this figure of speech, *pie in the sky* means an out-of-reach fantasy. You can read more about idioms and metaphors in Chapter 7.)

Abstract goals can be simplified by asking about times in the past when the client experienced similar thoughts or behaviors. If, for example, the client wishes to "be happier," you might help him or her get closer to a well-formed goal by saying something like, "Tell me about a time when you were happier. What was going on then? How were you different?" This "exception" question might lead to a more concrete description of what it means to the client to be happy, which then might be converted into a workable goal.

Using This Tool

Join with two colleagues to form a small group. One of you volunteers to be a client by sharing some goal in your life that you would like to achieve. As you describe this goal, however, be sure to begin by making it vague and assuming an external locus of control. Another person volunteers to help the client develop a well-formed goal according to the principles listed above. Finally, the third person serves as the recorder who observes the activity and leads the feedback discussion. Take turns until everyone has performed each role.

Clients and Commitment

Your job would certainly be easier if all clients came desiring to personally change and ready to devote their complete energies to doing so. But because of their reluctance to trade the known for the unknown and their uncertainty as to whether you are a trustworthy person, clients are usually not willing to take such a chance right away. With each client, you must discover the answer to the question, What does this person want for investing the time, making the effort, and taking the risks that are involved in counseling? You may begin the counseling relationship by suggesting that the client has come hoping to improve something in his or her life, and the client may indeed name something, but this does not mean that you can proceed as though you have a contract to help the client change. If you have not yet established a good working relationship, or if the client seems disinterested or disengaged, then you must listen to the client's story and wait to be invited.

Some brief therapists have come up with a useful framework for considering initial levels of commitment to counseling (de Shazer, 1988). This taxonomy is to be taken not as a diagnosis but rather as appraisal of your working relationship with a specific client at a particular moment in time. In this classification scheme, clients can be *visiting, complaining,* or *engaging fully* in their relationship with you.

A client who is visiting, or "window shopping," is not yet committed to the counseling process. It may be clear to others that this *visitor* "has problems," but he or she presently has little motivation to change. The best way for you to respond initially to someone who is just visiting is to listen respectfully, compliment and encourage when possible, but do not make suggestions for change, and be careful about offering counseling to this person.

A client who is predominately involved in complaining may elaborate at length on specific or vague problems. Clients who encounter you in this manner often present themselves as helpless victims of their circumstances and see others as responsible for making changes. It is not initially clear whether you are being invited to give advice or to help change someone else. In the beginning, your best option is to treat this *complainant* as a *visitor*.

A client who is fully engaged in the counseling process has made a commitment to be a *customer* seeking your services. This person comes with a complaint, gives a reasonably clear description of it, and is ready to work. In this relationship, you can quickly invite your client to move into productive goal setting and successful change. Furthermore, this client is willing to adopt what Teyber (2006) called "the internal focus." This means that the client realizes that changes must take place with the self rather than in others or in the troubling situation. Corey and Corey (2007) offered several questions that might be asked of the client in order to achieve an internal focus: "What specific feelings, thoughts, and behaviors are you most interested in changing? . . . What qualities would you like to acquire that you do not now have? . . . What kind of future do you want most for yourself?" (p. 166). *Customers* will generally respond to such inquiries with positive goal statements.

Sometimes, school officials, parents, or courts refer clients who are less responsive than those in the three categories listed above. The *involuntary* client is countercommitted because to comply or cooperate would be an admission of guilt or weakness. Becoming a customer would be a capitulation for this client. Obviously, the counselor has the most difficult time establishing a contract with the involuntary. This category of counselor–client relationship will be discussed in Chapter 13.

You should remember that the above categories (customers, visitors, complainants, and involuntaries) are really descriptions of the relationship between the counselor and the client. We use these terms as a convenient shorthand rather than as a way of labeling individuals. Some involuntaries, for example, will become fully engaged in the process with some counselors, while they never will with others. You stand a much better chance of having customers if you make sure you establish relationships with clients in which they are convinced that you are both competent and interested in helping. You must understand fully a client's goal in being with you and what he or she might "be a customer for." Never assume that clients referred by a third party are customers for the same goal as the referring agent, or that what you think they should be working on is what they desire to change. Unless the goal has been fully negotiated between you and your client, you will not have a *customer* relationship.

LISTENING IN ON A SESSION

Review the story at the beginning of the chapter. A resolution-focused counselor can help Jamelle to begin developing well-formed goals by engaging with her in the following way.

Counselor: (After they shake hands and introduce themselves to one another, they sit in comfortable chairs facing one another, and the counselor begins to speak.)

"Well, Jamelle, what is something in your life that you would like to improve by coming here?"

Jamelle: (She appears flustered by the counselor's words. She cuts short her breathing, squirms uncomfortably in her chair, tips her head in a quizzical pose, and softly chortles in a muted, high-pitched manner.)

"Mmm . . . *improve* in my life? Honestly, right now I'm only concerned about what my supervisors want. I don't even know what's going on, much less what people around here expect of me. I was hoping that maybe you could give me some advice on what to do."

Counselor: (She nods, offers a concerned smile as she leans forward, and uses a wave of her hand to indicate the management training program.)

"All the ambiguities that they build into this program have been really baffling and frustrating for you, and it sounds like that now you'd really like to find a way to get a better handle on what it's all about."

Jamelle: (She pauses, crosses her legs, smoothes the crinkles of her skirt, and finally looks up.)

"Yeah, that's right. I mean, in less than a month, I come up for a performance review and the rumor is that it's an all-or-nothing proposition. It's getting hard for me to sleep at night because I keep going over and over in my mind everything that's going on in my work and life, trying to make some sense out of it. The only thing I do know for sure is that this has been a really stressful time for me. If it's OK to go back to your original question, I guess the goal of this counseling for me is to get rid of this overwhelming stress."

Counselor: "Tell me, Jamelle, when this overwhelming stress is no longer present for you, what will you be doing differently and how will that change the way you feel?"

Jamelle: (She starts to answer, hesitates, considers for a moment, and then talks briskly.)

"Well . . . um . . . well, that's a very good question. (She pauses.) One of the useful things they've taught me here is to use what the management trainers call a 'delaying tactic' that gives you some time to pull together your thoughts."

Counselor: (She nods, smiles, and invites the client again.)

"You've got that management skill down nicely. So now that you've bought yourself some time to give that question more consideration, what will you be doing differently when you are no longer overwhelmed by stress?"

Jamelle: (She responds with a rueful smile.)

"Maybe I've mastered that delaying tactic, but I don't think it helped me all that much because I'm still not exactly sure what I would do differently. The one thing that flashed in my mind when you asked me again is that I would be acting more like one of the other trainees—Sophia—that I've met here. She's really got a different aura about her."

Counselor: (She tilts her head in a gesture of curiosity.)

"So when you begin to handle work and life more like this Sophia, what will you be saying and doing that is different?"

Jamelle: (She gazes off, lost in reflecting on this possibility.)

"I wouldn't be so uptight and worried all the time like I am now. I guess I would be acting with an air of serenity and a sense of purpose. Do you know what I mean? I'd be relaxed and focused, but still energetic and motivated."

Counselor: "When you become, as you put it, 'relaxed and focused, but still energetic and motivated,' who will be the first person to notice? What will that person see or hear that would be different about you?"

Jamelle: "My sister Harriet would have to be the one. I've been bugging her on the phone for weeks with all these complaints about stress at work and in my personal life. She would definitely notice if I told her that I decided that I'm going to get something out of this program—and my life— even if I don't end up as successful as others seem to be."

REFLECTING QUESTIONS

1. During this segment, in what ways is the counselor–client relationship changing?
2. In what ways are Jamelle's goal statements changing?
3. Write a possible counselor response to Jamelle's last statement.

Third-Party Goals

You may have noticed that when someone is referred for counseling, the referral is often saturated with problem statements. Usually, the only goal that is implied by the referring agent—be it a parent, teacher, or court official—is the wish that the problem behaviors be eliminated. Just as you do not accept the absence of something as part of a well-formed goal when speaking with your clients, neither should you accept a list of problem statements without well-formed goals from third parties who refer clients to you.

You can begin the relationship with your clients on a more positive note if you can also work briefly with third parties to develop well-formed goals. Not only will this help get your counseling relationship off on the right foot, but it will also change the relationship you have with referring agents. It is much easier to chart the progress someone is making toward a goal than to note the elimination of problem behaviors. Besides, some of the problem behaviors cited by third parties may not be seen by you or your client as problems, such as, "He grumbles when he has to take out the trash," or "He is not always on task in the classroom."

Be careful about accepting the client's "problem" as the referring agent defines it. If possible, normalize the problem definition by relabeling it, acknowledge that there is work to do, and talk about goals rather than problems. Change problem frames into goal frames by finding out what the referring party wants, and by minimizing the focus on the undesirable behavior. Whenever possible, change nouns that label the person into verbs that describe behaviors. For example, a "lazy" person "moves slowly," or a "belligerent" person "values his or her own opinion." There is no cure for laziness or belligerence, but "getting things done in a timely fashion" or "listening to the opinions of others" are workable goals.

Here's the bottom line: Never accept a referral that lists only problem behaviors! When consulting with the referring person to establish well-formed goals, you need to make explicit the target behaviors that will indicate to the referring person that the involuntary client is improving (Tohn & Oshlag, 1996). The following exchange between the counselor and the school official illustrates this point. The counselor, who is to work with a boy named Steve, asks the referring school official how the boy must change in order for the school official to believe that counseling has been successful:

School Official: "Staying out of trouble would help."

Counselor: "What would be some signs to you that Steve is beginning to do this?" (Tohn & Oshlag, 1996, p. 161)

Note that the counselor is not only asking for a specific behavior and the presence—rather than the absence—of a behavior but is also couching improvement as a "beginning" rather than a miracle cure. This not only helps to create well-formed goals that are clear to everyone, but it also tends to change the referring person's focus toward behaviors that will be improving. Kral (1986) suggested the use of a referral form that encourages the referring person to focus on goals rather than problems. Figure 4-1 offers an example of such a goal-oriented form.

Framing the Third-Party Referral

Iatrogenesis is a term meaning an outcome that is inadvertently caused by the treatment. Usually, this is stated in the negative—for example, a medication the doctor prescribed actually made you worse. For example, people who are given major tranquilizing drugs for schizophrenia often develop tardive dyskinesia, a Parkinson's-like disorder of the nervous system, as a side effect. People sometimes go to the hospital for something minor and die from a germ they contract from the hospital environment. Such events are unintended. But Milton Erickson (quoted in O'Hanlon and Weiner-Davis, 1989) said, "While I have read a number of articles on this subject of iatrogenic disease, and have heard many discussions about it, there is one topic on which I haven't seen much written about and that is iatrogenic health" (p. 51).

Usually, when someone is referred, or the counselor is called in for a consultation, the thing people want to know is "What's the problem?" It is amazing how, once the problem is named, many people seem satisfied, as if something has really changed after

```
┌─────────────────────────────────────────────────────────────────────┐
│                        COUNSELING GOALS FORM                          │
│                    (Completedby the Referring Person)                 │
│                                                                       │
│  Directions: Please place a check mark by either "DoingWell" or       │
│  "Desired Goal." If you desire a certain goal, then describe what      │
│  achieving this goal would look like for this student, so I can        │
│  communicate this to the client.                                      │
│                                                                       │
│  Name of Client: _____  Date: _____    │
│                                                                       │
│  Name of Referring Person: _____   │
│                                                                       │
│                                                                       │
│  Showing interest in schoolwork    ❑ Doing Well     ❑ Desired Goal    │
│                                                                       │
│      Description: _____    │
│                                                                       │
│  Working cooperatively with others  ❑ Doing Well     ❑ Desired Goal   │
│                                                                       │
│      Description: _____    │
│                                                                       │
│  Showing self-control               ❑ Doing Well     ❑ Desired Goal   │
│                                                                       │
│      Description: _____    │
│                                                                       │
│  Working well independently         ❑ Doing Well     ❑ Desired Goal   │
│                                                                       │
│      Description: _____    │
│                                                                       │
│  Staying on task                    ❑ Doing Well     ❑ Desired Goal   │
│                                                                       │
│      Description: _____    │
│                                                                       │
│  Treating others fairly             ❑ Doing Well     ❑ Desired Goal   │
│                                                                       │
│      Description: _____    │
│                                                                       │
│  Standing up for self               ❑ Doing Well     ❑ Desired Goal   │
│                                                                       │
│      Description: _____    │
│                                                                       │
│  My particular counseling goal for this student is: _____    │
│                                                                       │
│  _____  │
└─────────────────────────────────────────────────────────────────────┘
```

FIGURE 4-1 Goal-Oriented Referral Form.

a label has been applied to the problem or a cause has been offered. It is not uncommon for a counselor to have a referring agent report that the client improved after he or she had merely been tested or seen in an assessment interview.

This situation dramatizes the iatrogenic or placebo power of the referral itself and the referring person's belief that something is being done—whether it is or not. When this happens, you may feel obliged to explain it is unlikely that anything so far could make a difference because you have only evaluated, and not yet actually treated, the client. However, you are better off simply accepting that change has taken place. You have already accomplished that first step of helping the referring person to notice desirable behaviors in the client that had previously been overlooked.

There is a lot of mythology surrounding counseling. Most laypeople think they know something about it, but as to how it actually works, they haven't a clue. They often just assume it does work. We counselors want to keep them thinking this way! When someone who has referred a client comments that the client is better, accept that person's perception, even if it doesn't match your own, and ask for the referring person's elaboration on the noticed improvement.

Looking for Exceptions

Problems never always happen. Exceptions always do. Sometimes, when a client is in crisis or has been referred for a specific problem, you may find yourself urgently feeling that you need to immediately fix something. Corey and Corey (2007) stated that a common mistake they see in their counseling trainees is the tendency to jump into problem-solving mode.

Earlier in this chapter, we discussed the importance of keeping a lookout for client goal statements that involve the *absence* of something, wanting a problem or concern to go away. However, as we listen to clients' stories, we also look for *another kind of absence,* the times when the problem has not been happening. Such *exceptions* to the concern are usually absent in the client's story because he or she is so focused on the pain. If you can probe the story to find these exceptions, you will notice that they constitute part of the goal the client seeks.

Clients come to counseling expecting that all you want to hear about is the problem. They often describe it to you in excruciating detail. Furthermore, clients may report the problem to be constant and unwavering—always happening. As a result of this "problem focus," clients tend to ignore or dismiss as trivial the times when the problem is not happening. These times "are not seen by the client as differences that make a difference" (de Shazer, 1991, p. 58).

Finding exceptions is the quintessential technique of brief resolution counseling. The exception is a resolution that the client has already achieved, if only temporarily. Therefore, fully realizing an exception is the dramatic moment when the client both understands his or her own resources and gains a more hopeful attitude. The exception is Bateson's (1972) "news of difference"—the lubrication that "unsticks" the problematic story.

Trying to get clients to recognize exceptions when they are mostly focusing on problems is tricky. It must be done while still acknowledging the pain of their complaint; otherwise, it trivializes their concerns. Cade and O'Hanlon (1993) suggested that your responses should fit in with the severity of the clients' complaints. For example, you could say to a client, "Given what you have told me about your situation, I am really surprised that things are not much worse. How have you kept going?" (p. 99).

Murphy and Dillon (2003) stated that counselors must adopt a strengths perspective in which they pay particular attention to what their clients do well and attempt to enhance these strengths. As the counselor, you are much more curious about the strengths, resources, and resilience of your clients than you are about their problems and concerns. Your clients are coming to you able to see—in discouraging clarity and detail—their problems, personal inadequacies, and failures. However, they fail to notice their personal skills, talents, and resources—the clues for resolution.

By asking questions regarding their successes and competencies, you help clients become aware of these experiences and characteristics. You might, at a propitious moment, say, "Tell me about a time when this concern you are talking about was happening and you handled the situation differently. How did you get yourself to do that?" When your client names an exception, you are off and running. Your job is to capitalize on this opportunity by pursuing a description, at great length, of their exceptional behaviors and the nature of the situations when they were able to handle these problems. Using this technique also encourages clients to recognize their personal agency. It teaches clients that behaviors once thought to be out of control are truly within their control and, furthermore, that change is already happening!

You may also identify positive circumstances by asking, "What is different about the situations where this is less of a problem?" Or you may explore personal strengths by asking, "How are you different when this problem is not happening?" Of course, your questions are presumptive; you assume that there are such times. This should not be asked in a hesitant manner, such as, "Are there possibly times when the problem is not happening?" Clients who are so overwhelmed with the problem will simply say, "No." But, if you imply that the existence of exceptions is simply a fact, clients will search their memories for them. As we have stated, problems *never* always happen! Count on it!

LISTENING IN ON A SESSION

Let's return to this chapter's story and continue with the dialogue between Jamelle and her counselor. Look for ways that the counselor begins sifting through the client's story to find those nuggets of exceptions to the problem.

Counselor: "Jamelle, I'm puzzled about something. Given all the troubling ambiguities in this program, the intensity of your training, and the demands of your supervisors, how have you managed to hang in there and face all these challenges? As you know, a lot of trainees drop out."

Jamelle: "I've wondered that myself sometimes because it certainly hasn't been easy. I've thought about quitting dozens of times, but I guess I just decided that some way, somehow, I'm going to get something out of this program in spite of my own hang-ups and the craziness and pressure. I guess I'm just stubborn."

Counselor: "So your decision to make the most out of this situation, no matter how vague and stressful, has helped you stay determined, not just to finish the training, but also to take something from it. I guess that your use of that 'managerial delaying tactic' is one example of what you're taking from the training. Tell me, Jamelle, about a time when you've been able to remain relaxed and focused in spite of a lot of demands being placed on you."

Jamelle: "Maybe it's because I've already mentioned Sophia earlier, but one time that comes to mind is when I was talking to her just today after our training workshop. Our workshop leader had been really intimidating, but she stayed pretty cool, even when he was grilling her on new federal policies and procedures. Afterward, I told her how impressed I was, and she just shrugged, grinned this enigmatic smile, and started to joke about the workshop leader—she even nicknamed him 'Old Sergeant Rock'— being so full of it. She said she just imagined him sitting on the toilet. I couldn't help laughing and joining in with her. I guess turning a tyrant into a caricature helps remove the sting."

REFLECTING QUESTIONS

1. During this segment, how did the counselor encourage the client to look for exceptions to the problem?
2. What personal strengths and resources emerge from the client's answers?
3. Write a possible counselor response to Jamelle's last statement.

No Problems Are Ever Fully Resolved: Scaling

Since counselors are not healers, you cannot offer an absolute cure to your clients, and you therefore should not contract with clients to resolve their problems completely. If the client believes that the situation will not be improved until all problems have vanished, then you will be working with that client for a lifetime. What you seek in brief counseling is to get clients on the way to a place where they can carry on without you. In other words, you are trying to work yourself out of a job as soon as it's practical.

In working yourself out of a job, one useful strategy is to invite your client to participate in a scaling exercise (O'Connell, 2003). Scaling techniques can help clients in three important ways. First, participating in scaling can encourage clients to recognize that resolution is not an all-or-nothing proposition. Second, the activity can help them to envision their goals with greater detail and vividness. Finally, clients can use scaling to assess their progress in achieving these goals.

Brief counselors vary the specific details of this activity to fit their individual styles, but one general approach is to ask your client to imagine a scale that ranges from 1 to 10, with one representing the situation at its worst and ten representing the best possible resolution. Of course, self-report scales have been used for years to document perceived change and client satisfaction. Such scales have been part of pre-intervention and post-intervention assessment batteries that evaluate counseling effectiveness. However, our focus here is not on using such scales for documentation and accountability. Instead, we offer scaling as a valuable tool for encouraging therapeutic change.

You can invite clients to scale their current difficulties and then encourage them to explore possibilities. You begin by saying, "On a scale of 1 to 10, with 1 being that this concern you have been talking about is at its absolute worst and 10 being that it is completely solved, where would you say you are right now?" If your clients give you a number higher than 1, this means that they have already done something to keep the concern from overwhelming them. Whatever they have done is an *exception*. Be curious about that exception.

You might then respond by saying, "Wow! In spite of everything, you have somehow reached a [the number the client gave]. How have you been able to do that?" Get the client to elaborate this exception as much as possible. You can then ask, "If you were on your way to [the next higher number], how would you be feeling or behaving differently from now?" Out of such questioning you hope to get the beginnings of a goal for your work with the client. Furthermore, you are asking about an internal change in the client rather than some externally caused difference. Notice also that you do not ask what would be different if the client reached a 10. No one ever reaches a 10 in life.

As you attempt to set an expectation for the termination of your work together, you can ask, "When we get to the point where your problem is under control enough to let us know that we have accomplished our work together, that you can take it on your own from there, what will your number be then?" This question has the benefit of communicating to the client that there can be a certain ending point that can be anticipated for the counseling work, and that not everything has to be solved to be good enough.

Virtually anything can be placed upon a scale if the number has meaning for clients. You don't need to ask them to explain why a particular number has been chosen, nor do you have to understand the meaning of the number yourself. It is sufficient that a number has been indicated, and this number gives you a starting point in your search for a higher number that would symbolize improvement for the client.

This scaling technique can be used for most any content. For example, you can use scaling questions to assess a client's "self-esteem, self-confidence, investment in change, willingness to work hard to bring about desired changes, prioritizing of problems to be solved, perception of hopefulness, evaluation of progress, and so on" (Berg, 1991, p. 88). Using scaling questions, you also can "restrain" the client and keep expectations reasonable by saying, "Well, it would be great to go for a 10, but that's a lot to ask. What would you settle for in the next week?"

We have heard of school counselors being able to check in with their clients in the hallway by simply giving a signal that they wish to know how the client is doing today. The client responds by holding up the number of fingers that represent his or her current state. If there is progress, the counselor can give a thumbs-up gesture for a job well done. This exchange can all happen without a word being spoken, and this signal conveys to the client that they are in a secret club together, sending messages in code that others do not understand.

Walter and Peller (1992) pointed out that younger children sometimes have difficulty keeping the scale in mind. In such a case, more concrete devices may be used to help the child retain the idea. For example, you might ask, "If one crayon shows how you have been noisy and acting like you were 5 years old, but this whole box of crayons would stand for when you have been acting grown up and quiet in class, how many crayons did you have in your box this week?" With another child, you might say, "Draw a circle on the board to show me how hard you worked on your studies this week. A small circle would show that you didn't work very hard, and a big one would show that you tried really, really hard."

When clients are attempting to extinguish a behavior, there is a tendency for it to recur spontaneously. By predicting a relapse, and scaling the subsequent recovery from it, you can help the client avoid discouragement and the belief that he or she has failed. You might say, for example, "From time to time, you may find that you have slipped from a higher number to a lower one. That happens to all of us. You know the old saying, 'two steps forward and one step back.'" Or, you could observe, "So you found yourself slipping back from a 6 to a 5 last week. What will it take to get you back up to a 6?"

It is important to convey to clients that being on track toward resolution is success. The paradox of this is that, while it is the goal or solution that is being pursued, the real change is taking place in the successive approximation—the journey—toward the goal. Furthermore, the client will occasionally come up with ideas that could not have been anticipated, because the scaling technique does not dictate that particular events must take place in order to get to the higher number. A wonderful example of this idea was illustrated in the following vignette from Berg and de Shazer (1993). An 8-year-old girl, who had been molested by a stranger, was meeting with her counselor for the fourth session. When the counselor engaged her in the scaling activity, the girl placed herself at a 7. Then, continuing with the scaling procedure, the counselor asked her what it would take to move higher. The girl pondered the question for a while before shouting, "I know what!" "What?" asked the therapist. The little girl replied in a rather somber voice, "We will burn the clothes I was wearing when it happened." The therapist, amazed at this creative idea, said, "That's a wonderful idea!" (p. 23). The girl and her parents then carried out the ritual burning of the clothes and celebrated achieving a sense of resolution by having a family dinner at a special restaurant.

With the scaling technique, numbers are a language that roughly describes ineffable states that the client experiences, or expects to experience, and they do not necessarily point to an external reality. Numbers can stand for something that the client cannot fully articulate. These numbers can possess powerful meanings, and, so long as the client is master of the numbers, we counselors do not have to know precisely what the client means by their use.

Do Not Scale "SUDS"

The scaling technique we are advocating here should not be confused with the so-called "SUDS" technique. Some therapists ask their clients to use *SUDS* (subjective units of distress) to indicate a measure of the frequency, duration, and intensity of distress that they are experiencing. On this scale, higher numbers indicate more discomfort, and the goal would be to get the client to a lower number, by which he or she would be reporting less stress. In this case, *10* would be the most uncomfortable, while *1* would be a state of only mild discomfort and, therefore, the goal (Young, 1992).

The problem with the SUDS scale is that it seeks as its goal the *absence of something.* In other words, the counselor tries to get the client to a point where most of the stress has gone away. This would not fit our definition of a well-formed goal. Our aim is to establish the *presence of something.* The assumption in a resolution counseling approach is that, as the client accomplishes more of his or her goal (the presence of something), the numbers should increase to indicate that further levels of the goal have been achieved. Concomitantly, as the client's goal is more closely approximated, the less of that SUDS distress he or she will be experiencing.

The elimination of stress, in our model of counseling, is not the focus of the work. Our belief is that the lowering of the client's subjective level of distress will be a byproduct of the work. Just as we do not focus on the "pursuit of happiness," neither do we focus on stress reduction as the focus of our work. We assume that both these states—lower stress and more happiness—will ensue as the result of the client changing his or her viewing and doing of the situation. The scale we are discussing here would therefore have the opposite values of the SUDS scale. To restate our position on this technique, with our scale, *1* is the situation at its worst, and *10* would be the complete resolution of the concern. We work toward higher numbers, but we don't believe anyone ever gets to a 10.

LISTENING IN ON A SESSION

Once again, let's go back to this chapter's story and listen to some additional dialogue between Jamelle and her counselor. In this segment, see how the counselor uses scaling as a therapeutic tool.

> **Counselor:** "Jamelle, you've been sharing with me in our time together how you have been dealing with the stress here at work and in your personal life and how you have been working to cope. On a scale from 1 to 10, where 1 represents you feeling completely overwhelmed by this stress and 10 represents you handling this stress so well that you feel completely relaxed and energized, what number would you say represents where you are right now?"
>
> **Jamelle:** "Let's see, it's not as bad now as it was this morning, which was pretty close to being the worst I can remember, but things aren't dramatically better now. That would make it about a 3, maybe."
>
> **Counselor:** "So, between this morning and now, you have moved up the scale to a 3. How did you accomplish that?"
>
> **Jamelle:** "I think I am learning to get some distance on those things that normally cause me stress."
>
> **Counselor:** "Yes! You have obviously found a way to handle what was overwhelming to you this morning. So, if you were on your way from a 3 to a 4, how would you be different from now that would let you know this is happening?"
>
> **Jamelle:** "If I were going from this 3 to a 4, then perhaps I would . . .

REFLECTING QUESTIONS

1. During this segment, how did the counselor use scaling to invite the client to envision resolution possibilities?

2. What details about goals, strengths, and resources emerged from the client's responses to the scaling activity?

3. Write a possible counselor response to Jamelle's last statement.

Using This Tool

Divide into groups of three. One of you volunteers to share some aspect of your life that you would like to change, but you feel stuck. Portray your concern in a simplistic, self-defeating way by characterizing it as "all or nothing" and a "right or wrong" proposition. Another volunteers to listen, understand, validate, and, when appropriate, use the 1–10 scaling technique. Finally, the third person serves as the recorder who observes the activity and leads the feedback discussion.

Two Closing Comments

Have you ever noticed that when you read books like this on counseling or view a video of a therapy session, it always turns out well? We've noticed that, too. The vast majority of case studies offered for public consumption seem to be nearly perfect. Although these examples may be excellent models, they imply that, while the rest of us may bumble our way through counseling sessions with clients, the experts never mess up or make mistakes. That belief can be discouraging, so although in this book we present excerpts from counseling sessions that may demonstrate the use of specific brief counseling techniques, they are not meant to indicate that these interventions will inevitably arrive at tidy resolutions.

Finally, keep in mind that one of the goals of this book is for you to find your own voice as a brief counselor, not to parrot ours. As you read the sessions and suggestions in this book, please regard the counselor statements as examples to illustrate, not scripts to memorize. Consider each of our suggestions in the spirit in which we offer it: as an example of what you might say with a particular client in a particular situation. As you practice the brief counseling skills, you will learn to trust yourself to give expression to these strategies. Successful counseling requires authentic communication—not well-delivered quotes.

Summary

In this chapter, you explored how focusing on the future can change the present. Teleology and teleonomy are more useful ideas than etiology for conceptualizing your client's concerns. The dynamics of your relationship with a particular client can be characterized as that of a customer, complainant, visitor, or involuntary. This chapter offered a number of practical tools for helping clients to set goals. The idea that you can always find exceptions to client concerns—the time when the problem isn't happening—should be helpful as you listen to the story of trouble. A particularly useful technique is scaling, which helps clients to envision their goals with greater detail and assess their progress in achieving these goals.

SEGUE TO CHAPTER 5

Heraclitus, a Greek philosopher, once said, "You cannot step into the same river twice." It is also true that you cannot encounter your same self twice. Waking up this morning, having something to eat, and even reading the previous sentence are now part of your past. In what ways are you different from the person who woke up as you this morning? What has contributed to these changes? Is this amount of change typical in your life?

Resource

Brief Therapy Network
www.brieftherapynetwork.com

You will find that the Brief Therapy Network is a useful site that provides articles, interviews, and reviews of brief therapy materials. One by-product of exploring this site is that you gain a feel for the momentum of the field.

CHAPTER 5

Facilitating and Perturbing Change
Counseling and Chaos

"Human beings live not only poised at the edge of chaos,
but they work very hard 24 hours each day to maintain
that dynamic poise."
Mahoney and Moes

"As long as they are going to resist, you ought to
encourage them to resist."
Milton Erickson

CHAPTER GOALS

The goals of this chapter are to help you to understand and use the following ideas:

- Change is always happening. As a change agent, you are merely facilitating this change process by helping clients to alter their perceptions, revise their representations, and expand their openness to possibilities.
- Small perturbations can lead to dramatic change in complex systems, a phenomenon known as the Butterfly Effect.
- Instead of falling apart, complex adaptive systems come together out of chaos to reorganize themselves.

Reading about and practicing the tools in this chapter will help you to learn these valuable skills:

- Helping a client reframe the problem situation.
- Offering confusion techniques that help people to reorganize their thinking.
- Presenting counterintuitive interventions that perturb and encourage clients to think differently.

STORY

James's opening line to his counselor was, "I'm basically here because I think of myself as damaged goods." A week ago, when he had finally made the decision to seek counseling, James found himself mentally preparing for what he imagined would happen in the therapist's office. His image of counseling, based on the occasional scenes of therapy he had seen on television shows and in the movies, was that it was a narcissistic detective story, a self-centered process of searching for clues from one's own past—for a repressed memory or traumatic incident. If a mystery is a "who-dunnit," he thought, maybe counseling is a "why-I-dunnit." Frankly, James had serious reservations about embarking on such an endeavor, but he could no longer tolerate the sense of anguish that dogged him now.

Walking into the counseling center's waiting room, a parlor of an older house that was cluttered with old magazines and mismatched furniture, James recalled an event from his childhood that he hadn't thought about in years. James had spent most of his summers at a cabin with a front porch that was just as cluttered and old as this waiting room. The cabin, which had been owned by his family for three generations, was situated on the bank of a small river in the Shenandoah Valley.

One hot, sultry day when he was 5 years old, James had chased his cousin into the enclosed front porch, letting the screen door slam behind him, even though he had been reminded countless times to close the door quietly. His startled grandfather, who had been peacefully napping in the porch hammock, growled in exasperation at the boy's forgetfulness, "James Matthew! Let me ask you something, boy. Did you ever fall on your head when you were a baby?"

James had stopped in his tracks, intrigued by this seemingly irrelevant question about his medical history. With a perplexed expression on his face, James had felt his head for any tenderness and swelling, before giving his diagnostic opinion, "I don't think so, Grandpa," and then immediately resumed the chase after his cousin. His grandfather later told this story, to the amusement of the other relatives, at the family dinner table.

Now, as James waited to begin his counseling, he mentally checked himself for any psychological wounds that would indicate previous trauma. However, looking back on his life, he couldn't lay his finger on any dramatic instance of abuse, threat, or shock. Of course there had been tough times, painful losses, and ongoing hassles, but instead of any sharp specific pain, he only felt a dull, hollow ache as he reflected on the fact that he, nearing his 35th year, still felt that he was somehow an intruder on life. It was as if he were constantly barging in noisily on the lives of others, and never able to please the people who meant the most to him.

Contrary to his opening statement in the session, James certainly did not appear damaged to the counselor. James was a well-dressed, nicely groomed, and ruggedly handsome man who spoke with a bit more heartiness and self-assurance than required. He reminded the counselor of salespeople and "greeters" in discount stores. At first glance, James's manner, lifestyle, and circumstances seemed to epitomize the American dream. He had a good job managing a local grocery store, a fine family, comfortable home, and the family cabin by the river for holidays and weekends.

However, James's genial style seemed forced, as if he were the host of a dinner party, responsible for keeping the mood light and cheerful for all his guests. In spite of his efforts to appear confident, a few minutes into the session, he tilted his head slightly in a pensive manner, exhaled with a sudden sigh, and slumped back in his chair like a Raggedy Andy cast aside by a disinterested child.

REFLECTING QUESTIONS

1. What were your own reactions to this story?
2. What would it be like for you to work with this client?
3. What words would you use to describe this client?

OVERVIEW

For centuries, people have been intrigued with discovering the secrets of the change process. If there is one central idea in the counseling approach we are offering in this book, it is that your focus should be on change. In particular, you are in the business of helping to change a mind. When people are stubbornly resisting change, they often say, "My mind is made up." Reluctant to change their made-up minds, these people seem to repeat the same behaviors over and over—with the same results. If they are getting the results they desire, then they do not view themselves as having a problem. But often people repeat behaviors that do not get them what they want. Freud (1922/1961) called this "repetition compulsion."

Successful counselors help clients change chronically unproductive ways of viewing the world so they can find new behaviors that are more likely to yield desired results. While most of the techniques that we describe in this book are drawn from the various brief approaches to counseling, we recommend that you don't think of client concerns as "problems" in search of "solutions." Instead, we suggest you consider client concerns as their "stuck" or rigidified representations of experience that are in need of change.

Rather than solving a problem, you are helping your client to resolve the stuckness. By deconstructing clients' representations, you help them achieve a new resolution. As a result, your client becomes a newly resolute person, with his or her mind made up in a more useful way. As a brief counselor, you are working to accomplish this task in the most efficient way possible.

Brief counseling is done "on purpose." In other words, it is a method by which you guide or engineer change, rather than taking a nondirective approach. Such an intentional way of working will inevitably be briefer than if you were to wait for the client to attain a corrective emotional experience or a breakthrough insight.

IDEAS

Counselors as Change Agents

Counseling is a profession centered on change. Your clients often come living their lives in a "stuck place" or in a repetitive trajectory that creates unhappiness, much like that fly trapped in a bottle. If they have experienced a recent trauma, they have been thrown into a chaotic cognitive and emotional tailspin in which their cherished assumptions about life and the world have shattered. Other clients may come to you stuck in a rut, feeling discouraged and inert. Their lives have become gray, static, habitual, and without a sense of direction. Still others come to counseling because they are unable to break loose from patterns of repeated failure. Their attempts to find happiness always seem to end up in similar negative relationships or circumstances. Clients suffer from experiencing either too much or too little change in their lives.

As counselors, we should attempt to understand the change process as thoroughly as possible. Classical notions of change are inadequate to explain the dynamics of this process. The new sciences of chaos and complexity are beginning to inform us as to how change really happens. The idea of change is, well, changing.

As you work to help clients change, your main aim is to provoke a shift in the way they view themselves, their relationships, and their lives in general. Once they have come to this alternative view, their problems and concerns do not disappear, but they do become juxtaposed with new possibilities.

EXPERIENCING THIS IDEA

A good example of this type of shift is a Necker cube (see Figure 5-1). Stare at the Necker cube in the figure, and try to find the two ways in which it can be viewed. Did you see it shift? Once you have viewed this shift, then, as hard as you may try to maintain only one perspective, you can't do it. Once again, concentrate and allow it to switch again.

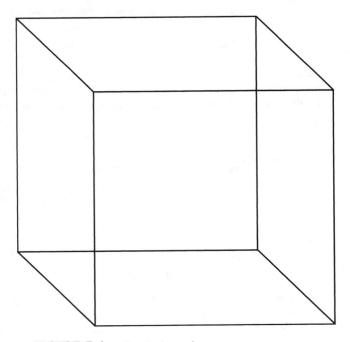

FIGURE 5-1   The Necker cube.

The pattern you saw the first time you looked at the cube was your automatic response to the situation. But when you took the time and tried to see another possibility, you were able to pull a different pattern from the cube. Did the cube itself change? No. Nothing regarding the facts of the cube were altered; you just suddenly experienced a change of mind. And now that you have allowed the two patterns to present themselves, you know that there will always be more than one way to view the cube. Even though you will have a tendency to see only one face of the cube when you first observe it, you are now armed with the knowledge that you may see the other face if you wish. What was once a hard "fact" is now a choice.

Clients come to counseling having fixated on only one view of their situation. You can help them change their minds by loosening this singular view, making it possible for them to see things another way, even if the facts of the situation itself don't change. This switch is known as a *bifurcation* in chaos theory. It is the point at which the whole system begins to reorganize.

The New Science of Change

We typically think of change as a fairly smooth and continuous process. One thing builds on another in sort of a straight line. Common sense convinces us that the ideas of continuity and cumulative change are inherent in all processes, and that small changes need time to amount to big changes. "The basic idea is that the patterns, processes and structures of daily life don't change very much if they are distorted or disturbed by a small amount" (Casti, 1995, p. 44). For example, a minor delay in a subway train's arrival normally only results in someone being a few minutes late for work, or baking a cake at slightly above the recommended temperature only results in a mildly overdone cake. Seen this way, minor alterations in initial conditions give rise to only trifling changes in outcomes.

However, Minsky (2003) stated that in highly complex systems, the kind in which all the parts interact with all the other parts, minor alterations "can lead to exponentially growing changes. . . . small differences can instantly cause drastic behavioral changes—for example, of the kind that *suddenly* happens whenever we get a new idea!" (p. 205, emphasis in original). If you saw either of the movies *Sliding Doors* or *Run, Lola, Run,* you have the idea of how small changes can result in major effects. The premise of each of these movies was that, if the main character were to miss the subway by just a few seconds or be delayed for a rendezvous only slightly, then these seemingly small lapses would end up being life changing. This is sometimes known as "sensitive dependence on initial conditions," but it is better known as the Butterfly Effect. As the saying goes, the mere flapping of a butterfly's wings over Beijing could drastically alter the weather in New York in subsequent weeks. A small perturbation can create unpredictable chaos. This is why chaos theory is the science of surprise (Casti, 1995).

A Few Concepts

The term *chaos* is really an unfortunate name for this new science, as it does not really mean disorder, randomness, or disaster. In fact, chaos is the process by which perturbations cause systems to reorganize. Chaos and complexity are the twin faces of this science. In this section, we help you make sense of the terms and new ideas associated with chaos and complexity theory and show how knowing about these recent discoveries can aid you in your work with clients.

Perhaps you are familiar with the science of chaos from watching the original *Jurassic Park* movie. In this film, the character played by Jeff Goldblum was a mathematician who was interested in nonlinear equations. In one scene, he seductively explained chaos theory to Laura Dern, as they sat in a sport utility vehicle waiting for those huge Jurassic creatures to make themselves known. Goldblum's character noted that chaos is the savage unpredictability of the universe, but "nature always finds a way" because it is a complex adaptive system.

"Complex adaptive systems are everywhere. They include insect colonies, immune systems, economies, political systems, the brain, and no doubt the human self-system" (Mahoney & Moes, 1997, p. 31). These are all dynamical systems. To put the theory succinctly, dynamic systems that are open, complex, and unstable can be thrown into disorder by the smallest perturbation, but they will self-organize in response to certain types of attractors (Davies, 2004; Gribbin, 2004; Strogatz, 2003; Ward, 2001). What in the world could all those odd terms mean? Let's see if we can unpack that statement and help you understand its implications.

First of all, a system contains parts that are so interrelated that a change in one part affects all the others (Hanson, 1995). Like sitting on a waterbed, you can't alter any aspect of a system without altering the whole thing. Counselors who work with families have long known this concept. You cannot simply "fix" the problem child (the identified client) that the family has dropped off at your office, because to change the child is to alter the whole family.

Second, to say that a system is "dynamic" is simply to observe that it is always moving and changing. In the case of open systems, the parts keep changing, but the pattern remains stable (Kline, 2003). For example, your body is constantly falling apart through cell death, but it is also replenishing itself by taking in energy from the outside and making new cells. Would you believe you get a new pancreas every day? (Capra, 1996). Physiologically, you are not the same person you were a few years or months ago, but, even though you are biologically a new you, the pattern that is you is constantly reorganizing. In 1900, William Bateson, who coined the term *genetics,* wrote, "We commonly think of animals and plants as matter, but they are really systems through which matter is continually passing" (in Lipset, 1980, p. 75).

Third, a system that is complex—as opposed to merely complicated—must be understood by considering it as a whole rather than by analyzing its parts. For example, you might be able to understand a complicated system like an automobile by knowing how all its parts function, because an automobile can be thought of as the sum of its parts. However, you could never understand a human being by analyzing all of its parts. And while you can take your automobile apart and put it back together, you cannot perform this procedure with a complex system without destroying it. Even Humpty Dumpty was more complex than he was complicated. All the parts to Humpty were still there after he fell off the wall, but a vital pattern was missing, and it could not be restored, even by all the king's horses and men.

Besides having each of its parts interacting with all its other parts, a complex system also takes its own output as input. When it behaves, its behavior changes its internal processes and changes its future behaviors. A toaster, for example, is only a complicated "trivial machine" because it behaves the same way every time you push the lever down—unless it is broken (Segal, 1986). Its behavior does not serve as feedback for future behaviors. But humans alter their behavior each time they behave, because the behavior feeds back into the system and changes the way the system operates. Something new emerges as a result of the system's behavior. Emergence is a property of the kind of system we are discussing. We might simply refer to this dynamic as *learning*.

Fourth, an "unstable" system is one that manifests sensitive dependence on initial conditions. A small change in the system can make a large, rapid, and surprising change of the entire system—the Butterfly Effect. Another way of talking about this effect is to say that such a system exists as nonequilibrium and is easily thrown into disorder or chaos by minimal perturbations. This type of system possesses self-organized criticality, always existing on the tipping point of chaos. The slightest nudge can send the system cascading into an unsettling process of change. However, this system can also be considered to exist on the verge of *order* because, as we discuss next, adaptive systems will always reorganize after a brief period of chaos (Ward, 2001).

Fifth, a complex adaptive system will *self*-organize. It does not have to be reformed by an outside force in order to pull itself together. It is like sculpture without a sculptor. If it is receiving the optimal amount of energy or information, it can proceed to organize itself according to a pattern that it "knows." Rather than behaving according to the second law of thermodynamics (the law of entropy), which would cause it to completely run down or fall apart, a complex adaptive system will become even more complex so long as it is receiving enough input of energy or information. Like that little tornado that forms over your bathtub drain, a self-organizing system uses the energy flowing through it to create its pattern. This type of system is sometimes referred to as a dissipative structure (Gribbin, 2004). You yourself are a dissipative structure. You are always changing and growing in some way.

Sixth, all systems respond to attractors. An attractor is not a force that acts on a system like a magnet (Davies, 2004). Rather, it depicts the system's teleonomic purpose or goal—where it is heading (Dembski & Ruse, 2006; Gharajedaghi, 2006). Three types of attractors affect systems (Fichter & Baedke, 2006). For simplicity's sake, let's call them *fixed, circular* or *periodic,* and the one already mentioned, *strange.*

A dynamical, or moving, system is always headed somewhere, and the type of attractor to which it is responding will create the type of system it is. A fixed attractor is like the pendulum of a clock that will eventually run down and fix on a single point if you leave it alone and don't wind it. This is the classic notion of entropy. Systems responding to a fixed attractor will eventually lose energy and suffer "heat death."

The circular or periodic attractor may perhaps be best understood by appealing to the metaphor of our solar system. With the solar system you have extremely large dead rocks running around in circular (or elliptical) patterns due to a dynamic tension that exists between them. They are held in orbit by the gravitational forces of the sun and each other and were originally set in motion by some historical force. They go round and round in rather predictable ways. (Note: There is some evidence that the solar system and the universe may really be responding to strange attractors, but this possibility should not disqualify our metaphor.)

The use of the term *strange* to describe this attractor simply means its trajectory cannot be known in advance, and it is therefore strange to us. A strange attractor results in surprising behavior because of the unpredictability of the system we are observing (Gribbin, 2004; Strogatz, 2003). Keeping in mind our previous discussion of the future causing the present, you can see that the future is an attractor of your current behavior. An attractor is thus *teleonomic,* moving the system toward a goal or end state, but not predicting exactly where it will finish. According to Casti (1995), the strange attractor is like "a ball of yarn or, even better, a bowlful of spaghetti (with sauce). Each strand of spaghetti in the bowl is one part of the strange attractor, the spaghetti sauce ensuring that no two strands ever quite make direct contact" (p. 29). Confusing? Of course, it's supposed to be; it's *strange.*

Finally, as the system (human or otherwise) changes, it passes through what is known as a *phase transition* (Gribbin, 2004; Kauffman, 1995), resulting in emergent properties. Just as in chemistry we think of H_2O moving from ice to water and on to evaporative gas (or the other way around), so too, do humans metamorphose from one phase state to another. The sequence of change we can expect from our clients will be movement from homeostasis (a place of relative balance), through a mild chaos or confusion after our perturbation, to an eventual self-organization (resolution).

The important thing to remember, however, is that such resolution cannot be designed or predicted exactly. Resolution emerges, meaning "the behavior of the overall system *cannot* be obtained by summing the behaviors of its constituent parts" (Holland, 1998, p. 122, emphasis in original). Nonlinear systems change, not in a straight line but in discontinuous and surprising ways.

Chaos and Counseling

At this point you may be wondering if this is still a book about counseling. Yes, it is! As you come to understand these new ideas about complex systems, you will gain fresh insight into your clients. Let's see if we can further translate the language of chaos and complexity into the language of counseling.

Consider, first of all, that people are complex adaptive systems, and, because to be human and alive is to be dynamic, we are always changing, learning, and growing. Humans are constantly altering their way of understanding the world and are always using the output of their behavior as feedback for changing future behaviors. Humans exist at the edge of chaos: Life itself is nonequilibrium and is always handing us new challenges for which we must muster our resources, and many of these challenges can knock us off course.

For example, when people are in crisis, they are perturbed so intensely that, while they struggle to settle down, they experience a chaotic situation in which they seek to find an equilibrium point. If their lives were attracted to a fixed point, they would end up feeling stuck and desolate. If they were to follow a circular or periodic attractor, they would go around doing the same thing over and over and expecting a different outcome. However, if they were to follow a strange and uncertain attractor to a conclusion, they would do more than merely adapt—they would reorganize themselves in the process. Instead of regressing or merely recovering, they would grow. They would move through the phase states of chaos, from victim to survivor to thriver (Echterling, Presbury, & Mckee, 2005).

You don't have to look for a cause that has led your client to his or her current troubles. Instead, you can deconstruct the client's story and perturb it in a way that will create "a difference that makes a difference." In other words, you increase the energy input in your interaction so that enough chaos is present to move the client through a phase transition to a new level of resolution or self-organization.

Since we humans are complex adaptive systems, until the moment our lives end, we are living within the struggle between stasis and crisis, between entropy and emergence. The really good news is that no matter how chaotic our lives and our minds may become, we are always capable of creating new patterns from that seeming chaos. Your aim as a counselor is to create the conditions for your clients that will foster the emergence of a new and more productive pattern of thought. Often, perturbing or confusing the client accomplishes this end. Don't be preoccupied with making your client too comfortable. Remember: You can't have an emergence without first having an emergency!

Implications of These Ideas for the Counselor

The ideas of chaos and complexity theory can make significant contributions to our work as counselors.

• You do not have to summon heroic interventions to have a rapid and dramatic impact on a client. Because the shift from chaos to self-organization often occurs quite suddenly, clients can often change long-standing patterns in a very short amount of time. They will reach this end state on their own. Your task is to nudge the system in the direction away from the fixed or circular pattern and to help your clients tolerate the process while they are reorganizing themselves.

• When clients are confused, they are in chaos, but they are not falling apart. Instead, they are on their way to coming together—achieving a new organization of mind. Whenever people are in the process of self-organizing, something new is emerging.

TOOLS

Mahoney and Moes (1997) stated their belief that "complexity studies will be among the most important concerns of 21st century psychology" (p. 187). Masterpasqua (1997) agreed and added that "Complexity theory may offer a revised scientific basis for describing and promoting optimal human development and mental health; that is, individuals most capable of adaptation and growth are those poised at the edge of chaos" (p. 37).

Orthodox psychotherapy is predicated on the idea that clients are disordered and that disorder is potentially dangerous. The obvious treatment that proceeds from this assumption is to eliminate, as quickly as possible, the source, or etiology, of the client's disorder. However, if you are working within the chaos/complexity paradigm, you are more interested in moving your clients toward resolution of their difficulties than in conducting an archeological dig into their past, establishing a baseline for the occurrence of their present problems, or revealing their unfortunate self-talk.

"What complexity studies offer . . . is a view of disorder that respects the role of ever-present cascades of disorganization in the living system's dynamic and lifelong development" (Mahoney & Moes, 1997, p. 188). When clients complain that they are falling apart or coming unglued, they are describing imminent chaos. Of course, you would not use your counseling session to explain chaos and complexity theory, but you can help your clients understand that they are experiencing a natural process.

In some circumstances, normalizing their experience of chaos may allow them to tolerate their discomfort. When you are normalizing, be sure not to offer trite or hackneyed comments such as "Everything's going to be all right," or "Everybody goes though this." Comments such as these only serve to trivialize client concerns. Simply convey, in your caring and empathic manner, that you are not alarmed or repulsed by their feelings of disorganization and that they will not have to struggle alone with their difficulties.

Solution Failures

Whether they are called paradoxical, counterintuitive, or ironic, interventions that perturb a client's patterns of thought and behavior will seem strange, because they go against common sense. Early in their work, the Palo Alto Mental Research Institute (MRI) group determined that what caused clients the greatest problems were the solutions they attempt. An example would be a client who suffers from insomnia, goes to the doctor, obtains a prescription for a sleep aid, and, after repeated use, becomes hooked. What began as a sleep problem now becomes a drug problem. Many of your clients' concerns are structured this way: There is an original concern (A) for which a solution has been sought, but the solution turns into an additional concern (B). Another example is someone who experiences anxiety episodes and then becomes an agoraphobic to avoid the embarrassment of possibly having a panic attack in public. Gharajedaghi (2006) offered a social-political example of how commonsense attempts to solve problems could lead to even greater trouble. He pointed out that the original purpose for making drugs illegal was to reduce the level of drug abuse in the United States. This intervention yielded paradoxical results. "Counterintuitively, it has produced a multi-billion-dollar crime industry, higher consumption, and an overburdened criminal justice system" (p. 49).

When you are working with a complex system in which every part interacts with every other part, you can't "just do one thing" (Becvar & Becvar, 2006). In the past, for example, we used DDT to reduce the number of insects that caused disease or reduced crop yields. Unfortunately, human beings, who are at the top of the food chain, then consumed plants and animals that had absorbed the insecticide. "The body does not discriminate between 'desired effects' and 'side effects'" (Becvar & Becvar, 2006, p. 363).

Two Types of Change

Years ago, the researchers at MRI wrote of first-order and second-order change (Watzlawick, Weakland, & Fisch, 1974). "First-order change occurs within the system, consistent with the rules of that system. Second-order change involves a change in the rules of the system and thus the system itself" (Becvar & Becvar, 2006, p. 294).

Have you ever tried to solve the famous "nine-dot problem"? It consists of three rows and columns of dots with three dots in each. The dots appear to form a square (see Figure 5-2). Your problem is that you are asked to connect all nine dots with four straight lines without lifting your pencil from the paper. Since the dots create what is obviously a square, the implicit rule is that you must also stay within the boundaries of the square while attempting to solve the problem. If you follow this rule, you now have two problems. First, you can't connect the dots with four straight lines without lifting your pencil, and, second, you have failed in your attempt to solve the problem. This is the state in which many of your clients arrive at your door. They had an original concern that they defined as a problem (A), and they have attempted many times to solve the problem and failed, so now they see themselves as a failure (B). They are helpless in the face of the original problem (A).

When it gets cold in one's house, it is logical to turn up the heat. When it gets dark, it is logical to turn on the lights. This is common sense. We do the opposite of the occurrence we are trying to solve, and this constitutes a first-order change. But sometimes with our concerns in life, "opposite equals more of the same" (Becvar & Becvar, 2006, p. 295). Thus, a logical or commonsensical attempted solution may serve only to escalate the original concern we had. To avoid the pitfall of trying to talk clients out of their difficulties by logic or common sense, it is helpful for you to keep in mind the distinction between first-order and second-order change.

First-order change is like rearranging the deck chairs on the Titanic in order to forestall the contextual problem. In counseling situations, first-order change appears when people are trying to "do the opposite" to solve a problem. This strategy certainly seems reasonable. For example, what could be more sensible to relatives and friends than to try to cheer up a depressed person, to remind him or her of all the good, enjoyable things in life, and to suggest going out to a ball game? Now the depressed person has a second problem: This intervention does not lift the depression, and, knowing that the relatives mean well, the person feels guilty for not responding as they had hoped, so the person sinks deeper into depression. You can't talk people out of their thoughts, feelings, and concerns, no matter how sensible your solution may be.

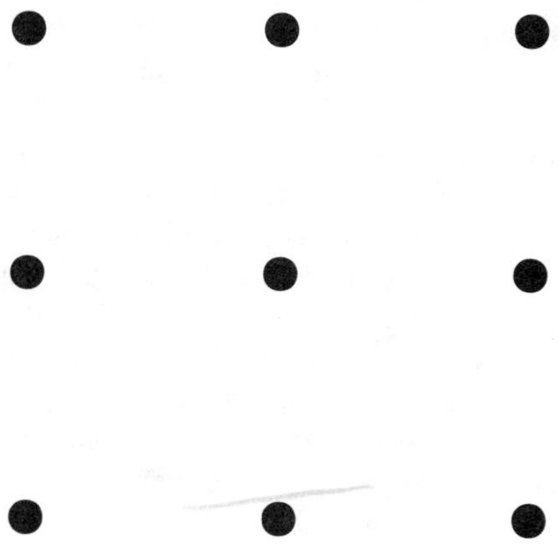

FIGURE 5-2   Nine-dot problem.

Second-order change is change that alters the system itself. It is change in the rules that govern the system and therefore interrupts the homeostatic balance and repetitive circularity of the system. The Palo Alto authors wrote that there are many things you can do in a nightmare: run, scream, hide, or fight, but these first-order behaviors do not alter the fact that they occur within the nightmare. Only waking up, a second-order change in your state, can transform the nightmare.

As a counselor, you should reflect on two important questions regarding your client's concern: What is being done in the here-and-now that perpetuates your client's problem? What can you do to disrupt your client's repetitive "solutions"? The client's solution is often reflective of the "Be spontaneous" paradox. Take the previous example, of the insomniac who has trouble falling asleep every night. With grim determination, the person goes to bed thinking, "I must *make* myself go to sleep." So, the insomniac's "solution" sabotages what should be a natural, spontaneous process of relaxing and quietly falling asleep. If you have ever tried it, you know it does not work. One possible second-order change intervention would be to suggest that the person attempt, by any means possible, to stay awake. This suggestion might lift the insomniac out of the paradox by a counterparadox that changes the rules of the game.

Delivering the Reframe

A frame is the class or category that we fit a thing or event into. A poodle fits into the "dog" category; a robin fits the "bird" category. Once we have found satisfactory categories to classify things and events, we tend to harden these categories. The category becomes the context that explains these phenomena. A *reframe* is a technique for perturbing hard categories so that alternative explanations are possible. For example, all animals in the mammal category meet certain requirements for membership, including giving live birth to their young. Is a platypus, which lays eggs but fits most of the other criteria for "mammal membership," truly a mammal? Is a kiwi, which doesn't have real feathers and can't fly, really a bird? The point is that all our categories or classes are arbitrary and do not perfectly sum up the things or events within them. We often confuse the category label with the thing. But it is possible to loosen categories with a reframe. Clients come to counselors with established frames for their concerns. The logical solutions they have tried have generally remained first-order, within the frame. If you can help the client reframe a situation, then a second-order change may be possible.

Suggesting a reframe to clients is not simply a matter of telling them how you see things or arguing against their point of view. You don't reframe a client's perspective—the client does. This is a point that novice counselors often misunderstand. An example of this misunderstanding came from one of our trainees, who in a supervision session proudly announced that he had used a reframe with his client. We asked for his account of the reframe, and he said, "Well, my client was complaining that he couldn't get to work that day because his car wouldn't start, and I said that he should be grateful that he even has a car." This "look on the bright side" form of counseling is not a reframe. Reframing results in your client making a second-order change, either a change of context or a change of rules.

Becvar and Becvar (2006) wrote of parents who brought their two children, a brother and sister, to counseling because of the deleterious effects of their "sibling rivalry" (a negative frame). In other words, the children frequently fought (the observed fact). The parents had tried repeatedly to get the children to stop fighting and eliminate their sibling rivalry (attempted first-order changes). However, it is possible to reframe sibling rivalry as the way children learn to become independent and stand up for themselves when others violate their boundaries (second-order change of the frame). Of course, you would not offer such a reframe in "one lump." Subtly changing labels during conversations begins to loosen the hard categories in which behaviors have been pathologized.

Decourting Another type of context change, used with couples who are on the verge of divorce, was developed by Carl Whitaker. He called this technique "decourting." He began by acknowledging that it looked like divorce would be the best thing for the couple, but then asked how long they had courted before they married. The couple might have, for example, said that they had dated for 8 months before marrying and had been married for 10 years. Whitaker would then say something like, "You have been with each other for 10 years and 8 months. Research suggests that in that length of time you have developed habits of living together that must be carefully separated. If you simply pull this marriage apart, it would be like tearing conjoint twins apart—with a lot of bleeding. I wonder if you might be able to avoid such a horrendous separation if you were to decourt your relationship for the 8 months you started with." Decourting involved the couple reliving their courtship. They would behave with each other in ways similar to their original dating period. In this context, a second-order change became possible, and some couples actually fell back in love and decided to stay married. Even if the decourting couple did ultimately divorce, they were likely to have a more civilized and congenial conclusion to their marriage.

Relabeling Once a category has been altered by a reframe, behaviors accrue different meanings. Watzlawick et al. (1974) explained that, once we do see things as possessing an alternate class membership, we can't easily go back to "the trap of the former view of 'reality'" (p. 99). Since relabeling can begin the process of reframing a category, you need to start thinking of alternate words for the negative terms clients tend to bring to their sessions. Bertolino and O'Hanlon (2002) offered a variety of helpful examples of relabeling. For example, if someone is labeled as "hyperactive," you can describe this person as "sometimes too energetic." If a parent labels a child as "ADD," you can depict the child as being "inattentive at times." Someone who is characterized as an "angry" person can be someone who "gets upset sometimes." A "rebellious" woman is "developing her own way," and a "shy" man "takes a little time to get to know people."

This small list of relabeling examples should be enough to give you the idea of how you would be changing the category rules in such cases. You take the client's hard-and-fast diagnostic and damning labels and turn them into process terms that are descriptive and normalizing. Of course, you must do this procedure gently, so delicately that the client hardly notices that you have changed the words being used. Relabeling is never a matter of debating with your client what a behavior is properly called!

The formula is this: After hearing the negative label, ask about the behaviors that account for it. When the client has given a description, you slip another word or phrase into the conversation as you refer to the behavior. These relabelings must make sense to clients as being roughly equivalent to the terms they have used. A single switch of a term may sometimes be the "bifurcation" needed to perturb the story and the system toward a possible reorganization.

USING THIS TOOL

Substitute a more benign term or phrase in the blank provided for the more abrasive label in the left-hand column.

1. Out of control _____
2. Abusive   _____
3. Raging   _____
4. Selfish   _____
5. Belligerent   _____
6. Violent   _____

LISTENING IN ON A SESSION

Review the story at the beginning of the chapter. In addition to communicating empathic understanding, a resolution-focused counselor could help James reframe his circumstances by transforming labels into descriptive processes in the following way.

James: "I'm basically here because I think of myself as damaged goods."

Counselor: (She is struck by his labeling of himself as "damaged goods," particularly since James' appearance and manner seem to be those of a confident and successful person.)

"It sounds like you may have been through some tough times, and now you're wanting to see about repairing the damage."

James: "Well, not exactly. I was just thinking about this in your waiting room and I'm definitely no poster boy for victims. To tell you the truth, I had a pretty happy childhood. My parents never beat me and I was never traumatized in a war or anything like that. I've got a great family and a nice job. It should be a good life, but I feel like one of those dented canned goods items at the store. You know, the ones we have to mark way down to unload 'em and even when somebody does finally buy one, they aren't really all that thrilled with what they bought. If people could afford it, they'd take the can that's in great shape and not put up with damaged goods."

Counselor: "So getting the dent isn't what's so bad. It's how people go on appearances and don't realize that what's inside is still just as valuable."

James: "Yeah, I feel like I've gotta work extra hard to show people that. In your waiting room, I was just thinking about this river cabin that's, well, been in our family for four generations. About 10 years ago, a flood carried it off. I was all for selling the property, but my dad had his heart set on rebuilding it. So, I worked like a dog helping him, weekends and evenings, for the better part of 5 years. It's been more trouble than it's worth, if you ask me, but now *I* own it 'cause my folks signed it over to me before they moved to Florida last year. Now the whole damn thing's on my shoulders."

Counselor: "So, you're carrying this heavy burden on your own now."

James: "That's part of it, but it's even more complicated than that. It got flooded out again 6 months ago and I was feeling so fed up that I didn't even want to go out to survey the damage, but I got a call from Ben, the guy who lives year-round in a neighboring cabin. All he says is, 'James, you'd better get down here quick' and then hangs up. When I get there, Ben's eyeing me like a judge about to sentence a child molester. 'I found your dog, James. He's dead. You let him die!' he says."

(James points his finger accusingly to punctuate each word of the accusation.)

"Well, of course, we didn't have a pet at the cabin, but there was a stray dog that came by sometimes and we took pity on it and threw it some scraps. Ben must have thought it was ours. I spent an hour trying to convince this stubborn old mule that we didn't own that poor mutt. What really gets me is that there I was—with a cabin I didn't want that's been washed away and a dog that's not mine that's been killed—and I'm feeling that it's all up to me to please everybody, even crazy old fools, and make everything OK, even if it's a mess."

REFLECTING QUESTIONS

1. Circle the labels that were applied to the client.
2. What relabeling techniques did the counselor use in responding to the client?
3. Write a possible counselor response to James's last statement.

USING THIS TOOL

Form a small group with two colleagues. One of you volunteers to role play a client whose self-labeling is sabotaging the potential for positive change. Another volunteers to listen, understand, and validate (LUV) while also turning those labels into descriptive process items. The third person serves as the recorder who observes and leads the feedback discussion.

Other Therapeutic Perturbations

One really nice thing about the Butterfly Effect metaphor for counseling is that all it takes is a seemingly insignificant perturbation of clients' current cognitions to set them on a path toward resolution. Rather than the disputation, countering, or annihilation of client thinking recommended by Ellis (1982) and other cognitive therapists, we advocate a more subtle method. When performed well, your perturbations will not seem to be challenges or confrontations. Milton Erickson (1967) believed that, rather than having an "adversarial conversation" with clients, attempting to confuse their thinking was the preferred technique (Bertalino & O'Hanlon, 2002). What is the benefit, you may be wondering, of confusing your clients? Aren't clients already confused enough? The short answer is that clients are often not confused at all but, rather, conflicted, caught between opposing or competing forces. They are systems on the edge of chaos, trying hard to maintain a homeostatic position in their lives.

Consider our earlier discussion of fixed attractors. Clients who feel thwarted in all their attempts to solve their difficulties are locked into a process similar to the clock pendulum. They may still be "in there swinging" and struggling to get better, but they are feeling inexorably dragged down by diminishing energy. Like a clock with its main-spring running down, they see their life heading toward a dead end. They may be victims of past recollections that portend a negative future, and they are leading entropic lives that are being drawn toward that fixed attractor. However, if you can find a way to stimulate their divergent thought processes and reallocate their energy, you can loosen their hard categories. Sometimes, these clients will say fatalistic things like, "I'm a marked man," or "I'm paying for my past sins," or "I'm just a screw up." You can hear in these phrases the constricting standards that these clients hold that have turned into self-limiting beliefs.

We have no hard-and-fast recommendations for what to say when attempting to perturb a client's hardening of the categories. You will need to use your own creative thinking in such situations. Perhaps, to the "marked man" you could say, "I wonder how that guy Cain, in the Bible, got rid of his mark, and found a wife, and lived a pretty good life thereafter." To the "sinner" you might say, "How many more payments do you have to make before you are finally paid up? What will you spend your energies on after that?" To the "screw up" person you might say, "What needs to happen to get you un-screwed? Can we begin that process here?" Such responses are mildly sardonic, and could throw the clients' metaphors into a slightly more confusing context. If you are successful, your clients may begin to discard some of their self-defeating concepts and start talking about getting past this "stuck place."

The client who has been drawn into a circular, or periodic, attractor is like that friend you once had who always chose relationships with abusive or indifferent partners. Each time the relationship ended in disaster, your friend sank into deep depression for a while, wondered what was wrong with him or her, and then sought out another relationship that seemed to be a replica of the last one. Cowan (2005) described this dynamic as a pattern of ever-increasing intensity where the client is essentially saying, "That didn't work, I think I'll try it again" (p. 289).

The metaphor for this repetition compulsion is that all attempts to escape this vicious cycle fail because of some unknown attractor. It is like our earth, which keeps trying to escape the sun's gravitational pull so it can head off in another direction, but it always ends up in orbit. While this circular (actually elliptical) orbiting of earth works well for those of us on the planet, such orbiting does your clients no good. Your work is to find a way to knock these clients off orbit, so they can overcome the circular attractor and finally realize their longing to be free of this compulsion.

Unfortunately, such clients come ready to play the game of "Why don't you?"—"Yes, but . . . " with you. Eric Berne (1964) originally described this game, but everyone knows it well. It begins when someone complains to you of a problem or concern and implies that he or she is asking your advice. You may believe that you see a way out of the situation, and, in order to be helpful, you offer your solution. The complaining person then responds by telling you that he or she has already tried that or gives several contextual reasons why your solutions would not work. Consequently, you then work even harder to come up with a better idea than had originally occurred to you. Sound familiar? No matter how many good ideas you come up with, the complainant can always add new information about the situation, proving that each of your solutions will fail. If you persist, you will be caught in a "game without end" (Becvar & Becvar, 2006), and you and your client both become victims of a circular attractor. Your clients expect you to give them good advice, and they will be confused if you don't—but don't!

Counterintuitive Interventions

Alfred Adler was perhaps the first person to use counterintuitive interventions with clients (Mozdzierz, Macchitelli, & Lisiecki, 1976). Adler believed that counselors should take care to avoid power struggles with clients and should instead side with client resistances—anticipating by decades Erickson's notion of utilization (to be discussed in the Utilization section later in this chapter). Clients typically expect that they must struggle against their symptoms until they overpower them. This counseling-as-combat metaphor appeals to the clients' intuition. If you should, to their surprise, side with their symptoms, the clients' intuition will be perturbed, and they will be confused.

Dunlap (1928) employed this technique with clients, calling it "negative practice." Instead of asking clients to fight against their symptoms and try to stop them from occurring, Dunlap asked his clients to practice trying to do the symptom better. Adler found that, if he gave the client permission not only to have a symptom but to embellish and refine it, the symptom came under the client's control and grew weaker—a counterintuitive result. You might say to your client, "I'm having a hard time getting the picture of how your problem works. I'm afraid I'm being a bit dense. Could you, between now and the next time we meet, try to do the problem a bit more, so you can explain it to me in a way that helps me 'get it'?"

Adler would sometimes predict a relapse, stating that, although the client might be experiencing improvement, he or she would inevitably "backslide." Students of behaviorism know that, any time we are attempting to extinguish a behavior, at some point the behavior will "spontaneously recover." Clients will, therefore, often report that the treatment has failed because the symptomatic behavior has returned. You might say, "Now that you have decided how you plan to handle this problem, what will you do when it tries to creep back up on you?"

Another counterintuitive device sometimes used by counselors is to declare helplessness. Clients often come with the expectation that you will say or do something that will miraculously change them or their situation for the better. The fact is that you cannot change another person; you can only help the person change him- or herself. Declaring helplessness places the responsibility on your clients for both the motivation and the strategy for change. Openly declaring this paradox decreases the possibility of a power struggle and assigns agency to your clients. In the famous "Gloria" video, Carl Rogers (1965) said to his client, "I sure wish I could tell you what to do." He went on to say that he would do his best to help Gloria find her own answer to her concern. In this way, he both declared helplessness and communicated that only she could change herself.

Bornstein, Krueger, and Cogswell (1989) discussed the technique of cautioning the client against changing. This is known as *restraining*. When your clients experience themselves as changing, they will be giving up a cozy (though problematic) pattern of behaviors for the uncertain prospect of a positive outcome. The technique of restraining addresses your client's ambivalent feelings about change and allows them to proceed at their own pace. When restraining the client, you imply that a drastic change might bring about a ripple effect that will affect all the client's relationships and create a general dissatisfaction with the status quo. In attempting to get the client to "go slowly," you could perhaps say something like, "It seems that now you are convinced that you want to get things straight with people in your family who have treated you badly, and you are ready to 'take them on.' What part of you worries that you might move too fast and create a disruption, rather than the resolution you hope for?"

All the above counterintuitive interventions will violate client expectations for how they should go about dealing with their difficulties and about what your role should be as a helper. These are mild perturbations that can serve as Butterfly Effects to get clients thinking about their situations in new ways and working toward alternative resolutions to their current struggles. Remember to insert these interventions into your conversations with clients as a nonexpert. You must offer them in the spirit of that curious and caring person who is "not from around here."

The Death of Resistance

We mentioned resistance in Chapter 1, but we return to it now to offer a more in-depth discussion, because a reconceptualization of resistance plays an important role in the technique of utilization. In 1984, Steve de Shazer declared resistance to be officially dead. He said the concept of resistance was the result of a wrongheaded notion that clients naturally resist changing and the counselor has to devise heroic strategies for overcoming the client's natural tendency to remain the same. For de Shazer, this thinking was based upon the old mechanistic notions of physics. He quoted Maruyama (1963), who contended that a "second cybernetics" (later known as chaos and complexity) operated on principles that declared that a system, when perturbed, will enter into a "deviation amplifying" process resulting in change that is disproportionately large compared to the initial perturbation.

According to de Shazer, we do not pay sufficient attention to the fact that whatever behaviors are exhibited in a counseling session take place within a system that includes both the client and the counselor. If the client is thought to be resisting, this behavior occurs within a "resistive" atmosphere. Instead of using the term *resistance*, de Shazer preferred to speak in terms of levels of "cooperation." Clients, he said, do the best they can to cooperate in the change process. Rather than either the counselor or client being to blame for the impasse, it is the way they are cooperating with each other that needs tweaking.

The chief benefit of declaring the death of resistance is an alteration in the counselor's attitude. Instead of viewing the client as resistive and seeing the overcoming of this resistance as combat, you can view the client's stuckness as not having yet reached escape velocity from those patterned interactions that have troubled the client. The staff of the Milwaukee Brief Family Therapy Center, headed by de Shazer, apparently considered the death of the idea of resistance to be such an important insight that, it is said, a funeral was held to mark its passing (O'Hanlon & Weiner-Davis, 1989; Young, 2005).

We could not find this funeral ritual cited in de Shazer's writing, but we thought it was a great story that dramatizes the importance of this change of attitude. In order to satisfy our curiosity, we emailed de Shazer, who responded by saying that the Center had indeed conducted a funeral for resistance, with a small coffin for it, and that they had buried it in their backyard. They even erected a tombstone, but someone stole it (de Shazer, personal communication, 1998). He went on to say that they had not publicized the event, because they did not want people to think they had murdered resistance, but rather that it had died a natural death. De Shazer believed that resistance can be utilized in ways that improve the therapeutic alliance and lead to better outcomes.

Dealing with "Resistance"

Dolan (1985) recounted the story of a man watching a butterfly emerge from its cocoon. The man, impatient with the slow progress of the butterfly, decides to help by prying away the impediment of the shell and thus allowing the butterfly its freedom. However, he fails to recognize the protective nature of the constricting, "resistant" cocoon. The butterfly, with the man's "help," is set free into the cold air prematurely. Deprived of adequate time to make the necessary adjustments within the cocoon, the butterfly crumbles into a helpless suffering heap. "The therapist must have reverence and appreciation for each client's personal rate of change, idiosyncracies, difficulties, vulnerabilities, and resources" (p. 3).

According to Welfel and Patterson (2005), there are two major reasons why people are reluctant when it comes to implementing change in their lives. One reason is that to enter into the uncertainty of change involves the risk of failure, which may prove more anxiety provoking than their current concerns. The second reason people "resist" change is that even problematic behaviors often "have rewards as well as difficulties." "Even though change may reduce the adversity, it may also reduce the rewards. These rewards are also referred to as secondary gains" (Welfel & Patterson, 2005, p. 115). Consider, for example, that someone who expresses chronic anger may find that this behavior keeps others at arm's length and provides the secondary gain of avoiding the terror of intimacy.

Resistance "is a natural self-protective expression of attempts to maintain the integrity of a system that experiences itself as being pushed too quickly or too far beyond the boundaries of its familiar functioning" (Mahoney & Moes, 1997, p. 181). When Bateson spoke of providing our clients with a "difference that makes a difference," he meant that confronting the system with information that is too novel or unfamiliar would produce too much oscillation and would bring about either resistance or diffusion (unnecessary chaos). On the other hand, too little difference would result in rapid assimilation, creating no bifurcations in the system, and therefore not lead to productive change.

Milton Erickson viewed resistance as an aspect of the client's total picture of symptoms and found ways to use it to the client's benefit. Like the butterfly's cocoon, resistance may temporarily slow a client's progress, but it expresses a protective wisdom that cannot be fully verbalized. If asked about their reluctance to change, clients can only say—if they can speak of it at all—that for some reason they are frightened to go farther or to talk of certain things.

The butterfly's helper in Dolan's example above would see this hesitation as a moment when stronger intervention is required. Tearing off the covering and exposing the interior is considered by many to be the most efficient and useful thing to do. The paradox of this intervention is that often the counselor's efforts to speed up the therapeutic process produce the opposite of the desired effect. As Erickson (1975) put it, for the therapist to know the correct treatment is not sufficient for success. The client must also be "receptive of the therapy and cooperative in regard to it. Without the patient's full cooperativeness, the therapeutic results are delayed, distorted, or even prevented" (p. 212).

The Ericksonian notion is that the resistance of the client should be honored and that the counselor should go along with the client's flow and pace, rather than rush the process. Not only will this lead to better understanding on the part of the client, who then discovers everything for himself or herself, but it further cements the bond between counselor and client, making them allies rather than adversaries.

Utilization

"Too many psychotherapists take you out to dinner and then tell you what to order" (Erickson & Rossi, 1973; quoted in Dolan, 1985, p. 6). Following on Erickson's metaphor, we must make sure that we allow the client to slowly peruse the menu and then to select only those items that look tasty. We may wish that clients order full-course meals when they desire only appetizers or desserts. We may worry that clients will not be getting all the essential food groups, but, if we allow them to be the experts on what they need, they may eventually end up eating nutritious and satisfying banquets.

Utilization is the Ericksonian term for taking whatever the client brings to the table and using it. You must carry out this action without direct or implied criticism of your client's style or choices. Dolan (1985) suggested three requirements that utilization must meet in order to be helpful. First, you view the client's reluctant behavior as a communication about the way the client views the world. Second, you welcome this cautious behavior as a valuable therapeutic resource. Finally, you communicate that the client's guarded approach to change is honored and respected. Resistance represents the client's way of defending against unpleasant realizations. Much care and creativity has been invested in these defenses, so you should appreciate the client's artistry in erecting them. To disrespect a resistance is to disrespect the person who created it.

As Dolan stated, it is useful to assume that resistant behavior plays a functional role for the client. Siding with the client's resistance is often the most useful behavior you can display. Rather than getting clients to change, you must help them find ways that allow them to change—their way. According to Dolan, a counselor can fully accept the client only if he or she is willing to set aside personal judgments and view the client's model of the world as a valid and accurate representation of the client's experience. It is only when we understand the client's need to remain the same that we can help the client change.

Summary

The concepts of chaos and complexity offer us insights into the mysterious process of change. For example, the Butterfly Effect can alert us to the many opportunities we have to offer small perturbations that can lead to dramatic change. Conceptualizing our clients as complex adaptive systems can reassure us that, instead of falling apart in counseling, they can reorganize themselves. Helping your clients to reframe a problem situation and think differently about it can lead to cascading changes.

These intriguing ideas can help you to use strange and powerful techniques that at first seem counterintuitive. Keep in mind that such techniques are not mind games or manipulations. In fact, such paradoxes abound in counseling. One fundamental paradox is that clients come to you seeking your counsel, but you rarely offer them advice because they are likely to reject the advice you would have given them. Paradoxes can vex, confuse, and annoy us while, at the same time, capturing our attention like an itch we can't scratch.

Segue to Chapter 6

To help you gain a feel for the ideas and tools in the next chapter, do this experiment. The next time you go into a store, pay close attention to the *positive* aspects of your experience. For example, you might notice the helpfulness of a clerk, the cleanliness of the store, or the quality of the products. Ask to speak to a manager or supervisor and offer a sincere compliment. Notice this person's reactions.

Resource

The Milton H. Erickson Foundation
3606 North 24th Street
Phoenix, AZ 85016
602-956-6196
www.erickson-foundation.org

The Milton H. Erickson Foundation is dedicated to promoting and advancing the contributions made to the health sciences by the late Milton H. Erickson, MD, through training mental health professionals and health professions worldwide.

CHAPTER 6

Constructivist Counseling
Invented and Imposed Realities

"What you see is what you get"
saying from the 1970s

CHAPTER GOALS

Reading and experiencing the ideas in this chapter will help you to understand these fundamental constructivist concepts:

- People construct subjective realities that can either sabotage or promote their well-being.
- Social constructions are the worldviews, expectations, and stereotypes that culture imposes on individual members.
- Deconstruction is an essential process in any significant change in our thinking.
- Constructed ideas can be deconstructed.

Reading about and practicing the tools in this chapter will help you to develop skills in using the following techniques based on constructivist and social constructionist points of view:

- Helping clients to deconstruct and reconstruct their worldviews so that they contain more possibilities.
- Using the miracle question to create positive constructions.
- Offering the encouragement triad to help crystallize positive worldviews.

STORY

Her husband used to tease her, "No one could ever claim that gardening is just a hobby for you, Honey. It's clearly a crusade." Mrs. Thompson didn't have a violent bone in her body, but she certainly assailed weeds, bugs, and other threats to her flowers and vegetables with fervor. Dressed in a dilapidated straw sombrero that had been a souvenir from Tijuana, a pair of patched Oshkosh ("B'Gosh!") overalls, plaid shirt, and work boots, Mrs. Thompson would march into her garden with a glaring intensity that rivaled General Patton. Her husband used to sometimes gently needle her with the comment, "Well, dressed like that, dear, you definitely don't need a scarecrow." Year after year, she had worked the soil early in the spring, coerced the plants to thrive in spite of unfavorable conditions, and then harvested her impressive vegetable bounty every fall.

On this particular day, Mrs. Thompson attacked the weeds with a ruthless, take-no-prisoners ferocity that she had never shown before. She wielded her gardening tool like it was a bayonet, jabbing the dirt with a rhythm that punctuated her mutterings. "What a fool I've been!" she grumbled as she stabbed the earth. "After all that I've done for them, how could they be so mean?" Each time Mrs. Thompson ended the refrain, she ripped some weeds out by their roots and flung them aside in disgust.

These words were the only ones that Mrs. Thompson seemed to be able to form. Each time that the words forced their way through her clenched teeth, Mrs. Thompson felt slapped once again by the stinging, stunning statements of her three grown children at the meeting with her minister. Certain aspects of her repeated litany seemed to stir up particular emotions all over again. The word *fool* would trigger another wave of the shame that had blindsided her at the meeting. The word *all* would provoke once again her sense of righteous anger and outrage over the unfairness of it all. But the final word *mean* would bring out emotions that she had rarely expressed during her 72 years: hurt and vulnerability. She found herself emphasizing those three words in her repetitions— "What a FOOL I've been!" and "After ALL that I've done for them, how could they be so MEAN?"

Mrs. Thompson was sure that her youngest daughter had been the mastermind. That realization finally nudged her into a new theme for her mutterings. "That *mastermind* should've minded her own damn business, instead of poking her nose where it doesn't belong. I'd like to *mastermind* her for airing all our dirty laundry in front of the Reverend." Mrs. Thompson finally stood up, surveyed the results of her work, massaged her back, and carried her wooden stool and gardening tool to her back porch.

Whoever had been the mastermind, all three children—hardworking, successful, and loving—had shared with their mother AND the minister how concerned they were. They had detailed the times she had been so bitter and sarcastic during the past three years. They explained that they had tolerated her cutting remarks because they understood that her forced retirement at 69 and the sudden death of her husband a few months later had been terrible blows. But neighbors, old friends, and other relatives were not as patient, and one by one they had drifted away from her.

It was only when her children brought out the heavy guns at the meeting that Mrs. Thompson finally agreed to see a counselor. Her children told her that recently the grandchildren had begged to be left at home so that they wouldn't have to endure her caustic and cutting remarks. Mrs. Thompson didn't see how counseling would do any good, but not being able to see her grandkids would be unthinkable.

The following week, Mrs. Thompson steered her vintage, mint-condition Buick Skylark into a parking space behind the community mental health center. As she stepped out of the car, she realized that she was feeling the same queasy apprehension that she had experienced when she faced her last dental appointment. She stalled for a few minutes, unfastening the seat belt, tidying the interior of the car, carefully making sure that everything was shut off properly. As she stepped out of the car, she had an overwhelming urge to flee. While she was reaching into her purse for the car keys, her billfold fell on the pavement. While retrieving it, she saw the school pictures of her grandkids.

Sighing, she muttered, "You big scaredy cat! For cryin' out loud." She reassured herself gruffly, "This counselor's surely not going to take a drill to me."

REFLECTING QUESTIONS

1. In what ways did Mrs. Thompson create her psychological world?
2. In what ways was her construction of the world imposed upon her?
3. How might you begin your work with this client in her current state of agitation?

OVERVIEW

This chapter, along with Chapters 7 and 8, explores important facets of making meaning, a process that lies at the heart of any significant change. We begin in Chapter 6 by examining the constructivist and social constructionist perspectives that portray how individuals and cultures create mental realities that have a powerful and pervasive impact on how we think, feel, and act. This conceptual foundation presents humans as constructing their phenomenological realities. In this chapter, we will frequently be referring to stories as one of the primary ways we create our psychological and cultural worlds. We continue with this theme in Chapter 7 by exploring in greater depth the concepts of narrative theory that concentrate on how we use stories to give voice to our experiences. Finally, in Chapter 8, we turn to the core concept of meaning, which is the focal point of both constructivist and narrative theories.

Although we have divided these ideas into three separate chapters, they are all variations on the same theme: Humans make meaning of their experiences. This chapter offers an alternate way of looking at reality. It is known as *constructivism* and is sometimes seen as opposed to *empiricism* (Prochaska & Norcross, 2007). There are two important positions taken by constructivists that can have a tremendous impact on how you view counseling.

The first fundamental assumption of constructivism is that one can never fully know another person's reality from an objective stance. Therefore, as a counselor, you cannot make sense of a client's experience through disengaged, "objective" approaches involving diagnostic or scientific methods. Only by encountering the client in an authentic relationship can you gain awareness of that person's experiential world. The LUV Triangle we described in Chapter 2 and the empathic connection we discussed in Chapter 3 take on even more importance now. If all knowledge is relational, then listening, understanding, validating and empathizing not only help you develop a trusting relationship, they also are essential if you are ever to come to truly know your clients.

The second assumption is that human knowledge of an objective reality is not possible. Instead of our perceptions providing a veridical copy of reality—sometimes called the "immaculate perception"— human beings can only construct their own rendition of "reality." Consequently, when you take a constructivist position as a counselor, your goal is not to get clients to become more rational and better adjusted to reality. You are trying neither to "straighten out" the thinking of clients nor to dispute the facts that clients offer as their life stories.

Instead, you are helping clients to deconstruct the way they are representing themselves and their world. As part of this process, you assist clients in recovering hidden facts, overlooked themes, and "unstoried" experiences that suggest a different, richer, more liberating portrayal of reality. In order to carry out this task successfully, you must listen for your client's constructs of self, others, and the world, while beginning to deconstruct the negative and destructive features. Two particular techniques for reconstructing a new mental reality are asking the miracle question and offering the encouragement triad.

IDEAS

A Mental Reality

In his book *Reality Isn't What It Used To Be,* Walter Anderson (1990) summed up the view of constructivists and social constructionists on the nature of reality: "Whatever is out there . . . remains for all time out there, and all our systems of thought are stories we tell ourselves about something that remains essentially unknowable" (p. 13). It is never possible to truly know whether the glass is half empty or half full. You only know your own glass story.

One of the first psychologists to make this claim was George Kelly, who developed the psychology of personal constructs. "Whatever exists", he insisted, "can be reconstrued" (in Anderson, 1990, p. 137). Kelly considered people's lives to be "shaped by their distinctive language *maps* of reality" (Blume, 2006, p. 185). People's lives are formed by language and constructed into stories they tell, and these stories may have less to do with the actual experiences they have gone through than the meaning they have assigned to them.

The good news for you as a counselor is that, if we remember all the events of our lives as constructed stories, then we can deconstruct them. As a counselor, you can assist your clients in re-authoring stories of discouragement and despair by transforming them into narratives of resolve and hope. Reality isn't what it used to be. The old idea of a fixed and immutable past, together with an inevitable future, turns out to be malleable instead. You can co-construct with clients new stories that will help them toward a successful resolution of their concerns.

Ways of Knowing

Does this idea of equivocal experiences strike you as unrealistic? After all, you have grown up in a socially-constructed tradition that holds that facts are facts. If someone has an experience, it is what it is. However, as long ago as the eighteenth century, the philosopher John Locke proposed a famous demonstration to show that experiences are not this clear cut. Take three bowls, he suggested, and fill one with cold water, another with hot water, and a third with lukewarm water. Place your right hand in the hot water and your left hand in the cold water. Of course, your right hand feels hot and your left feels cold. However, when you place both hands into the third bowl, your left hand will feel warm and your right hand will feel cool. The sensation of temperature is not a property of the water but comes from your experience.

The confusion takes place when you attempt to determine from your experience what the temperature of the water in the middle bowl *really* is. In this case, your experience creates a dilemma: Is the water warm or cool, or both? Facts may be facts, but we can change our interpretations of the facts and the meanings associated with them. It all depends on how we tell our story. The so-called "facts of the matter" depend on the narrative of the experiencing person. We have often heard adult siblings who were near the same age, comparing notes about their experiences as children in their family-of-origin and remarking, "It's like we were raised in totally different families with different parents!"

In his 1990 book *Acts of Meaning,* Jerome Bruner suggested the existence of two prominent ways of knowing. He called these two modes "paradigmatic" and "narrative." *Paradigmatic* knowing is involved in the process of constructing abstract models of reality, while narrative knowing makes sense of the world by constructing stories. The former is the language of science, while the latter is the way we deal with everyday life. Science has always attempted to ascertain the facts about objective reality without the necessity of an observer. *Narrative* knowing is the storied account of an observer who has experienced the events being discussed. This narrative is "re-collected" or "remembered." Because it is not a scientific account, it contains the biases and emotions of the observer, and because it is a construction, it is not strictly true in an objective sense. This narrative is, however, true for the author, the person telling the story. It is a story constructed from experience, and it is influenced by the context in which it is told.

Constructivism

As we previously stated, the idea of *constructivism* is that individuals create the world in which they live. *Social constructionism* is a slightly different concept. It asserts that our notions of reality are indeed constructed, but they are imposed upon us through our dominant culture. As a brief counselor, it is helpful for you to know that these two terms are related but do not have the same meaning.

The core claim of constructivism is that one cannot know "reality" as it actually is; there is no reality independent of the individual knower. No human has a "God's eye" view of objective reality. This does not mean that we simply "dream it up," but constructivists do suggest that we create reality rather than discover it. "That is not to deny the reality of concrete objects or a physical existence. Constructivists walk on the same ground and bump into the same walls that everyone does" (Prochaska & Norcross, 2007, p. 452).

When your clients come to you, their concerns are not about physical objects. Instead, they are bumping into psychological walls that keep them from achieving their goals and fulfilling their lives. The way that they have constructed their realities has led to a hardening of their categories. Their inflexible, confining, and limiting constructs have created a subjective reality that undermines their self-esteem, damages their relationships, and undercuts their potential for achieving a resolution of their concerns.

Social Constructionism

Although a constructivist would say that the individual creates reality, a social constructionist would emphasize that our culture imposes a reality on us. Both these processes are at work when clients tell you the stories of their lives. Neither of these "realities" are objective records of events in the world.

A social construction arises from the cultural ethos, paradigm, or zeitgeist into which we are born. Social constructionism is a fundamental assumption of a multicultural perspective (Sue & Sue, 2003). You see the world differently from someone in another culture because your particular cultural perspective drives your ideas. If, for example, you believe that capitalism is good, that private property rights should be respected, that people should work for a living, and that the accumulation of wealth is a worthy pursuit, then you were likely born into a contemporary Euro-American culture. Such beliefs are influenced not only by geography but also by historical period.

Until recently, people in the Soviet Union and the People's Republic of China did not hold that the belief in capitalism or private property was either natural or true. On a more local level, what you believe about marriage, how families should be configured, how friends should treat each other, what a successful person looks like, and what is beautiful or ugly have all been heavily influenced by the culture in which you have been reared. They are social constructions. Once we have accepted the values and views of our culture, we have difficulty imagining that there is any other way to see the world.

Obviously, social constructions have also influenced how women, Blacks, Latinos, homosexuals, and others have been treated in our culture. Since you will be counseling clients who have different social constructions, it is vital that you enhance your multicultural competencies (Sue & Sue, 2003). Social constructions are collectively held beliefs that change over time, but are generally not deliberately or consciously adopted. They are the stories that have been told to us that we continue to tell ourselves. Who we personally are, relative to cultural expectations, affects our self-esteem and our general happiness. It becomes a narrative "in which we prune, from our experience, those events that do not fit the dominant evolving stories. . . . Thus, over time and of necessity, much of our stock of lived experience goes unstoried" (Day, 2004, pp. 353–354).

Counseling and therapy from a social constructionist standpoint are based on the assumption that you must approach all taken-for-granted knowledge with a critical eye. You must also recognize that knowledge is time-limited and culture-bound: One person's way of knowing is not inherently superior to another's. Because social processes construct knowledge, everything that you consider to be "truth" has been produced by "daily interactions between people and daily life" (Corey, 2005, p. 386).

As a counselor, your challenge is to understand your client's world as a social construction and attempt to loosen the grip that this assumed reality has on the client. As Corey (2005) put it, "change begins by deconstructing the power of cultural narratives and then proceeds to the co-construction of a new life of meaning" (p. 386). You encourage your client to tell some of those "unstoried" events in which he or she has succeeded, felt beautiful, overcome barriers, been resilient, or has coped with society's challenges, fought oppression, and opposed stereotypes.

Memes: Units of Social Construction

The basic unit of biological transmission is the gene, while the basic unit of cultural transmission is the *meme*. Oxford English Dictionary defines a *meme* as an element of a culture, or accepted belief that may be considered as passed on by non-genetic means. Richard Dawkins (1976) coined the term "meme" from the Greek *memetic*—that which is imitated—and he gave as examples such things as tunes, ideas, catch-phrases, clothing designs, and social conventions.

Memes make themselves known in all aspects of our lives. Some memes emerge merely as fashions; they come on the scene, bask in the limelight of the meme pool for a while, and then die out. They may even come back again, like bell-bottomed pants or long sideburns, but they eventually fade again into the cultural background. At the time of this writing, words and phrases such as "twenty-four, seven" (meaning all the time), "efforting" (trying hard), and "stepping up to the plate" (accepting a challenging task) are very popular in everyday usage, enough to be a bit nauseating. By the time you read this, these utterances may be out of style. If you are relatively young, you probably have never heard the phrase "Kilroy was here" or been told a "little moron" joke. Most trendy memes appear in common usage seemingly overnight and then disappear just as rapidly.

Like genes, our memes have no long-term interest in our survival once we have passed them on to our offspring. As Dawkins (1976) put it, genes and memes are selfish. From the standpoint of biology, you and I are only vehicles that carry our selfish genes, and, as far as they are concerned, we only exist to help them replicate. It is not quite accurate to call them *our* genes. It is we who belong to them, not the other way around. We are simply the conveyance that exists to ensure their survival. As Samuel Butler once put it, "A hen is only an egg's way of making another egg" (in Stanovich, 2004, p. 2).

Similarly, our memes, which are our acquired attitudes, beliefs, rituals, and other conventions, exist selfishly in their attempt to get us to pass them on. In this sense, we are merely cultural vehicles whose only value to the memes is our ability to communicate with other humans, who may as a result be infected by our meme transmission. Of course, genes and memes do not literally "desire" to replicate themselves through us as vehicles, but they have found us to be proper hosts and transmitters, even though they are themselves quite mindless.

The first rule of memes—and of genes, for that matter—is that their replication is not necessarily good for anything. Just as there are "junk genes," so are there many junk memes. Susan Blackmore (2003) views human beings as meme machines. Memes are the units of the social construction (culture) in which we find ourselves. Our drives to imitate, learn, and communicate are impelled by memes that wish to survive and replicate themselves. "[H]uman development is a process of being loaded with, or infected by, large numbers of memes" (p. 24).

The memes that have constructed our culture will, in turn, affect all who live in this culture. For example, in spite of legislation enacted to prohibit discrimination on the basis of gender, women are still woefully underrepresented in positions of power. The dominant culture still encourages adolescent girls to conform to certain stereotypes regarding submissiveness and standards of beauty. Pervasive socialization processes and oppressive conditions have an enormous impact on women's body image, self-concept, and overall sense of well-being (Sue & Sue, 2003). Men, too, are constrained by prescribed gender roles that are passed to them by the memes of their culture. Once established, a meme can become an idea of "truth" in someone's head, a habitual piece of behavior, or an artifact in general use—a wheel or computer, for example.

Obviously, memes such as science, democracy, and equal rights, to name a few, appear to have a positive influence on those who are lucky enough to have been born into such social constructions, or "meme-plexes" (Dennett, 1991). If the memes of our socially constructed beliefs about the world have turned out to be life affirming, self-esteem-enhancing, and resolution-building, then being born into this happy memetic environment has given us a firm foundation for our mental health. The stories we tell about ourselves and the world would thus be filled with confidence, resolve, and faith in a positive future.

Unfortunately, because of the circumstances of their particular socially-constructed environments, many of your clients have been infected by memes that produce negative narratives. They may see themselves as incompetent or unlovable and the world as a hostile place.

We mindlessly acquired most of the memes that have taken possession of our beliefs and continue to shape our experience without our awareness (Stanovich, 2004). However, we can, with insight and effort, surmount the power memes have over us. As a counselor, your mission is to hear the stories that people tell of their lives and deconstruct the memes that are restricting their potential. One way to begin this process is to adopt the guileless attitude of a person who is "not from around here," and ask, I wonder where *that* idea came from?

Peanuts, Pizzas, and Pluto

When the authors of this book were in elementary school, we remember having to learn the names of all the planets in order of their distance from the sun. Perhaps you did, too. Our teachers designed mnemonic devices to help us remember this otherwise not very meaningful information. One such method is to put the items to be remembered into a sentence using the first letters of each item. Thus, the names of the planets in order—Mercury, Venus, Earth, Mars, Jupiter, Saturn, Uranus, Neptune, and Pluto—can become "My Very Empty Mouth Just Swallowed Up Ninety Peanuts" or "My Very Eager Mother Just Served Us Nine Pizzas." This method definitely helped us to regurgitate this information on tests and even stayed in our memories for years.

Here's a problem: In August 2006, little Pluto was voted out of the planet club by an international group of astronomers. Its status as a planet has been revoked. What then becomes of our constructed mnemonics that had served us so well? Now what has our empty mouth swallowed up? What has our eager mother served us? Peanuts, pizzas, and Pluto are suddenly gone! If we want a new mnemonic to replace our now "deconstructed" one, we are going to have to think hard to come up with it.

You have probably never actually seen the former planet Pluto anyway, but you always believed that it was there, orbiting around at the end of that line of planets. We still believe that Pluto is in fact out there, don't we? The *fact* has not changed, but its *meaning* is now entirely different. The important point to consider about this revision of our original belief in "planet Pluto" is that this belief was originally socially constructed anyway. And now, this belief has been deconstructed. The story of the planets has changed.

Our Storied Cultures

Culture is a world of stories (McLeod, 2003), and the above astronomical example illustrates that even science is a story. By embedding ourselves within some stories and rejecting others, we create our personal identities. Often without question, we accept as real the stories of our culture, and we interpret our experience through this worldview. We may take on these stories wholly as our own, building our personal identities with the raw materials of these myths, legends, and tales. If we never question or challenge these assumptions, we abandon our unique individuality and, instead, become two-dimensional characters in our culture's dominant stories, inhabiting their settings and following their prescribed plots.

Ask yourself, What does it mean to be a man? or What does it mean to be a woman? Some definite images and attributes of gender roles will probably come to your mind. Then ask, Where did I get these ideas? You will realize that because you were born in a particular place, in a particular family, and had certain experiences, your ideas about gender have formed. Had all these contextual and cultural experiences been different, your ideas about who you are, and how you should act, would be different. This is the social constructionist perspective of narratives. Our lives are lived within the dominant narratives of our families and cultures. The dominant narrative can restrict or impoverish our lives.

Deconstruction Defined

Deconstruction is a process that forces us to alter our beliefs and meanings regarding the facts of our experience (Hanna, 2007). This process is the very essence of continued learning. Piaget (1970) suggested that when we receive information that fits well within our already existing schema, we simply *assimilate* it; we do little more than add it to our store of information. The learning involved in assimilation is at best minimal. We easily assimilate everyday details by merely accumulating data, acquiring tidbits of information, and gathering trivia.

However, when we come across information that will not fit into our representational system, we must *accommodate* to it. We have to change our schema. The dissonance of this conflict between the new experience and our old schema is jarring. We feel blindsided by the unexpected, and suddenly the world no longer makes sense within our existing constructs.

Such a jolt to our representational system stirs us to somehow find a way to reconcile the clash between the novel and the known. The struggle may be a puzzle that plays on our assumptions, so that we have to "think outside of the box." Or, the challenge may be a traumatic experience that causes us to question our basic assumptions about our self-worth and the goodness of life (Janoff-Bulman, 1992).

Achieving a successful reconciliation requires flexibility, creativity, and willingness to set aside our familiar and comfortable constructs for new ones. When we successfully achieve this resolution, we then have a wider representational system that is more open to new possibilities.

Our entire lives are a cyclical process of assimilation and accommodation. In other words, we construct our realities based on our experience, and then, when new and different experiences come along, we deconstruct the old realities and reconstruct new ones.

Clients often come to you stuck between the old and new realities. McLeod (2003) pointed out that the stories that your clients tell you reveal the underlying structures of the cognitive schemas through which they interpret the world. As the person retells the story of an event, the multiple drafts of the narrative will occasionally conflict with each other. For example, a tale of ultimate tragedy conflicts with one of hope. It is your role to help in this process. You will be asking for details that might be left out of the victimization story so that the narration turns to one of survival.

As a counselor, you can help your clients reflect on the conflict in their narratives and achieve a higher level of understanding. By constructing a higher-order story, your client can come to a richer, transcendent story that subsumes the previously conflicting accounts. Your client can then use this new story as a guide for change and resolution. In the Tools section of this chapter, we offer practical techniques for deconstructing and reconstructing your clients' realities.

The Cognitive Revolution

When the field of psychology underwent a "cognitive revolution" in the 1960s, and the mind once again became a legitimate area of study, there developed within this revolution a divergence among psychologists and counselors regarding how to conceptualize mental processes. One group, having assumed that reality is something external to us to be faithfully copied by the mind, held that an individual's mental representation must be brought into correspondence with the reality out there by a combination of logic and empirical investigation. Another group, having adopted the constructivist position, placed its emphasis on the meaning that events have for the individual. Constructivists did not accept mere mental alignment with, or correspondence to, an external reality as the criterion for mental health.

Mahoney (1988) called the former of these views the "rationalist" position and the latter the "developmental." Albert Ellis and Aaron Beck are two therapists who personify the rationalist view. From the *rationalist* perspective, failure to take a clear picture of reality is the result of a defective lens, bad film, or inadequate exposure. If someone's picture of reality is distorted, then that person is thinking irrationally.

Your work as a counselor would then be to help this client adjust the photo-taking apparatus in order to obtain a veridical copy of reality. The result would be what Mahoney and others have called the "immaculate perception" (1988, p. 158). From the rationalist's point of view, the brain is "a curator of information gleaned from sense data . . . [but] constructivists . . . tend to portray the brain as an active sculptor of experience" (Mahoney, 1988, p. 162). Knowledge, in this sense, always implies a participating knower.

The rationalist considers the client as someone needing to adjust to an external reality. The *developmentalist,* on the other hand, sees the client as needing to change and grow. Rather than viewing the client's cognitive schema as distorted, the developmentalist would characterize such schema, or constructions, as outmoded and in need of a more flexible accommodation to the client's experiences.

Do not confuse *deconstruction* with *demolition.* You work to help your clients metamorphose, transcend, or rise above their current troubling positions toward more liberating ones. As you facilitate the change process, keep in mind that growth is not destruction but transcendence.

Implications of These Ideas for the Counselor

Constructivism and social constructionism have rich and important implications for the practice of counseling. Adopting these perspectives opens up a number of exciting possibilities for you as the counselor:

- In this way of working with clients, you are not interested in trying to align someone's thinking with an objective reality.
- People's realities are constructions based on experiences they have had and the meanings they have assigned to these experiences.
- Being born into a culture imposes meanings on people that they may never have examined. The counselor helps to bring some of these meanings to light or assists the client in loosening the grip of negative meanings.
- Whatever your version of reality, you should not attempt to sell it to your clients. Instead, you must seek aspects of the client's story that are more hopeful and more filled with possibilities.

TOOLS

Deconstructing Is Not "Dissing"

We have found that when novice counselors are first introduced to the idea of deconstruction, they immediately think that the technique involves talking the client out of his or her beliefs. As we have said before, when clients tell you their stories, you must *validate* the version they are telling you.

Some of the rationalist approaches to therapy advocate a frontal attack on clients' discouraging beliefs and maladaptive attitudes. However, deconstruction is the process of helping your clients to experience what they previously had considered to be "givens" as filled with overlooked "possibilities," what they had held as unquestioned "facts" as merely "perspectives," accepted "realities" as "interpretations," and "closed cases" as "works in progress."

You are probably familiar with the slang term *dis,* which according to Merriam Webster's Collegiate Dictionary means ". . . treat with disrespect or contempt: insult . . . to find fault with: criticize" (Feb. 2, 2007, http://www.m-w.com/dictionary/dis). There are a vast number of ways you can communicate to your clients that you are "dissing" their stories of reality. Words such as *disagree, disapprove, disallow, disbelieve, discredit, disconfirm, discount, dismiss, disparage, dispute, disregard,* and *distrust* are all "dis" words that, when communicated to your clients, will disrupt your working relationship. If there is a hint of any of these in your responses to your clients, they will likely become hesitant to tell you everything.

Techniques of Deconstruction

Lay the foundation for deconstruction work   Although we focus in this section on several specific deconstruction techniques, keep in mind that all the tools you have learned in previous chapters actually contribute to the deconstruction process. For example, in Chapter 4 you read about techniques for helping your clients envision a future. Engaging in goal setting automatically begins to deconstruct any narrative of hopelessness that your clients may have brought to counseling. In Chapter 5, you practiced reframing, which involves using another schema to view an experience.

In fact, the techniques from Chapters 2 and 3—providing a LUVing and empathic relationship—not only are the foundation for any successful counseling but also are the most fundamental tools for deconstruction work. When your clients feel truly heard, understood, and validated, then you have impacted their constructs regarding human relationships. Alienated clients begin to unconsciously reconsider their initial portrayals of other people as uncaring, disengaged, and rejecting. By communicating empathically and authentically, you create opportunities for shared subjective realities with your clients. These therapeutic encounters themselves can facilitate the deconstruction and reconstruction process.

Listen for self-sabotaging constructions   Your clients' stories will contain countless constructions (Neimeyer, 1993). As a counselor, your role is to focus on those important schemas that characterize *self, others,* and the *world* (Janoff-Bulman, 1992). If you are sensitive to these three fundamental areas, you can be alert to those constructs that are self-sabotaging and limiting. Then you can watch for openings that yield deconstruction possibilities.

• **Constructing self.** Your clients can, for example, characterize themselves in cultural stereotypes according to their gender, age, or ethnicity. They may ignore their unique individuality by limiting their personal identities to their roles in their families, work settings, peer groups, or communities. Or your clients may slap destructive labels on themselves. These tags may include such global portrayals as *bum, idiot, loser,* and *neurotic.* In Chapter 7, you will also read about the damaging metaphors clients may use in describing themselves.

• **Constructing others.** Be alert to your client's constructs that portray other people, particularly significant others, as negative caricatures, such as bigots, nerds, cheats, liars, or tyrants. Pay close attention to how your client uses constructs to interpret other people's intentions or motivations. Some examples of these might be, "She is an insecure person," "He doesn't care about me," "She is out to get me," or "He is narcissistic." Such one-dimensional and pessimistic portrayals can not only undermine important relationships but also block any potential avenues for genuine fulfillment in the future.

• **Constructing the world.** Notice when your client characterizes the circumstances of life as meaningless, overwhelming, hopeless, demoralizing, and damaging. Possible examples include, "Life sucks and then you die," "My entire life has been such a complete disaster," or "I have no future." These portrayals allow no possibility of change, transformation, or fulfillment. Such characterizations sap your client's motivation and sense of hope.

Ask for a description of the construction   As you listen to client narratives, you tune into those constructs that are especially problematic and sabotaging. You then ask your client for a concrete description of the particular construction. At this point, it is particularly important that you adopt a *not-knowing,* "not from around here" attitude regarding your client's story as you work to bring their global construction down to a workable level. An example of such a transaction follows:

> **Client:**   "My entire life has been such a complete disaster!"
>
> **Counselor:**   "I'm not sure I understand what's happened to lead you to this conclusion. What would be an example?"
>
> **Client:**   "It's just one damned thing after another."
>
> **Counselor:**   "What was one thing?"
>
> **Client:**   "Well, take my love life for example. I am always attracted to guys who seem, at first, to be looking for a real relationship, but in the end, they can't commit."
>
> **Counselor:**   Yeah, that sounds like you would end up getting hurt and feeling deceived after you had invested a lot yourself into the relationship."
>
> **Client:**   "Exactly!"
>
> **Counselor:**   "So, are you saying that you need to work on fine-tuning your radar so that you can spot these losers before you get sucked into a relationship with them?"

Remember that, although you are helping to deconstruct and co-construct better stories along with your clients, they ultimately are the authors of their life stories. You must be careful not to impose your interpretation. This error is common among beginning counselors who fail to recognize that clients are always the experts on their own life stories. Rather, your expertise is in changing minds, that is, in perturbing your clients' representations of the world so that their narratives will have gaps or holes that must be filled so that their stories are coherent.

It is when these gaps are present that your clients are open to change. Therefore, at these times, ask for a more detailed and descriptive narrative. For example, you might say, "It sounds like you're saying that you won't be a success unless you become a manager with a corner office," or "In what ways does your husband show his narcissism?" Getting to the bottom of the attribution will begin the deconstruction process. Then you can respond in a way that will relabel, reframe, or call an assumption into question without disrespecting your client's worldview. Since all our worlds are constructed, either by social constructionist processes or person constructs, they are all open to revision.

Clarify with a wedge   The next step to deconstruction, after getting a description of what your client means by any assigned meaning in the construct, is for you to clarify with a wedge. In other words, while you are attempting to make sure you have completely grasped the client's circumstance and its assigned meaning, you are, at the same time, driving in the "wedge" of a possible alternative interpretation of the issue under discussion.

What you are doing is giving voice to your client's construct in such a way that it is seen as a proposition, not a law carved in stone. You are acknowledging that the client's story is just that: a personal account that your client is offering at this particular time and place, implying that it may be open to future revision.

Here are just a few examples of how you might begin the "clarification wedge" deconstruction process:

Constructs about self

- "Let me check something out with you, it almost sounds as if you believe a real man wouldn't cry in that situation."
- "So you believe that unless you are a size 4, you cannot be an attractive woman."

Constructs about others

- "Sounds like you are saying that his forgetting to wrap your birthday present could only mean that he really does not care about you."
- "So, because your son is a teenager who doesn't have fully-developed frontal lobes yet, and often forgets to phone to say he will be late, then he must not respect you at all."

Constructs about the world

- "It's almost as if you've been somehow convinced that because several of those events have turned out badly, all of life is totally hopeless."
- "So, if I'm understanding you correctly, failing that test has somehow convinced you that your entire life has been a complete disaster."

Capitalize on "sparkling moments"   In spite of containing constructs that can confine or oppress, all narratives have their "sparkling moments." You want to enter into your client's story and pan for the gold nuggets of resilience within it. When you notice any instance of creativity, resilience, grit, or courage in your client's story, then become a more excited listener. Use the reverse empathy technique presented in Chapter 3, and highlight these events. Provide an animated "voice over" that narrates these scenes depicting your client's unacknowledged strengths and overlooked resources. Similarly, be on the lookout for the unstoried constructs. These are the experiences that your client may be ignoring because they do not fit cultural stereotypes or the person's dominant schema.

Invite re-authoring   As you work to help people re-author their impoverishing constructs, you must remember to stay with the material that your client gives you. Avoid injecting cliché phrases as you attempt to reconstruct the narrative. Offering reassuring aphorisms from the dominant culture, such as "When the going gets tough, the tough get going" or "When life deals you lemons, make lemonade," is useless and restricting to people who are trying to tell their stories with an individual and authentic voice.

However, anytime you can get a wedge into your client's construction, you then have the opportunity to open the conversation for alternative meanings. Keep in mind that this approach is not argumentation or debate. Deconstruction is finding opportunities to agree with your client's rendition while adding a comment that will loosen the negative schema the client has created.

The natural tension between your client as the storyteller and yourself as the audience can ultimately result in the re-authoring of a liberating story. Real men do cry without being "sissies." Real women can succeed in business without being "ball-busters." The new story will be workable if it continues to fit to some degree within the culture, while freeing the individual from the constraints of a restrictive myth.

LISTENING IN ON A SESSION

Review the story at the beginning of the chapter. At some time during their first session, a brief counselor might use the following deconstruction techniques with Mrs. Thompson.

Counselor: (He had started the session with an invitation to offer a goal statement. However, when the client quickly turned to her account of how she was encouraged to seek counseling, the counselor listened and validated. He now explores possibilities for deconstruction by using the following question.)

"Mrs. Thompson, as you were sharing with me the meeting you had with your children and minister and your time in the garden going over all your reactions, I was really curious about something. How in the world did you get yourself to come here for counseling? You've never been to counseling before in your life."

Mrs. Thompson: "Well, I may seem like a hateful old bitch to my grand-kids, but I actually do love 'em all. The oldest one used to throw a fit if she couldn't come to visit her 'Grammy Rose'—that's what she used to call me. I'll do anything to change so the grandkids want to see me again."

Counselor: "I couldn't help but notice that you called yourself a 'hateful old bitch.' Let me check something out with you. It sounds like you have been through the worst time of your life. First, you were pushed out of your job in which you were so successful and from which you drew so much satisfaction. And then your husband, with whom you had shared a long, deep, and abiding love, suddenly died. It almost sounds as if you think that a woman shouldn't feel angry, even in such painful and awful times."

Mrs. Thompson: "Well, you're certainly right about those being some of the worst days I've ever had in my life . . ."

(She pauses, sighs, and brushes a tear from her eye before continuing.)

"I really have no idea how I made it through those horrible days. My husband was such a loving, kind soul who was always doing the sweetest things . . . He was the romantic one—buying me flowers, even though I had a garden full of them, and writing love notes for me to find, even though he hadn't even left the house. I guess that lately it's been real hard for me to just keep my damn mouth shut and not nag my grandkids about how stupid they look with earrings stuck where they don't have any ears."

1. In what ways has the counselor clarified with a wedge?
2. How might you respond to the client's final comment?

Fantasy and the Hypothetical

In his 1991 book *Learned Optimism*, Martin Seligman suggested that optimists and pessimists are made, not born. In other words, the experiences one has in life will tend to give a valence to how the person views the future. Since the only thing we have before us is the future, it seems that it would be more pleasant to look forward to it with optimism. And, since optimism is learned, our job as counselors is to work with client stories in order to "tip the balance" toward a positive future outcome (Echterling, Presbury, & McKee, 2005). The future has not happened yet; it exists only in the minds of people. The future is by definition a hypothetical. The way people predict it determines their attitudes and moods in the present. By helping clients envision an optimistic future, we might help them improve their current condition.

If clients persist in the belief that their goals in life will never be realized, they see no reason to put much effort into trying to achieve them. This discouragement leaves them stuck. The first step toward changing a story of hopelessness into one of optimism is for you as the counselor to restate their current vision of a negative outcome differently and hint at possibility:

- "*So far,* you have not seemed to be able to come up with a way of handling this situation the way you'd like."
- "You haven't *quite* settled on a plan of action here."
- "You're not sure how you're going to do it, but you *still* really want to make the most of this painful situation."

(Echterling et al., 2005, p. 127)

Notice that each of these statements implies a future in which things will be better. This successful hypothetical future, being presumed by the counselor, tends to lift the restrictions of the gloomy present. Studies have shown that when people strive for positive goals, they experience higher levels of well-being than those who attempt to avoid negative outcomes (Emmons, 1999). We all hope for the "happy ending." If clients can have inklings that greater happiness is indeed achievable, their entire life stories become altered.

The use of the hypothetical frame temporarily relieves the client of the responsibility of changing immediately and tends to imbue the situation with a hopeful yet tentative quality through the use of fantasy. "Fantasy is an expansive force in a person's life—it reaches and stretches beyond the immediate people, environment or event which may otherwise contain him [sic]" (Polster & Polster, 1973, p. 255). Fantasy is a vicarious form of enactment; people can imagine themselves behaving differently and feeling differently as a result. If people have become discouraged and stuck with regard to their desires and goals, then as Minkowski (in Ellenberger, 1958) pointed out, their future becomes an impossibility; they foreclose on tomorrow and live in a "dammed-up" present. When liberating fantasies emerge in counseling, the client's energy increases and gives the client a new sense of self. The dam begins to leak.

It is important for you, the counselor, to be an optimist. If you are, you can infect the client with your confident attitude about the future, and you will easily come up with presumptive questions and statements that portend a promising resolution to their current situation, such as the following:

- "When this problem is resolved, how will you see the world differently?"
- "From what you are saying, I sense that you still believe that you will eventually find that special person in your life."
- "I have heard you say that there was a time you lived your life in Technicolor, and that you hope to do so again."
- "How is it that despite the situation you now find yourself in, you can still struggle like a determined butterfly in a cocoon to be liberated?"

In the Necker cube exercise you saw in Chapter 5, recall how suddenly the picture changed and how you were then no longer able to imagine only a single view. If optimism and pessimism can be considered as the two faces of the Necker cube, once we can get our clients to hypothetically imagine a positive future, the negative aspects of their concerns won't have disappeared, but will be juxtaposed with possibility. Change can sometimes come about so suddenly that no rational explanation can be offered for it. Just as you cannot say how it is you switch the faces of that cube, neither can your clients fully explain how imagining a better future can change their life story. The world suddenly seems more welcoming and the future more hopeful, though nothing has really changed in the client's present circumstances. Now, a bittersweet longing for resolution comes to propel the client toward possibilities that did not seem to have been there before.

Pretending Miracles

When you ask your clients to enter the hypothetical frame, you are offering the opportunity for them to artistically create a future that will contain both a solution path and a resolution of their former difficulties. You ask for the best-case scenario—the one in which they live in fantasy. One of the best techniques for accomplishing this is the famous "miracle question" developed by de Shazer (1985) and his associates. With this intervention, the client is asked to imagine that, while he or she was asleep, a miracle happened that resolved the client's issues. You then ask for a detailed description of what the client—who was asleep at the time and did not know the miracle had happened—would notice that is different. The miracle question is used when clients are unable to identify any exceptions in their problem pattern.

We have found, when attempting to train our counseling students in the use of the miracle question, that they tend to go too fast. This question needs to be delivered in a slow, hypnotic style. As you set the scene, watch the clients' breathing (look at the rise and fall of the shoulders, not the chest) and try to match the delivery of this image to their rhythm:

"Imagine that tonight, after this day of lots of activity, you go home and find that you are extremely tired. Maybe you watch a little TV or try to read, but you find that sleep is calling you. You go to bed and fall into a deep, refreshing slumber. During the night, while you are sleeping, a miracle happens, and the miracle is this: All these difficulties that you have been talking about and that have held you prisoner are gone! You are free of all these problems.

But, of course, since you've been asleep, you don't know that this miracle has happened. So, when you wake up, what is the first thing you will notice that is different, that will make you say, 'I think a miracle has happened!'"

Of course, as is true of all the suggestions, we offer that you might say to your clients, you must put the miracle question into your own words and fit it to your client's circumstance. Also, it is important to ask your client's permission before offering the miracle question: "I'd like to ask you something that might help us move along in our work together. It will take some imagining on your part. Are you willing?"

Most clients will say that they are willing if you have engaged their trust by acknowledging their concerns (with the LUV Triangle) and have created a working alliance. Once the client begins to respond to the miracle question, you can help make the image as clear and concrete as possible by presuming the miracle: "Please tell me everything you are doing that is different than yesterday, now that this miracle has happened, and how you are seeing things in a new way." Keep asking "What else?" until the client runs out of ideas.

O'Hanlon (1995) suggested that children sometimes respond better to the notion of the therapist using a "magic wand" or a "magic pill" to solve the problem. Erickson (1954) employed the hypothetical as a "crystal ball technique." While clients were in a trance, Erickson would ask them to look into the crystal ball and see a future in which their problems had been eliminated. Then, he would have them peer back to the present from their place in the future and identify how they had been able to accomplish this change.

In any case, the idea is to follow up the hypothetical solution with inquiry about how the person will be different when the negative situation is resolved. Whatever the client says about the difference, it will serve as a road sign on the path to a well-formed goal statement and, ultimately, toward resolution of his or her current difficulties.

LISTENING IN ON A SESSION

Review the story at the beginning of the chapter and the dialogue between Mrs. Thompson and her counselor in the previous section. A counselor might use the miracle question with Mrs. Thompson in the following way.

Counselor: (He leans forward again and prefaces the miracle question by briefly asking for permission and taking care to call the client by her preferred name.)

"Let me ask you something, Mrs. Thompson. What if you went home after this session, spent a typical afternoon of gardening, maybe having something to eat, perhaps reading for awhile, and then went to bed. Suppose that, while you were sound asleep in bed, a miracle happened that resolved your situation so you could live the life that you desire and have the kind of relationships you seek. However, since you were sound asleep, you didn't even know that this miracle had taken place. What would be the first thing that you would notice when you woke up in the morning that would show you that this miracle had happened?"

Mrs. Thompson: (She hesitates, with her eyes gazing toward the window, and appears pensive.)

"Well, I'm not sure . . . I believe that there would be a lilt in my voice. Back when my husband was alive and I was feeling in particularly good spirits, he would say that I was his bluebird of happiness because I had a lilt in my voice, a bounce in my steps, and a cheerful smile on my face.

(She stops and a tear glistens in her eye as she smiles faintly.)

I guess if that miracle did happen, I wouldn't feel guilty anymore about enjoying my life without my husband. I would realize that he would have wanted me to be the person that he loved—his bluebird of happiness."

REFLECTING QUESTIONS

1. How has Mrs. Thompson envisioned her miracle?
2. How has the counselor used the miracle question?
3. How might you respond to Mrs. Thompson's last statement?

USING THIS TOOL

Divide into groups of three. One of you volunteers to share some aspect of your life that you would like to change. Another volunteers to listen, understand, validate, and, when appropriate, pose the "miracle question." Finally, the third person serves as the recorder who observes the activity and leads the feedback discussion.

Encouragement versus Praise

Jerome Frank (1985) said that many people who seek counseling are demoralized. He described demoralization as a state characterized by one or more of the following: "subjective incompetence, loss of self-esteem, alienation, hopelessness (feeling no one can help), or helplessness (feeling that other people could help but will not)" (p. 56). According to this view, clients seek not only to alleviate problems and symptoms but to decrease feelings of discouragement (Young, 2005). Resolution counseling focuses on dissolving concerns and deconstructing narratives but also expects that people will become more encouraged by the process.

In order to accomplish this re-storying of the client's demoralizing narrative, you must adopt what Schmidt (2002) called "the encouraging stance." You must believe that, even in the darkest of times, good things are on the horizon. A counselor must believe that, no matter what, people can change. "To think otherwise, weakens our resolve. . . . the hallmark of a truly caring relationship appears when, under frustrating circumstances and difficult conditions, we maintain a positive direction and persevere unselfishly" (p. 56).

We have found that counselors in training often are so moved by their clients' plight that they are quick to try a "look on the bright side" intervention and attempt to argue clients out of their pain. This is not an unselfish intervention. The counselor is also trying to decrease his or her own discomfort. The encouraging stance provides a "holding environment" (Teyber, 2005) in which clients are free to talk of their pain, knowing that you will not be overwhelmed by it. But while acknowledging their concerns, you also stand ready to become enthused about their successes. Encouraging statements are different from praise, gratuitous compliments, or pep talks. They are designed to reflect an internal positive state existing within the client. Witmer (1985) stated that encouragement is used to inspire, hearten, and instill confidence, while praise is designed to maintain the strength of a specific behavior. Encouragement is intended to increase a sense of personal agency and efficacy, while praise runs the risk of increasing the client's feeling of dependency on external control.

If, for example, a child displays a desired behavior, the praise response might be, "Great job!" or "I'm really proud of you!" or "You get an 'A' for that one!" On the other hand, the encouragement response might be, "I noticed you were really trying hard on that, and you did it!" or "How in the world were you able to do such a difficult thing!" or our old standby, "How did you get yourself to do that?" In the latter responses, the evaluation is more of in the form of an observation in which the agency remains with the child. You are expressing awe and excitement at his or her accomplishment.

There is certainly nothing wrong with praising, complimenting, or cheering when someone does well. It is just that such behavior is not as effective in building autonomy, an internal locus of evaluation, or a sense of personal power in the client. Remember, you are a significant other for your clients, and the way in which you respond will affect the way they see themselves. If you wish to help improve the client's self-concept, then encouragement is superior to praise or reinforcement.

The encouraging stance is accomplished when you strike a balance between acknowledging the client's concerns and listening for accomplishments and possibilities in the client's story. You can acknowledge concerns without encouraging the client to stay with problem-saturated talk by keeping a respectful evenness in your own emotional arousal as you employ the LUV Triangle. If you appear too interested in the client's story of demoralization, then the client will tend to dig more deeply into his or her discouragement. Someone has said that when your clients are in a discouraged state, they always imagine that you secretly despise them. What they talk about is what they experience. If you probe their pain and negative self-image, you may be reinforcing their sense of worthlessness. Just as you must watch your language with clients, you must also watch your reactions to their language. It is when clients' stories turn to reporting success—actual or hypothetical—that you should appear enthusiastic and intensely curious.

Compliments, Praise, and Encouragement

Walter and Peller (1992) correctly contended that you must "observe for positives" in your client's story. They referred to this tactic as "complimenting" the client. It is important to note, however, that most of their compliments were in the form of encouraging statements rather than praise or positive reinforcement. The difference between encouragement and praise is in the goal of such interventions. As we have said, if one wishes to strengthen the behavior under consideration, then praise is appropriate. The operant-conditioning behavioral literature has stressed this strategy.

Conversely, if your goal is to increase a client's self-esteem, you should use encouraging statements. Encouragement focuses on the client's inner direction, internal control, and effort, while praise emphasizes your evaluation of the adequacy of a client's performance against some standard. Encouragement is more likely to promote the client's feeling of competence and independence, but, as we pointed out, praise or reinforcement may "develop a strong association, perhaps dependence, between a specific reinforcer and a behavior, [and may be] less likely to generalize to other life situations" (Walter & Peller, 1992, p. 142).

LISTENING IN ON A SESSION

Let's return to the session with Mrs. Thompson. Continuing with their interaction, the counselor can turn to "getting by" questions.

Counselor: "You know, Mrs. Thompson, one of the amazing things I have found in working with people on their concerns is that by the time they come for the first session, they have often already started something new that seems to be helping. What is one small thing that you have noticed yourself doing differently between the time you made the appointment and now?"

Mrs. Thompson: "That's interesting that you should ask me that question because I honestly do believe that I've been making an effort not to be a pain in the butt with my grandkids. I dropped off a birthday present for one of them and he grabbed it, tore off the paper, and ran off playing with this electronic toy he had wanted without thanking me. If that had happened last month, I would have yelled at him to march right back to me, give me a hug and a kiss."

Counselor: (He leans forward to listen more closely and pauses to invite her to continue.)
"And now you would instead . . .?"

Mrs. Thompson: "Well, instead, I just tried to keep my thoughts to myself. I didn't like being ignored, but then again, I seem to stick my foot in my mouth every time I try to help. Heck, I wasn't that careful with my own kids and they turned out all right."

Counselor: (Displaying increased interest)
"I'm still thinking back to when you said that you would have yelled at your grandson. I could tell by the way you just said it that you had really strong feelings at that moment. I don't know many people who could have pulled that off. How did you get yourself to do that?"

Mrs. Thompson: "I just reminded myself that it's HIS gift and not MY present. After all, he's only 8 years old—what do you expect? I mean, I can feel good that he's so excited about it—even though he didn't use good manners—and be satisfied that at least I picked out a good gift."

REFLECTING QUESTIONS

1. In what ways is the counselor continuing to use questions?
2. How might you respond to the client's final comment?

USING THIS TOOL

Divide into groups of three. One of you volunteers to share some successful experience. Another volunteers to offer encouragement (rather than reinforcement) in the listen, understand, and validate process. Finally, the third person serves as the recorder, who observes the activity and leads the feedback discussion.

When a Client Focuses Positively (The Encouragement Triad)

Any time the client moves from problem-saturated talk to a positive focus, you will want to attempt to increase the vividness of the focus. If the client utters a goal statement, states an exception, or reports a success, you must try to, as they say, "make hay while the sun shines." Ask the client to elaborate the scenario, using the "fly on the wall" or "video-talk" techniques or any type of request for detailed information that fits your style. "If I were a fly on the wall, what would I see you doing differently?" "If I were to follow you around with a video camera, what would be on the DVD that hasn't been there before?" "What else?"

Then, attempt to insert as many of the "encouragement triad" responses as you can into your reaction to the client's positive statements. The three points of the triangle (see Figure 6-1) will serve to remind you of how you can get the most out of your client's positive focus. First, get excited and do everything you can to communicate your enthusiasm for the client's content. In other words, display *energy*. This message of excitement over what is being discussed has the effect of *reverse empathy* (discussed in Chapter 3). Clients also have empathic responses to the counselor, and your enthusiasm about their success can be contagious. Second, pump the client for all the details. Make sure that you get a complete picture of what the client is talking about, every bit of its concrete minutia. For example, if you are exploring exceptions, you might ask what the client said or did, how other people responded, what was different, where the event was taking place, what it felt like, and so on. In other words, you strive to have the client give as complete an account of the *imagery* (visual, kinesthetic, and acoustical) as possible. Make the scene as real for the client as you can by persistently asking for a complete description. In addition, make every attempt to use presumptive statements that assign *agency* to the client. In what way is the client responsible for the change or the positive turn of the situation? Try to

FIGURE 6-1   The encouragement
                 triad

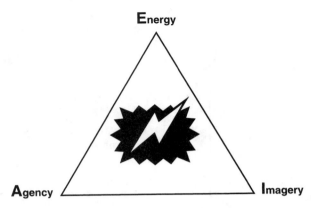

reflect each "external locus of responsibility" statement back on the client, so that you communicate your belief that the client was, or will be, in control, rather than being the passive recipient of munificent fortune or someone else's good deed: for example, "So, how were you able to get him to respond differently this time?"

USING THIS TOOL

Divide into groups of three. One of you volunteers to share a recent success experience. Another volunteers to engage the client in elaborating on the success by being enthusiastic, encouraging imagery, and promoting agency. Finally, the third person serves as the recorder who observes the activity and leads the feedback discussion.

SUMMARY

Based on our knowledge of constructivist and social constructionist theories, we arrive at several powerful tools to use with clients. The miracle question technique is a way of inviting clients to construct a detailed scene in which they have resolved the major concerns of their life. We have also introduced you to the process of encouraging, rather than praising or reinforcing, client behaviors. The use of the encouragement triad (energy, imagery, agency) helps clients focus on success, develop a clearer picture of what they desire, accept that they are responsible for past successes, and believe that they can—and will!— be successful again.

SEGUE TO CHAPTER 7

To help you gain a feel for the ideas and tools in the next chapter, think of a time when you were hoping to gain something. In other words, you didn't have it yet but you had the hope of getting it. How were you different while you had this hope?

Resource

Constructivist Psychology Network
www.constructivistpsych.org

The Constructivist Psychology Network (CPN) is an organization of persons interested in constructivist approaches to psychology, relationships, and human change processes. It publishes a newsletter, sponsors a journal, and organizes an international biennial conference.

CHAPTER 7

Narrative Counseling

Clients' Lives as Stories

"We all live in suspense from day to day; in other words,
you are the hero of your own story."
Mary McCarthy

CHAPTER GOALS

Reading and experiencing the ideas in this chapter will help you to understand the following key ideas:

- Narrative concepts offer new insights into the cognition of humans, the only species who are storytellers.
- Metaphors are not just tools for poets and artists. Clients use them as they portray their concerns, and counselors use them to communicate empathy and promote reframing.

Reading about and practicing the tools in this chapter will help you to develop skills in using the following techniques based on a narrative point of view:

- Externalizing the problem.
- Listening for metaphors to understand how clients perceive the world.
- Using metaphors to respond empathically and promote resolution of client narratives.

STORY

"William" was the name that appeared on his birth certificate, but people never called him that. His mother, who was notorious for giving nicknames to her children, decided that this youngest child—the runt of the family—was much too short for the seven-letter name they had selected originally, so she started to call the baby by his initial, "W." But even this abbreviation, with its three syllables, seemed too long and cumbersome for such a tiny thing, so she quickly shortened his name even more to the single sound "Dub."

Even when he had grown to a lanky six feet, two inches, a height that certainly could justify a longer name, people continued to call him "Dub." Dub never actually complained about his nickname, but he began to resent it when he was 13. One day he realized that his name was distinctively odd. Sure, many of his friends and relatives had nicknames that often bore no resemblance at all to the names that appeared on their birth certificates. But "Dub" was different because it wasn't a word. In fact, it wasn't even a letter—just a sound that started a letter. It was as if he wasn't worth more than just a simple utterance. Dub thought about asking people to call him "William," but it seemed such a minor issue to trouble others over.

Since graduating from college a year ago, Dub had come to the realization that the nickname issue—what to call himself—was only part of much larger and more fundamental questions. Who was he? What did he want to do with his life? Where was he heading? Dub really had no idea. He was working as a waiter, but that was just to support himself until he found some answers. He had lived much of his life without thinking about these questions, but now they intrigued and even obsessed him.

Dub had never before been introspective. Instead, he had been an outgoing guy who was more interested in tinkering with motorcycles than in figuring out what made himself tick. For some reason, however, he lately had been keeping to himself, playing his guitar, and making up song lyrics. Coming home from work, Dub would squat on a tiny wooden stool he had kept from his childhood days, hunker over his guitar as if he were cradling a baby, and experiment by combining different chords with his lyrics. After several hours, he sometimes would throw aside his guitar, disgusted with himself when the words rang so maudlin and his fingering seemed so awkward that they would never capture the depth and intensity of his feelings.

Many of Dub's friends were also in temporary jobs, taking it easy and biding their time while their lives were on hold. They seemed to enjoy the respite from the grind of school and were in no hurry to enter the real world of adulthood commitments and responsibilities. But Dub began to feel a sense of urgency tugging at him and distracting him as he waited on tables. Even partying, which used to be so much fun, now seemed to be just a diversion that left Dub feeling even more empty and dissatisfied with his life—and wondering if he would ever be able to change it. In fact, it was after a party that he decided to make an appointment to see a counselor.

REFLECTING QUESTIONS

1. What do you think Dub is searching for?
2. What would it be like to work with Dub as his counselor?
3. How might Dub tell his own story?

OVERVIEW

In Chapter 6, you read about the constructivist ideas that focus on how clients create their phenomenological worlds. Moreover, you also learned how social constructionism creates our cultural expectations and worldviews. One specific way that humans construct a meaningful framework for their experiences is through storytelling. In fact, as you saw in the previous chapter, many theorists and practitioners use the concept of story as an important element in understanding clients' lives. This chapter, in which we turn our attention to the narrative process, is an elaboration of the constructivist theoretical assumptions. In Chapter 8, we will explore the concept of meaning in greater depth. For now, we will examine stories and metaphors, which are the basic tools people use to create meaning from the raw material of their life experiences.

From a narrative perspective, people organize their lives into stories. Although we create these stories about our past experiences, our stories take on enormous psychological power in directing our present and future lives. Clients often come to you with stories that are outdated, tragic, and rigidified. As a result, they experience their lives as repetitive, negative, and unchangeable. Your challenge as a counselor is to help your clients create new and therapeutic narratives.

While clients are not to blame for all the disappointments, failures, and catastrophes that may have befallen them, they are responsible for rewriting their life narratives so that they can break out of the "stuckness" in which they find themselves. Taking this assumptive position frees both your client and yourself from the endless cycle of looking for causes. Instead, using such techniques as externalizing the problem can help turn the client's concern into a personified external influence that attempts to lure the client into unproductive thoughts, emotions, and behaviors. You then can ask for "news of a difference"—those times during which the client has succeeded in not being lured into trouble by this malevolent external entity.

One of the most compelling narrative tools is the metaphor, which gives power, clarity, and luminosity to our stories. Metaphors turn abstract and vague ideas into concrete images. You may not be a poet, but you unconsciously use metaphors every day, particularly when you share any experience that has stirred your emotions. As a counselor, you can listen for the metaphors that your clients use to characterize both their concerns and themselves. You can then use these same metaphors to communicate your understanding of your client's worldview and to offer vivid and enchanting reframes. Using your client's metaphors helps you in building a relationship, but it's also a powerful tool for therapeutic change (Lyddon, Clay, & Sparks, 2001).

IDEAS

Outdated, Rigidified, and Tragic Stories

People seek counseling because the story in which they are living has colored or restricted their experience to the point that they are suffering under its weight. The story may be *outdated*; the person is repeating the same story over and over, even though the context in which the story was originally constructed has long ago vanished into the past. The characters in the story may have changed to the point that they are no longer recognizable and do not fit their roles in the old story.

For example, parents will sometimes treat their adolescent child as they did when the child was much younger. As a result, there is friction in the family because the adolescent will not accept his or her role in the outdated story. The parent, in this case, may have "frozen" a story in time that portrays the child as dependent and in need of a great deal of instruction and protection. When children reject the ideas of their parents and resent the control of "overprotective" adults, they are sometimes viewed as rebellious, incorrigible, or perhaps even insane by parents who are living an outdated story. The child's behavior, which, in another context, would be seen as a normal adolescent stage, cannot be accepted as such until the story has been brought up to date.

Similarly, married clients whose stories fail to take into account that their spouses are continually growing and changing might say, "You're not the person I married!" The accusing spouse has failed to accommodate to the other's natural metamorphosis over time. When clients are caught in *outdated* stories, we must try to understand their reasons for clinging to the past. We might be tempted to say that they are attempting to return to a time that was happier, and our initial disconfirming response might be Thomas Wolfe's (1934/1998) admonition: *You Can't Go Home Again.* But what is the meaning involved in giving up an outdated story for the client? What is the consoling aspect of the old story that gives solace to the client? You must try to find out, lest you find yourself faced with a resistant client.

Rigidified stories are the result of adopting beliefs about how things are supposed to be and failing to take into account that life rarely fits well into ideal categories. A typical example of a rigidified story not fitting the experiences of some people is what might be called "the pursuit-of-happiness myth." People somehow get the idea that if one works hard, saves money, and obeys the laws of the land, then happiness will be an inevitable outcome. But many find that the harder they pursue happiness, the emptier they feel. Despite material success, many people experience an existential vacuum in which such success leaves them unsatisfied. On the other hand, many people set their goals so high as to be unattainable and, as a result, view themselves as unsuccessful.

We have all heard about the proverbial CEO of a Fortune 500 company, never stopping to smell the roses, who ends up disenchanted and disappointed. Buddha taught that people make themselves miserable by doggedly focusing on the attainment of their desired goals and failing to recognize the importance of the journey. So long as people remain aware that life is teleonomic, and not fully teleological, then they can modify a life story as their experience dictates. But if their story remains rigid, and their goals are a horizon that constantly moves away, they will suffer from an unfulfilled life. These people are often victims of social constructionist criteria that dictate the nature of success. They may have been taught that if, and only if, they attain certain levels of education, income, position, or marital status, they will be happy. Otherwise, they will have missed the mark. The paradoxical good news is that seeking these goals has not made them happy—which was the original goal—so you can help them search for a new scenario that might lead in the direction of happiness.

Many people suffer under *tragic* stories. When they construct stories in which they are unhappy protagonists who face ruinous outcomes, they tend to incorporate all new experiences into this plot. In your work with clients, you may find such tragic stories to be the most difficult. There is often a heroic quality to the role of the protagonist in tragedy, and clients are often reluctant to give up their roles. To be "long-suffering," for example, is to view oneself as bearing up in circumstances over which one has no control. Like Job in the Bible, when events cannot be changed by the protagonist, the heroic behavior of enduring the suffering may be seen by this person, as well as by others, as an admirable quality. In Chapter 8, we will discuss the dynamics that make it difficult for people to give up such stories.

Stories Needing Revision

There are other types of stories in need of revision that your clients may bring to counseling. Bertolino and O'Hanlon (2002) identified several common recurrent themes that need to be "re-storied" if clients are to achieve successful changes in their lives. These included stories of *invalidation, nonaccountability,* and *impossibility.*

When your clients use stories of *invalidation,* they cast themselves as fundamentally wrong or abnormal. They characterize their perspectives as out of touch with reality. "I shouldn't feel this way," or "I must be crazy to think this," or "She doesn't really mean anything she says," are examples of invalidating comments associated with this type of story.

In contrast with stories of invalidation, clients who rely continually on stories of *nonaccountability* portray themselves as hapless victims of overwhelming circumstances. Consequently, they claim that they should not be held responsible for their actions. Their accounts typically contain phrases such as "He made me do it," or "I was drunk," or "When she said that, I couldn't help but hit her." This type of story externalizes the responsibility for one's actions.

Stories of *impossibility* have as their main theme that there is little that people can do to truly change themselves or their situation. "What can you expect from a kid with a family like that?" and "Considering the chronic nature of this type of disorder, we cannot expect much change," are two comments that are often heard in impossibility stories.

Seligman (1991) pointed out that the stories your clients tell about bad events in their lives reflect their thinking. He identified three important dimensions to clients' explanatory styles that he labeled with the following alliterations: *permanence, pervasiveness,* and *personalization.*

Permanence is your client's belief that negative events will persist and will continue to affect one's life. Words like *always* and *never* reveal this attitude. In crisis situations, people may be rendered temporarily helpless, but those who bounce back see the situation simply as a momentary "punch in the stomach." On the other hand, those who harbor the permanence attitude will ruminate on the event. They nurse their grudges, sometimes allowing petty grievances to fester into emotional wounds and harboring feelings of resentment until they become rancorous and bitter.

The *pervasiveness* dimension is a generalization from the negative event. Words like *everything* and *nothing* are associated with this attitude. This style of attribution may cause people to "bleed all over everything." "They catastrophize. When one thread of their lives snaps, the whole fabric unravels. People who make *universal* explanations for their failures give up on everything . . ." (Bertolino & O'Hanlon, 2002, p. 46).

Personalization refers to whether one locates the blame for an event on self, others, or accidental circumstance. People who persistently self-blame tend to feel more helpless and hopeless in negative situations: "He hit me because I deserved it." But those who characteristically externalize blame are in no better position, because they are suggesting that they have no control in noxious situations: "She won't listen to anything I say. She is trying to give me a heart attack!" Externalizers will tend to be pessimistic and predict a future that will simply happen to them without their ability to shape it.

Those who have, as their default style, this negative attribution triad of permanence, pervasiveness, and personalization, tend to get depressed easily, underachieve, suppress the functioning of their immune systems, and take less pleasure from life. When you are attempting to help reconstruct people's narration of troubling events, you must pay attention to the words they use in the telling of the story. Words will reveal the attributions that people are placing on the event being discussed.

Where Limiting Stories Come From

The stories in which we live can imprison us. They can restrict the possibilities that we are able to envision for ourselves. You will remember that the root metaphor for our type of brief counseling is helping the fly out of the bottle. Oddly enough, Shira White (2002) cited research showing that if you capture ordinary houseflies and keep them in a jar for a few days and then remove the lid, most of them will *not* fly away. The lid is off, and their way is open to freedom, but the flies apparently "cannot think outside the jar," so to speak. They seem "committed" to remaining trapped. White suggested that this condition is like humans who have made what psychologists call a "premature cognitive commitment" that places their problems in a tight frame beyond which they cannot venture. This unfortunate commitment becomes a foreclosure on their future and keeps them contained within a limiting story. Life stories, and the beliefs that they entail, can be either liberating or oppressive. You can help your clients loosen the boundaries of their coercive stories so they can choose to free themselves from their subjugating beliefs.

Sometimes, when we hear clients tell stories that are holding them prisoner, we wonder where they could have gotten such limiting ideas. If you remember our discussion of "memes" as units of social construction, you can understand that ideas often take possession of us without our permission. Selfish memes are contagious (Lynch, 1996). They can infiltrate our thoughts and deterministically influence our life stories. Nunn (2005) pointed out that most of our stories are imposed on us: "They originate in our societies. We do have some choice about which ones we incorporate in ourselves, but the majority get into us whether we like it or not" (p. 188). Nunn emphasized the power of stories to shape our lives by suggesting that they are not *our* stories per se, but rather we are theirs. Two chapter titles in his book illustrated this assertion: "Stories and Their People" and "On Being a Story."

Nunn (2005) worried that the long tradition of uplifting stories that had previously existed in the myths and fairytales of our society were being replaced by "impoverished tales in the tabloid press, purveyors of TV banalities, trashy movies, sick computer games, and the like" (p. 191). Some time ago, social learning theorists warned that observing "models" performing antisocial behaviors tended to seduce onlookers into identifying with these actions. If the observed models have their behaviors rewarded, the observer will tend to adopt these same behaviors. Clients who have been influenced in this way may see themselves as outlaws or rebels on the fringe of society. They may identify with disaffected loners who seek revenge for real or imagined persecution or for the indifference of others to their plight. One example of this dynamic was the Columbine, Colorado, High School massacre in which two students who experienced themselves as outsiders adopted a "Goth" manner of dress and took revenge on their schoolmates for perceived insults directed at them. The story they were living had only one possible ending, so they committed suicide after killing many students.

Even socially constructed stories that are designed to help people live happier lives can become isolating and create social conflict. For example, some religious traditions that have as their central belief the humane treatment of other people may nevertheless develop what Lynch (1996) called the "adversive mode." Those who are "nonbelievers," "heretics," or "infidels" will be treated with contempt or pity, and social interaction with these people tends to be avoided. In extreme cases, war seems necessary in order to preserve the story that sustains their religious beliefs. In addition to becoming socially isolated, such religions also tend to refute new ideas that run counter to their beliefs. For example, Lynch (1996) wrote that "When Benjamin Franklin introduced the lightning rod, his idea seemed blasphemous to many clerics thundering from pulpits and presses—all because the populace still saw lightning as punishment from God" (p. 8).

People who have been raised in ghetto areas of the inner city, where poverty, violence, and drug abuse may be seen as the norm, are often living stories of limitation in which they see themselves as unable to participate in the American Dream. They may develop *adversive* attitudes that keep them from even wishing for another lifestyle, because that would mean identifying with the abusive dominant culture. Social welfare and other assistance programs are certainly useful for helping them maintain survival at a minimal level, but such programs do little to alter their story of degradation and isolation from the mainstream.

As we pointed out in the previous chapter, stories are largely socially constructed, and they are powerful influences on how clients see their futures. "Stories create our personhood and our worlds" (Lynch, 1996, p. 191). Stories of limitation portend a future with few prospects, and people attempting to free themselves from such stories are like Houdini struggling to get out of a straight jacket. Your clients will often present with stories that have isolated them from ideas that could be liberating for them, and you can help clients become open to new possibilities without triggering their "adversive" defenses. You do this by validating their stories while at the same time deconstructing it with a subtle wedge.

Making Sense of Narrative

People usually come to counseling ready to tell their troubling stories, and they do their best to offer up the upsetting facts in a narrative sequence. Initially, you probably do not need to ask many questions in order to hear their tale of anguish. You just need to be an empathic listener. Neimeyer (2000) stated that counselors should also listen for the narrative structure of the story in order to know how to help the client deconstruct and reconstruct it in more positive ways. The basic concepts of a narrative form are setting, characterization, plot, and themes. As you become sensitive to these components of storytelling, you will find clues in one or more of them for how to intervene.

Setting A narrative's *setting* is the account of the where and when of the story. It can be located in actual experience, an image, or a dream (Corey, 2005). It can be focused on either a past or future time or place. As you begin to deconstruct the client's narrative, it is important to hear about times when the concern was not happening or was less problematic, and to assume that the negative events do not take place in all settings and cultures. The client may tend to portray him- or herself as always the same in every situation, and the concerns as present everywhere in the world. Taking a multicultural perspective is particularly helpful in considering the setting for your client's story. "A common theme in competitive societies such as the United States, particularly common among people who have come in for counseling, is the theme of failure" (Blume, 2006, p. 191). Not being successful enough, and the shame associated with this belief, plagues many people in more individualistic cultures. However, this concern is rare in cultures that prize interdependence.

The question to ask is whether this belief applies to all situations and at all times. Counselor inquiries such as, "Tell me about a time when you did okay at that," or "What is something that you feel you do well?" or "Who is someone that believes in you?" serve to alter the setting of the story in which the client feels inadequate. You have now placed it in a more successful time or place or with more supportive people. A multicultural perspective enables your client to consider settings that offer a different, more liberating story for their lives.

Characterization In a narrative, the *characterization* is a portrayal of the players or actors. Usually, the client is the protagonist in the story. Others may be antagonistic or benign characters, predators or prey. The behaviors and motivations of the characters in the narrative are usually described. Everyone, including your client, is an amateur psychologist. We all conjure up "attributions" of why people do what they do. We believe that people are in some way *caused* to behave.

As clients tell their story, you should be alerted to what has come to be known as the *fundamental attribution error* (Jones & Nisbett, 1971). This concept refers to the fact that clients often explain their own behaviors as happening due to situational factors, but they may characterize the behavior of others as emanating from their personalities. Blume (2006) offered examples of both attributions: "'the traffic was so bad I couldn't help driving aggressively' [but] 'he's always blowing up at things, it takes nothing to set him off'" (p. 181). Both causal attributions explain aggressive behavior, but the fundamental attribution error separates their motivation. One couldn't help it, while the other is predisposed to such behavior. Clients often defensively externalize the responsibility for their actions. For this reason, the technique of externalization is quite useful for deconstructing narratives.

Plot The way the story has unfolded is its *plot*. Weingarten (2001) wrote that clients most often present with "regressive" or "illness" narratives. Everything is going wrong and the client is getting worse. Be careful to listen carefully and acknowledge the client's version of reality (listen, understand, and validate—LUV). File away the elements of the narrative, but do not jump too quickly in an attempt to deconstruct the story. "If one's illness story is not heard, the chaos and pain of the illness are compounded by isolation" (Blume, 2006, p. 190).

Occasionally, the story may be told in a haphazard manner, and episodes are disconnected. "Sometimes the therapist helps the client put the episodes together in a manner that is coherent to the client" (Corey, 2005, p. 577). As you will see, a well-constructed plot has a beginning, middle, and end. In regressive narratives, the end is an implied catastrophic or discouraging outcome.

As you attempt to clarify your understanding of the plot, ask the client to fill in gaps. Occasionally, you can creatively misunderstand and offer your veiled insight: "Oh, I see. You mean when he said that, you kept silent, but you really wanted to . . . ," or "If I'm getting this right, a lot of your identity is wrapped up in what she thinks of you." Simply forcing the client to construct the narrative so that the plot makes sense will serve to change some aspect of the story in the client's mind.

Themes   The narrative's *themes* are the meanings that the client creates by punctuating certain events and weaving them into a pattern of recurrent episodes. These themes include the client's view of the reasons that the events took place. "These themes may go undetected by many listeners, who are distracted by the fascinating events and colorful descriptions . . . [but] others who are familiar with a theme may pick up a recurring message—" (Blume, 2006, p. 191). If you do not listen for the message behind the message, you may be distracted by the content of the story and then be tempted to go sight seeing, probing for information merely out of curiosity.

The episodes in your client's story convey a theme that may be contained in metaphors or repeated words. Certain verbs with prepositions, such as *put down, blown off, let down, left out,* or *passed up,* usually support a negative theme in our culture. But do not simply assume you know what theme these phrases point to. "What is the meaning for the storyteller? What is the client's emotional experience in telling the story? It is the client's understanding of the story, not the therapist's, that is the focus" (Corey, 2005, p. 578).

EXPERIENCING THIS IDEA

Think of a poem or piece of prose that you wrote at some time in your life under the influence of some inspiring muse. Remember the ecstasy (which is from the Greek for *crazy*) you felt when you had finished it? Remember also how compelled you felt to find an audience? And remember how crushed you were if they seemed only to wait to talk, rather than to really listen as you read your work to them?

Narrative Therapy

Narrative therapy is most closely tied to the work of David Epston and Michael White, two psychotherapists from "Down Under." Epston is from New Zealand, and White hails from Australia. Epston started out as an anthropologist, which he said gave him an "intellectual poaching license" and "disrespect for 'disciplinary' boundaries" (White &

Epston, 1990, p. xvi). White traced his own interest in psychotherapy to the writings of Gregory Bateson, himself a poaching anthropologist. Epston and White have emphasized the importance and the power of written communication in therapy. They often used letters, proclamations, and certificates, for example, in their work with clients.

The core of narrative therapy is the constructivist view that all knowing is an act of interpretation. In order for one to change one's narrative, he or she must receive "news of a difference" (Bateson, 1979). In other words, the client must incorporate new information into the narrative, resulting in an alteration of the plot. A narrative is a metaphorical map, never the territory. Have you ever seen one of those old maps that showed what the country looked like before it had been completely explored? Imagine trying to find your way across the country with one of those maps! Furthermore, try finding the interstate highways on a map that was published in 1950! These highways did not exist at that time. Even the road map that you used on your last vacation probably has errors and omissions. Moreover, a map that you can hold in your hand is quite small as compared with the territory it represents. Likewise, personal narratives always leave out important details.

When you ask clients for their stories, you are asking them to put themselves into the role of the story's protagonist and to "perform" the story as if you were the theatergoer and the client were giving a one-person show. In this process, not only must the story be retold, it must be re-experienced. Each time people retell stories, they have reauthored them. "The evolution of lives is akin to the process of reauthoring, the process of persons entering into stories, taking them over and making them their own" (White & Epston, 1990, p. 13).

Your first act is *witnessing*—you become the audience and set the stage for change. Your client, as performer of the story, reads your reactions as the audience and makes adjustments according to how you are receiving the performance. From the client's standpoint, things that seem to go over well may be kept in, while the clunkers may be marked for a rewrite.

Metaphors and the Stories of Our Lives

People use metaphors to help shape their experiences into the stories of their lives. When you first engage with your clients, they typically want to tell you their stories of tragedy and despair. Your initial task is to listen carefully, acknowledge their stories empathically, and look for the metaphors they use to describe both their pain and their longing to find relief.

Just what is a metaphor, anyway? How does it differ from a statement of fact? What is the value of a metaphor to anyone besides a poet or artist? According to Sheldon Kopp (1985), there are only three basic ways of knowing. The first is rational, which involves our use of logic and scientific reasoning. The second way is empirical, which is achieved through our sense perceptions. And finally, the third way of knowing is metaphorical, which offers an intuitive grasp of situations and their coexisting multiple meanings.

In general, conceptual metaphor theory takes the position that people make sense of abstract concepts and events through concrete experiences (Wickman & Campbell, 2003). For example, you can see life as a journey, a person as a traveler, a goal as a destination, the

means for achieving it as a road, difficulties as roadblocks, choices as crossroads, and counselors as traveling companions (Bulkeley & Bulkeley, 2005).

People normally think of metaphor as a literary device in which one thing is expressed
in terms of another. For example, one person may be described as having "a heart of stone,"
while another is "a breath of fresh air." Metaphors are comparisons that illuminate. They
have a figurative, poetic quality about them. While English teachers may decry our lack of
precision, the authors of this book lump all these comparisons, such as similes, aphorisms,
idioms, proverbs, and analogies, under the general heading of metaphoric language. The results of two studies can help you appreciate the pervasiveness of idioms. An analysis of political debates, psychotherapy sessions, and other forms of communication found that
people used about four idioms each minute (Pollio, Barlow, Fine, & Pollio, 1977). Another
study found that idioms were even more frequent in television programs and that compre-
hending their meaning was crucial to understanding the plots (Cooper, 1998).

EXPERIENCING THIS IDEA: THE METAPHOR READINESS QUIZ

Below are 10 common statements that clients make. Following each statement are two
possible interpretations. Check the metaphorical interpretation of the client's communication. Once you have completed the quiz, determine your readiness score by following the scoring instructions.

1. "I've been down in the dumps lately."
   _____Recently, I have been spending my time at the landfill.
   _____Lately, I have been feeling depressed.
2. "She's such a princess."
   _____That young woman is the daughter of a king and queen.
   _____She is spoiled and feels entitled.
3. "He's been keeping me at arm's length."
   _____That person has maintained a proximity of about one yard.
   _____He has been emotionally detached from me.
4. "I have a bone to pick with you."
   _____I am inviting you to share a meat dish with me.
   _____I have a complaint regarding your behavior.
5. "I guess I wear my heart on my sleeve."
   _____The organ that pumps my blood is situated on the garment that covers
   my arm.
   _____I show my feelings easily.
6. "It was just a case of sour grapes."
   _____The legal matter brought before the judge concerned berries that were tart.
   _____The person devalued something she desired after not getting it.
7. "Well, now it's going to get down and dirty."
   _____We presently are descending into an area that is soiled and grimy.
   _____People will soon become combative and unrestrained.

8. "What a pain in the ass!"

_____ My goodness, I certainly have a soreness in the buttocks region.

_____That person is extremely annoying.

9. "You should never look a gift horse in the mouth."

_____Avoid inspecting the oral cavity of any equine present.

_____When you are given something, don't be ungrateful.

10. "Well, I could read the handwriting on the wall."

_____I am an adept interpreter of graffiti.

_____I am aware of signals that portend bad news.

Scoring: All second statements are metaphorical interpretations, so give yourself 1 point for each correct answer. A score of 10 indicates you are on top of your game. A score of 8 or 9 indicates that you are knocking at the door of success. A score of 7 or below indicates that you are not quite ready for prime time. (Of course you noticed the metaphorical nature of each of these three outcomes.)

Fuzzy Metaphors

Metaphors are, by definition, "fuzzy" thinking and are literally false (MacCormac, 1985), but "like poetry . . . metaphors can express emotive meaning; the tension that they produce is the very expression of meaning" (p. 26). Using his own colorful metaphors, Hofstadter (2006) asserted that analogy is at the center of human thought. He called analogy "the very blue that fills the whole sky of cognition—analogy is *everything,* or very nearly so, in my view."

Strictly speaking, a metaphor is not factually correct, but if a person suspends disbelief, a metaphor can have the ring of truth and the clarity of real enlightenment. A cardiac specialist, for example, can assure us that it is not possible for someone to literally have "a heart of stone." However, if we have experienced this person as unfeeling, unloving, and uncharitable, we will stand by our metaphor as true, even if it's not medically accurate. Another important point about metaphors is that their meaning may not be immediately obvious, and their initial ambiguity is often the source of metaphors' emotional clout. The evocative nature of metaphors compels one to reflect and mull over their message until they are "digested," or incorporated into the experience of the listener. Kuang Ming-Wu (2001) stated that using metaphors is an effective way to communicate across cultures by building a highway of communication where there is no previously shared way of thinking. He called this method of understanding a "cultural hermeneutic."

Experiencing This Idea

You can sensitize yourself to metaphoric speech simply by making it a habit to "tune in" and listen for metaphors in everyday conversation. Metaphors, however, may present problems for those who wish to think precisely. If you consider yourself to be "metaphorically challenged," you can loosen up and stretch your thinking a bit by using the following recipe for constructing a metaphor.

Just remember that a metaphor is simply associating one idea with another that normally would not seem to be related. For this exercise, join with three or four colleagues to form a small practice group. Take turns selecting one of the concepts below and linking it to a different object in the room. Once you have paired the concept with an object, explain their metaphoric relationship to your colleagues. For example, you might say, "Depression is like that reclining chair, because the longer you lie in it, the more difficult it is to get out of." Or, you might say, "Anxiety is like this carpet, because you worry what sort of vermin might be lurking in it." Continue taking turns until you have completed the entire list.

Problems are like _____, because _____.

Solutions are like _____, because _____.

Counselors are like _____, because _____.

The future is like _____, because _____.

The past is like _____, because _____.

Relationships are like _____, because _____.

Worries are like _____, because _____.

Parents are like _____, because _____.

Friends are like _____, because _____.

Happiness is like _____, because _____.

Anger is like _____, because _____.

Once you have completed this activity, take some time with your colleagues to discuss the experience. What reactions, such as curiosity, emotion, surprise, or laughter, did you have to the metaphors of others? What intriguing parallels did you discover? How would your group process have differed if you had engaged in a rational or empirical discussion of these concepts?

Implications of These Ideas for the Counselor

The ideas of meaning making and narrative can have significant consequences on your work as a counselor:

- Narrative knowing is metaphoric and constructed. People organize their meaning into narrative life stories that are not "true" in the logical sense, but are the stuff of the way we develop our world hypotheses. There is more power in a story than in a fact.
- As a counselor, you can help clients alter the outdated, rigidified, and tragic plots of their lives in two important ways: You can serve as the audience for their retelling of the story, and then you can help the client to reauthor the story in ways that lead to resolution.
- You need to tune into your client's metaphors because they provide not only an empathic bridge for you to form a therapeutic alliance but also material for co-constructing a story of resolution.

TOOLS

Externalizing "Problems"

There are two meanings of the term *externalization*. The first meaning describes the defensive style of a client who takes no responsibility for the problem situation and who blames everyone else. This style is similar to the fundamental attribution error discussed above. Parents fostering a sense of personal responsibility are particularly skilled in smoking out this defensive style and insisting that their children "own up" and accept that the problem lies within them. Teaching accountability rather than blaming others is their goal.

The second meaning of externalization—and the one emphasized here—is that it is desirable for you to help clients separate their problems from their self-image. When your clients identify with their problems, they can feel discouraged and disheartened about the possibility of changing (Blume, 2006). This externalization technique, developed by Michael White (1988) is meant to keep the client from identifying with the problem. The motto is, "The person is never the problem—the problem is the problem."

There are several advantages to adopting this attitude regarding the difference between the client and the problem. First, the client usually comes to counseling already trying to externalize the problem, so this technique fits with the client's portrayal of the story. Second, the client may feel powerless to control the problem, and may feel guilty for not being able to overcome it. This dynamic usually results in a sense of shame for the client. Problem one is the problem; problem two is inability to rise above the problem. Third, by characterizing the problem as external, the counselor can enter into a "conspiracy" with the client against the problem, inviting more cooperation. This type of intervention increases the strength of the working relationship. Finally, the client can achieve a sense of agency as he or she battles the external problem. This action avoids the defeating diagnostic merging of client and problem—"I *am* a Conduct Disorder, this is what I do," or "I *have* depression, I can't help myself"—which robs the client of a sense of personal agency.

Based on O'Hanlon's (1995) suggestions, the procedure for externalizing the problem involves several simple steps.

• Begin by speaking of the problem, even naming it, as if it were an *entity* that is plaguing the client. For example, you can personify the problem or characterize it as having a mind of its own. You may refer to jealousy as a "green monster," anger as "blind rage," or depression as a "blue funk." You will find that clients often come to counseling having coined their own metaphorical terms. In this case, use the clients' terms. As you listen to their characterization of the difficulty, you can often get a clue from their label for it. You will remember that in our discussion of metaphor we said that using the client's own metaphors is far more effective than your attempting to come up with one that fits.

• Next, characterize the problem as having *malevolent* motives. In other words, the problem "desires" the downfall of the client by trying to get him or her to think or do certain things. It is important, however, not to accept the narrative as the problem "making" the client feel or behave in negative ways. You are attempting to co-construct a story in which the problem might "sneak up on the client" or "whisper in the client's ear," but you do not want the story to convey the idea that the client is powerless in the face of such events. Sometimes, when the client describes a feeling of low self-esteem or incompetence, you might ask, "When you hear that voice telling you that you don't measure up or that you will never succeed, whose voice is it?" Very often, the client will name a parent or another significant person who has repeatedly sent the message that the client is a "loser." Whether you are able to personify the message as coming from a particular person or as just a vague message, you have already externalized the problem entity from the client.

• Third, continue the externalizing procedure by asking the client about the *ways* in which this external entity attempts to fool, influence, trick, or seduce the client into certain thoughts or behaviors. For example, you might ask, "What does that voice say when it tries to get you to feel bad about yourself or attempt to sway you toward the belief that you will not be successful?" As you carry out this process, be sure *not* to give the problem the power to *cause* the client's behavior—only to suggest or influence it.

• Fourth, ask presumptively about the times when the problem has attempted to influence the client and the client has *ignored* the problem or forged ahead in spite of this attempted manipulation. For example, you might ask a child who has problems with anger, "When have you told that temper tantrum to take a hike?" It is important to inquire about a time when the problem tried, but failed, to alter the client's mood or behavior.

• Finally, once the client has identified an exception, ask, "*How did you get yourself to do that?*" You can also explore details of a future in which the client will be dealing successfully with this externalized problem. Perhaps you could say something like, "So, a year from now, after our work has been successful enough for you to regularly resist this negative influence, what strategy will you have developed to weaken its power and keep it at bay?" Then, you might ask a client, "Which one of your friends would be the first to notice these changes? What would this person say to you about these differences?"

Externalizing the problem can be a very powerful tool in your attempt to influence the client to tell his or her story in a different way. Kleinke (1994) pointed out that we are continually attempting, as counselors, to increase the client's sense of efficacy in the face of a situation he or she has defined as a problem, and in which a sense of helplessness has formerly prevailed. No matter what school of therapy you subscribe to or what your personal biases may be, your primary aim is to help clients toward a sense of freedom. You want to help the client realize a sense of "I can" (Kleinke, 1994, p. 34).

When you seek exceptions to the client narrative through the use of the externalization technique, you help clients to realize that the problem is not them, not "I *am*." Furthermore, not only might they come to believe "I *can*," but also they might realize, once they have rediscovered their past success experiences, "I *already have*." Clients overcome their problems often. There are many times when problems are *not* happening. It is your job to help clients remember and include in their stories these times, and to get back in touch with the successful strategies they were using to prevent the problem from influencing them.

LISTENING IN ON A SESSION

Review the story at the beginning of the chapter. A resolution-focused counselor might work to externalize Dub's concerns in the following way.

William: (After the counselor introduces himself, William explains that his nickname has been Dub all his life, but that he would like for the counselor to call him William. When the counselor invites William to talk about what he would like to get out of counseling, William tilts his head slightly and gazes out the window.)

"To tell you the truth, I don't even know exactly why I made this appointment. That's one of my problems, I guess. I just don't think I know *anything* anymore. I didn't even know how to introduce myself to you. I'm sick of being called Dub, but people give me such crap when I've asked them to call me William. They act like I'm putting on airs and trying to act superior or grown-up. Some are nice about it and call me William once or twice, but then they slip back into Dub. I feel guilty about bugging them, so I just say to myself, "Aw, to hell with it. Why should I make such a big deal over this. I mean, what do I know?"

(He shrugs his shoulders dismissively and pauses before he begins with a new idea.)

"What's totally weird about this is that I used to be kind of a smart-ass, know-it-all guy when I was in college. I really got off on showing people how much I knew about motorcycles or NASCAR or music, even sports trivia. But now, I don't know crap. I don't know why I'm here. I don't know who I am, and I sure as hell don't know where I'm going with my life."

Counselor: "So, lately, your life has been feeling like a real mystery to you and you've decided that it's finally time to look for some answers."

William: (He nods his head slightly and smiles wryly.)

"Yeah, it's like I'm searching for something, but I have no idea what it is, or where it is, or even if I'll recognize it when I find it."

(He pauses and waves off that idea.)

"Wait a second, that's not exactly it, either. It's like for my whole life, y'know, I've been riding along this highway. Don't get me wrong, it's been a pretty fun ride, but now I'm wondering if this is the highway I'm really meant to be on. I don't even know where this highway's taking me. Maybe I want to turn on a different road for a change."

Counselor: "So it's like there's a traffic cop that keeps directing you on down that old, familiar highway. He doesn't care about where *you* really want to go—he just wants to keep traffic moving down that highway and he even wants you to keep your old name on your driver's license. What's this traffic cop been telling you to keep you traveling down that same highway?"

William: "Oh, he'll say that my friends will wonder, 'Who the hell does Dub think he is?' or he'll say something like, 'Dub, why don't you come along with your friends?'"

> **Counselor:**   "Tell me about the times that you've been able to follow your own road and not listen to this traffic cop."
>
> **William:**   "Well, I guess that instead of tinkering with my Harley or partying, which is what I always used to do in my spare time, I've been keeping to myself more and tinkering with my mind lately. I try to put all this crap I'm going through into my music."

REFLECTING QUESTIONS

1. How has William shaped his story?
2. How has the counselor used externalization?
3. How might you respond to William's last statement?

USING THIS TOOL

Divide into groups of three. One of you volunteers to share some present concern. Another volunteers to listen, understand, validate, and, when appropriate, help the client externalize the problem. Finally, the third person serves as the recorder who observes the activity and leads the feedback discussion.

Life Stories and Metaphors

Schank (1995) said that when people are faced with universal human concerns we sometimes speak about them in proverbs or what he called "culturally common stories." Douglas Hofstadter (2006) referred to these proverbs as "situation labels" and suggested that we keep hundreds of them tucked away in our unconsciousness to explain difficult situations to others.

As we reflect on our life stories, we humans tend to view ourselves as the protagonist within the sphere of our life. Life itself, in order to be successful, must be lived meaningfully. Truly fulfilled individuals not only participate fully in life but also strive for personal understanding of "what it's all about." Religion and science can provide helpful guidance and information for us along the path, but, in the final analysis, we make our own lives—we write our own stories.

Stories are, by their very nature, metaphors. Metaphors have a loose structure, so an individual can supply the meaning. The metaphor is a powerful teaching tool because it invites the listener to bring his or her own emotional experience to the understanding of it. Jesus, for example, used metaphors as devices with which to teach. "Instead of putting forward his teachings in scholarly texts, Jesus spoke in metaphors and parables. Bible scholars counted 65 of them in the four gospels" (Ehrenwald, 1986, p. 257). Parables and allegories are useful ways to teach moral lessons. They exist in many forms of literature, from mythology to Aesop's fables. When Shakespeare said that all the world was a stage and all the men and women players, he opened up a parallel system for understanding the structure of events which take place among humans. It is when metaphors parallel life events that they add to our meaning.

As you begin to listen to your clients' stories, they will be teaching you about their lives. You can employ their metaphors to open up their restricted accounts so that there is room for fresh meaning and new realizations.

USING THIS TOOL

Writing down a client's metaphors is a useful strategy so that you can use the exact words when acknowledging his or her concerns. The main thing to remember is that you are not collecting facts or data in the way a scientist would do, but, rather, you are collecting metaphorical insights into your client's world.

Join with two colleagues to form a practice group. One of you volunteers to talk for about 5 minutes about a recent experience that stirred up some emotions, either positive or negative. Another volunteers to actively listen for metaphors and take notes. Finally, the third person serves as the recorder who observes the activity and leads the discussion of the process. Now switch roles until everyone has had an opportunity to practice.

Responding to Conceptions, Descriptions, and Associations

Freud (1911) distinguished between two modes of thought: primary and secondary process. Primary process is metaphoric, visual, irrational, and "timeless, contradiction-less, permitting opposites to be maintained simultaneously . . . mostly pictorial or imagistic rather than verbal . . . metaphor is deeply rooted in the primary process" (Siegelman, 1990, p. 10). Secondary process, on the other hand, is a rational mode of thought. "Words are used denotatively rather than connotatively: The meaning is narrowed down as precisely as possible . . . Something cannot be itself and not-itself at the same time" (p. 10). Since client stories contain both modes of thought, you can consider narratives as existing along a continuum from metaphorical narratives (deeply primary) to rational narratives (objectively secondary). On this continuum, metaphors are expressed as primary process *associations,* facts are expressed as mid-level *descriptions,* and rules are expressed as secondary process *conceptions.* People who are held prisoner by their rules cannot see a way to escape. They are like those flies in the lidless jar that have accepted their fate.

When clients tell their stories, they often make assertions in the form of propositions regarding the "truth" of their situations that tend to create negative predictions for their futures. For example, the proposition, "Without a college education, you can't be a success in life," must be logically either true or false. If you were to hear your client making such a statement, and you believe it to be false, you might be tempted to argue with the client and point out someone like the billionaire Bill Gates who never finished college. But argumentation is not counseling. Client *conceptions* are the categorical rules that clients have interpreted from their experiences, and these rules tend to be absolute, rigid, and powerful determiners of client attitudes. They amount to "hardening of the categories." Never allow yourself to be drawn into a debate regarding the client's conceptions, although it is ultimately these conceptions that you are attempting to change.

At the next level down are *descriptions*. When you enter the conversation by asking the client for descriptions of experiences that have led to the stated conceptions, you are more likely to get concrete responses that are amenable to your attempts at story revision. At this level, you do not have to deal with as many propositional assertions, because the client is trying to give you the facts. As clients offer descriptions of their experiences, you can ask for details that might alter the story: You can "misunderstand" by changing the labels or frames of the story, or you can attempt to call out facts (exceptions) that run counter to the negative story. The very experience of telling the story, with you as the appreciatively inquiring audience, will change the way the client tells it without your having to do much of anything to influence change, so long as you try to reduce conceptions to descriptions.

When clients use metaphors (associations) in the telling of a story, they often do so with little awareness that they are expressing this type of primary process thought. Metaphors are generally implicit and much closer to the client's emotions and sensory experience than either descriptions or conceptions. For example, anger is "hot," happiness is "light," sadness is "heavy" or "dark," and so on. While the client's conceptions may have created a limiting story, if you ask instead for descriptions and associations, the story will tend to loosen up and contain more possibilities. Conceptions are the "rules," descriptions are the "facts," and associations are the "experiences." Conceptions that are hard categories cannot be directly altered. For example, try arguing someone out of his or her political or religious beliefs. But changing the facts and experiences can soften conceptions. Since metaphors are associational primary processes, and are therefore "contradictionless," you can couple your positive metaphorical response with the client's negative metaphor without having to argue the point. "Down" can seek to be "up," "dark" can seek to be "light," "dirty" can seek to be "clean," etc. Metaphors do not exist as "either-or" in the way that conceptions and their propositions do. Freud (1911) said that there is no "no" in primary process thought.

Here we offer our suggestion for how to work with client stories: Ask for *descriptions* of all *conceptions* and tune into client metaphorical *associations* while trying to turn them in a positive direction.

Listening for Client Metaphors

The personal metaphor someone adopts tends to color everything that takes place within the narrative space that is his or her particular life (DeJong, 2004). Think for a minute about the root metaphor you use to summarize life. What is it? Here is a possible list of some of the positions that people might adopt: Life can be viewed as a trial, mythic quest, cross to bear, accident of nature, box of chocolates, battle, journey, veil of tears, a bitch and then you die, gift, curse, mystery, problem to solve, learning process, blessing, or losing proposition. Is your own metaphor for life among these? Perhaps just considering this list will help sensitize you to the fact that each of us carries with us a summary idea in the form of metaphor for our lives, our problems, and our hopes and dreams.

Most of the time we are unaware of our own metaphors, and we are even less conscious of those of others. Therefore, you must deliberately listen for the metaphors of your clients in order to truly hear their experience of the situations they are reporting. They may mention that their life concern is like being caught in a trap, drowning, suffocating, or trying to climb a mountain. We might overlook such metaphors because, as Siegelman (1990) put it, "These clichés may have been born out of bodily experience that was once vivid and compelling. But now the figures appear worn out—like coins so thumbed one can scarcely distinguish the buffalo's head on the old nickel" (p. 45).

Client metaphors can range between "pale" and "vivid" in terms of the emotions they immediately summon for the person using them (Wright, 1976). A pale metaphor has become *cliché*, a French term that refers to a stereotype plate used in printing multiple pages. In other words, a pale metaphor is one so worn and familiar that the meaning and impact may be lost on both the client and the counselor. But even such automatic metaphors may simply be slumbering (Siegelman, 1990). You must listen for, and note, the metaphors used by your clients as they describe their concerns. Then, you need to employ their exact terms in your feedback, while seeking alternative congruent metaphors that will enhance the possibility of resolution of your clients' negative narratives.

When client metaphors turn from negative narratives of discouragement to positive metaphors of longing, then it becomes your job to capitalize on these novel metaphors and help expand them. Siegelman (1990) called such novel turns "key metaphors," and she suggested that you do little more than stay with these metaphors to encourage their continued use in the client narrative. As she describes the process, "It is more a question of attentive receptivity. I often feel I am functioning as midwife, 'catching' the psychological baby as it emerges" (p. 78).

USING THIS TOOL

In order to give you a better idea of the terms you will be looking for in client talk, we have put together a short list of the metaphors that clients sometimes use to depict themselves. These are such common expressions that you can complete them by filling in the blanks.

"I don't have any more options. My life is a _____ end."

"I allow people to treat me like a _____ mat."

"When I get angry, I can't help blowing off _____ ."

"I'm so overwhelmed. I can't keep my head above _____ ."

"I'm caught between a _____ and a _____ place."

Once metaphors such as these have become summary ideas, they are then conceptions that color the client's story, and they dictate behaviors and expectations. These conceptions must be deconstructed so that alternative responses are possible.

Working With Client Metaphors

Many client metaphors involve the body. According to Siegelman (1990), the body is equated with the self more than any other object, and this leads to what Lakoff (1987) called the bodily kinesthetic schema of "the container." For example, when we are "full," we tend to be satisfied, but when we are "empty," we tend to experience ourselves as in need. On the other hand, someone else might consider us to be "full of ourselves," or "full of crap." They may also see us as "empty headed" or in some way deficient—"one brick short of a load." When we are "hot," we tend to feel unsatisfied. We may lust after someone, or we are angry and want to lash out by "fuming" or "blowing our cork." When we are "cool," we are content with our image or we are in control of our emotions—"chilled out." Furthermore, the various sensations involving the locations or positions of our bodies can be metaphors for our psychological state. We may be "backsliding," "falling," "feeling down," or we may be "flying," "lighter than air," or "cruising." We may be "crushed" or "ten feet tall." Clients will produce such metaphors without fully realizing that these are not literal descriptions. From these metaphors, you will be able to pick up clues as to their experience of the world.

Your job as a counselor is to become more sensitive to metaphorical expression than you currently are. You fine-tune your instrument so that clients' metaphors become more obvious to you as you hear the story they are telling. Then, you use their metaphors to help co-construct a less limiting narrative.

USING THIS TOOL

Think of some recent event that stirred up some significant emotions, positive and negative, for you. What are these emotions, and what part of the body might be most involved in feeling or expressing these emotions? For example, expressing anger might be "giving someone a piece of my mind," or feeling annoyed might be considered to be having a "pain in the neck."

Generate a list of five metaphorical phrases that involve emotions and their location in the body. The main thing is to begin to think in metaphorical, rather than logical, conceptual terms.

1. _____
2. _____
3. _____
4. _____
5. _____

Opening up your own mind to new possibilities will help the client to do the same. Not only will the client be able to find new cognitive connections, but he or she will be helped to get in touch with his or her emotions in a less threatening way. Metaphors tend to place emotions in an "as if" context and thus make them easier to talk about. As Caruth and Ekstein (1966) put it, "like the repartee of the cocktail party, [a metaphor] permits a kind of freedom and license which is recognized by both parties to be meant and not meant at the same time" (p. 38).

Capturing Client Metaphors

Emotions are more closely connected to metaphor than to other forms of language. Siegelman (1990) stated that this deep connection exists because the experience of the emotion is bodily and nonverbal in the first place—a primary process experience—and ordinary language is inadequate for its expression. One has only to consider that people rarely speak in complete sentences when making love or expressing rage to realize the primitive nature of what is being felt. Clients who are in crisis will be experiencing emotions intensely, and their language will not always make logical sense. As you listen to the metaphors clients use to describe their situation, you will discover that they are often metaphors of loss, failure, guilt, and anguish. These metaphors will predominate the conversation. You should also expect to hear metaphors of longing: the way they wish things could have been, the way things used to be, or the way they wish things will work out. You can then use their negative metaphors when acknowledging with LUV and their longing metaphors when attempting to enhance the images of their future.

In Chapter 11, we will discuss how you can construct a metaphor to use as an indirect influencing technique. This procedure usually comes after the "consulting break."

LISTENING IN ON A SESSION

Review the story at the beginning of the chapter and the two previous dialogues between William and his counselor in earlier sections. At this point in the session, a resolution-focused counselor might highlight William's metaphors in the following way.

William: (He sighs.)

"I never had any illusions that I was going to be making a living from my music. That's really OK with me. I was just hoping that I might make some sense out of my life's journey with the music. I tried to be honest and realistic with it, 'cause that way maybe I could find something out about who I am. But my music's turned into a total dead end—just like my whole life. It's all been really depressing. I mean, what's the point? At least before, when I was in college, I was heading somewhere, but now I'm just stuck and going nowhere fast."

Counselor: "With all these feelings that your music's come to a dead end and that you're stuck in a life that seems pointless, how in the world did you get yourself to make the decision to come in here and search for some answers?"

William: "I really don't know for sure. Maybe it had something to do with how I feel when I do hang in there long enough to come up with at least a chord or phrase that seems to ring true for me. There's something in here (William taps his chest.) that tells me I've got to keep on keepin' on. I told myself that talking with a counselor might be another way of coming up with something else that rings true."

REFLECTING QUESTIONS

1. Circle the metaphors that William used in telling his story.
2. What metaphors did the counselor use in responding to the client?
3. Write a possible counselor response to James's last statement.

The Charismatic Use of Metaphors

Erickson, Rossi, and Rossi (1976) believed that the therapeutic use of metaphor and analogy created a far more powerful message for the client than direct explanation. The mechanism for this was seen as unconscious re-patterning and the subsequent ability to view something differently. If clients' metaphors are negative, it might be possible for you to become a spin doctor for them. Spin doctors are political spokespersons who follow up on speeches and debates by placing the most euphemistic interpretation on what has taken place. Successful spin doctors, preachers, teachers, and counselors are charismatic, a word that comes from the Greek word meaning *gift of grace*. The "Graces" of mythology were goddesses who brought joy and beauty to human lives. In the New Testament of the Bible, Paul speaks of charisma as the possession of spiritual gifts from God, such as prophesy, the working of miracles, and the gift of healing.

You can charismatically use metaphors in several ways. First, you can identify the metaphors your client uses in the story and employ them in your acknowledgments. Second, you can put a spin on your client's metaphor, changing the portrayal in some positive way. Third, you may compare the client's situation and its resolution to some well-known situation, for example, playing tennis, climbing a mountain, or building a house. Better yet, you might find something that greatly interests your client and build a metaphor on that topic.

It is not necessary to get fancy with the use of metaphors. If you are sensitive to the client's metaphors and you think about the client's situation in metaphorical terms, the appropriate metaphors will naturally come. Sometimes phrases from well-known literature or popular songs are found by clients to be compelling, so long as you are not delivering them pedantically.

SUMMARY

In this second of three chapters dealing with meaning, we portrayed clients as storytellers. A narrative perspective emphasizes your important role of bearing witness to your client's experiences as the audience of the story. It also alerts you to key elements of stories, including setting, characterization, plot, and themes. The narrative tools include externalization and using metaphors. Finally, taking a narrative perspective reminds you of the power of story to transform our life experiences into meaning, which is the focus of Chapter 8.

SEGUE TO CHAPTER 8

Think of those times in your life when you have "lost yourself" in something that completely involved you. What were you doing at the time? Did you find the experience rewarding? What changed in your way of viewing things as a result of this experience?

Resource

The Brief and Narrative Therapy Network (BNTN)
www.brieftherapynetwork.com

BNTN offers information on training opportunities, sponsors a listserv for interested participants, publishes interviews with brief and narrative therapists, and promotes the *Journal of Systemic Therapies.*

CHAPTER 8

Meaningful Stories, Meaningful Lives

"Meaning, not raw facts, is what humanity seeks."
Alvin Kernan

CHAPTER GOALS

Reading about and experiencing the ideas in this chapter will help you to understand the following concepts:

- Meaning gives significance to our lives.
- Our level of happiness has much more to do with our personal character than our life circumstances.
- Events, particularly crises and traumas, can challenge our basic assumptions about life.

Reading about and practicing the tools in this chapter will help you to learn these valuable skills:

- Using appreciative inquiry to explore for strengths.
- Questioning discrepancies in meanings.
- Honoring your client's transderivational searches.

STORY

Even though there were closer ones on the aisle, John spotted the one empty window seat near the back of the crowded bus and squeezed his husky frame into it. He sat by the window whenever possible because he liked to absentmindedly gaze outside as the bus lumbered along. The muffled bits of conversation he overheard, the scenes of street life flashing by, and the rhythm of the bus made such a hypnotic combination that John typically relaxed to the point of falling asleep. But today there was too much on his mind for relaxing. Instead, he soon found himself entering a deep reverie.

On doctor's orders, John was on his way to his first appointment with a counselor. Since his heart attack 9 months ago, John has made regular follow-up appointments and endured countless medical tests to keep his truck-driving license. At his last check-up, his doctor was worried because John's health had deteriorated markedly. When the doctor questioned him, John admitted that he was no longer following the strict nutrition and exercise regimen that he had religiously observed for 6 months. John confided that it didn't seem to be worth the effort since his third wife had left him. That's when the doctor laid down the law. Unless John agreed to attend a heart attack survivors' support group, eat better, exercise regularly, and see a counselor, the doctor would not permit John to drive his rig.

Unlike any other truck driver he knew, John enjoyed riding public transportation. Letting someone else worry about driving felt so luxurious to him. But this day was different. John felt humiliated, ashamed, and outraged that he was being ordered to see a counselor. At one point, he was jolted by a sudden fantasy that he would be interrogated, judged, and found guilty by the counselor of ruining his marriages, abandoning friendships, and destroying his health. John's punishment would have to fit the crimes, so since he had lost everything else, he would surely lose his job. The only other time John had felt this scared, and had so much at stake, was over 40 years ago.

As the bus carried him to his current destination, that entire episode of years ago began to replay itself with the vivid detail of a video. It was the fall of 1956. General Dwight D. Eisenhower had just been reelected President, and the Korean Conflict had ended, but the United States now found strife within its own society. For the first time in history, the "teenage" years were considered a distinct and troubled age—rock and roll was in its infancy, teens dressed in outrageous costumes, and *Rebel Without a Cause* was in the movie theaters.

Although it was a school day, and a desolate November one at that, John had awakened chuckling to himself. He was celebrating a rare victory over his hypervigilant mother. Tonight he finally would be allowed to stay overnight at Leo's house. After two weeks of conniving, he had convinced his mother to accept two outrageous falsehoods. The first lie was that he and Leo were assigned to work together on a project in Mrs. McCormack's Latin class that was sure to take all of Friday night and most of Saturday to finish. The second untruth was that those rumors about Leo's wild adventures were largely unfounded. If the truth were told, Leo and John had secretly finished the project earlier in the week, and Leo was indeed the master of his unsupervised universe.

After school, the boys played pinball, drank cherry Cokes at the drug store, shot three games of snooker at the bowling alley, and made themselves *personae non gratae,* as their Latin teacher would say, at cheerleader practice in the school gymnasium—all before 5 o'clock. On the way to Leo's house, they stopped at a playground and began an impromptu game of follow-the-leader on the jungle gym. As they tried to outdo each other with various gravity-defying contortions, a young, slightly built 7th-grade girl brushed past them. Leo called after her in that taunting way that only 14-year-old boys can do justice to, "Hey, little girl, where are you going in such a hurry?" She seemed upset and wailed over her shoulder, "Just shut up, Leo!"

John defused the situation by chiding Leo for his unsophisticated way of dealing with the opposite sex and thought to himself that apparently his mother wasn't the only female in town who was not a big Leo fan. Just then a large man in an overcoat walked across the asphalt basketball court. Even though he passed within a few feet, he ignored Leo's wiseacre greeting and hastily moved past them.

Stung by the affront, Leo proposed, in a low voice, another contest to John. "I bet that I can throw a rock closer to that guy than you can, without actually hitting him." In spite of the alarm that sounded in John's head, he took the dare. After all, how could he turn down a dare from the number one daredevil in school? He'd never live it down. As he grabbed a hefty flat rock, John had an inspiration. If he were to aim to the right, he would be assured of a missing the mark, most likely losing the contest but definitely keeping his honor intact. By now the silhouetted figure of the man was at least 30 yards away, and John knew there was no way he could throw his rock that far.

John hurled the rock with all his might to the right of the stranger and followed its arc. He held his breath as he silently prayed for divine intervention. But the throw turned out to be magnificent, with the rock seeming to sail forever and then hooking to the left. The sharp flat edge of the missile caught the man right behind his ear with a sickening thud. Howling in rage, the man pressed his hand against his neck, blood spurting between his fingers, and reeled to charge the boys.

Leo and John had never run as fast as they did that day. They ran up the street, across back yards, and down alleys, finally hiding in the woods on the outskirts of town for what seemed to be hours. The rush of adrenaline had dissipated by the time they finally made it back to Leo's house, and, after wolfing a couple of peanut butter and jelly sandwiches, they fell asleep in their sleeping bags in front of the television.

Leo and John decided it would be in their best interest to keep the incident to themselves. They vowed to tell no one, no matter what. On Monday, both boys were sitting in their Latin class when a student assistant knocked on the door and told the teacher that Leo and John were ordered to go immediately to the principal's office.

Both boys, red faced and sweating, made their way down the hallway, with the catcalls of their classmates still ringing in their ears. At the office door, the principal greeted them stiffly, but their eyes were immediately drawn to the others seated in the room—two police officers, Sharon, the 7th grader from the playground, and her mother. The woman had her arm around Sharon, who looked about as scared as John and Leo. The principal asked Sharon if these were the two boys from the park. The girl's eyes quickly darted from Leo to John, and then she nodded her head with a sense of urgency. For John, suddenly the room took on the stark, vivid stillness of an image that's been captured by a flash camera.

REFLECTING QUESTIONS

1. What is your reaction to the ending of the story?
2. How did the meaning of this story evolve as you read it?
3. What meaning does John make of his life as he makes his way to the counselor's office?

OVERVIEW

Building on Chapters 6 and 7, this chapter offers ideas and tools for helping your clients transform their experiences into something meaningful that promotes successful change. No matter what concerns or problems your clients bring to you, they are always rooted in the implicit philosophy of life that your clients have adopted. Therefore, one of the fundamental points of this chapter is that your clients, as meaning makers, are not passive victims of their troubling circumstances. Instead, they are on active quests to seek meaning as they attempt to find a resolution to their concerns. Unfortunately, clients often come to counseling with stories that may make meaning of their experiences but sabotage their potential to achieve a greater sense of satisfaction in life. In this chapter you will learn to use appreciative inquiry techniques and other questions to help clients in their quest for meaning. People who are discouraged have foreclosed on their dreams for the future. Nevertheless, their longing for a better life is always there. In order to tap into this longing, you need to become sensitive to those times when the client is experiencing a transderivational search. It is during these moments that the client is more open to co-creating new meaning.

IDEAS

Meaning and Happiness

Victor Frankl was fond of quoting the philosopher Nietzsche, who said a person who has a "why" to live can bear almost any "how" (Corey, 2005). Frankl's approach to counseling was called *logotherapy*, which means "therapy through meaning" (p. 134). All of us have a basic survival instinct provided by an innate biological desire to preserve our lives, but what gives our lives the zest, the élan for living, is the sense we make of our existence. It is *meaning* that supplies the "why" of our life and gives significance. In order to find meaning, we must carefully explore ourselves, discover our values, and determine what noteworthy activities make life precious. As early Greek philosophers put it, "The unexamined life is not worth living."

Long ago, the philosopher Aristotle said that finding happiness is our greatest quest in life, and the framers of the Declaration of Independence agreed, stating that people have the right to pursue happiness. The novelist C. P. Snow countered this American notion when he grumbled that *pursuit of happiness* is a ridiculous phrase. "If you pursue happiness," he said, "you'll never find it" (Lemley, 2006). Likewise, Frankl observed that it is one of life's most fundamental paradoxes that happiness, when we pursue it, actually eludes us. Happiness can only *ensue* from the kind of lives we live.

As a counselor, you will likely see clients who have successfully sought the American Dream of rugged individualism and material accumulation but who nevertheless complain that they are unhappy, that their lives seem meaningless. In spite of having performed well in the game whose rules state "the person who dies with the most toys wins," their lives are an existential vacuum (Prochaska & Norcross, 2007). They echo that old Peggy Lee song: "Is that all there is?"

As we discussed in a previous chapter, Martin Seligman has, over the course of his career, turned from the study of learned helplessness to learned optimism. His current research into the nature of happiness has led him to declare that "optimism is happiness about the future" (in Lemley, 2006, p. 65). When you work with your clients, this optimistic view of the future is precisely what you are trying to help them achieve.

Seligman's research has identified two "happiness-creating interventions" that fit well with our brief resolution counseling approach. He asked people to write down three good things that had happened to them over the course of a week and their causes. Follow-up data documented that this simple procedure lifted the happiness level of participants for a full six months. The second intervention involved asking participants to use what they considered to be their greatest personal strength in a new or different way for a week. Seligman found that this activity boosted their happiness level for an even longer time.

As a result of their studies, researchers of positive psychology have developed an equation for happiness: $H = S + C + V$. In the equation, H represents a person's enduring level of happiness, S is the contribution of the person's genes or biological makeup, C is the life circumstance in which the person exists, and V represents the factors under the control of the person (Lemley, 2006).

The biological makeup of the person, S, seems to remain fairly stable, although we would contend, along with Cozolino (2002), that counseling with a positive orientation may alter the brain's neural networks that can enhance mood, and may even control what genes are expressed.

C, the life circumstances of a person, has a surprisingly small effect on the level of happiness. One group of investigators found that, beyond a certain minimum requirement for such things as health, education, safety, and wealth, life circumstances contribute little to one's enduring happiness. They discovered that "altogether life circumstances count for no more than 8 to 15 percent of the variance in happiness among people" (Lemley, 2006, p. 65).

V, the element in the equation that is under a person's control, accounts for about 40 percent of the happiness quotient. These findings regarding the happiness formula provide encouraging news. Biology is not destiny, life circumstances contribute less than we thought, and personal control—the part we counselors are attempting to improve—accounts for almost half of someone's enduring happiness. When you help your clients talk about their positive experiences in the past, their hopes for the future, and their strengths they can use now to achieve their optimistic goals, you are eliciting a positive view of life in your clients.

Seligman (in Lemley, 2006) identified three levels of happiness. The first he called "pleasure," which includes the sensory enjoyment of such things as good food and sex. The second level of happiness is "flow," which involves becoming fully absorbed in a productive task (Seligman & Csikszentmihalyi, 2000). The third level is "meaning." People who experience meaning are using their greatest strengths in service to something larger than themselves. In other words, happiness may not be brought about by the rugged individualism of the "me generation," but rather as the result of transcending oneself for a higher calling.

In a 2001 issue of the *Journal of Psychosomatic Medicine,* it was found that poets who committed suicide, such as Sylvia Plath, used the words *I, me,* and *my* much more frequently than *we, us,* and *our.* They also tended to use fewer terms like *talk, share,* or *listen.* Many years ago, Alfred Adler stated that the quintessence of mental health was "social interest" (Day, 2004). We humans are social creatures. Selfishness brings us little happiness, and not much meaning. Investigators have found that people who are high in social interest "are more altruistic, trustworthy, socially adjusted, nurturant, and helpful. . . ." "Individuals high in social interest also report less depression, anxiety, loneliness, narcissism, and hostility toward others" (Ryckman, 2004, p. 116).

The attainment of meaning answers the important "why" of living, and it appears that much meaning can come from devoting oneself to the improvement of the lives of others. Since you have chosen to be a counselor—someone whose interest is in helping others—it is likely that your social interest and service to something larger than yourself will confer significant meaning and happiness to your life. We, the authors of this book, are certainly optimistic about *your* future.

The Problem of Meaning

In his now classic book *Existential Psychotherapy,* Irvin Yalom (1980) pointed out that the central concern we humans ponder is about the meaning of our existence. *What is the meaning of life?* we ask. This question, along with *What is my purpose in being here?* seems to bewilder and nag us during our time on the planet. In their most cynical moods, hard-nosed scientific reductionists, such as Richard Dawkins (1976) or Keith Stanovich (2004), might reply, "Don't worry about it. You could possibly be nothing but a vehicle that exists to allow selfish genes and memes to replicate themselves, and this replication may be all that life means." But even these skeptics seem to recognize that there is something about us humans that transcends our biological and socially constructed states, something that allows us even to pose questions of meaning. If we succumb to our selfish genes and memes, says Stanovich (2004), we become wanton robots that are driven by physical and cultural forces whose "meanings" were never our own. Stanovich's formula for overcoming these external forces and finding our own meaning is "rational self-determination" (p. 275). We think Stanovich overvalues rationality while giving emotional intelligence short shrift, but the partial truth contained in his assertion is that a harmonic blending of primary process with secondary process thought (Freud, 1911) seems to create personal meaning in our lives.

Of course, the ultimate meaning of life and the outcome of our futures will never be certain. For this reason, many existentialists contend that we must develop "the courage to be" (Corey, 2005). Without this courage, we may not confront life's fundamental questions, and we might not adopt a philosophy of life that is authentically our own. Obviously, since existential concerns are lifelong, and you are attempting to work briefly with clients, you will not be addressing life's entire conundrum in depth. However, it is important to keep in mind that, no matter what concerns or problems your clients bring to you, they are always rooted in the implicit philosophy of life that your clients have adopted.

Charles Starkey (2006) has conducted an investigation into what constitutes a meaningful life for people. One conclusion that he reached was that people who live fulfilled lives create their own meanings. Starkey also asserted that "engagement," allowing oneself to be fully involved, is a basic component to a meaningful life. This concept is similar to that of "flow" or "optimal experience" (Csikszentmihalyi, 1993). People who report their experiences while in flow tend to characterize this state as meaningful, fulfilling, and gratifying. Flow appears to be more of a sensation or emotion rather than a rational state. It occurs when people are fully engaged in an activity and are stretching their cognitive and emotional resources to the limit. They report being completely involved, focused, and concentrating on the task at hand and being absorbed in the moment. They speak of an inner clarity, of knowing what needs to be done and how well it is going. They feel composed and competent, that their skills are adequate to the demands of the situation. A sense of serenity accompanies this experience, with no worries about self and a lack of awareness of the passing of time. Rather than seeking approval or reward, people in flow are inspired by intrinsic motivation; whatever produces flow becomes its own reward. While people in flow are usually deliberate in their pursuit of a goal, the experience of flow is not brought about by an act of will; it accompanies the total engagement of the individual in the task at hand. However, engagement does not always bring happiness. Activities to which people dedicate themselves may sometimes involve stress, exertion, or sorrow, but if such activities are seen as having worth, then they can be meaningful.

Meaningfulness is a larger concept than happiness. Caring for a terminally ill loved one, for example, is not likely to make you happy, but you could see it as meaningful. Fighting against political oppression would involve you in difficult, stressful, and frustrating work. Those with vested interests in the status quo may criticize or even threaten you. Under these circumstances, you would probably feel angry, fearful, and disappointed, but you would nevertheless find your own behavior to be meaningful. Closer to home, our counseling students often describe their supervision sessions with a faculty member as challenging, anxiety provoking, and intensely emotional. In spite of the fact that this activity does not make them "happy," our students tend to view it as important and meaningful, crucial to their development as counselors. When clients come for counseling, they would probably all say that their goal is to be "happier." Happiness and meaningfulness are not necessarily mutually exclusive. Of course, we would all prefer to be living lives that are both happy and meaningful, but we sometimes gain meaning from unhappy events.

The Meaning Behind Client Stories

In Chapter 7, you read about the outdated, rigidified, and tragic stories that clients often bring to counseling. You will recall that those stories persisted because they held profound meanings for the clients, even though these meanings were holding them prisoner. In this section, we explore still other restrictive meanings of stories that may limit client growth. Janoff-Bulman (1992) proposed that the core of many people's preferred "assumptive world" is predicated on three basic beliefs:

> The world is benevolent.
> The world is meaningful.
> The self is worthy. (p. 6)

With these beliefs as the basis of the assumptive world, if people live a moral life, they can proceed with supreme confidence that the world will provide what they need, they will always find their efforts fulfilling and meaningful, and they deserve all the successes that come to them. These beliefs are based on the assumption that the world is just, and they offer an optimistic view of the future for those who follow their tenets. What then, can be the meaning of suffering in a just world?

Janoff-Bulman suggested that the biblical story of Job, in which God visits countless troubles on a good and righteous man, is the prototype for undeserved human suffering.

One way to make sense of bad things that happen to good people is to attribute suffering to a test from God as to the faith of the individual. For example, you will recall that God asked Abraham to kill his son Isaac as proof of Abraham's worthiness. Luckily for Isaac, God withdrew the order before the action was completed. The idea is that, if people can suffer for their faith, this is proof of their goodness, and they will profit in some way. Nietzsche had an explanation for this circumstance, too. He said, "That which does not kill me, makes me stronger" (Corey, 2005, p. 134). We also hear people say, "God would not give me a burden too heavy for me to carry." On the one hand, this way of making meaning seems heroic and worthy of respect. On the other hand, if people become trapped in a story of martyrdom by their assumptive world and believe that they are not allowed to be happy, such an attitude portends a grim future.

A crisis or traumatic event can shatter one's basic assumptions (Janoff-Bulman, 1992). If their belief in a just world has been exploded by an unexpected event, they may turn a formerly optimistic life into one of fatalistic pessimism. They may then assume the following:

The world is unkind and hostile.

Nothing makes any sense.

I deserve all the pain and suffering that has been visited upon me.

With such a set of assumptions, people no longer see the world as a hospitable place, they are constantly confused by events, and they see themselves as unworthy of happiness. The long-term danger is that they will accept these negative assumptions as their new life story. Given such an assumptive world, people can easily lose hope and see the meaning of life as nothing but suffering. Why would anyone be reluctant to give up this set of assumptions when they obviously give life such negative significance? One explanation might be that there is some "secondary gain" in remaining within the negative story. *Secondary gain* is a term meaning that, although the client would appear to be in pain, there is something rewarding in the situation that is not obvious to us. But what could be the secondary gain in adopting such a position?

Movie characters, such as *Spartacus*, Obi-Wan Kenobi in *Star Wars*, Gandalf in *Lord of the Rings*, and William Wallace in *Braveheart*, who battle against all odds and are ultimately killed by their enemies, appeal to our sense of heroic martyrdom. There is meaning, but not happiness, in such scenarios. People who see their own lives in this way will sometimes say such discouraging things as, "It's a jungle out there," "Life is nothing but a veil of tears," and "You can run, but you can't hide." They view themselves as facing up to a life that is a losing proposition, but they have vowed to fight until the bitter end. We have referred to this type of tragic life story as the "Invictus Syndrome," after the poem written by the nineteenth-century poet William Ernest Henley:

Invictus

Out of the night that covers me,
Black as the Pit from pole to pole,
I thank whatever gods may be
For my unconquerable soul.

In the fell clutch of circumstance,
I have not winced nor cried aloud.
Under the bludgeonings of chance
My head is bloody, but unbowed.
Beyond this place of wrath and tears
Looms but the Horror of the shade,
And yet the menace of the years
Finds, and shall find, me unafraid.
It matters not how strait the gate,
How charged with punishments the scroll,
I am the master of my fate:
I am the captain of my soul.

Another tragic story involves the person who has grieved for a lost loved one for an unusually long time. The length of this person's period of mourning can be viewed as overt testimony to the strength of their love for the departed person. If the mourner should decide to revise this tragic story by expressing hope for a new life, this change may at first feel like an act of disloyalty.

There are also clients who find meaning in their roles as the victims of other people's insensitivity, callousness, or violence. The reasons for their behavior can be quite complicated, but suffice it to say that, while they do not enjoy being victimized, they may find it difficult to give up the role. Keep in mind, however, that this self-destructive story is much more complex than the simple idea of secondary gain. Find out, if you can, what holds the person to this tragic life. If you ask an abused woman why she stays with the abuser, you will often hear her say, "Because I love him." You must consider this justification to be only a "level one" explanation. Deeper down there exists a level of meaning that anchors your client to this situation.

Whenever you find yourself baffled by a client who seems to be tenaciously holding to a story that seems to you unwarranted and with unnecessary suffering, this means you have not yet understood the client's meaning. Keep in mind that *meaning* is more important to people than *happiness*. As you attempt to influence a change in people's stories or narrative life plots, you are asking them to give up something important in the bargain. If they relinquish an *outdated* narrative, then they may need to grieve the loss of a time gone by that will never come again. If they give up a *rigidified* narrative, then they must abandon a sense of certainty or an ideal outcome for their life. Finally, if they renounce their position as the heroic but *tragic* protagonist, they must find an alternative meaning for their role that—although no longer tragic—could be equally heroic and just as romantic.

If it is everyone's human nature to tend toward adopting optimistic assumptions, then the good news is that you may find a way to co-construct a life story with your clients that is both meaningful and happy. However, if you "side" with a story of hope without communicating your understanding of the client's meanings that are involved in the negative story, you are violating the basic principles of LUV and empathy. As a result, your efforts will ring hollow, and your counseling will be unsuccessful.

Resistance and "Siding"

We repeatedly caution our counselors-in-training to be careful about "siding." We point out that more police officers are killed responding to domestic disputes than in any other type of confrontation. Sometimes the "perpetrator" kills them, but on other occasions it is the "victim" who is protecting the perpetrator who does the killing. Once you side with one or another person in a dispute you are in trouble. We tell our students that, as they listen to a client's story in which another person is portrayed in negative terms, they need to take the position of being *by* the client's side rather than *on* the client's side. You will find that when you are attempting to "be with" a client who is complaining about mistreatment by a significant other, if you buy into the idea that the other person is mean or uncaring—and you say so—the client will jump to the person's defense. At such moments, the client seems to need to protect that person against you, hence the reason we tell our students not to take sides.

Similarly, when clients state goals that are positive, your first impulse is to enthusiastically support these goals. However, remember that, whenever clients seek change, this means they must give up something. A part of them wants to get better, to be happier, but another part wants to stay the same. They would not be simply giving up a behavior; they would be giving up something meaningful, so naturally they "resist." As we have previously stated, "resistance" is a relationship. They are resisting *you* and your optimistic siding against their story of anguish.

Clark (2005) believed that counselors should reframe resistance by considering certain "negative" behaviors as doing something important for the client. Asking how these behaviors "offer support, relief, and gratification can help resolve resistance" (p. 253). As we discussed in Chapter 1, you should recognize that clients may be hesitant but are never "resistant" in the conventional sense. You need to respect and honor the ideas and behaviors that have served a protective function for the client (Cowan & Presbury, 2000; Teyber, 2006).

Our colleague Eric Cowan (2005) suggested that counselors often move too quickly in siding with the prosocial or healthy part of clients, while ignoring the "symptomatic" part. In his book *Ariadne's Thread*, he wrote of a client who was a self-destructive "cutter." She regularly mutilated herself with sharp instruments, beat herself black and blue, and was at times suicidal. Obviously, a goal of therapy would be to find a way to stop this sort of behavior; right? However, Cowan found that the more he sided with the part of her that wanted to quit these behaviors, the more she would act out in destructive ways. It was only when he began to inquire about the aspects of these behaviors she found reassuring, helpful, and meaningful that the therapy took a different turn. Cowan discovered that siding only with the part of his client that wanted to stop injuring herself set up a contest between the therapist and the part of her that needed these behaviors.

Resistance, in this sense, can be viewed as "the client's 'space suit' in an environment that is seen as alien or inhospitable for survival" (Cowan, 2005, p. 141). The moment the therapist sides with only one part of the client, the games have begun, and the client usually wins by losing. Years ago, Fritz Perls understood this phenomenon when he wrote that each client has within a "top dog" and an "underdog" (Prochaska & Norcross, 2007). Top dogs metaphorically admonish underdogs regarding what they should or ought to be doing better, but the underdog always collapses and claims incompetence.

Perls believed that therapeutic progress could not be made until each of these parts was given a voice. As Blume (2006) pointed out, we experience ourselves along dialectical dimensions—opposites in a constant and enduring tension. If you remember the two faces of the Necker cube, this dialectical notion will make sense. When we try to deconstruct old stories while co-constructing new ones, we must realize that the negative face never goes away, but it can be incorporated into a new and more complete meaning system. While meaning and happiness are not the same thing, they can coexist. This is the kind of resolution we hope for in our clients.

Implications of These Ideas for the Counselor

These concepts, many of which are taken from the recent movement in positive psychology, have a number of implications for your work with clients:

- Clients seek meaning as they attempt to find a resolution to their concerns.
- Clients are not hapless victims of their circumstances. They have the power to achieve happiness, or meaningfulness, in spite of catastrophic events.
- Clients come to you with stories that may make meaning of their experiences but sabotage their potential to achieve a greater sense of satisfaction in life. You must be careful not to side with only the positive aspects of the story.

TOOLS

Appreciative Inquiry

The major tool you can use to help your clients make new meaning in their lives is a question that seeks out strengths and resilience: an appreciative inquiry. The appreciative inquiry is based on an affirmative approach to change that, like positive psychology, turns its attention to strengths and resilience (Cooperrider & Whitney, 1999). It involves asking questions that strengthen people's capacity to tap into and heighten their positive potential (Cooperrider, Sorensen, Whitney, & Yaeger, 2000).

When you offer an appreciative inquiry, you communicate that you value your client's inherent wisdom and resources, and, at the same time, you are asking a question that is designed to bring these strengths into the conversation. The root of *question* is *quest,* which means an adventurous journey. This image seems an appropriate metaphor for our work as counselors. When we *question* our clients, we do so in an attempt to initiate their *quest* for a better life. The term *inquiry* is also appropriate because, since we adopt the position of being "not from around here," we are obligated to inquire into the client's worldview.

The major skill you must develop when asking questions is how to conduct an inquiry without conducting an inquisition. You must acknowledge the client's story of pain and limitation while you seek exceptions and possibilities. Once a goal has been named by the client, you can say, "I imagine that while there's a part of you that really desires this goal, there might also be another part that is hesitant to go for it." This way, you can refrain from "playing favorites," which would make the client feel that immediate change is the only option. This is the technique of *restraining* in which you communicate that you are willing to wait until the client reaches escape velocity.

The Quest for Meaning

Clients often struggle with issues of meaning when they encounter horrific life-changing experiences or suffer serious crises (Echterling, Presbury, & McKee, 2005). No one will be able to turn back the clock on these tragic situations, but as the counselor, you can help your clients to make new meaning out of these experiences. Your clients may never have reflected on their own meaning systems, but these meanings nevertheless form the foundations for all their thoughts, feelings, and behaviors (Ivey, Ivey, Meyers, & Sweeney, 2005; Lazarus & Fay, 2000). Asking questions can invite your clients to examine and articulate what gives meaning to life—their values, hopes, dreams, and sense of mission (Ivey & Ivey, 2007). For example, you might ask,

"What did that situation mean to you?"

"What sense did you make of what happened?"

"Reflecting on your life, what do you care about the most?"

"What have been the important lessons you've learned from dealing with other crises in your life?"

"What do you see as the overall mission of your life?"

Our meanings reflect the cultural worldviews that we have learned from society. Most of them came to us as received knowledge that we rarely questioned when we were children. In fact, we swallowed these meanings whole. We often do not even know what these meanings are until they are called into question. Sometimes we find that our meanings and values, like our feelings, are in conflict. If this conflict becomes explicit and obvious, we then seek what Pinker (2002) called a "'cognitive dissonance reduction,' in which people change whatever opinion it takes to maintain a positive self-image" (p. 265).

Sometimes, as the counselor, you will seek to be a "sower of discord" (Egan, 2007) in order to create a perturbing cognitive dissonance. Egan sees a difference between confronting clients and challenging them, because the latter is less hard-hitting. Remember that it takes only a butterfly-like perturbation to send a system into chaos and thus toward a reorganization.

Questioning Discrepancies in Meanings

In Chapter 6, you read about tools for deconstruction that can help clients to revise their worldviews. Then, in Chapter 7, you examined narrative tools that can help clients re-author their life stories. Here, we continue with this general theme, but we now focus on the meaning behind these worldviews and stories. Since clients' unexamined meanings are often in conflict, discrepancies will begin to turn up in their constructs and narratives. As Egan (2007) put it, "sometimes clients believe in things they don't believe in" (p. 178). Many authors have written about the human tendency to create an ego ideal, the person we wish to be. We then accept the values that cluster around this ideal as our own, even if we do not act on them. However, if you profess a value that you have not acted on in the past year, it is probably not really yours.

When you challenge your clients' meaning discrepancies, you can do this without a hint of moral superiority if you remember that we all engage regularly in self-deception. In order to guard against the dissonance that arises when we experience our values and meanings to be in conflict, we use self-deluding defenses that lead to blind spots in our self-awareness. Consider the "three *Rs*" of self-delusion: reaction formation, repression, and rationalization. *A reaction formation* is when we claim to have thoughts or feelings that are diametrically opposed to the actual, but unacceptable, desires or urges we experience. When we proclaim not to have such desires or urges, as Shakespeare put it, we "doth protest too much." *Repression* is when we automatically deny unacceptable desires or urges, not allowing them to become conscious. It's as if we cry out, "Who, *me?!*" We engage in *rationalization* when we offer plausible, but untrue, excuses for our behavior, such as saying, "I meant to do that!" when we make an egregious error. "As Jeff Goldblum said in *The Big Chill*, 'Rationalizations are more important than sex.' When his friends demurred, he asked, 'Have you ever gone a week without a rationalization?'" (Pinker, 2002, p. 264).

When you hear what seem to be blind spots in your clients' narratives, proceed cautiously. Detecting a discrepancy, you might say something like, "I'm a bit confused by what you are saying. You told me earlier that having a committed relationship is very important to you, and now you say that not being tied down to one person is essential to your independence. Help me see how these go together."

When it seems that your client is leaving something meaningful out of the story, you might deal with this omission by saying, "I think I may have missed something here. I probably had what they call a 'senior moment' just now. Would you please go back and tell me again how that incident took place, so I could put together the sequence of events?"

Sometimes, clients avoid dealing with meaning by becoming vague or abstract as they tell their story. In this case you might respond to this avoidance by saying, "I'm not quite getting this. Would you please give me a specific example of how that works?" or "You're going to think I'm a little dense, but would you tell me what it was that struck you as significant about that?"

Notice that each of these challenges to the client's rendition of the meaning of these events keeps the focus on you. Instead of calling the client to account, you "take one for the team," as one of the authors of this book (J.E.M) is fond of saying. You and your client are indeed a team, and both win when the client begins on the path to a happier, meaningful life.

Other Meaning-Making Questions

The effect of any question is greatly influenced by the manner in which you ask it. As we mentioned earlier, your style of inquiry should be low-key, gentle, and touristlike ("I'm not from around here, and I need some help"), as compared to the interrogator's know-it-all, distant, rapid-fire approach. Questions beginning with *what* and *how* are open-ended questions that encourage clients to talk more, explain further, go deeper into their feelings, and explore the meaning of the events under discussion.

You may also want to use an *open-ended lead*, which is a statement typically describing your own experience and perceptions, rather than a question. Like questions that "take one for the team," open-ended leads begin with the first-person pronoun *I*. For example, instead of asking, "How did that make you feel?"—a hackneyed phrase at best—you could say, "*I am wondering what that must have been like for you,*" or "*I want to make sure I get this right. I thought you were saying . . . .*"

Questions are powerful meaning-making devices. They usually cause clients to pause, consider the inquiry, and give some sort of response—even if they do not wish to answer. Your clients are likely to feel some obligation to search for a response when you question them. This desire increases emotional arousal and sometimes stirs the client to enter into new and uncharted territory of meaning. Questions "dig up" experiences in the client.

Here are some questions that you will want to ask your clients:

"What do you want from counseling?"

"How will what you want make a difference in your life?"

"How will you know when your goal has been reached?"

"How much of what you want is already happening?"

You will want to ask questions that encourage images of meaningful success or possibility rather than "why" questions or those that probe additional pain. Because of the power that questions hold for people, remember: Before you ask that question, think!

Useful Goal-Directed Questions

Our major source of meaning in life is a sense of mission and purpose. As you read in Chapter 4, helping your client envision a goal gives direction to your counseling work. Even more important, having goals gives meaning and brings momentum to your client's life. As you begin your counseling work, ask goal-oriented questions (O'Hanlon, 1995). These questions set expectations for success and focus your clients on resolution rather than on what holds them back. Some examples that elicit positive expectations for the counseling might be as follows:

"When you get to the place where you are on track to your goal, and can carry on by yourself, how will we know?"

"What changes will have taken place when you get to that place?"

"How will you be different?"

To help your clients create a vivid and detailed image of a successful outcome, you can ask for "a video description" (O'Hanlon, 1995, p. 6): Encourage your client to give an elaborate portrait of the future as if you were following your client around with a video camera and capturing the new behaviors that your client will be exhibiting when the counseling has been successful.

As previously mentioned, you can also ask questions that focus on your client's resources that have in the past helped the client in dealing with difficulties:

"Tell me about a time when you experienced a similar difficulty. How did you handle that problem?"

"What about those times when this problem started to come up, but you headed it off so it didn't happen?"

"How about a time when you did something positive and you were surprised by your ability to do it?"

"When was a time that you acted completely out of character and it turned out well?"

It is useful to ask what clients have tried in order to resolve their difficulties, because you don't want to offer suggestions for remedies they have previously attempted that haven't worked. For example, you might ask, "What are some of the things you have tried to solve this situation that have not worked quite as well as you had wished?"

LISTENING IN ON A SESSION

You may need to review the story at the beginning of the chapter before you turn to this segment. A resolution-focused counselor can use appreciative inquiries and meaning-making questions in the following ways.

John: (As he sits down, he immediately begins speaking with a sense of urgency and agitation.)

"OK, let's cut right to the chase; I'm in one of those lose-lose situations that Oprah and Dr. What's-his-name talk about on TV. I've been sentenced to counseling. You and I both know that I wouldn't be here if my doctor hadn't threatened to flunk me on my physical so I wouldn't get my license. Now I've got to sit in here and spill my guts about how I've screwed up my life just so I can keep my license. In fact, I thought I was going to have another heart attack on the bus ride to your office 'cause I got really scared that once you got to know me you'll find out just how screwed up I am then I'd lose my permit anyway."

(He shakes his head and chuckles mirthlessly to himself.)

"That's pretty much the story of my life all right, 'lose plus lose equals loser.' Hell, I might as well salvage what little dignity I have left and catch the next bus home."

Counselor: "John, I want to check something out with you; what you just said doesn't quite fit for me. When I was talking to your family doctor last week by phone," (John squirms noticeably in the chair at the mention of his physician) "he said that a lot of people look up to you in the community. He also mentioned your being an athlete and a Little League baseball coach. What do you say to those kids when they get on a losing streak?"

John: "I tell them that if they work harder on the fundamentals, they can expect to get better."

Counselor: "So, if I'm hearing you right, it sounds like you don't tell them that they are a bunch of losers."

John: "No, I tell them that playing the game right, knowing how the game is played, and playing together are more important than winning. I learned that when I played and I try to teach the kids that. In fact, years ago, Doc was one of my players and now he's telling me what to do. Funny, huh?"

Counselor: "I was struck by the way your face lit up when you were talking about coaching and playing the game right. I think I'm starting to understand what it must be like for you to be sent to counseling against your will and forced to work on *your* fundamentals. I find myself wondering how you were able to talk yourself into that?"

John: (He is silent for a minute, then smiles as if he had discovered something.)

"I know! You're going to tell me that Doc is just doing what I taught him, following the rules."

(The counselor doesn't respond but continues to wait patiently for further explanation.)

"Yeah, but this is different. It's like this nightmare where someone is making me play a game that I know I'm not going to be any good at 'cause I don't even know the damn rules! And I can't ask because that would be stupid or crazy and that's against the rules, too. And it's the same way with the dietitian and the stupid exercise physio-whatever. Hell, I'm an athlete. I never had to worry about my body and what I ate."

(John sighs and his head droops noticeably.)

"I guess I've kind of gone to pot after my heart attack and most of my friends have kind of given up on me." (He sighs again.) "Well, not all of them anyway."

REFLECTING QUESTIONS

1. How might you respond to John's last statement?
2. How did the counselor help John to make meaning in his situation?
3. How effective were the counselor's appreciative inquiries?
4. How did the counselor side with John's "resistance" at the beginning of the session?

USING THIS TOOL

Write two *goal-directed questions* that you could ask the client in the story. In order to increase their power and impact, make the questions specific to the story. Remember: A useful constructive question is one that helps the client conjure up images of success or possibility.

Presumptive Questions and Leads

In the literature on brief therapy, there appears to be some disagreement as to whether questions should be put to the clients in a presumptive manner. Our position on this is that open-ended questions or leads that presume strengths and resilience are powerful change devices. For example, if you were to ask, "Is there a time when the problem is not happening?" the client has the option of taking the easy way out and dismissing your question with a simple "No."

However, if you were to say, "Tell me about a time when the problem is not happening," or ask, "When was a time that this problem was not happening?" the client will likely feel more pressure to come up with something. Use presumptive questioning anytime that you wish the client to search for exceptions to the problem (a time when the problem is not happening) and when you are asking for the client's vision of success.

USING THIS TOOL

Write two *presumptive questions* or *leads* that you could ask the client in the story. In order to increase their power and impact, make them specific to the story. Remember: A useful constructive question or statement is one that helps the client conjure up images of success or possibility.

The Circular (or Relational) Question

The idea of the circular question comes from Gregory Bateson's notion of "double description" (Penn, 1982). An individual's world must be described and understood, not only as the person's unique perspective, but also from the imagined perspective of others. We want to know how our clients see themselves being seen by others. Family therapists have long used the technique of the circular question in order to make sense of the interactions within a family system and to add a new dimension of understanding for the family members. For example, the family therapist might ask a child to describe the relationship between the mother and father or between the mother and another child. On hearing the description, the other family members are forced to take into account this additional perspective on their family's problem and to perhaps alter the meaning of their family's interactions. This alteration might be called a change in the "family self-concept."

Brief counselors (De Jong & Berg, 2002) use similar questioning techniques that they call "relational questioning." In this sort of questioning, you ask clients to take the perspective of important persons in their lives and to see themselves through the eyes of these significant others as they change for the better. The result of this type of questioning can be the elevation of your client's self-concept. The main difference between relational questioning and the standard circular question is that your client will imagine being seen differently by others when a positive change has happened. This is "double description" from the "inside out." If clients can imagine someone seeing them in a better light, or saying positive things about their change, then these clients will be simultaneously changing their "meta-perspective": their way of seeing themselves through the eyes of others.

In order to be helpful in this process, you will want to ask the client questions such as the following:

"When this change in your life has happened, who will be the first person to notice? What will he or she say is different about you?"

"If your mother were here and I were to ask her what had changed about you, what would she say?"

"When I talk to your teacher and she tells me that you are doing better, what exactly will she talk about?"

"What will your boss say you are doing more of than before?"

"What will it take to convince her that you are a changed person? What will she have to see to be convinced?"

Not only are all these questions designed to concretize the goal statements of your clients and to give a clear picture of the desired behaviors, but they also offer the opportunity for your clients to begin to see others seeing them differently. As clients' behaviors (the doing) come into alignment with the images of success (the viewing), the clients' belief in the way they will be seen—and positively valued by others—is strengthened.

USING THIS TOOL

Write two *relational questions* that you could ask the client in the story. In order to increase their power and impact, make the questions specific to the story. Remember: A useful constructive question is one that helps the client conjure up images of success or possibility.

"Getting-By" Questions

Miller (1995) suggested that sessions might begin with the use of "getting-by" questions. He borrowed this idea from Berg (1994) and Weiner-Davis (1993), who claimed that in the first session, two-thirds of the clients they saw, had already begun to improve the situation that brought them to counseling. Sometimes, asking about changes that have happened before the first session took place can speed up the process "by focusing the conversation on changes that are already working." "It is also a way of helping clients redefine themselves as problem-solvers" (Miller, 1995, p. 77). Even if your clients cannot come up with anything, you can imply that a change has happened but they simply have not yet noticed. This gets the session started off with change as the focus and with the notion that it is your client who is to bring about improvement. Therefore, you might ask, "What have you noticed that has changed for the better after you made the phone call for this appointment?"

In the case of the survivor of a crisis situation who is still focusing on him- or herself as a victim of the event, you can assume that this person has surely done something right, or you wouldn't be speaking together. The rape survivor was not murdered, the flood survivor did something to avoid being drowned, and the survivor of a death in the family (notice that the obituary always states, "The deceased is survived by . . .") has probably found a way to take care of funeral arrangements. In these cases, the "getting-by" question—"How did you do that?"—can be asked with genuine astonishment by the counselor who, imagining him- or herself in the same situation, is not sure he or she could have done as well (Echterling, Presbury, & McKee, 2005).

Questioning the Use of Questions

Ivey and Ivey (2007) offered the following disclaimer regarding the use of questions in counseling: "*we believe in questions, but we also fear their overuse*" (p. 112, emphasis in original). Brief and narrative counselors ask many questions, as do we. These questions are, however, not asked out of idle curiosity or to probe for an "underlying problem."

Questions are powerful devices in conversation. Most people feel pressured to answer when a question has been asked. Because of this dynamic, questions can be wonderful intervention tools for helping clients make meaning of their lives, but their use should include a label: "Warning! Questions can be hazardous to your relationship."

Many authors in the field of counseling and psychotherapy have cautioned that the use of questions can be problematic (Egan, 2007; Welfel & Patterson, 2005). Questioning sometimes makes clients less spontaneous and less fluent in the information they provide. They may sit back and wait for you to ask the *right* question. As a consequence, your questioning may paradoxically undermine your attempts to gain information (Sommers-Flanagan & Sommers-Flanagan, 1993). It appears that the most egregious type of question that you can ask is the "why" question. Benjamin (1987) suggested that clients interpret a "why" question as connoting disapproval or displeasure. If clients were able to construct a satisfactory story as to "why" they think, feel, or behave as they do, they probably would not need to see you for counseling in the first place.

The point we are stressing here is that questions—if they are not used mindfully and deliberately—are potent techniques that can alter the course of the interview in ways you may not intend. As Benjamin (1987) put it, "The question is a useful tool when used delicately and sparingly. Too often, I fear, it is employed like a hammer" (p. 156).

Therefore, follow these guidelines when you use questions:

- Be *aware* that you are asking a question.
- *Challenge* the question you are about to ask and weigh carefully the desirability of asking it.
- *Examine* carefully the types of questions you tend to use.
- *Consider alternatives* to asking a question.
- Be *sensitive* to the questions the client is asking, whether he or she is asking them outright or not.

Flow and the Transderivational Search

Mihaly Csikszentmihalyi (1993), a collaborator with Martin Seligman, has spent decades researching the subjective experience of people involved in creative and joyful states of mind. He characterized the experience of being totally immersed in an activity while losing the sense of time and surroundings as "flow." This absorbing experience is Seligman's second type of "happiness" mentioned above. One does not necessarily need to be performing a task to experience flow. People who are daydreaming often engage in such activities in their imagination. An observer of someone in this state might be tempted to say that the person is "off task," not realizing that there is much work being done while this person is in flow.

Because everyone has experienced flow from time to time, you are no doubt familiar with the phenomenon. The elements of flow involve immersing yourself into the process of achieving a goal, concentrating completely and feeling in control of the situation, setting aside your self-consciousness, experiencing an altered sense of time, and taking pleasure from the sheer involvement in the activity. Flow is sort of an enchanting state, and, when a person is absorbed in it, intrusions are very frustrating. It's like being jerked awake from a wonderful dream. Once awakened, you cannot simply pick up where you left off, because the spell has been broken.

You will be able to observe flow happening in your clients during what is known as a *transderivational search*. This term was coined by Milton Erickson to indicate a process by which the client can experience "downtime" and "go inside" to organize his or her experience in a more coherent way. In brief periods of preoccupation, your clients will appear to go blank, usually right after you have asked a question about times when their problem isn't happening or how they have been able to overcome certain past difficulties. Your question prompts the flow involved in their search for personal resource. Erickson believed that during these moments clients are engaging in a productive internal search. They are searching for meanings and resources of which they were previously unaware. They are in a hypnotic state. Their eyes will fix in a stare, their pupils will dilate, their bodies will remain relatively motionless, their breathing will deepen, and their skin tone will change.

So long as people stay in "uptime," when external events demand their attention, they do not allow unconsciously stored memories to be brought into awareness and sorted out (Grinder, DeLozier, & Bandler, 1977). Conscious short-term memory is very limited in the amount of information it can process at one time. It is only when we allow our mind to wander away from its vigilant state that useful memories can arise. When working with clients, be alert for these moments when your clients seem to "leave the room" and sink into that "downtime." At such moments, you should proceed slowly and allow sufficient time for them to stay with a thought or feeling and pull from it a deeper, richer level of understanding.

The transderivational search is also used in Gestalt therapy. When the client seems to have trouble responding or pauses pensively, the Gestalt therapist might say something like, "I would like for you to stay with those feelings and even intensify them. Now allow yourself to think of some other time when you felt exactly the same feelings."

Another similar technique is employed in Gendlin's (1996) focusing approach. "Focusing is an experiential strategy that uses the body as a source of information on emotions" (Seligman, 2004, p. 82). Clients are asked to focus on a "felt sense": a vague and indistinct feeling that comes to them from the periphery of experience. While focusing, they are usually able to get in touch with emotions that have been previously denied or otherwise have remained out of awareness.

The most important aspect of the transderivational search is that it allows your client time to access deeper sensations and ideas. Unless you pause and allow these times for introspection, your clients will resort to a well-rehearsed way of describing themselves and will not learn anything new about their inner experience. When people come to their senses, they can find new meaning.

The Common Everyday Trance

The transderivational search is a brief and mild form of the common everyday trance. When you read the word *trance,* you may automatically think of stage hypnosis. If you do, you may expect people under trance to be hapless victims who can be forced to perform embarrassing acts such as removing their clothing or quacking like a duck. Contrary to this popular misconception, someone in trance is not under the control of another person's will. In fact, the situation is quite the opposite: Trance can be an opportunity for people to discover their inner resources and exercise more fully their own personal power.

Another misconception is that hypnotic trances are abnormal, bizarre, and unusual phenomena. In fact, you are probably in a state of hypnosis several times a day, but you may think of these times as simply being distracted, such as when you absentmindedly put the carton of milk into the microwave when you intended to return it to the refrigerator. If you could see yourself at these moments, you would notice that your face loses its animation and your eyes are devoid of their usual sparkle. For some reason, another thought process that has seized priority over getting the milk into the right place has captured your attention. As you reached out for the microwave, you stopped—transfixed—your arm floating in the air, your hand holding the milk as if captured in a still photo. At that point, you are in a state of mild catalepsis, an everyday type of trance. Maybe you heard an old song on the radio that took you back to a special time in your life, or someone may have rushed in to tell you an intriguing story, or you may have been captivated by a news flash on television.

Whatever the distraction, you were immediately engrossed in the song, story, or news. You were now reliving your past, caught up in some curious tale, or concerned about a late-breaking event. Such an episode is the "common everyday trance" (Erickson, Rossi, & Rossi, 1976), familiar to all of us. A trance viewed in this way does not seem at all mysterious. You can recognize it as an often-occurring experience. Another common example of an everyday trance that you are likely to have experienced is traveling miles on the interstate highway system without recalling anything about major milestones of the trip. You may have suddenly "awakened" when you realized you had passed your exit because you were lost in thought. In fact, a popular expression describing this experience is "highway hypnosis."

These examples are dissociative experiences—situations in which you are present, and yet not present, at the same time. There is nothing particularly mysterious about it. When your clients have these experiences in your counseling sessions, they are more open to possibilities because they have dropped their guard, set aside the censors that keep away any dissonant information, and are embarking on transderivational searches. When the client enters this trance state, you know that the question you have just asked is accessing previously untapped meaningful information rather than some easy answer to your inquiry. At other times, clients will simply stop in midsentence and go into such a trance. Erickson advised that the client is, at such moments, engaged in an inner search of unconscious processes, and that you must be careful not to ruin this "precious" interlude. What you should do is stop talking for a while and then perhaps say softly, "That's right," or "Stay with that thought." You may even notice that your own rate of breathing begins to synchronize with your client's at those times and you sense an empathic rhythm between the two of you.

When your client "returns" from this trance, you will notice a change in demeanor. Your client reorients, as if on awakening, and looks expectantly at you. This is the creative moment. This instant is when your client is most open to engaging with you in a nondefensive way by co-creating a vision of new possibilities. If you can "catch the rhythm" of your client's reorientation to the present, you will know when the moment is right to inquire about trance experiences.

LISTENING IN ON A SESSION

Scan over the opening story and earlier segment of this counseling session. A resolution-focused counselor can use common everyday trance in a number of ways.

Counselor: "A minute ago you were saying that some of your friends still believe in you. I'd like to hear more about that."

John: (He turns his eyes to the ceiling, tilts his head, shrugs his shoulders in an exaggerated fashion.)

"Man, that's hard to talk about." (He pauses.) "On the way here I remembered a time that my high school buddy Leo—we played ball on the same teams, too—and I were involved in this freaky incident one Friday evening. We had made this stupid bet and I wound up accidentally hitting a man in the head with a rock I had thrown. God, there was blood gushing all over that guy."

"Anyway, we were able to escape from him that night, but the next Monday we were called into the principal's office. Man, we were so scared! There were even a couple of cops at the meeting and we thought we were dead meat."

"Then we heard one of the cops tell the principal that if it weren't for our quick thinking, this girl might not have been able to escape a stalker who had tried to molest her. Her mom reported him to the police and a cruiser picked up this guy who was running around the neighborhood, mad as hell, and holding a bloody handkerchief to his head. Leo and I thought they were hauling our asses off to jail, but then they called us 'heroes.'"

"Leo and I used to kid each other about that for years . . ." (John laughs, shaking his head ruefully, then stops, sighs, gazes out the office window and is silent.)

Counselor: (After 5 or 10 seconds of silence, the counselor offers an acknowledgment in a soft, affirming tone of voice.)

"Yeah, there's sure a lot there to sort through."

John: (He pauses for a few more seconds, then squints his eyes as if there had been a sudden glare on the window. John looks toward the counselor, blinks rapidly several times, and begins to chew his gum again.)

"Yeah . . . Leo and I kinda drifted apart the past few years, but somehow he heard about my heart attack and called me at the hospital. The first thing he said to me was, 'Hey, how's your throwing arm—still got that wicked curve ball?'"

(John smiles and pauses again, staring vacantly at the pattern on the parquet wood floor and rubbing his right arm like a pitcher preparing to toss a few warm-up pitches. After a few seconds of silence, he raises his head to face the counselor and continues.)

"God, it felt so good to hear his voice then. When I had my heart attack, I felt like some big thug had come up, stomped me in the chest, and shook me like I was a rag doll. Even later in the hospital, I was feeling pretty frantic and wondering if this was the end. But when Leo called, I began to think that maybe I was actually going to make it."

Counselor: (The counselor winces as he listens to John's account of his heart attack.)

"Whew! I'm struck by how powerfully you just put that—your heart attack was like being physically attacked by a thug. Whether it was that sex stalker when you were in high school or a death stalker a few months ago, you've somehow managed to survive . . . and you had Leo around both times."

John: "You know, I need to call Leo . . . and another guy from the army, Randy. He called me, too, in the hospital. On my bus rides, I've been thinking a lot more about my life now that I almost lost it and I realized that I don't have time to waste anymore. Life threw me a curve, but guess this time I got a hit. I'm still in the game, and if I don't take advantage of it today, I may not get the chance tomorrow."

REFLECTING QUESTIONS

1. What was your reaction to hearing the resolution of John's earlier story?
2. How do you deal with silence in a counseling session?
3. How might you respond to John's last statement?

SUMMARY

Human beings are the only meaning-making species. As clients pursue a successful counseling outcome, they must first place their goals within a meaningful framework. Clients are not helpless victims of their circumstances. Rather, they have strengths that emerge in challenging times. Using appreciative inquiry to explore the resilience and hopes of your clients can serve as a catalyst for positive change. Honoring the trans-derivational searches of your clients can provide a safe haven for this productive process.

SEGUE TO CHAPTER 9

Think about the scariest movie you ever saw. Now think of the most boring lecture you ever attended. If someone were to videotape your reactions at those times, what could be seen of your emotional expression?

Resource

Positive Psychology Center
University of Pennsylvania
Solomon Labs
3720 Walnut Street
Philadelphia, PA 19104-6241
215-898-7173
www.ppc.sas.upenn.edu

The Positive Psychology Center, directed by Martin Seligman, is located at the University of Pennsylvania. The Center promotes the scientific study of the strengths and virtues that enable individuals and communities to thrive.

CHAPTER 9

Brains, Emotions, Thoughts, and Counseling

Cool Reason and Hot-Wiring

"Reason is and ought to be a slave of the passions"
David Hume

"Lovers and madmen have such seething brains
Such shaping fantasies, that apprehend
More than cool reason ever comprehends."
Shakespeare

"In the small matters trust the mind, in the large ones
the heart."
Sigmund Freud

CHAPTER GOALS

Reading and experiencing the ideas in this chapter will help you understand that

- When you are counseling, you are counseling a brain.
- Discoveries in neuroscience are inspiring innovative counseling techniques.
- Emotions must be appropriately engaged in order for clients to think productively.

Reading about and practicing the tools in this chapter will help you learn to

- Manage your client's emotional arousal in the session to promote therapeutic change.
- Use immediacies and gentle interpretations to move the counseling process forward.

STORY OF CARLA

Although it had only been 6 months since her sudden and painful separation from Sandy, the only truly emotional expression that Carla would allow herself was a small, hesitant gesture. On those rare occasions that she came across one of her ex-partner's photographs, Carla found that she couldn't help touching it. It was only then that her eyes might glisten and she would exhale a hesitant, guttural sigh.

A camera buff, Carla had once read how the actual light that imprinted someone's image in a camera had touched the person first. Somehow, that thought gave a tactile, almost intimate, quality to any of Sandy's pictures—from grainy, unfocused snapshots to the one well-crafted, professional studio portrait she had coaxed Sandy into having done.

Whenever Carla encountered these photos among the belongings that now cluttered her efficiency apartment, her hand would be drawn almost magnetically to Sandy's face, where she would tentatively stroke the image of her former lover's cheek. The gesture was a miniature imitation of one she had used on Sandy. Too late (that was the story of her life!), Carla realized that the stroke had been one of the few affectionate gestures that she would use to express her feelings toward her partner. It was the only clear and consistent barometer of her mood. When she was playful, Carla had followed the stroke with a gentle pat or two. When she was feeling sensuous, her hand had lingered to caress Sandy's jaw line and neck. Carla couldn't remember when her partner had stopped responding to the gesture, but it must have been months before their separation. Sandy's failure to react to that gesture was only one of many warning signs that Carla had missed during that time.

For the past 6 months, Carla has felt stuck, her life put on hold, her existence frozen like the image of her ex-partner in one of her photos. At work, she has tried to jump-start herself, psych herself up, and become once again the energetic and confident person she used to be. Instead, she has found herself procrastinating, making excuses for missed deadlines, and avoiding her supervisors. Although this behavior has been so unlike her, Carla has been even more surprised by her uncharacteristic attitudes of indifference and passivity regarding her poor performance. At one time, she had thrived on accepting challenging tasks and other demanding commitments, but now nothing has seemed to be worth the effort.

As bad as the work situation has become, Carla's social life has been worse. She has spent nearly all of her free time alone in her apartment. Just as she has often gone to the office with resolutions to finish long-overdue projects, Carla has arrived home with the intention of calling an old friend, going out with an acquaintance, or joining a club. However, each evening she has sat curled up on an old sofa, listening to music, listlessly paging through magazines, thumbing through old photographs, and delaying taking any action until it was too late.

Last week, Carla's supervisor sat her down and expressed concerns regarding her poor work performance. Carla acknowledged these problems were serious and admitted that she had been fooling herself by dismissing them as only a temporary setback from the separation. Reluctantly, she accepted the recommendation that she make an appointment with a counselor to deal with these concerns. Carla now enters the counseling room with a quiet, uncertain, and restrained manner.

STORY OF BOB

Bob was referred to the counseling agency by his minister, who had decided that Bob was not having a "crisis of faith," but perhaps needed to work with a counselor on some "lifespan issues."

Fifty-five-year-old Bob began the session by announcing that he did not know what the hell a "lifespan issue" was. "It's probably just another new age BS term that was invented by some damn yuppie shrink to create a new insurance category to bilk the public out of more money."

The counselor began to acknowledge Bob's upset feelings but was interrupted by a torrential outpouring of red-faced, blustering anger.

"I don't know how you're going to be able to help me. Hell, I'm old enough to be your father. Just don't talk so loud! Young people think because somebody wears a hearing aid that we are deaf and stupid. I was in a store last week and the clerk asked me in a placating voice if I wanted to buy the product I laid on the counter. I felt like telling her that I wouldn't have brought it to the damn cash register if I hadn't wanted to buy it. Things like that happen all the time."

Bob paused and shook his head disgustedly, then continued.

"I trained a kid 10 or 12 years ago who was no great shakes, but now he's my damn boss . . . No, that's not true—it's worse than that. He's my boss's boss! I feel like the world has passed me by. Last month at the office Christmas party, people huddled around in groups talking about the latest TV sitcoms, movies, or the Internet. I'm sure people got tired of my asking who somebody was. Whatever happened to interesting conversation? Doesn't anyone read any more?"

Bob's voice trails off, and he seems to shrink down into his chair.

"Herbie—I guess I should call him *Mr.* Parker—made me feel like such a dumb-ass when he suggested that I needed to get up to speed. Everybody got a big kick out of that."

Bob stiffens, sits up straighter, and all but shouts, "Up to speed, my ass! Herbie wouldn't have lasted through his probationary period if it hadn't been for me wiping his nose for him when he first came to work here. The hell with him and with the rest of them, who cares!"

REFLECTING QUESTIONS

1. What were your own reactions to these stories?
2. Which client is more similar to you?
3. With which client would you rather work?

CHAPTER OVERVIEW

People often think of emotions as residing in the heart and cognitions in the brain, but it is the amygdala, an area of the brain, that is primarily responsible for our emotions. Furthermore, emotions are not messy contaminants to effective problem solving; they are essential to good judgment. When you are successful in your work with clients, you have, as Cozolino (2002) put it, "rebuilt" their brains. You are helping them reintegrate dissociated neural networks. In particular, co-constructing more optimistic narratives helps to reintegrate your client's amygdala and hippocampus.

In this chapter, you will learn the techniques for managing emotional arousal during your sessions so that clients benefit from the optimal cognitive-emotional connection. The Yerkes-Dodson Law—the inverted-U hypothesis—suggests that people are most productive when they are moderately emotionally aroused, but their efficiency of thought declines as arousal increases past the optimal level. Because too little or too much emotional arousal is counterproductive, your work as a counselor is to maintain your clients' arousal in the optimal "zone." We will also explore the use of immediacies and interpretations in the counseling process.

IDEAS

Rebuilding Brains

Many counselors and psychotherapists have a bias against neuroscience: "They describe it as confusing and irrelevant to their work" (Cozolino, 2002, p. xvi). We counselors deal with psychology—with the mind—and not with the functioning of the brain, right? But remember, the mind *is* what the brain *does*. This assertion does not mean that all future interventions into human concerns will take place at the brain level, leaving talk therapy in the dust. The interaction between brain and mental processes goes both ways; one affects the other.

In the sixth edition of their book *Intentional Interviewing and Counseling,* one of the most popular texts on microskills training for counselors, Ivey and Ivey (2007) have included many findings from brain research that they believe counselors should know: "It is becoming apparent that effective counseling not only affects cognitive growth but also impacts the brain's development" (p. xviii). Cozolino (2002) referred to counseling as "rebuilding the human brain." In fact, whenever your work is successful in bringing about positive change, then you have altered your client's brain. Early in his career, Freud (1895) saw the project of psychology to be the uniting of neurological and psychological research. Over 100 years later, the time for Freud's project may be at hand.

When people consider the brain, they typically think of the neurons (nerves), numbering over 100 billion, that reside inside our heads. But brain activity consists of more than neurons. There are also a great number of chemical neurotransmitters and hormones that facilitate brain function, and each of the brain's neurons can have huge numbers of connections with other neurons, creating vast neural networks.

A simplistic example of a neural network is a billboard sign with pixels that actively spell out messages or display pictures at the ballpark. Like neurons, each pixel is limited to being on or off, but all these lights working together can create movement on the screen. At one instant, you may see Barry Bonds on the screen and, the next, his record-breaking home-run record, followed by an ad for a popular beer. The possibility of what can be on the screen is not limited to the number of pixels: It's patterns, not pixels. Likewise, the brain's 100 billion neuronal "pixels" can make a nearly infinite number of patterns.

Counseling actually changes those brain patterns because it offers an enriching atmosphere for clients to enhance their ways of thinking, manage their emotions, and learn new ways of coping (Cozolino, 2002). Borrowing a term from Fritz Perls (1977), Cozolino stated that counseling provides a "safe emergency" in which stressful learning alters neural networks. In fact, your support, empathy, and encouragement promote learning "through the enhanced production of dopamine, serotonin, norepinephrine, and other endogenous endorphins that support neural growth and plasticity" (Cozolino, 2002, p. 300). In addition, during productive work clients must be experiencing a moderately stressful safe emergency so that their brains are perturbed. The brain is a complex adaptive system that must be nudged into mild bifurcation and chaos, which, as you read in Chapter 5, can result in a new organization.

As clients experience the counseling relationship, their brains are "rewiring" themselves. For example, when the counselor attends to the client's story and helps the client focus on certain aspects of it, definite areas in both brains (counselor and client) become more active (Posner, 2004). This activity can be monitored with EEGs or functional MRIs. Such dramatic changes reflect the *neuroplasticity* of the brain, which can develop new neural connections throughout the lifespan and can respond to new situations or experiences (Draganski et al., 2004). Experience changes brains. Obviously, the brain's neuroplasticity has profound implications for the power and impact of counseling.

Emotions and Thought

Historically, most psychological researchers ignored emotions because they saw feelings as confusing and ephemeral, unnecessary for theory building, and incompatible with the dominant paradigm (Blume, 2006). This "dominant paradigm" held that emotions interrupted good thinking and that it is dispassionate reason that prevails in sane people. When the philosopher René Descartes said, "I think, therefore I am," he implied that thought is all there is to being. However, neuroscientist Antonio Damasio (1994, 2003) argued that Descartes's omission of emotions in the enterprise of good thinking was an error. From his research, Damasio concluded that there is an intuitive-emotional side to knowledge, which, if missing, can seriously hinder the reasoning process. In other words, we make the best decisions when our thoughts and emotions are integrated.

Damasio (1994, 2003) wrote that feelings known as *somatic markers* aid good judgment. Against conventional wisdom, which had considered emotion and feelings to be atavistic and useless contaminants of good decision making, Damasio asserted that they are an indispensable part of our cognitive process. When our thoughts and feelings are in harmony, our decisions are much more likely to turn out well. Too little emotion renders rational thought incapable of dealing with many of our most important problems. Successful thinking involves both the neocortex and the older areas of the brain.

When we reason in the manner of Descartes, we engage in "high reason." Rationality is the stuff of this process, and emotion is considered its adversary. High reason, unsullied by passions, is the holy grail of thought to which many intellectuals aspire. The somatic marker is, on the other hand, a felt sense. The *soma* (Greek for *body*) develops a "gut feeling" about the options under consideration. It marks the experience. If the feeling is negative, then an alarm goes off; if the feeling is positive, then we sense a satisfying confirmation, attraction, and perhaps elation. Somatic markers increase the accuracy and efficiency of the decision process. People with frontal lobe damage sometimes lose their ability to use their somatic markers. Although their decision making may strictly follow Descartes's ideal for pure, unemotional reason, their decisions are often grossly impaired, even bizarre.

Denying Emotion

Another neuroscientist, V. S. Ramachandran (2004), described an eerie condition, known as Cotard's syndrome, that some brain-injured people must endure. This disorder seems to be the result of the person's experiences being disconnected from the emotional centers of the brain. For such a patient, "nothing in the world has any emotional significance, no object or person, no tactile sensation, no sound—nothing—has emotional impact" (p. 91). The conclusion such a person must draw from this absence of emotional contact with the world is that he or she is dead! This unfortunate person has ceased to be. Without information coming from the emotional centers of the brain, notably the amygdala, otherwise rational people can believe that they do not exist.

While it may be difficult for us to relate to someone with such a bizarre condition as Cotard's syndrome, we have all experienced what Ramachandran called "mini-Cotard's." At times when you have been very ill, or have been extremely sleep deprived, or profoundly anxious or depressed, you may have experienced derealization or depersonalization. In such a dissociated state, your sense of being in the world is greatly diminished, and you may feel as if you are in a dream or that you cannot quite believe your experiences.

Ramachandran cited the famous case of the African explorer David Livingstone who described his experience while being viciously mauled by a lion. Livingstone said that he was completely detached from it all, as though he were seeing it from a distance, and he felt no fear or pain. Sometimes, rape victims or soldiers in combat describe similar reactions. Ramachandran suggested that during those moments, activities of the amygdala and other emotional centers of the brain are suppressed, while "the anterior cingulate activation generates extreme alertness and vigilance in preparation for any defensive reaction that might be required" (2004, p. 92).

Cozolino (2002) described such experiences as the dissociation of the brain's neural networks. If Dr. Livingstone had been flooded with emotion at the moment of danger, he might not have been able to act in order to bring about his survival. He could have been paralyzed with fear. Livingstone's sense of being at the crucial moment in his encounter with the lion was only vaguely experienced, and that was a good thing. But if such dissociation continues, the person loses vivid contact with personal experience. Occasionally, you will see clients whose presentation appears quite flat, and they will speak of a seemingly painful experience in a manner that seems so distant it could have happened to someone else.

Traumatic events affect people in different ways; one person "goes numb," while the other "falls apart." Too little emotion can negatively affect thinking, while too much emotion can do so as well. Your job is to manage extremes of emotional arousal so that the client may be able to work productively with you in counseling and begin to reintegrate those dissociated neural networks. In the Tools section of this chapter, we will offer some suggestions as to how this might be done.

The Amygdala and Hippocampus

Deep within the temporal regions of the brain, in an area some call the limbic system, are situated two very important structures: the amygdala and the hippocampus. The amygdala, so called because of its almondlike shape, is the key to our processing of strong emotions such as fear (LeDoux, 2002).

When people are in situations that provoke a fear response, they form a "figure-ground" memory of the event. For example, say you are held up at gunpoint while in a strange city. LeDoux pointed out that the salient feature of your memory, the figure that stands out, is the guy with the pistol pointed at you. However, the context of the robbery is also important. Anytime that you enter a comparable situation—a similar street corner, a strange city, or a different country—you may find yourself feeling afraid. The original fear associated with the robbery has generalized to the context, the environmental surroundings.

The hippocampus, which is important for learning and memory (Hawkins, 2002; Ivey & Ivey, 2007), is a loopy structure near the amygdala that some claim resembles a seahorse (Turkington, 1996). The amygdala and hippocampus are really neural networks, rather than single structures, and we all have these networks in both hemispheres of our brains.

The amygdala and hippocampus engage in an important and complementary balancing act. The amygdala is more responsible for implicit emotional memory, while the hippocampus serves the conscious, or explicit, part of our memory. The amygdala stimulates our hair-trigger emotional reactions to aspects of the environment, while the hippocampus inhibits these responses. The function of the amygdala is to generalize, and the purpose of the hippocampus is to discriminate. For example, if you see a spider, your amygdala may cause you to be initially startled. However, your hippocampus will help you recall that the particular spider is not poisonous, so you can relax (Cozolino, 2002). Sometimes, however, this stimulation–inhibition interaction between these two systems breaks down and they become dissociated from one another.

We know of a Vietnam veteran who had served as a medic in the war. He suffered from post-traumatic stress disorder (PTSD) and often found that seemingly innocuous sensory events would panic him. Sudden noises, helicopters in flight, and other cues could send him scampering for cover, despite the fact that he intellectually knew they posed no threat. He had administered medical aid to countless wounded men during the war, and he reported that now, when he would enter the front door of a supermarket, he could smell the meat department and would immediately experience great discomfort. His hippocampus was not doing its discriminatory and inhibitory job, and his amygdala had generalized the context of war to many aspects of his peacetime life. He would say, "I know it's nuts to be this jumpy around things that can't hurt me, but I can't help it."

It is by way of its connections with the prefrontal cortex of the brain that the hippocampus accomplishes its fear-reduction work (LeDoux, 2002). When we ask clients to tell their story of events that have been troubling to them, we are engaging the prefrontal cortex and the hippocampus. This intervention alone can help dampen or regulate the anxiety that has accompanied their concerns. We are asking them to employ their memory in piecing together the story so that it is cohesive and makes sense to us. As we respond to the story, besides acknowledging the negative aspects of it, we are pulling for overlooked details of a positive nature. This counseling process should serve to dampen an overactive amygdala, enhance the functioning of the hippocampus, and employ the prefrontal cortex in forming a coherent narrative with a more hopeful ending.

The hippocampus appears to encode "explicit memories" while the amygdala creates "implicit emotional memory" (LeDoux, 1996, p. 202). In a stressful situation, the amygdala primes us for action and registers an emotional memory of the event, while the hippocampus lays down a conscious memory of the situation. While memories are not actually stored in these two areas of the brain, damage to either will result in long-term memory impairment.

When someone is in a chronic state of emotional arousal, the amygdala and the hippocampus are at war with each other (LeDoux, 1996, 2002). The amygdala is stimulating the production of stress hormones throughout the body and brain, while the hippocampus is attempting to slow down this production. Engaged in such a conflict, the hippocampus may be unable to carry out its usual functions that support explicit memory. In fact, there is some evidence that the continued flooding of the hippocampus with stress hormones eventually even kills neurons in the hippocampus. Studies of people who have suffered prolonged stress show a marked degeneration of the hippocampal area.

EXPERIENCING THIS IDEA

Join with four or five colleagues. One of you volunteers to share a time when the amygdala overtook your reason. While telling the story, use a sculpting activity with two colleagues. Shape your colleagues into statues whose postures, gestures, and expressions indicate the depth of your affect. Then ask them to freeze for a few seconds as you explain the sculpture to the group. Then reshape the statues to illustrate the strategies that you used to manage your feelings. As time permits, continue with other volunteer sculptors.

Emotional Arousal and the Yerkes-Dodson Law

Optimal stress levels can help in the formation of explicit memories, making them stronger (Cozolino, 2002; LeDoux, 2002). Memory is likely to be enhanced under conditions of moderate stress due to the facilitatory effects of adrenaline, but too much adrenaline will block memory formation. In addition, moderate stress will increase attention, while intense stress may fragment awareness. How can stress both help and hinder cognitive functioning? This paradox is sometimes called the Yerkes-Dodson effect.

There exists a curvilinear (inverted-U) relationship between levels of emotional arousal and efficiency of performance (Martindale, 1981). The Yerkes-Dodson Law, first articulated in 1908, reflects this relationship. Simply put, the quality of performance on any task, physical or mental, is a function of the level of emotional arousal. Very low levels of arousal produce little in the way of efficient performance, while extremely high levels produce scattered and inefficient performance. Optimal performance occurs when emotional arousal is sufficient to motivate, but not so high as to fragment production. Our counseling students have dubbed this optimal area "the zone."

Imagine that emotional arousal proceeds from left to right in Figure 9-1. Someone who is at the extreme left would be comatose, while someone at the extreme right would be on the verge of a crack-up. When your clients merely talk about emotions or describe seemingly emotion-producing situations in a flat narrative style, then they are operating closer to the left end of arousal. They are not sufficiently aroused to do productive work with their concerns. Because such clients have defensively withdrawn any emotional awareness from their narratives, any change brought about at this level will be sterile and intellectual. Your job will be to perturb their emotional arousal.

Head Scratching

Sometimes when people are momentarily confused by an event they have witnessed we hear them saying, "That situation left me scratching my head." Of course, this is a metaphorical statement; they don't necessarily mean that they were really scratching their head. But did you realize that every time you *do* scratch your head, this movement makes a loud internal sound? Go ahead, try it! You heard the sound, didn't you? Most of the time when we scratch our heads, this sound occurs outside our awareness, and we hear it only when it is called to our attention—like just now.

When we become aware of previously unnoticed events, alternate pathways in our brains are turned on (Hawkins, 2004). This can occur in two ways. The first is a signal from the cortex, our higher brain, and the second is a powerful and surprising signal from our lower, more primitive brain. Your first awareness may have occurred when we asked you to scratch your head and hear the sound. This signal is a *cognitive* stimulation. The second type of stimulation would probably occur if your amygdala were

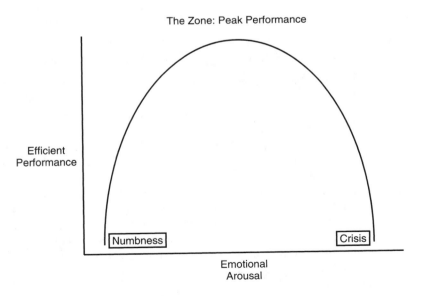

FIGURE 9-1 The Yerkes-Dodson Law.

prompted to action by the realization of novelty or error: "There's a big bump on my head!" This would be an *affective* stimulation, which Hawkins characterized as a "wake-up signal."

Hawkins (2004) offers a good example of these two types of signals. When you view a portrait, you activate a neural pathway that is involved in face recognition. This neural pathway does not arouse any intense emotions. However, if the face had a severe wound on it, you would first recognize it, but suddenly you would be alerted through the lower pathway that something is horribly wrong, and you would immediately be overwhelmed by a powerful emotional reaction.

When we are attempting to deconstruct a client's telling of a problem-saturated story, sometimes we attempt to cognitively redirect their attention to the possibility of exceptions to problems. This cognitive strategy is like asking them to scratch their heads and tune in to other aspects of the events they are relating to us. At other times, we attempt to perturb them by bringing surprise to their telling of the story, stimulating the affective pathway. We pursue this affective strategy by raising emotional arousal.

If we can work on both these pathways—cognitive and affective—our chances of creating what Bateson called "the difference that makes a difference" in the clients' narratives are increased. They will then have to consider their stories in a new light, and we may be able to, in effect, leave them scratching their heads.

The Neural Substrate

Just below the surface of that head scratch on your skull is a universe of neural networks. Some have called the brain a "frontier" that, when explored further, will yield rich treasures and deep understandings. Counselors who attempt to learn more about neuroscience will come to appreciate that, when they are counseling, they are simultaneously altering brain processes (Cozolino, 2002). Regardless of their theoretical orientation, successful counselors promote neural growth and integration of neural networks throughout the therapeutic process. From the initial stage of counseling, establishing a safe and trusting relationship, to the final stage, of termination, you engage your client in processes that enhance brain functioning.

Implications of These Ideas for the Counselor

The recent neurological research regarding psychotherapy and the brain has significant implications for our work as counselors.

- In order for clients to make good decisions in most situations, their emotions *must* be involved. Therefore, you need to notice when your client is displaying emotions in the session.
- You should observe where your client is in terms of emotional arousal in the session. Your goal is to keep him or her in "the zone." If the client is too far to the left of the Yerkes-Dodson curve, then perturb. If too far to the right, soothe.
- When you are counseling people, you are engaging their brains as well as their minds. Counseling actually alters brains.

TOOLS

Counseling Brains

In a counseling session, when your client becomes emotionally aroused, the reticular activating system at the brain's stem lights up and sends stimulation to the rest of the brain. At the same time, selective attention, or focus, stimulates areas in the thalamus, which acts as a spotlight shining on the stimulus. When you are counseling, you are focusing the client's attention on certain aspects of the story and ignoring others. You are also trying to manage the client's emotional arousal, so that it is in a range (or "zone") that is most supportive to the client's productive thinking.

When you are attending to the client's story, be careful to allow the client to lead, while you adopt your "not from around here," nonexpert attitude. This is important because the client is drawing on memory, and we know from the studies of Loftus (1997) and others that memory is constructed. Our job is to co-construct the client's story so that it includes more possibilities. We are not trying to insert memories of events that have never taken place, but we are trying to help clients retrieve previously overlooked memories of events when they successfully engaged their resources and resolve.

Also keep in mind that your questions can actually suggest new ways of thinking (Ivey & Ivey, 2007). When you ask, "When you have handled this sort of challenge in the past, how did you deal with it?", you are inviting your client to search for positive memories of successes. The ideas you wish to put in a client's head are of strength, resilience, and resourcefulness. You want to help clients retrieve memories that will counter their stories of despair and to insert the possibility of remembered events that have not previously been in their awareness.

You need to take care not to explore for painful material, because, by doing so, you may be putting even more negative ideas and emotions into the conversation. While you attend and acknowledge the client's story of pain, you should not exacerbate the agony. The "safe emergency" that we mentioned above is a matter of pacing and leading. When clients are engaged in problem-saturated talk, you provide a safe environment by pacing, tracking, and acknowledging their stories. Then, when the timing seems right, you can begin to lead by asking for exceptions to the story that illuminate your client's strengths and prompt talk of resilience to emerge into the conversation.

As you listen to the client's story, you should offer a faint understanding smile. Smiling is a primary way of communicating warmth and acceptance (Restak, 2003). Also, the recent research on mirror neurons, which we discussed in Chapter 3, suggests that when your clients see you smile encouragingly their brains automatically respond with a sense of pleasure. Like that researcher picking up a raisin, when you pick up your interest and energy, your client tends to mirror it. However, because smiles can communicate many messages you do not wish your clients to receive (such as mocking or sardonic smiles), you may want to practice your accepting smile in the mirror and ask your supervisor to comment on how your smiles look on video recordings of your counseling. Research suggests that positive feelings stimulate areas of the frontal cortex and serve to calm turbulent emotions, such as fear and anger, that the amygdala encodes in the limbic system.

The frontal cortex also organizes our more complex emotions into layers that sometimes contradict each other (Kolb & Wishaw, 2003). An example of these multilayered emotions is when a beloved person gives you a gift that you don't like. Perhaps it is your birthday, and your partner has given you a new vacuum cleaner. At one level, you may feel irritated at this gift giver for not recognizing that something more personal would have been nice. At another level, you appreciate the fact that your partner remembered your birthday at all, and you also feel guilty for not acknowledging that "it is the thought that counts." At still another level, you worry that your lack of enthusiasm on receipt of the gift will betray your disappointment and make your partner feel foolish and ashamed. Finally, all these conflicted levels of emotion could fire off in your amygdala and result in you blowing a fuse (Ivey & Ivey, 2007).

Obviously, many different areas of the brain will have been stimulated during this hypothetical event. It is important for you to remember that emotions and brain activity do not come in only one "flavor." This is why we caution our counselors-in-training not to ask clients, "How did that make you feel?" Feelings are much more complicated than the simple answer your client is likely to offer in response to that question.

New discoveries in brain research have encouraged counselors to be more positive (Ivey & Ivey, 2007). For example, positive feelings are necessary to manage the negative emotions, which are embedded deep within the brain. Therefore, if your client speaks only of painful events and difficult interactions with others, the networks that stimulate negative emotions remain activated. Your mission as the counselor is to see if you can alter the conversation toward the affirmative, helping to give the neural circuits that support hope and resolve a chance to be stimulated.

Extremes of Emotional Reaction

Examples of the two extremes of the emotional continuum might be the alexithymic at one end and the "slave to passion" at the other. The term *alexithymia* comes from the Greek meaning "having no" (*a-*) "word" (*lexis*) for "emotion" (*thymos*). Most people with this difficulty appear flat and unflappable, without feeling. Though they rarely cry, when they do, alexithymics spew copious tears. When asked to explain the tears streaming down their cheeks, they are befuddled because they "are utterly lacking in the fundamental skill of emotional intelligence, self awareness" (Goleman, 1995, p. 51). Like small children who have not yet developed nuanced terms for their feelings, the best alexithymics can do is describe their feelings as good or bad, happy or sad. Ramachandran and Blakeslee (1998) wrote of a man who had suffered a stroke that severed the connections between his amygdala and higher cortical areas. To the observer, it was often obvious when this poor man was having emotional reactions, but he reported feeling nothing.

On the other hand, people who are chronic slaves to passion seem always at the mercy of their overactive amygdalas. It takes very little to set them off. They regularly erupt either in fits of rage or pitiful bouts of emotional lability. Their passionate outbursts often follow a pattern. First, they perceive some threat, whether to physical well-being or self-esteem. Then, a limbic surge is triggered, releasing catecholamines that generate the rush of energy we know as "fight or flight." Finally, the amygdala-driven release of additional chemicals, such as adrenaline and cortisol, excites and agitates the brain. The calming influence of the hippocampus and frontal lobes is then overwhelmed by the strength of the emotion.

Both extremes, being either emotionally "clueless" or emotionally overwhelmed, render a person unable to make good social judgments. Somewhere between the alexithymic and the slave to passion lies the middle ground of emotional intelligence. Too little experience of emotional feeling creates the "zombie" with a seemingly hollow core. Too much emotion brings chronic worry, suspicion, rage, and depression. While your clients may not suffer such extremes of emotional flooding or deprivation, knowing about such disorders should serve as a reminder that you need to manage emotional arousal in clients as they speak of their concerns.

In cases of trauma, the usual reactions are those of overwhelming pain, suffering, and fear. At these times, when the emotions are flooding in, the person has difficulty thinking clearly and mobilizing resources effectively (Wilson, 1989). If the trauma survivor reacts with outcries, tears, and wails, the person's distress is sharp and obvious. However, in some instances of extreme emotional intensity, a few people remain unaware of the emotional events taking place within their body. Their presentation may be decidedly flat, unexpressive, and numb.

When clients are feeling emotionally overwrought about their current circumstances or are reacting to a recent traumatic event, your approach will be to soothe them. Their emotions are running too high for them to do productive work in the counseling session. Until their emotions are calmed to the point of being back in the zone, it is best to offer emotional support to your clients. Never try to reason with people who are in a strong emotional state. In the case of dampened or numbed clients, you work to increase their emotional responses by challenging or perturbing them in some way. The goal in either case is to move the client into the zone by managing emotional arousal.

Managing emotional arousal in your clients is very important to your eventual success with them. You may find it helpful to imagine that you are viewing the client through a screen on which is located the Yerkes-Dodson curve, and that you are watching a moving needle indicating where your client is on that curve from moment to moment. Assessing the client's emotional arousal is, of course, more art than science. You can't see the neural networks changing connections, but when you are helping to manage the emotional arousal of your client, you are actually changing brain functioning (Vaughan, 1997).

Lowering Emotional Arousal

If you are seeing someone who has recently experienced a major crisis, or if you are talking with a client who appears to be quite stressed or agitated, then you will have to employ some "quieting" techniques with your client (Young, 1998). Most quieting methods are "safe and quickly lead to positive experiences by clients" (p. 221). You will have to make an assessment of your client's level of emotional arousal as you speak with him or her, and determine whether he or she is too aroused to be in the zone. If you consider this to be the case, then you will want to engage in behaviors that are comforting to your client. Obviously, the first step is to communicate to your clients by word and behavior that they are *safe* in their relationship with you. All of the suggestions for establishing the relationship with your client that were discussed in the Chapters 2 and 3 regarding the LUV Triangle and empathy apply here. You must not behave in any way that suggests that you are disagreeing or wishing to contest your client's point of view.

Speak in *soothing* tones and work slowly. Your voice should be slightly less loud than your clients', though your decibel level should rise and fall with theirs, so as to match their fluctuations of emotional expressiveness. Also, match your client's pace and rhythm by paying attention to the person's breathing, rate of speech, metaphors, and tonal variation. Be sensitive to how your clients are reacting to moments of silence in the session. If they seem calmed by silence, then they are experiencing "formless quiescence" (Cozolino, 2002), a feeling of momentary solace and respite from their concerns.

Your clients will sometimes lapse into what is known as a transderivational search in which their neural nets are integrating and forming new awarenesses. It is important for you to refrain from impinging upon these moments. Simply allow your clients to engage in reverie, and you will be able to note the moment when they "come back into the room." There will be a slight shift in their bodies and their eyes will appear as if they have just awakened. You could then say something on the order of, "It looked like you were coming up with some good ideas just now." Often, their response will be that they had thought of something not previously in their awareness. If that "something" is negative, acknowledge it; if it is positive, capitalize on it.

You must determine how *physically close* to your client you should be in order to maintain comfort. Some clients want you to be quite near to them, while others will "need more space" and may experience closeness as a threat. The same goes for how much *eye contact* you maintain while talking with them. Some clients may want a lot of eye contact to confirm that you are paying close attention. Others may not want you to look at them, because they believe that they "look a mess" or that you will easily detect their sense of shame or guilt.

Until your client is soothed enough to be entering the zone, you should not use any influencing techniques. Initially, employ only your attending skills, and wait to be invited to help. As clients tell their stories, if they experience you as listening, understanding, and validating, they will begin to feel less overwhelmed and will often afterward report that a "weight has been lifted off their shoulders." Once clients realize that you are interested in hearing their stories without judging or arguing, they will become comforted. After all, how often do any of us experience another person's willingness to focus exclusively on us without putting in their "two cents' worth"? Once clients learn that you are such a person, your very presence will lower their emotional arousal.

You will, of course, acknowledge that your client has been suffering, but you will not be displaying undue interest in the details by exploring this turmoil. This is what we call "sightseeing," and it serves only to intensify the negative mood. Acknowledge the pain and then attempt to move on. If you have not acknowledged enough, the client will let you know by returning to problem-saturated talk, in which case you must acknowledge further before once again attempting to move toward resolution-focused talk. When clients are engaged in problem-saturated talk, manage the associated emotional arousal by keeping it toward the left side of the zone of the Yerkes-Dodson curve.

LISTENING IN ON A SESSION

Review Bob's story at the beginning of the chapter. A counselor might work to reduce the client's arousal in the following way. We pick up the dialogue with Bob's final comment.

Bob: "... The hell with him and with the rest of them, who cares!"

Counselor: (While the client has been telling his story, the counselor has been looking Bob in the eyes, leaning forward, shaking his head and reacting with empathic grimaces to the accounts of upsetting events, and nodding to the client's complaints. The counselor speaks and gestures with some energy and expressiveness, but slower and softer than Bob.)

"You've really been feeling pissed off and fed up with the way people've been treating you."

Bob: (This time, he allows the counselor to finish his comment.)

"You damn right! And I hate the way that they look at me, like I'm some useless relic who's just taking up space and the way they make me the butt of their snide comments. Of course, they say that they're just joking and that they don't really mean anything they're saying, but I'm not the doddering idiot that they take me for. I'm still sharp enough to notice when somebody's not treating me right. In fact, I didn't like it when Reverend Cummings told me I should come here. I'm not senile and I'm not 'going postal,' either."

Counselor: (At the start, his voice has an edge that emphasizes "sick" and "tired" to convey the intensity of Bob's emotions.)

"You have been feeling *sick* and *tired* of being typecast as 'the bitter old man.' Now you'd like to find a way to help people realize how hard you've had to work and how valuable your contributions have been over the years."

Bob: "Bingo! But how the heck can I do that? Every time I think about how I'm treated, I get worked up and my good intentions go out the window. I'm sure that sometimes I do sound like some cranky old buzzard."

Counselor: (Smiles at the "Bingo!" comment. He earnestly leans forward and looks directly at Bob for a moment.)

"Bob, before we talk about how you're going to find a way to do that, I'd like to thank you for being so open and up front with me, even though I'm probably about the same age as these people at work. How did you get yourself to take that risk with somebody who's young enough to be your son?"

Bob: (He chuckles.)

"Hell, it's not that hard—you're paid to be nice to me."

REFLECTING QUESTIONS

1. Where was Bob on the inverted-*U* figure when he entered the session?
2. What did the counselor do to influence Bob's emotional arousal?
3. How might you respond to Bob's last statement?

USING THIS TOOL

Form a small group with two colleagues. One of you volunteers to role-play, with emotional intensity, a character similar to Bob from the chapter story. Another volunteers to listen, understand, and validate while also using the above techniques to lower emotional arousal. Keep in mind that although your words are important here, your body language and tone of voice are essential influencing factors. Finally, the third person serves as the recorder who observes the activity and leads the feedback discussion.

Raising Emotional Arousal

Unlike approaches to therapy that attempt to evoke the clients' repressed and painful memories so that they abreact events that have been troubling, we are simply trying to raise emotional arousal so that clients can work productively with their concerns. Young (1998) enumerated the benefits of increasing emotional arousal and expression as stimulants for change. He stated that emotional arousal and expression tend to promote greater self-understanding by making more real what would otherwise be merely an intellectual experience. Arousal can "melt down old attitudes . . . therapeutic change being an 'unfreezing and refreezing' process, meaning that the client's world view can be catalyzed by emotional arousal" (p. 231).

For clients, the counseling situation can have inherently arousing aspects. Just the experience of coming to a counselor's office for the first time brings with it an emotional tension. It is a bit like being sent to the principal's office. The client is not sure whether you will be friendly or punitive or whether you can be trusted at all. Furthermore, if you are doing your job correctly, you have placed the onus on your client to account for what has brought him or her to counseling, and it is not clear just what you want to know. Clients wonder whether you might decide that they are to blame for their situation or perhaps that they are mentally ill, and they speculate as to what sort of power you have to cause them harm. Merely coming to counseling is emotionally arousing!

Other aspects of the counseling situation are stressful for your client, such as an unaccustomed amount of silence between verbal utterances, more eye contact than your client is used to, and finding that he or she is the person who is the focus of the entire conversation. For these, and other reasons, it is not difficult to raise the level of emotional arousal in the first session with the client. The initial task, then, is to provide a reassuring environment so that arousal does not zoom past the zone and become crippling anxiety.

In subsequent sessions, however, as the client becomes more comfortable, you may need to deliberately raise the client's stress level. Many new counselors are overly concerned with making their clients comfortable and do not realize that a client who is too relaxed will sink back into unproductive, intellectual, and sometimes rambling conversation.

LISTENING IN ON A SESSION

Review Carla's story at the beginning of the chapter. A resolution-focused counselor can work to increase her emotional arousal in the following way.

Carla: (She glances occasionally at the counselor, gestures haltingly to emphasize a point, and speaks in a hesitant manner.)

"To be frank with you, this . . . was not my idea. My supervisor at work strongly recommended that I make an appointment. Don't get me wrong—I don't blame her and I'm not here under protest. She's always been very caring and supportive . . . and I know she's been worried about me the past few months. Besides, things are such a . . . mess in my life right now that I have to agree with her that something has to be done."

Counselor: (She speaks with a little more expressiveness than Carla and at a slightly quicker pace.)

"So you have been unhappy with how things are going in your life and you're here now to do something about it."

Carla: (She gives the counselor a quick, tight-lipped smile and raises her eyebrows.)

"Yeah, but I've had plenty of good intentions and grand ideas before for turning my life around . . . and I'm still in this same mess. I'm reluctant to naively think that counseling is going to . . . magically change all that."

Counselor: (She leans forward, continues to speak with more energy, and looks directly at Carla.)

"Yes, but if you did turn your life around this time, how would it be different?"

Carla: (She tilts her head to one side and nods.)

"I need to give that question some thought. Like I said, I've had some grand ideas these past few months, but that's where they've stayed—at the idea stage. It's been so rough with Sandy gone from my life that sometimes I wonder if I'll ever be able to turn it around. I've never been through such a painful time in my life."

Counselor: (She maintains eye contact, pauses before speaking, and gestures to emphasize the feelings.)

"You've been going through a time of *heartbreak* and *grief* that's been the worst that you've ever endured. How have you been able to hang in there through all this?"

Carla: (Her eyes glisten with tears.)

"I have wondered about that myself."

1. Where was Carla on the inverted-*U* figure when she entered the session?
2. What did the counselor do to influence Carla's emotional arousal?
3. How might you respond to Carla's last statement?

USING THIS TOOL

Form a group with two colleagues. One of you volunteers to role-play a character similar to Carla from the chapter story. In particular, try to duplicate her lack of emotional intensity. Another volunteers to listen, understand, and validate while also using the above techniques to raise emotional arousal. Keep in mind that, although your words are important here, your body language and tone of voice are essential influencing factors. Finally, the third person serves as the recorder who observes the activity and leads the feedback discussion.

Making the Implicit Explicit

New clients will be fearful that you are going to call attention to something that had not consciously occurred to them, and that they will feel foolish for not seeing it sooner. Too much surprise is unwelcome. Imagine, for example, that you are out on a date with an extremely attractive person and doing your best to appear sophisticated and urbane. At dinner, as you smile alluringly and lean in closer, your date breaks into laughter and points out that you have broccoli stuck in your front teeth. How humiliating! This is the metaphor for client worries about being caught off guard.

Whenever something that is unconsciously or implicitly known—but not explicitly in awareness—is forced into our consciousness, we may experience it as repugnant. "Yuck!" is often our immediate response. Consider two examples offered by Combs and Avila (1985). If you accidentally cut your finger, you might automatically stick it in your mouth. As a result, you might drink some of your own blood, but you probably would do so without much awareness or concern. However, after bandaging your finger, you would probably be revolted by the suggestion of licking any blood then— "yuck!" A second example is one that occurs even more frequently. Throughout the day, you are regularly swallowing your own saliva without any reaction. However, if this saliva were collected in a glass for you to swallow, you probably would have a strong negative reaction!

Fearing that you will bring something into the client's awareness that will create feelings of foolishness or yuckiness, the client will likely react defensively. Making implicit knowledge explicit is a powerful tool for raising emotional arousal, but it is not without risk. When the client believes that you are not simply trying to make a fool of him or her or win some "putdown" game, the client will be more open to your arousal-producing feedback.

Empathic Immediacy and Interpretation

Sometimes, clients seem to behave in discrepant ways. For example, as they tell their stories, they may display incongruity between verbal and nonverbal messages, between their stated values and behaviors, or between two inconsistent verbal statements (Young, 2005). It may occasionally be helpful to call attention to these discrepancies in order to clarify the client's story or to check on the interpersonal process between you and your client. However, you must always do so in the spirit of the naïve listener who is attempting to fully understand rather than convey your skepticism or disbelief in the story. You will be making implicit behaviors explicit, but, if you take care, your client will not be humiliated by this move.

Two techniques that might be helpful in this regard are immediacy and interpretation. An *immediacy* (also called a *process observation* or *metatalk*) is a here-and-now comment highlighting the encounter between you and your client. You are calling attention to what is happening in the moment (Teyber, 2006). Such comments bring the topic of conversation "into the room." Immediacies call attention to client behaviors, highlight interactions between you and your client, or express your private reactions that are helpful for the client to hear.

An *interpretation* takes place when you provide feedback on what you are hearing your client say (or seeing your client do), but you add something to the reflection from your own frame of reference. Interpretations work best when they proceed from an observation of something happening here and now in the relationship.

Anytime you are attempting to deconstruct the client's story, you are, in effect, interpreting. Such techniques as relabeling, reframing, creative misunderstanding, or adding possibility statements to acknowledgments (Rogers with a Twist), are all interpretations because they add your perspective to the content of the client's story. These interpretations, if skillfully delivered, are rather subtle and do not jeopardize your stance as a nonexpert who is "not from around here."

However, sometimes a more obvious interpretation is necessary. A cautious interpretation should be "combined with empathic interventions to provide support and encouragement and reduce any threat presented by the interpretations . . . [and be] carefully timed so that the client is receptive rather than resistant" (Seligman, 2004, p. 201). Interpretations should be offered tentatively. Be sure to "own" your interpretation, and be prepared to "take it back" if the client seems unwilling to accept it. Some more directive therapeutic approaches refer to the technique of interpretation as "the therapist's scalpel." We prefer to think of it as more of a pinprick. You can use a mild interpretation to focus the client on what is happening in the session, raise emotional arousal, and add alternatives to how the client's story can be told.

When clients present in an incongruent manner or tell a discrepant story, they may be (a) reluctant to fully realize their emotions, (b) compartmentalizing their thoughts to avoid cognitive dissonance, (c) trying to keep themselves from being hurt or exposed, or (d) simply struggling to put their story together in a coherent manner. Most of the time, these behaviors are unintentional.

Sometimes, however, this way of behaving is quite deliberate. Do you remember a time when you went to a job interview and struggled very hard to manage the impression that the employer would have of you? Do you also remember how exhausting it was to keep up this behavior? Mark Snyder (2003) coined the term "high self-monitor" for those people who are good at deliberate emotional expression designed to make a desired impression on others. He quoted W. H. Auden, who wrote of "the image which I try to create in the minds of others in order that they might love me" (in Snyder, 2003, p. 130). This process of impression management can lead to striking gaps or contradictions between our public appearances and our private realities. Those who excel at this impression management ability are good at picking up cues and quickly learning which behavior is appropriate in social situations, and they exercise good control over the way in which they are perceived.

The empathic counselor can detect this incongruity in the client's presentation style. You can usually see through this display and know that the client is simply attempting to get you to think that he or she is a likeable person, a good and compliant client, and not too crazy. An untrained person would simply dismiss this impression-management attempt as deception. All of us offer our façade in social situations with which we are unfamiliar, but if a client persists in this form of self-monitoring, the message may be that he or she believes that the true self, with its true emotions, is unacceptable and must be masked by a social self. Years ago, Carl Rogers characterized this attitude as originating under "conditions of worth" (Presbury, McKee, and Echterling, 2007).

Instead of receiving the message that they are acceptable just as they are, children are sometimes placed in a condition of being "sculpted" by their parents or other significant people. During their developmental years, the message they have received from others is, "I will love you if—and only if—you become the person who is acceptable to me." The problem that arises from these conditions of worth is that if people learn to live as others wish, and deliberately attempt to behave according to an external standard, the resulting false self may eclipse the sense of who they are. They may ultimately fool even themselves into believing that their mask is their true self.

When your clients attempt to manage your impressions, they are telling you that they believe that you can accept only their false self and that it is too dangerous to reveal their actual self to you. They are willing to "sell out" for a good impression. So, what are you to do with a client who offers an inauthentic face in the session? Has your empathy—your ability to sense the true client—backfired on you? How can you maintain a caring relationship and a positive regard for clients when they are hiding their true selves?

Remember that all clients are reluctant to let themselves be known and that this hesitancy inhibits their freedom when interacting with you. At first, they may attempt to manipulate your perceptions of them. They will use the well-rehearsed defensive style that they have developed to hide the shame of being "unacceptable." They may present as "the respectful client," "the helpless client," "the tough-guy client," or "the know-it-all client." Your task is to offer acceptance of who they are behind their masks so that they become more willing to be authentically self-disclosing.

Consider the following possible offerings of immediacies combined with interpretations:

- To the "respectful" client, you might say, "I notice that you compliment me a lot, and today you have brought me a gift. It's almost as if you think I wouldn't, or couldn't, like you just for you."
- To the "helpless" client, you could comment, "You seem to be saying that you are unable take that first step toward your goal. I wonder if it feels to you like I am pushing you too hard."

- To the "tough-guy" client, you can observe, "This is the third time today you have said that this problem really doesn't bother you. It's almost as if you don't feel I am quite convinced that you are a strong person."
- And to the "know-it-all client," you could share, "It seems to be really important to you that I get the facts right about what you are saying. I'm glad that you're comfortable straightening me out on important things that will help me to understand you better."

Once clients realize that you will not respond to them with scolding, shock, scorn, or moral indignation, they will be encouraged by this lack of expected censure, and may then begin to reveal themselves more authentically. You will then have created a condition that Carl Rogers (1961) termed "unconditional positive regard." When Rogers said that he "winced" at the idea of "reflection" of client feelings, he meant that it is not the technique that is important. It is your own authentic manner of communicating that you actually *do* care. When the client gets this message, you have effectively communicated your empathic feeling for the client's predicament and your desire to be helpful. Keep your instrument tuned up, and this caring will come through without effort, and you will obtain permission from the client to push a bit harder toward the client's goal.

Sometimes, your clients will be experiencing involuntary emotional states that are inhibiting progress in the session. They will seem frightened, angry, or depressed. You can productively use immediacies and interpretations in order to call attention to what is happening in your relationship, and to tentatively offer your understanding of what your client might be experiencing but has not mentioned. When you employ these techniques judiciously, they will offer an opportunity to move the process along in productive ways that simply tracking your client's comments cannot do. They are especially helpful when talk of unspoken emotions is needed in the relationship.

For the sake of simplicity, you can think of negative emotions as three different colors: yellow, red, and black (Echterling, Presbury, & McKee, 2005). *Yellow emotions*, like the traffic light that signals caution, are characterized by anxiety, fear, and reluctance. Clients are often experiencing yellow emotions in the counseling session. Apprehension and anxiety can be highly adaptive, even essential, in threatening circumstances, because they prompt behaviors that can sometimes avoid unpleasant outcomes. However, while it makes very good sense to hold your breath while swimming under water, it is not adaptable behavior after you have climbed out of the pool. Many clients allow yellow emotions to pervade all their relationships, even when no threat is present. Your client may appear "tight as a coiled spring" and may find it difficult to relax and be at ease. At such times, there may be something in your relationship that is threatening to your client. Sometimes, an immediacy and interpretation from you may help relieve this tension. For example, you might say, "As I see how you are holding your arms across your chest, and being a bit vague in your manner of speaking, I am thinking you look on edge today . . . almost as if you expect that I might act in some way to injure you." Often, this intervention produces a change of mood in the client and a response such as, "It's not you, I'm just worried about . . ." If this happens, you have turned the defensive display of caution into a discussion of what is bothering the client.

Red emotions are anger, resentment, and hostility. Certainly, anger can be a very appropriate and valuable emotional response to adversity, physical threat, and personal violation. Outrage and fury can energize people to protect themselves and others, persevere in overcoming obstacles, and mobilize resources. At times, however, anger can be maladaptive. Chronic anger leads people to feel resentful, embittered, and mad at the world (Novaco & Chemtob, 1998). The commonsense notion is that anger must be "gotten out," or vented. This idea seems to come from the old notion of catharsis, based on a steam boiler metaphor: Heat builds under the boiler, and pressure increases to the point that, if not released, the boiler will "blow." This metaphor makes it seem obvious that expressing anger is therapeutic.

But Williams and Williams (1998), in their book *Anger Kills,* stated that venting anger is not always good for us. Their research suggested that if we have a really good reason, and an effective (nondestructive) response, then we should go ahead and express our anger. However, people sometimes have a chronic "edge" that comes through as irritation and suspicion in most situations. Besides creating problems in their relationships, this type of anger compromises people's immune systems and sets them up for illness.

Clients may bring this type of anger to the counseling session. In such cases, you could find yourself becoming defensive. An immediacy and interpretation may be useful when you are presented with a client's generalized anger, only, in this case, your interpretation will be a "creative misunderstanding." "I notice as you are talking, your facial muscles seem tense and your fists are doubling up. I wonder if there is something I have said or done that has made you angry." Like the "yellow emotion" example above, the client is likely to respond by explaining that the anger has nothing to do with you, which will then open up the conversation to resolving the client's issues. On the other hand, if the anger *is* directed at you, this offers the opportunity for you to "clean up the mess" that was otherwise going unstated and affecting your relationship. When you respond to a client's anger in a way that is different from others in the client's world, you have set the condition for a corrective emotional experience (Teyber, 2006).

Black emotions are the depression, hopelessness, shame, and grief that many people in counseling are experiencing. The psychodynamic explanation is that these emotions are really anger turned back on the self. While we do not wholly subscribe to this explanation, we do think that when discouraging events go unprocessed, they tend to build into an amalgam of confusion, depression, and self-blame. Sometimes, these events are not major traumas but are simply the buildup of day-to-day niggling annoyances; they are like being nibbled to death by ducks. The brain's amygdala will encode hurtful emotional memories that must later be cognitively processed in order for the person to gain some rational control over them. If these emotions go unprocessed, they will remain a torment to the individual. Eventually, such emotional accumulation can take its toll, even on brave and self-possessed individuals who believe they are unaffected by these small insults.

Hans Selye's (1976) classic research on chronic stress suggested that we tend to accommodate to repeated stressful events so that we barely notice that we are stressed. This is the "numbing effect" described above. Eventually, however, if we allow the tension to build, we inevitably collapse into exhaustion either physically or emotionally, or both. Some clients may present with the "John Wayne syndrome"—a reluctance to admit any physical or emotional pain. Bravado, however, serves only to make the emotions less accessible.

Successfully managing emotions involves experiencing and working through these feelings, rather than suppressing them (Gross, 1998). Some clients may just seem "blah" and slow to respond, as if they were functioning under water. This may be *anhedonia*, which often accompanies depression. Anhedonia is considered the absence of joy or energy for living.

Occasionally, it seems you must serve as a surrogate amygdala for the John Wayne or anhedonic clients and help them reconnect with the emotions that have been buried. As they speak of stressful events in their lives about which they seem unaffected, you can tune into your own experience and imagine what you would feel if these same events had happened to you. An immediacy, in the form of a self-disclosure, and an interpretation, in the form of a hypothesis, can help in such situations. For example, you could say, "As you are talking about what happened to you, I am feeling a profound sense of sadness, and, since that happened to you and not me, I can imagine that you are feeling even worse. Tell me if I'm right about that," or "I am kinda mystified by looking at you as you talk of this. I don't see or hear in your voice the sadness that I am feeling. I wonder if I am way off base here."

SUMMARY

Contrary to the assertions of poets, emotions do not come from the heart but from the older parts of the brain such as the amygdala. And contrary to public opinion, emotions actually improve our thinking and judgment. Recent brain research has demonstrated that successful counseling can rebuild a client's brain by helping reintegrate dissociated neural networks. As a counselor, one of your important strategies is to influence your client's emotional level to benefit from the Yerkes-Dodson Law. Too little or too much emotional arousal is counterproductive, so you strive to maintain your clients' arousal in the optimal zone.

SEGUE TO CHAPTER 10

Think of a movie that you have seen recently that involved a crisis somewhere in its plot. In fact, it's difficult to think of a movie, even a comedy, that does not include at least a minor crisis as a turning point. How were the characters feeling during that crisis? How did they resolve it? How were they changed as a result of the crisis?

Resource

LeDoux Laboratory
Center for Neural Science
New York University
www.cns.nyu.edu/home/ledoux/

On this home page, you click on the pictured amygdala to enter this informative and fun website. It describes research projects, gives information on upcoming conferences, and even has a theme song about the amygdala—"All in a Nut!"

CHAPTER 10

Counseling People in Crisis
Promoting Resilience and Resolution

"Only through experience of trial and suffering can the
soul be strengthened, vision cleared, ambition inspired,
and success achieved."
Helen Keller

"Great emergencies and crises show us how much greater
our vital resources are than we had supposed."
William James

CHAPTER GOALS

The goals of this chapter are to help you understand the following fundamental ideas:

- Crisis is a concept that emphasizes a crucial turning point, a decisive moment of both danger and opportunity.
- Factors that promote resilience include social support, meaning making, managing emotions, and envisioning possibilities.
- The goal of crisis counseling is to help victims become survivors who can go on to become thrivers in their lives.

Reading about and practicing the tools in this chapter will help you learn to

- Adapt brief counseling techniques to crisis situations.
- Reach out with LUV in a crisis, find the survivor, help the survivor take heart, and help the survivor to begin moving on.

STORY

Back in the 1970s, when they were young children, Hoang's parents did not know each other, but, though their lives would not cross paths until later, they endured remarkably similar adversities. They had been "boat people," refugees who had risked their lives sailing on overcrowded, unsound vessels to flee the chaos and turmoil of Vietnam when the American troops had withdrawn from the war. After that ordeal, their families then had to navigate equally dangerous and uncertain bureaucratic currents, spending months in refugee camps before they found sponsors for their immigration to the United States.

Finally arriving in this country, the families of Hoang's parents eventually settled in the familiarly humid climate of Biloxi, Mississippi. Their ancestors had always fished for their livelihoods, so it was only natural that they, along with many other refugees, would become shrimpers. At first, the Vietnamese suffered the racism of the mostly Anglo shrimpers as they scratched out a living on tiny boats. As their hard work translated into profits, they bought larger trawlers and began to flourish.

Hoang's mother Thuy and his father Giau grew up only blocks apart in the village-like Vietnamese shrimping community. As children, they had shyly stared at one another when their mothers chatted at the market or noodle house. They played together at the Buddhist Center, began dating as teenagers, and married young. Alongside her own mother and sisters, Thuy "headed" shrimp at the processing factory while Giau continued working on his family's Gulf trawler.

At 15, Hoang was Thuy and Giau's oldest child. He grew up loving the natural rhythms of the Gulf—the rising and falling of the tides, the usually gentle waves, and the rolling clouds overhead. When school was not in session, Hoang went with his father on the trawler. He worked hard to be an important member of the crew and quietly savored every one of the compliments Giau would offer him.

Certainly, Hoang had seen hurricanes on TV. He sometimes teased his father, who vigilantly followed all the weather developments, even when ashore. "Dad, you're a Weather Channel junkie," Hoang would say with a playful smile. "You know that's the MTV channel for old people." But the typical TV scenes of whipping winds, high waves, and flying debris did not prepare Hoang for the enormity of Hurricane Katrina.

When Katrina was bearing down on the Mississippi coast, many of the Vietnamese families rushed to gather their relatives together on their boats. As the adults frantically collected essentials, Hoang was placed in charge of watching a half-dozen neighborhood children, along with his brother and sister. He had always been a favorite of the kids, so he was the natural choice.

In the midst of all the chaos, Hoang organized an impromptu day care around the dining room table with some toys, snacks, and drawing materials. For a couple of hours, he did his best to entertain the children, who were fearful and concerned. One particularly anxious 4-year-old girl, Kim, clung to him the entire time, following him around the table or sitting on his lap whenever Hoang had a chance to rest. Grasping two large crayons, Kim carefully drew a picture that she presented to Hoang, saying, "Here, I made this for you."

Hoang absentmindedly said, "Hey, thanks for the cool-looking heart." But his young neighbor patiently explained to him that her drawing might look like a heart, but really it was two angel wings. "You can wear these wings," she encouraged. "Then you can fly away from Katrina."

Soon, she fell asleep in Hoang's arms, and, when her mother came to retrieve her, Kim stayed deep in her slumber. Hoang thought that it was funny how, even though she was asleep, Kim's tiny fingers stayed curled—dainty and birdlike—around the crayons she had been using.

Once the neighbor children were gone, Hoang's father decided to leave immediately and sail upriver, where they would ride out the hurricane in one of the back bays. When Katrina struck, the entire family was horrified by its ferocity. Hoang felt like he was on a toy boat that was being pounded mercilessly by a giant, impulsive, and cruel toddler. Once the winds finally began to ease, Giau tried making radio contact with the other boaters. That's when they heard the terrible news. Some of the shrimpers had died when their trawler was rammed against a bridge and sank. Among the bodies that floated to the surface the next day were those of Kim and her parents.

Hoang's entire family was shocked. They had been feeling so relieved that they had made it through the horrible storm and were anxious to hear that others were safe and sound, even if they were scattered throughout the area. They had resigned themselves to the probability that their homes were seriously damaged, but they had assumed that, somehow and some way, everyone they knew and loved would survive. Now, that assumption was shattered.

They slept on the boat for three weeks because they heard that their lovely little home, just steps from Biloxi Bay, had been reduced to a bare slab of cement. When Hoang's father saw the rubble that had once been their community and the splintered shards of wood that had once been shrimp trawlers, he flashed back to the war scenes of An Loc in 1972. It looked like B-52s had bombed their homes and boats. He never dreamt that he would ever see such utter devastation again—not in America.

Hoang and his family now live in a tent on their property. Giau, Hoang's father, has nightmares of fleeing Vietnam. "Katrina has uprooted us and made us boat people again," he said to his wife. Hoang is withdrawn and subdued. He still has Kim's drawing that he had absentmindedly slipped into his pocket. In his mind's eye, he keeps seeing Kim's body being tenderly rocked by the bay water, her dainty fingers still curled around her crayons.

REFLECTING QUESTIONS

1. What are your own reactions to Hoang's story?
2. What signs of resilience are you noticing in Hoang?
3. What brief therapy concepts and techniques have potential for helping Hoang?

OVERVIEW

As a counselor, you will regularly deal with people in critical circumstances. Even if your community agency, mental health center, school, or private practice does not emphasize emergency services, you will find yourself frequently performing some form of crisis counseling. Although people may have been dealing with serious concerns for months, it is only when these difficulties reach a critical mass that many finally seek counseling. Therefore, your first contact with a client may be when he or she is in crisis. In fact, you may have noticed that several of the stories we have presented in this book have involved clients in crisis.

Crisis intervention is any rapid, brief collaboration to assist someone in surviving and resolving a crisis (Echterling, Presbury, & McKee, 2005). Wherever and whenever crises confront people, you can offer interventions that are based on the concepts and techniques of brief counseling. You will find that these principles offer you a valuable perspective in emergency situations. For example, the positive psychology concepts that emphasize strengths and resilience (Pedersen & Seligman, 2004; Snyder & Lopez, 2002) can be particularly helpful when you are dealing with someone in crisis. The purpose of this chapter is to help you engage with individuals in ways that promote successful resolutions to the crises they are facing. The techniques we describe can be done on the fly and can be implemented in virtually any setting, however primitive the conditions.

IDEAS

The Concept of Crisis

There is an important distinction between the concepts of trauma and crisis. *Trauma,* which comes from the Greek word for *wound,* refers to a serious psychological injury that results from a threatening, terrifying, or horrifying experience. Psychological traumas can have a profound impact on a person's cognitive abilities, emotional reactivity, behavior, and even neural functioning (Le Doux, 1996). Conventional wisdom suggests that counseling is necessary for such people in order to prevent post-traumatic stress disorder (PTSD).

However, many studies of psychological trauma have found that resilience is much more common than was once believed (Ryff & Singer, 2003). For example, Kessler, Davis, and Kendler (1997) documented that the majority of children who experience severe traumas, including sexual assault and death of a parent, do not develop psychiatric disorders. In fact, many people report post-traumatic growth (PTG) (Calhoun & Tedeschi, 2006). It is likely that you have studied psychopathology and the various disorders listed in the Diagnostic and Statistical Manual (DSM-IV-TR; American Psychiatric Association, 2000). In addition, many texts on personality development grimly describe how traumatic experiences can result in subsequent dysfunctional behavior. However, "there is no Diagnostic Strengths Manual" (Saleebey, 2001, p. 13). People often come away from traumatic events having gained a new perspective on life and having achieved important understandings. Focusing exclusively on the possible negative results provides a narrow perspective that can blind us to other phenomena, such as resilience, if we rely only on trauma and its impact to provide our entire conceptual framework for emergency situations.

The concept of crisis provides a useful complement to that of psychological trauma. The Greek word *krisis* means a decision or turning point. The Chinese symbol for crisis paradoxically combines the figures for danger and opportunity. Therefore, a crisis is seen as a pivotal moment of decisive change that involves both peril and promise. A crisis is a turning point in our lives, a brief but crucial time in which there is both the opportunity for dramatic growth and positive changes and the danger of violence and devastation (Wethington, 2003). Looking back on their crisis experiences, survivors often describe them as "marking the end of one chapter and the beginning of another" (McAdams, 1988, p. 144). Because as a crisis worker you intervene at such an important crossroad in an individual's life, a seemingly small intervention can make a profound difference for years to come. Concepts such as the Butterfly Effect, which we have discussed in Chapter 5, are especially relevant to crises.

Schemas, Crises, and Sandpiles

Piaget (1954) described a *schema* as a pattern of thinking that people use to make sense of the environment. Usually, when new information presents itself to us, we tend to *assimilate* it by "incorporating it into current schemas" (Rice, 1995, p. 45). So long as all our experiences fit into our schemas, we adapt well to our environment. But what happens when these incidents don't fit? At those times, we have to *accommodate* to strange, new information by creating new schemas. Assimilation is much easier and less stressful than accommodation. When our previous schemas are thrown into chaos and we are temporarily left with no way of making sense of our situation, we are in crisis.

Erik Erikson, who coined the term "identity crisis," proposed that we humans face continual crises as we develop throughout our lives (1964). Each stage of our development is a crisis that challenges the consolidation of our self-image and our world. Crises are turning points that create a tension between progress and regression. When faced with sudden change that requires our accommodation to events, our first impulse is to endeavor to restore the world as it was before. In Piaget's terms, we try to assimilate it. This regression is a failed attempt that leaves someone longing for a past that will never come again.

Progress is a creative act that brings about a new self and world. A crisis is an event in which someone's thoughts and emotions become destabilized. It is a period of chaos. Eventually, the person in crisis arrives at a place where the ground is more solid and the events are more predictable. But it is a new place, rather than the reconstruction of a former state. "Erikson optimistically believed that the general tendency in human nature is toward the resolution of crises in a way that moves people toward a strong self-identity" (Ryckman, 2004, p. 176).

As you read in Chapter 5, our view of how change takes place involves a process of disruption, followed by a state of chaos, and then the development of a new consolidation or organization. Piaget (1954) called this new organization "equilibration," which is the achievement of equilibrium between schemas and accommodation. Both Erikson and Piaget saw the desire for equilibrium as a motivating force that propels people upward through stages of cognitive development (Rice, 1995).

Think of when you were on the verge of becoming a full-fledged adult. Your struggle was between progress and regression. You wanted to be independent and self-sustaining, but a part of you longed for your lost childhood and a time when you were dependent and nurtured. You were in a developmental crisis. You needed to accommodate to the uncertain world of adulthood, and to realize that change will always be present in your world.

Stacey (1996) wrote that we are all pulled toward stability, but we are doomed to failure if we seek absolute certainty. "Success lies in sustaining an organization in the borders between stability and instability. This is a state of chaos, a difficult-to-maintain dissipative structure" (p. 349). In this sense, all of life is a crisis. Each day, we all face turning points of danger and opportunity as we make decisions about our lives.

Jacob Bronowski (in Fichter & Baedke, 2002) stated that all complex systems evolve through a series of stratified stability. Systems in nature go along for a time in a state of relative stability until the moment they are thrown into chaos by unexpected events. In the midst of their chaotic process, they struggle for a new stability—which eventually comes—and then they settle down again until the next crisis. All open systems tend to operate at the edge of chaos, a condition that he termed self-organized criticality. All living systems—especially humans—live at the edge of chaos. Often, we are perturbed by small changes (butterflies). But sometimes, we are rocked by cataclysmic events from which we must seek, not recovery, but reorganization.

The physicist Per Bak likened this process to that of a sand pile (Lewin, 1999). Imagine a thin stream of sand, flowing grain by grain onto a round plate. With enough grains on the plate, the sand will begin to pile up in the shape of a cone—wide at the base and peaked at the top—as if reaching up for the source of the stream of sand. When the limitations of the plate as a base, the downward pull of gravity, and the height of the sand pile reach a critical state, then one more grain of sand dropped onto the pile can cause an avalanche. Most often, the avalanche is small; a few grains of sand will go trickling down the incline of the pile.

However, every now and then, just one more grain of sand added to a pile that has reached the critical state will cause the entire sand pile to collapse. A very small perturbation of a large system can sometimes create monumental changes. In everyday parlance, it is called "the straw that broke the camel's back." After the collapse, if the stream of sand continues to be added, the pile will eventually regain its shape, but this time it will have a wider base and will be able to reach higher. It is not the same sand pile after its collapse.

Per Bak intended the behavior of the sand pile to be an analogy that would extend to humans: "A personality reaches the critical state; then the impact of each new experience reverberates throughout the whole person, both directly, and indirectly, by setting the stage for future change" (in Fichter & Badke, 2002, p. 38).

Minor avalanches occur in our lives all the time. When we encounter information that is novel enough to cause us to have to accommodate our pattern of thinking to it, this is what Piaget called learning. When the many small abrasive encounters in our everyday life make us feel like we have been "nibbled to death by ducks," we experience these minor avalanches. We make adjustments to life events constantly, and this is our everyday creativity at work. But following a major collapse of our sand pile, in the midst of the chaos, it remains unclear as to whether we will be able to build up again and transcend the crisis.

Chessick (1999) suggested there are two fundamental paths we might take after such a major shake-up of our world: The neurotic path and the creative path. Neurosis is resistance to change that uses repetition, freezing, and stagnation. Creativity involves embracing change by originating new, bold, and enterprising ways to cope. Although one approach may characterize more than another our general style of problem solving, in a crisis we often fluctuate between neurosis and creativity. Both are ways that we may try to resolve the fragmentation of the chaos and seek a stable state. The neurotic path is an attempt to reassemble things the way they were, but the creative path tries to make something new from the situation.

When a crisis event changes our world so that we suffer the loss of stability, our loved ones, our prized possessions, and our belief in a just universe, then obviously we want to have our old world back. When working with people in crisis, you must honor this universal tendency toward repetition and freezing. However, somehow you must also provide the support for the person to go on, reconstruct, and have the courage to face an uncertain future.

What is necessary for a positive outcome, said Chessick (1999), is "dancing near an abyss and developing a creative life" (p. 267). There is creativity in all of us. Otherwise, we would not be able to solve the smallest problems that come up in our day-to-day lives. A major crisis, however, calls for the summoning of all the creative resources a person has in order to build that sand pile with a broader base and a higher reach. Perhaps the biggest mission you have as a crisis intervener is to help the person in crisis get back in touch with his or her own creative power.

Resilience

Resilience is the ability to "bounce back" after significant adversity and risk. Instead of studying the dangers that crises pose, many researchers are now exploring the opportunities that they offer. As you read in Chapter 3, positive psychology (Aspinwall & Staudinger, 2003; Keyes & Haidt, 2003; Seligman & Csikszentmihalyi, 2000; Snyder & Lopez, 2002) is a recent conceptual shift that is adding momentum to this movement. For decades, the focus in psychology has been on studying deficits and disorders, but now there is a new interest in exploring human strengths, positive experiences, and resilience.

Focusing on only the victim can blind you to the survivor. From this bleak perspective, people in crisis are seen as poor, pitiful victims in desperate need of rescue instead of coping survivors who are doing their best to achieve some resolution. Consequently, you may believe that, as the counselor, you must be the rescuer who takes heroic measures to save these pathetic casualties of circumstances beyond their control. In your counseling relationship, you may unconsciously take on too much responsibility for developing crisis resolution strategies. You may be tempted to offer simplistic reassurances, lecture your client on unnecessary details, or give trite suggestions on how to cope with the situation.

Unfortunately, such attempts at rescue, however well intentioned, can sabotage your client's sense of confidence and personal efficacy. At the very least, you are overlooking people's dormant and underlying potential for resolving crises in their own creative and personal ways. Of course, individuals in troubled times often are confused, overwhelmed, and distressed. Nevertheless, they also possess unappreciated strengths, unnoticed talents, and unrecognized resources. As they begin to experience their own sense of empowerment, recognize their untapped capabilities, and reconnect to sources of sustenance and nurturance, they can build the scaffolding for a successful resolution to the crisis.

When you recognize and value the resilience of people in crisis, you then presume that they are survivors who can go on to thrive in their lives. Therefore, your approach to your clients remains respectful, empathic, and collaborative.

From Surviving to Thriving

Whatever the ultimate outcome of an emergency situation, people do not emerge from a crisis unchanged. If there is a negative resolution, the crisis can leave alienation, bitterness, devastated relationships, and even death in its wake. However, if the crisis is resolved successfully, a survivor can develop a deeper appreciation for life, a stronger sense of resolve, a more mature perspective, greater feelings of competence, and richer relationships. Such survivors achieve a level of transcendence in which they can become thrivers. With the lessons they have learned and the discoveries they have made from their crisis experience, thrivers can go on to engage more fully in life, savor it more deeply, and take advantage of its many opportunities.

Researchers are now exploring how people can flourish under fire. For example, in an extensive review of the literature, Ryff and Singer (2003) concluded that most people were able to prevail in times of crisis to forge lifelong personal strengths and values. Tedeschi and Calhoun (1995) focused on the positive changes and personal growth many survivors of trauma can achieve. In their later work, Tedeschi, Park, and Calhoun (1998) offered an overview of how cultures throughout history have recognized that people can change in dramatically positive ways as a result of encountering devastating events. More recently, Calhoun and Tedeschi (2006) summarized the extensive research on transcendence and described clinical practices that promote positive change. They proposed the term post-traumatic growth (PTG) to serve as a contrast to the field's heavy emphasis on post-traumatic stress disorder (PTSD) as the consequence of trauma.

EXPERIENCING THIS IDEA

You have been through your own crises—if not accidental crises, then certainly developmental ones as you have gone from one stage of life to another. Choose a crisis from your past that you have successfully resolved and take a few minutes to recall the details of your resolution experience.

REFLECTING QUESTIONS

1. How did you manage to resolve the crisis?
2. In what ways are you a different person as a result of that experience?
3. What important lessons about life did you learn?

Social Support

In Chapters 2 and 3, you read how supportive, caring, and empathic relationships are essential in helping people deal with their life concerns. In fact, from birth to death, people's lives are interwoven in an intricate tapestry of relationships that nurture, protect, enliven, and enrich them. Humans are not islands unto themselves. We are all social beings who have a basic need to be in relationship with others.

The power of these relationships is even more important in troubled times, because people typically do not resolve their crises alone. They are likely to turn to others for support, comfort, and assistance (Berscheid, 2003). In particular, people have a profound need to quickly share their stories with others. Rimé (1995) found that people revealed a vast majority of their emotional experiences—over 95 percent—within a few hours of the crisis event. When survivors disclose their crisis stories with others, they typically experience immediate and positive physiological changes, including reduced blood pressure and muscle relaxation (Niederhoffer & Pennebaker, 2002). Research on social support has consistently found that relationships offer many vitally important resources such as affection, advice, affirmation, information, assistance, and nurturance (Reis, Collins, & Berscheid, 2000).

The dominant culture in the United States values rugged individualism to such a degree that we typically do not appreciate just how embedded we are in a complex web of interdependence throughout our lives (Berscheid, 2003). At a fundamental level, successful crisis intervention can take place whenever a person in crisis comes into contact with someone who is not in crisis but who happens to care. The sooner that a survivor makes such contact, the better.

Meaning and Survival Stories

As you read in Chapter 8, meaning plays a crucial role in our lives. When people are in crisis, they are also experiencing a crisis of meaning (Janoff-Bulman, 1992, 2006). Crises can destroy people's basic assumptions about their world, undermine the sense of meaning in their lives, and sabotage their feelings of self-worth. As a counselor, one of your most important tasks is to help a survivor make meaning of the crisis.

We make meaning in our lives by creating stories. Telling one's crisis story offers the survivor an opportunity to face, acknowledge, accept, and express powerful emotions. The narrative process helps a person begin recognizing the enormity of what has happened and its consequences. The act itself of telling the story helps people organize the information needed to assess the practical impact of a crisis and to think more clearly and completely about the current circumstances. Perhaps most importantly, the process of telling one's story helps the person find some meaning in the catastrophic event that has taken place.

Not only do we tell stories, our stories tell us (Echterling, Presbury, & McKee, 2005). In other words, the life narratives that we create do more than organize our experiences. Stories are the way we put events in order, and these stories, in turn, organize our minds. They influence us to take on certain roles, behave according to particular values, and choose some options over others (Nunn, 2005). By transforming our crisis narratives into survival stories, we are able to reach a successful resolution—and go on to thrive in our lives. Just as we all strive for stability in our lives, we also seek happy endings. When you hear the story of someone who is in crisis, you can capitalize on these innate motivations and help the story turn out well.

Managing Emotions—Taking Heart in Troubled Times

When a crisis confronts someone, the typical emotional reaction is one of overwhelming and intense distress. The person may be sobbing, screaming, crying for help, fleeing, or striking out in rage. As alarming as these reactions are, such distress can serve an adaptive purpose in crisis resolution by spurring a survivor to take immediate and extraordinary action. However, as we discussed in Chapter 7, too much distress can hinder the person's ability to perform the essential tasks involved in resolving a crisis. As a crisis counselor, your job is to help people to find their "zone," their ideal state of arousal. At this optimal midpoint of the Yerkes-Dodson curve, the different brain structures are working together successfully.

Crisis is a time of heightened emotional arousal, but a common assumption is that people in crisis have only negative feelings—those yellow, red, and black emotions that we described earlier. Recent research has demonstrated that people going through times of loss and adversity actually experience positive as well as painful emotions (Larsen, Hemenover, Norris, & Cacioppo, 2003). In fact, acknowledging and giving voice to the gamut of emotions—both negative and positive—can promote a positive crisis resolution. For example, in one study, caregivers told their stories shortly after the deaths of their partners by AIDS (Stein, Folkman, Trabasso, & Richards, 1997). Although their narratives were deeply poignant, nearly a third of the emotional words that caregivers used in their accounts were positive. At follow-up 12 months later, the survivors whose stories expressed more positive feelings showed better health and well-being. They were more likely to have developed long-term plans and goals in life.

There are many feelings that people experience as they go through the process of resolution. For example, three emotions that reflect flourishing under fire are courage, compassion, and hope. *Courage* is the feeling that survivors draw on to face the threat and deal with the danger, while all along managing the anxiety. *Compassion* for one's fellow creatures is an emotion of resolve that tempers the rage, serves as an empathic bridge with other survivors, and strengthens the emotional ties that make up a sense of community. *Hope* is the optimistic feeling that a resolution is possible in spite of overwhelming odds and frustrations. People with high levels of hope are better adjusted, enjoy more social support, and have more meaning in their lives (Snyder, 2002). Magai and Haviland-Jones (2002) considered emotions to be the "primary agents or energetic movers of human personality development . . . comprising a dynamic, self-organizing, and self-defining system" (p. 498). Their contention is that emotions propel people through chaos toward new self-organization. Even powerful displays of grief or anger signal the movement of people in crisis toward resolution.

Listen nondefensively with LUV to their expressions of emotion. Once you sense that they are soothed enough by your empathic acknowledgment to be in "the zone," you can capitalize on these emotions and guide the telling of the story in the direction of compassion, courage, and hope. Who do they care about? How did they summon the nerve to survive the crisis? What do they long for, and what possibilities do they see? You too, must be experiencing compassion, courage, and hope in the presence of the person you are attempting to help. If you care about this person, have the courage to persevere in the face of strong emotions, and are confident that the person can go beyond surviving to thriving, then you will be an influential companion for the person in crisis.

EXPERIENCING THIS IDEA

Think about a time in your life when you were in "the zone" as you successfully dealt with a crisis. Take some time to remember the specifics of where you were, what was going on, what you were doing, and how you were feeling.

1. How did you "psych" yourself up to perform your best?
2. How did you lower your anxiety when it threatened to interfere with your performance?

Envisioning a Future

When you work with people in crisis, you will find that they may initially be in a frame of mind that makes it impossible for them to envision any possible resolution. If you ask them for a goal, their first reaction may simply be to say that they wish the crisis would go away or, better yet, that it had never happened.

You will also find that, if survivors do articulate a goal, it will likely be an immediate one: To feel safe, to know where they are going to sleep tonight, to get some clothes, or to connect with people they know. Depending on the situation, their immediate goals are likely to be at the foundation of Maslow's hierarchy—the basic survival needs. Beyond these basic needs, survivors usually wish for their lives to quickly resume as close as possible to the way they were before the crisis.

However, as you hear their crisis narratives and begin to co-construct a survival story, goals will begin to emerge. You then can invite people to turn their focus from the crisis experience in the past to the resolution possibilities in the future. Once they envision a future, survivors gain a sense of direction and hope, become more motivated, and increase their momentum toward resolution. Studies have found that people who strive to attain positive goals have higher levels of well-being than those who try to avoid negative goals (Emmons, 1999).

To gain an appreciation for the power of envisioning, look at Figure 10-1. At first glance, what does this figure look like to you? Perhaps you see it as a meaningless assortment of blocklike shapes of different sizes. Or maybe the figure seems like a maze without any particular beginning or end.

To envision something more meaningful than blocks or a maze, you don't really need to force it to happen. Instead, just relax and focus your eyes on one specific point in the figure. It doesn't matter where, just as long as you stay focused. As you begin, you may experience the same sense of doubt and frustration that you have when you look at one of those "Magic 3-D" pictures and can't see any hidden figures. But, by keeping your attention tuned into that one spot for 20 or 30 seconds, something meaningful seems to pop out of the chaos; everything comes together into a unified vision. If you didn't have much luck with that strategy, move 5 or 6 feet away from the figure and look at it. What word appears?

Implications of These Ideas for the Counselor

These ideas about resilience and resolution have important implications for your work with clients.

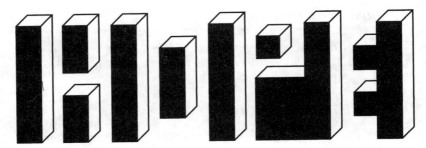

FIGURE 10-1   Create a vision of hope.

- You are not a rescuer. You are facilitating a positive resolution to this crisis.
- When you counsel someone in crisis, your role is to contribute to the factors that promote resilience: Social support, making meaning, managing emotions, and envisioning possibilities.
- In crisis counseling, focus on the resolution not the precipitating event.

TOOLS

When your client is in crisis, you can use any of the therapeutic tools you have been learning in this book. Of course, as you would with any client, you need to adapt these techniques to address specific needs and circumstances. In this chapter, we highlight a few techniques that are especially relevant to crisis counseling, but other tools, such as scaling and reflecting teams, can also enhance your effectiveness.

In this section, we begin by describing two vitally important and essential techniques of crisis intervention. In fact, with many people in crisis, these two strategies may be all that you need to promote a positive resolution. The first, and most fundamental, tool is offering the LUV Triangle, which we introduced in Chapter 2. The second technique is using questions that help survivors conjure up images of resilience and possibilities for resolution. We have discussed various applications of this approach in many of the previous chapters.

These two tools may seem woefully inadequate and feeble compared to the intensity and severity of a crisis. How can merely listening to someone make any possible difference in the person's struggle with seemingly overwhelming odds? What impact can questions have? Shouldn't you be providing *answers*?

The reason that these two techniques are fundamental—and so powerful—is that they recognize and value the resilience of a person in crisis. As a crisis counselor, your role is neither of the rescuer with all the power nor of the expert with all the answers. By taking the attitudes of "not rescuing" and "not knowing," you invite people in crisis to share their stories and to create their own positive resolutions.

Individuals in crisis are more likely to be resilient when they are reaching out to others for support, making meaning of the crisis experience, taking heart by managing their emotions, and moving on by actively coping with these challenges (Echterling, Presbury, & McKee, 2005). Therefore, we have organized our techniques according to these four essential processes that promote resilience and facilitate successful resolution.

Reaching Out with LUV

The purpose of *reaching out* interventions is to offer psychological support and comfort to survivors as they embark on the journey toward resolution. When you offer LUV, you are attending carefully to the crisis story, communicating that you comprehend, and bearing witness to the enormity of the crisis experience that this survivor has been enduring. If someone does not feel heard, understood, and accepted, then your interventions, however elegant, can appear to be only scheming manipulations or, at best, meaningless gimmicks.

Keep in mind that you are neither the expert with all the answers nor the sage who dispenses glib advice in troubled times. Instead, by offering your supportive presence, you offer a safe space, a psychological refuge in this threatening storm. Fundamentally, crisis intervention takes place whenever the person in crisis is able to make contact with someone who cares. Your LUVing encounter with someone in crisis is the most powerful intervention of all.

One specific point to remember is that people in crisis may be making less eye contact with you as they share their story. When they are fully engaged in their transderivational search for meaning in the crisis event, survivors are not "present" in the here and now, so they do not need to focus their eyes on their immediate surroundings. Instead, they are there and then—back to the crisis event. As you offer LUV, you should take care to look toward their faces because people will regularly glance to check that you are still connecting with them.

Furthermore, as they speak of what has happened to them, crisis survivors are likely to use "you," rather than "I." For example, they might say, "When something like that happens to *you, you* feel . . ." Do not press them for "I messages," because they are still needing to create some distance between themselves and the horrific event. After a while, they will return to the use of the personal pronoun "I."

Looking for the Survivor

In addition to offering LUV, as the crisis story is unfolding, you are constantly looking for the survivor: The strengths, talents, and resources that this individual possesses. In fact, by your manner and questions, you are inviting the person in crisis to join you in this search.

To help you look for the survivor, you will be using questions, which can be powerful crisis intervention tools. Questions gather information, of course, but, more important, they communicate important messages. By asking about strengths and coping, you will be inviting a person in turmoil to pause, reflect, and dig for material that can be used to piece together a response that holds promise for resolving the crisis. A crisis is, by definition, an emergency. During an emergency, the possibility for the emergence of something new is always present. Your questions should be designed to help the person in crisis create the emergence of new understandings.

You may feel tempted to use questions to gather details about the crisis. And you may be curious about who was involved, exactly what the circumstances were, and precisely how these events unfolded. However, such probing can be counterproductive because it focuses on the victimization rather than the resilience of the survivor. Besides, people typically need little encouragement to talk about the sequence of events that make up their crisis experiences. Questions motivated by your curiosity about the events are "sightseeing" questions, something we cautioned against in Chapter 9. Therefore, your questions should explore strengths, resources, successes, and possibilities. These questions encourage the person in crisis to envision vivid and powerful images of surviving and thriving, rather than detailed portraits of victimization or despair. What you *are* curious about is how this person has survived. As you listen to the story, continue to acknowledge "crisis talk," and also persist in seeking "survivor talk."

"Getting through" questions   No matter how recently the crisis event has occurred, by the time that somebody has contacted you, he or she has already engaged in the active process of surviving. Somehow, some way, the individual has managed to chart a course through the chaos, turmoil, and dangers to connect with you. Asking about the ways that someone has been able to get through up to this point is a way of focusing your intervention on what is working instead of what is broken. Such questions help crisis victims to begin seeing themselves as survivors. Remember: The fact that the person is alive is incontrovertible evidence of his or her ability to survive.

You are asking questions that underscore the fact that the person has surely done something right or you wouldn't be speaking together. The rape survivor was able to come up with some way to find refuge, the flood survivor did something to avoid being drowned, and even the person considering suicide has found a way to choose life long enough to connect with you.

Some common "getting through" questions are the following:

- "How did you get yourself to do that?"
- "How did you manage to handle the crisis the way that you did?"
- "What did you draw from inside yourself to make it through that experience?"

With most crises, you can ask these questions with a sense of genuine astonishment and awe. Imagining yourself in that situation, you must certainly wonder if you could have done as well.

Making meaning   Helping people make meaning of the chaos, pain, and turmoil of a crisis offers them an opportunity to begin to give form to raw experience, gain some sense of cognitive mastery over the crisis, and make important discoveries about possible resolutions. The themes that emerge from their stories eventually shape their own sense of personal identity and family legacy. In other words, the narratives that people create do more than organize their life experiences. They affirm fundamental beliefs, guide important decisions, and offer consolation and solace in times of tragedy (Neimeyer, 2000; 2006).

Transforming crisis metaphors   As they tell their stories, many survivors automatically turn to metaphoric language to give voice to the intensity of their crisis experiences. Like poets, they strive to express themselves in more figurative ways than merely stating the facts in detached, concrete, or objective terms. For example, in their account of the events, they may describe themselves as "being caught in a trap," "feeling lost," or "carrying a heavy burden."

Pay careful attention to the metaphors that the person is using. Sometime later in your intervention, you can transform these metaphors of crisis into those of resolution. For example, "falling apart" or "coming unglued" can be later linked to "putting the pieces back together." This technique accomplishes two important objectives. First, by using the language of the person, you are communicating that you are listening carefully and engaging in a dynamic process of building on his or her ideas. Second, by revising the metaphor to express resolution, you are inviting a survivor to contemplate future coping strategies.

When people use some of the common crisis metaphors mentioned above, you can transform them in the following ways to encourage survivors to explore a future resolution:

- "And when you begin to make your escape from this trap, what will be the first thing you'll be doing?"
- "As you begin to find your way again, what's one of the first things you will notice that will let you know you are handling this situation?"
- "When you decide to share some of this heavy burden, who will you be turning to for help with this load?"

Note that these questions are presumptive. Instead of asking "if," you ask "when." Instead of "might," you use "will."

LISTENING IN ON A SESSION

Review the story at the beginning of the chapter. An outreach disaster counselor, whose regular practice is as a community mental health therapist, strikes up a conversation with Huang when his family came to the local disaster assistance center. Like many people in crisis, Hoang has a need to share his story, so the first 10 minutes of the session involve his crisis narrative. As their conversation continues, notice how the crisis counselor uses both the LUV Triangle and questions in this segment to create an empathic encounter and to promote meaning making.

Counselor: "Hoang, how in the world did you get yourself to talk to me, a stranger, about all this painful stuff?"

Hoang: "Mmmm . . . Well, I'm not really sure how I did that. I guess that I just decided that I'd better talk with somebody fast 'cause I was starting to kinda sink into this pit that I couldn't see any way out of."

(He pauses before continuing with a pained expression.)

"My mom says it's because of the *ac mong*. That's some old Vietnamese saying for a terrible experience, a tragedy, I guess you'd call it."

Counselor: (Checking her understanding by being immediate and then offering a reflection.)

"First of all, I want to say how sorry I am that you had to endure that nightmare you and your family went through. As you talked about it, I could see in your eyes how horrible and frightening that experience was for you. I can't imagine what it must have been like to go through it.

(She continues, her voice characterized by a soft, sincere, and inviting quality.)

From what you are saying, it sounds like you're still having to deal with a lot of troubling things."

Hoang: "Yeah, I'm just all mixed up, I guess. I'm glad my family all made it, but I'm feelin' really bad that some of the other shrimpers and their kids died. How come they died and we didn't? I guess I feel kinda bad about that.

(After a pause, Hoang continues, the frustration and anger rising in his voice.)

My dad had worked his rear off to come to this country and he took a lot of crap from some of the local rednecks, but he stuck it out. And just when he gets the house paid off and it looks like I may get to go to college in a few years . . ."

(He waves his hand dismissively as if he's brushing away a fly. As Huang's voice trails off, he sighs deeply, shakes his head, and twists his mouth in an expression of dismay and regret.)

Counselor: (She waits a few more seconds before speaking.)

"I guess that even though Katrina is over, inside it must still feel almost like the same kind of turmoil. I imagine at first there was relief and maybe even happiness that you and your family were safe, but later it sounds like you were so shocked and saddened that you lost friends, your house, and nearly all your belongings."

(The counselor leans forward and continues.)

"Hoang, I'm wondering how you're able to get out of bed every morning and go on in spite of all these losses."

Hoang: (He offers a wry smile, shakes his head, looks off to the side as if he's gazing at a distant horizon of the sea.)

"Well, when Katrina hit our trawler, I'd never been so scared in my life. We almost capsized twice. The waves were over 12 feet and the winds were blowing at almost 100 miles an hour."

(He glances at the counselor with a sheepish smile.)

Anyway, my dad said I became a man that night. I guess that a real man doesn't give up even when he's down."

REFLECTING QUESTIONS

1. What kinds of information would you try to get from Hoang about his survivor story?
2. How would remembering the details of those successes help Hoang?

USING THIS TOOL

Form a group with two others. One of you begins by sharing an experience involving a crisis that you have resolved successfully. Another member reaches out with LUV and looks for the survivor by using "getting through" questions and making meaning. The third person serves as the recorder who observes the activity and leads the feedback discussion. Once you have completed this process, rotate roles until each person has practiced.

Taking Heart

As a crisis counselor, your job is not to provoke emotional catharsis. Instead, you help survivors to regulate their emotions by reducing distress, soothing themselves when they are upset, enhancing feelings of resolve, and staying in the optimal emotional zone. Successful athletes talk of being in the zone when they are performing at their best. At these times, they're energized yet focused, emotionally charged yet poised. Individuals are more likely to survive troubled times if they are in this ideal state of emotional arousal. The purpose of the following techniques is to help survivors take heart and manage their emotions productively.

Reduce distress   As you intervene with someone in crisis, tune into the person's current emotional level to check if he or she is too aroused to be in the zone. If a survivor is still in a state of intense distress, you can use the following techniques to reduce this heightened emotional arousal:

• **Address basic needs.** When someone is deeply distressed, you must respond quickly to address basic needs. Ensure the person's safety from threat and take steps to offer physical comfort, shelter, food, important information, and opportunities to contact loved ones. Offer assurances such as, "You're in a safe place here," or "Let's see what we can work out together to deal with this situation."

• **Rely on LUV.** We discussed this tool earlier, but we remind you of it here because, when someone is feeling overwhelmed with distress, you may forget the power of this technique. Remember that one of the purposes of emotional expression is to send a signal of distress to others—to sound the alarm. Once survivors feel heard and see that others are rallying to their call for help, they feel less distressed and more hopeful.

• **Acknowledge feelings of distress.** The most important response you can offer to someone who is in distress is to recognize these feelings with openness and concern. The best way to acknowledge feelings of distress is to reflect them. Offering a reflection is an essential helping skill in which you serve as an emotional mirror to someone. Mirrors usually only show people their outer appearance, but as a crisis intervener, you can reflect back their specific inner feelings. The following are possible reflections that you could offer someone in extreme distress:

"It sounds like you're still feeling shocked and scared."

"Those tears tell me that you have a powerful sense of sadness about your loss."

"You're feeling outraged that someone has treated you so terribly."

Although you are reflecting the survivor's distress, do not force the person to re-experience the crisis by probing for details about the suffering. Remember, your role is not to compel someone to endure a painful ventilation of emotions. Instead, you are offering the comfort of an empathic ear. Reflecting the person's feelings is a powerful way to help normalize the intense distress that people typically experience during times of crisis. Putting these emotions into words and communicating them back to the person in a nonjudgmental, respectful, and accepting manner suggests that these feelings are normal and natural.

Enhancing feelings of resolve   In times of crisis, people often feel demoralized, discouraged, and overwhelmed by the black, red, and yellow emotions. However, as a crisis counselor, you need to develop antennae that are also sensitive to people's positive emotions. Your job is not only to reduce distress but also to help survivors recover their "rainbow" emotions. When people recognize and enhance their feelings of courage, compassion, and hope, they regain their sense of resolve.

Feelings of resolve create a positive momentum for a survivor. Just as no one can "empower" another person, neither can you give someone a sense of resolve. Like meaning in life, people must discover and nurture resolve for themselves. Obviously, you must convey your own compassion and hopefulness, but this process is not like giving blood: You cannot transfuse resolve from yourself to another person. Instead, your job is to "mine" the debris of someone's tale of agony for the small gems of courage, compassion, and hope that will shine through in spite of the chaos and confusion.

Below are specific techniques that you can use to promote a survivor's feelings of resolve:

• **Look for exceptions to the distress.** Mixed in with the distress-saturated talk will be comments indicating relief, resilience, and perseverance. For example, survivors might say, "Without even thinking about it, I suddenly was in the water, pulling him to the shore," or "I don't know how I came up with that idea, but it seemed to work."

You can spotlight these statements by checking your understanding with the person and emphasizing them. For example, you might say, "Let me make sure I've got this right. You're saying that you *dived* into the water and *rescued* him from drowning?" or "You mean that in the midst of all that turmoil, the light bulb turned on in your head and you came up with that idea?"

• **Be presumptive about resolve.** As you learned in earlier chapters, you can safely presume that a person in crisis has some feelings of resolve, even though he or she may not be aware of them. As mentioned above, you would not be asking, "*If* the situation changed for the better, how would you be feeling?" Instead, you would phrase the question presumptively, "*When* the situation changes for the better, how will you be feeling?"

• **Reflect emotions of resolve.** Whenever you are picking up on positive emotions that someone is experiencing, reflect them. All counselors are taught to use reflection as a technique, usually as a way of mirroring negative feelings. However, reflecting feelings of resolve can be a powerful way of helping a survivor become aware of such emotions. Although they are often keenly in touch with their shock, rage, and pain, survivors may not be conscious of their feelings of determination, fortitude, and inspiration.

Some examples of reflecting emotions of resolve are the following:

"It sounds like you truly love your daughter with all your heart and would do anything in your power to keep her safe."

"You seem to have been determined to do whatever you could to make a positive difference in the middle of that chaos."

"I get the sense that you had a glimmer of hope at that moment, and realized that maybe you could prevent something worse from happening."

• **Ask "taking heart" questions.** "Taking heart" is a phrase that captures the essence of the feelings of resolve. When someone takes heart, the person feels hopeful, determined, inspired, and encouraged—in spite of the pain and suffering. No matter how much distress people endure, they turn to positive emotions to buoy them through these tough times, stir them to cope somehow, and comfort them in their grief. In crisis, survivors take heart.

Whenever you notice any signs of positive emotion, such as humor, love, joy, elevation, or gratitude, ask "taking heart" questions. Invite the person to give detailed elaborations of the circumstances, nuances, sensations, and images associated with these emotions. For example, you might ask,

> "How did you find the courage to put yourself at risk to rescue your friend?"

> "What was it like for you to tell your daughter how much you love her?"

> "How did that feel to finally believe that there might be a way out of this mess?"

Moving On

At least temporarily, crises rob people of their dreams for the future. As a crisis counselor, you can help them envision new possibilities by inviting them to create positive goals. Once articulated, goals serve as beacons that light the way for the resolution journey. In this section, we describe techniques that can help survivors begin the process of rebuilding their lives.

Keep in mind that, even though your clients may not have resolved a crisis, somehow they have successfully survived it. You can invite them to explore the achievements that they have already accomplished. By drawing attention to these instances of eluding dangers, dealing with challenges, and finding refuge, you can assist survivors in discovering unknown strengths, appreciating unrecognized resources, and achieving a sense of hope. These strengths and resources form the foundation for a successful resolution.

Using "moving on" questions   Most traditional crisis intervention approaches have focused on the past: The precipitating event and the survivor's reaction to it. Certainly, survivors have a need to tell their crisis stories, but you want to listen carefully for some kind of sign or evidence of an emerging resolution. At this point, you can begin to ask questions that invite the survivor to begin thinking about the future.

Earlier, we discussed "getting through" questions, which explore the strengths of the person instead of his or her experience of victimization. While these questions looked to the past to find nuggets of resilience, you can use another kind of question to explore the future for clues of possible resolution strategies. Therefore, "moving on" questions are open-ended, future oriented, and presume an inevitable resolution. They implicitly predict that what is emerging is something positive. These queries are excellent tools for inviting the survivor to envision a resolution. Sometimes, instead of a question, you may offer a "moving on" lead, such as the request, "Now that you've begun rebuilding your life, tell me about the next step that you'll take." The lead also could be a simple statement (a disguised question), such as, "I'm wondering what are some of the things that you'll be doing as you embark on this new chapter in your life."

Inherent within these messages is the presumption that the person *will* be resolving the crisis in some way. You're merely expressing curiosity about how this particular person will be achieving this resolution. Such questions and statements encourage the person to explore the future as he or she embarks on the resolution journey.

Some common "moving on" questions are the following:

- "As you begin to resolve this painful time in your life, how will your life be different?"
- "When you leave here, what do you see yourself doing right away?"
- "As you embark on your journey of resolving this crisis, what will be your next step?"

A "moving on" lead might be this:

- "In a year from now, when you have successfully overcome this situation, I wonder what advice you would have for someone who is where you are right now."

Even if the person has no advice to offer now, your lead has implied that he or she will be in a different place later, and may even be able to be helpful to someone who has suffered a similar crisis.

Asking "what if" questions   In Chapter 4, you read about the "miracle question" developed by de Shazer (1985) and his associates. This technique is not appropriate for people in intense crisis circumstances because of its mystical and enchanting premise. Such a portrayal can tap into someone's desperate search for a miracle that will make the crisis disappear. Instead, we prefer a more mundane and less dramatic approach of asking "what if" questions. One example would be,

> "What if you woke up tomorrow morning and, without even realizing it,
> you were one step closer to living the kind of life you want to live again.
> How would you know? What would be different?"

Once the person responds, you can help make the image as clear and concrete as possible. Whatever the survivor says about the difference, it can serve as a road sign on the path to a well-formed goal statement and, ultimately, toward resolution of his or her current difficulties.

LISTENING IN ON A SESSION

Let's return to the intervention. Continuing with their interaction, Hoang begins to show an emerging resolution process. Note how the counselor makes use of "taking heart" and "moving on" questions, but interweaves these questions with offering comfort, reflecting feelings, and presuming resilience.

Hoang: "I'm still having nightmares just like my dad—well, not just like his because mine are more like dreams about Kim, the little girl that died."

Counselor: "You mean the little girl who drew you the picture of the wings, right? And now Kim's appeared in some of your dreams. You know, one image that keeps coming back to me right now is that of you holding that girl in your lap."

(She leans forward, gesturing as if she's cuddling a child. Then the counselor gestures more broadly and speaks with growing force as she continues.)

"With Katrina bearing down and so many people panicking in the midst of all that chaos, how were you able to be so *comforting* and *soothing* like that?"

Hoang: (He offers a wan smile and shrugs his shoulders.)

"I guess that I figured I couldn't stop Katrina, but I could at least take care of Kim."

Counselor: "I'm wondering in what other ways you're making a difference in people's lives right now."

Hoang: (He begins to speak with more energy as he recounts his experiences.)

"Well, my dad's kinda depressed and he's been lyin' around the tent a lot and Mom and I can't get him to help clean up the lot, much less talk about rebuildin' our house and repairin' our boat. All he does is say, '*Da an may ma con doi xoi gac*' over and over whenever Mom or I try to get him to do something. It means something like, 'Stop crying for the moon.' I even got online at the Center and found out about no-interest disaster loans for small businessmen like my dad. But all I get is '*Da an may ma con doi xoi gac.*'"

Counselor: "As you talk about all these things you're doing, I'm remembering something else you said earlier—the night your dad told you that you had become a man. Now it sounds like even though he's feeling discouraged right now, you've done whatever you can to keep hope alive. You're cleaning up the lot and finding ways to get the family back on its feet. What's helping you make your way out of what you called 'that dark pit'?"

Hoang: "I know this is going to sound silly, but I keep Kim's drawing in my backpack."

(He shows the picture to the counselor and tears glisten in his eyes.)

"See how it kinda looks like a heart, but they're really wings."

REFLECTING QUESTIONS

1. How should the counselor respond to Hoang's last statement?
2. How did the counselor enhance feelings of resolve in the client?
3. What metaphor for resolution is emerging in this interaction?

USING THIS TOOL

As you did in the previous exercise, select two colleagues and form a group. Again, one of you begins by sharing an experience involving a crisis that you have resolved successfully. Another member takes on the role of intervener by helping the person in the process of taking heart and moving on. The third person serves as the recorder who observes the activity and leads the feedback discussion. Once you have completed this process, rotate roles until each person has had an opportunity to practice this technique.

The Importance of Believing

In order to be an effective resource for people in crisis, you must take care to take care of yourself. Because really bad things sometimes happen to good people, you will find yourself being profoundly affected by the pain that has been inflicted upon those you attempt to help. Corey and Corey (2007) caution that if you are involved in doing a great deal of intensive crisis counseling, you "may suffer *compassion fatigue,* a stress-related syndrome that results from the cumulative drain on the helper's capacity to care for others" (p. 363, emphasis in original).

Working with people in crisis can take its toll. You will be struck by the unfairness of the brutal vagaries of life, and tempted to become bitter and pessimistic about the future. If you don't believe that survivors of crises can grow and thrive in spite of negative events—and even because of them—your growing cynicism will contaminate your work.

Like swimming, crisis work requires a buddy system. "Crisis workers need to develop strong professional support systems. They need people to talk with about their clients, to get angry with, to weep with, and to celebrate with" (Moursund & Kelly, 2002, p. 147). As we have previously stated, self-care is crucial to maintaining your instrument. In order to be effective, you must sustain an optimism that is infectious and that inspires hope.

There is an old joke (author unknown) that dramatically illustrates the necessity of remaining positive in the face of overwhelming events. The proud parents of twin boys immediately noticed that they had widely differing personalities. One seemed to be constantly fearful and cried easily, while the other cooed and smiled, content with most any situation. While the latter was initially considered to be a good trait, when the smiling infant became a toddler, he displayed an undiscerning trust in everyone, and his parents worried that he might go to any stranger who beckoned and, in this way, be kidnapped. The fearful child displayed no such tendencies, always clinging to his mother for support and bursting into tears at the mere sight of any stranger. The parents were concerned for both boys. But the pediatrician said what pediatricians usually say: "They'll grow out of it."

They did not grow out of it, however. By the time the boys were 8 years old, the parents decided that both were in need of psychotherapy. The parents' goal for the therapy was that the "pessimistic" one would become more trusting and hopeful, while the "optimistic" one would be less gullible and more wary. The therapist designed a treatment plan for each boy based on the parents' goals: The overly pessimistic boy was to be placed in a room with an enormous quantity of wonderful toys and games and told he could do with them whatever he liked, while the optimistic boy was given a shovel and told that he was to spend the day cleaning out horse stalls. The therapy was to last from early morning until late afternoon.

Toward the end of the day, the parents looked in on the pessimistic boy to find him sobbing in a corner of the room with all the toys still in their packages. When he was asked what was wrong, he explained that the toys were so marvelous that he was sure that, if he played with any of them, he would destroy them all and never be able have them again. On the other hand, when the parents went down to the horse barn, they found the optimistic boy whistling with a broad grin on his face. The boy had finished cleaning several stalls and had just opened the door to the next one, which was filled nearly to the ceiling with horse manure. When asked why he seemed to be so happy and optimistic in the face of such a task, he replied, "With all this shit, there's got to be a pony in here somewhere!"

If you are going to be able to assist people in "finding the pony" in spite of the awful things that your clients have experienced, you must maintain your belief in positive outcomes. A philosopher once remarked that we always live in the best of all possible worlds. Sometimes it is hard to see the good in it when people are suffering so greatly. If you stay positive, you can provide the light as the survivor of a crisis struggles in the dark to find the path to resolution. People are resilient, and they can work toward a new and better organization of their lives. They can be happy again. Believe it!

SUMMARY

Most of the ideas and tools we have discussed in previous chapters for use in brief counseling apply just as well in crisis intervention. You do not have to be an expert or someone who has sage advice in order to help survivors of crisis move toward thriving. People have an innate drive toward the positive, and they simply need to connect with someone who will listen for their resources and strengths. As they tell their stories, you can respond in a way that highlights their efficacy and points the way toward a new level of understanding and hope.

SEGUE TO CHAPTER 11

Think about a time when you had a concern and needed to talk about it. You asked someone to listen, but, instead of listening, the person seemed to be waiting for you to stop talking so that he or she could offer you advice. Did you find yourself resisting the advice, even if it made sense?

Resource

Creating Hope and Resolve in Troubled Times (CHARTT)
http://collegeprojects.cisat.jmu.edu/chartt/

The CHARTT website offers mental health providers and survivors of disasters information about effective techniques for discovering strength, helping others, and building bonds that promote hope and resolve.

CHAPTER 11

The Reflecting Team, Consulting Break, and Offering Suggestions

"Find out what they want to do and advise them to do it."
Harry Truman

"Advice is seldom welcome, and those who need it the
most, like it the least."
Lord Chesterfield

Chapter Goals

Reading and experiencing the ideas in this chapter will help you to understand these things:

- A reflecting team can add a powerful feedback experience to your counseling session.
- The consulting break can serve several useful functions.
- Suggestions are different from advice because they are more subtle and tailored to the client.

Reading about and practicing the tools in this chapter will help you to develop skills in

- Being an effective reflecting team member.
- Using a consulting break well.
- Designing successful suggestions.

Story

As she ground her way home through the gridlocked Friday afternoon traffic, Dolores tried to have pleasant thoughts about the upcoming weekend. She was still feeling the afterglow from the regional meeting she had attended. Everyone liked her ideas on the new project, and afterwards she received high praise from her boss and coworkers.

If only she were as successful at other things. It was as if she lived in two completely different worlds: hardworking, capable, creative, and a wonderful manager at work but, according to her teenaged daughter Dulcinea, a cruel, nagging witch at home. Maybe she and Dulcinea would be able to work out their problems soon, and there wouldn't be any more scenes over money, clothes, boyfriends, curfew, homework, grades, meals, bedtime, visitors—the list was endless. Dolores and her own mother had disagreed over similar issues 25 years ago, but there had been no screaming, swearing, or running away back then.

Two weeks ago tonight, Dolores had muttered the hoary ultimatum, "As long as you are living in this house, young lady, you'll obey my rules." A 20-minute shouting match ensued, followed by a 2-hour search through the neighborhood for her daughter. Things had been quieter but chilly between them ever since.

As Dolores pulled off the interstate and drew closer to her neighborhood, a numbing resignation began creeping over her like fog through a mountain hollow. Things would only get worse. She had tried everything she could think of and had spent hours talking on the telephone about these problems with her friends, coworkers, mother, and sister. If Dulcinea were only like her older brother Dario, Dolores told her confidantes, things would be fine. He's the perfect child. He never complains about what other families have. He reads all the time and makes good grades, does his chores—and sometimes Dulcinea's, too—and only gets mad when Dulcinea teases him about being "the golden child."

She had wondered many times what things would be like between her and her 13-year-old daughter, if Alfonso had not left them. Her eyes began to moisten, and she missed her turn. She swore angrily and, for an instant, was tempted to get back on the interstate and hit a couple of "happy hours" out by the airport. But she sighed and felt her shoulders slump forward as they once again took on the heavy weight of responsibility. Dolores arrived home to an empty house.

According to a hastily scribbled note on the refrigerator, Dulcinea had made plans for an overnight stay at her best friend's house, and Dario was away on a weekend camping trip with the Boy Scouts. She began to worry if she should have given her permission for Dario to go since the weather was turning cold. She also wondered how she could check up on Dulcinea without starting World War III.

Someone had left the television on, and Oprah was just giving a recap of that day's show. Apparently, the program had been about the conflict between teenage daughters and their mothers. With a little time to kill before the end of the program, Oprah gazed at the audience and asked them how many of them filled their own cavities at home without bothering to go to the dentist. Two or three hands went up, and everyone else laughed and shook their heads. "Anybody overhaul your automobile transmissions when they go out?" received a similar reaction from the audience. Then in a slow deliberate voice, she looked into the camera and asked the studio audience and the millions of television viewers how many of them knew their families were in need of some professional help but had tried the do-it-yourself approach instead? She concluded with a quiet thought, "Think about it."

As the audience clapped its approval and the credits rolled, Dolores realized that it wasn't just Dulcinea who needed help; they all did. Within a few days, Dolores, Dario, and Dulcinea were referred to a family counselor by her pastor. Dolores did most of the talking—and crying—during the first half of the session as she described her concerns and frustrations. Dulcinea sulked, but grudgingly answered the questions that the counselor had asked her directly. Dario often stared at his shoes and regularly insisted that things weren't all that bad, and, besides, his mother and sister never have gotten along anyway, and they probably never will. After they had met for about 35 minutes, the counselor invited the family to take a break and to observe a reflecting team discussing their observations of the session so far.

REFLECTING QUESTIONS

1. What are your impressions of these three clients?
2. What are your recommendations regarding intervention?
3. How might you describe the session?

OVERVIEW

This chapter offers ideas and tools for dealing with the latter portion of the counseling session. First, we discuss the reflecting team—a strategy for involving other counselors in your work to increase its impact. We urge you to set up such a team and observe for yourself the benefits that can result. If you are working alone, you may wish to employ the consulting break. This technique involves leaving the room for a few minutes to either consult with an available colleague or to reflect on your own. During this break, you can decide on a therapeutic suggestion to offer your client.

Suggestions are not the same as advice. Advice is when you "just tell 'em." As we pointed out in Chapter 1, this approach is ineffective. Suggestions are more subtle and tailored to your client's style. We discuss this important difference and offer guidelines for offering successful suggestions.

IDEAS

The Dual Perspectives of the Counselor

If you are lucky, you will be working in a setting where colleagues are available for consultation on your counseling cases. Or, if you are even luckier, your colleagues can be watching behind a one-way mirror, able to consult on an immediate basis. No counselor should ever attempt to work completely alone, even if this means simply consulting with a colleague after the session. Not only do you miss many cues and dynamics that are immediately happening with your clients, but also you are unable to maintain a reflective stance when you are so absorbed in the moment-to-moment counseling relationship.

You have probably already noticed that being present with your client is quite different from watching the session on a video recording. Later, you see things you were unaware of before, you can make sense of things that had you stuck or baffled in the session, and you are better able to formulate a plan once you have the luxury of a bit of psychological distance from the event.

Think back to a time when you went to see a movie and found yourself totally absorbed—living it as though you were the protagonist, losing all sense of your surroundings, and being emotionally overwhelmed by the experience. For you, that was a truly effective movie. You were in "flow"! The movie did what all movies should: It involved you totally. However, when friends asked, "How did you like the movie?" you found it hard to find words to convey the depth of your experience to them. It was one of those "you had to be there" experiences.

But maybe you decided to go to see the movie a second time because you hoped to recapture the experience that you originally had. It didn't quite work, did it? Somehow, the second viewing seemed to have lost some of its power to involve you the way the first time did. You may have felt disappointed and may have mourned the loss of that first-time experience. Unfortunately, that's the way it is with all "first times."

The good news, however, is that the second time you see a movie you see it from more of a distance—with an observer's perspective. This change makes it possible to see things you did not realize the first time you saw the movie. You may, for example, notice how well the dialogue is written, how well the characters are developed in the script, the special devices or techniques used by the director to make the experience real for the viewers, or you might begin to grasp a subtext or symbolism in the story that completely eluded you the first time around.

Both these levels of experience are important in counseling. Being fully involved with your client will help you make that vital connection between the client's world and your own. You will intuitively understand and gracefully convey your empathy. Unencumbered by self-consciousness and doubts, you will find yourself really listening—rather than merely waiting to talk. But lost at this level is your ability to analyze what is important in your relationship dynamics or the full impact of your interventions. Fully engaged, you cannot reflect on where you should be going next and what strategy might be the most beneficial for your client's growth.

Of course, as you develop as a counselor, you will find yourself better able to toggle back and forth between these levels of presence and distance as the counseling session is unfolding. But this switching of levels is like the Necker cube you saw in Chapter 5: You can never see both faces of the event at the same time, so it is likely that you will miss something of the unattended level at any given moment. If you are analyzing, you are not empathizing. When you are totally involved, you do not fully understand what is happening.

As you continue to practice the techniques in this book, they will slowly become second nature, and you will not have to think as much about how and when to use them. The awkwardness you may now feel in the use of these new techniques will eventually fade. This emerging comfort will allow you to really "be with" your client. But you will also find that, even if you possess the most amazing set of skills, there are times—many times!—when you experience yourself as stuck, confused, and uncertain what to do next with your clients. At such times, you may be able to grab a colleague in the hall for quick discussion, present your case at a staff meeting, go back to the books and study, or find a quiet spot and simply reflect. All these are useful options, but as Friedman (1997) suggested, the most helpful and, paradoxically, even the most cost-effective option would be to enlist colleagues as members of a reflecting team.

The Reflecting Team

Any time you can employ a reflecting team in your work, you will find this method to have profound impact on your clients (Bertolino & O'Hanlon, 2002; Lipchik, 2002). In fact, Michael White (1995) claimed that one reflecting team session is worth about five sessions of regular counseling. Many of our clients have reported to us that hearing what their reflecting team had to say was the single most potent event in their counseling sessions.

The purpose of a reflecting team is to supply new information, from another perspective, to both the client and the counselor. As an adjunct to therapy, the team may watch through the one-way mirror and phone in to the counseling room when they see something the counselor misses, or they may be available for immediate consultation when the counselor feels stuck. In the latter case, the counselor takes a break, leaves the room, speaks with the team for a few minutes, and then returns to the counseling session.

This technique is often crucial when the counselor is working with a family, a situation in which so many dynamics are at work that it would be impossible for any one person to simultaneously attend and respond to all of them. The session may also be designed so that a break is scheduled, whereupon the counselor and client(s) leave the room and take up a position behind the one-way mirror, while the team sits in the counseling room, discussing their observations of the session they have been watching.

Friedman (1997) cited years of research (Berlyne, 1960; Fiske & Maddi, 1961; Hebb, 1946; Hunt, 1965) suggesting that, when people are confronted with large amounts of novel or unexpected information, they become overwhelmed and distressed. However, when given information that is neither too novel nor discrepant with their experience and expectations, these same people will be receptive to altering their points of view. As we discussed in a previous chapter, such "news of difference" (Bateson, 1972) inspires people to expand their views, consider novel or previously denied information, and soften up old rigid categories. Tom Andersen (1991, 1997), who first wrote of the use of a reflecting team in therapy, characterized the reflecting team's intervention as a way to unstick "stuck systems."

Although the reflecting team is a relatively new practice in counseling, the dramatic technique of the Greek chorus has been recognized for centuries as a powerful tool in theater (Wilson, 2000). The chorus, a supporting group of performers who sang or spoke in chants, fulfilled many functions in a drama. One was the practical task of providing the principle actors a break and giving time to change the scenes. More important, the chorus gave expression to emotions and themes that had been left unsaid by the characters. It gave a rich spectacle to the unfolding drama, provided commentaries about the action that took place on the stage, and evoked the visionary experience of the dramatic arts. The rhythmic beat, verbal cadence, and changes in pitch intensified the emotional impact of the play and promoted a bond between the audience and characters.

In counseling, the reflecting team carries out functions similar to that of the Greek chorus (Papp, 2005). Like their dramatic ancestors, members of a reflecting team can offer a break to the therapeutic process. More significantly, they can weave narratives of resilience and resolve about the clients, who in fact are the protagonists of their own life stories. The members of a reflecting team can highlight strengths, reveal overlooked resources, and point out undiscovered opportunities. Clients who may have felt mired in a tragic narrative can feel surrounded by a new narrative of hope and possibilities.

The Consulting (Reflecting) Break

For most counselors who have been traditionally trained, the idea of taking a break toward the end of the session may seem awkward and disruptive. It did to us also, until we came to realize the powerful benefits that such a break can provide. If you are working alone—without a reflecting team—some of the benefits can still be captured by employing the consulting break. Most brief theorists offer little in the way of a rationale for the break, but we have found at least three ways in which the break itself can positively affect the counseling session.

First, the break affords you the opportunity to get your thoughts together. When you are in the midst of the session, it is often difficult to reflect on the significance of what your client is saying because you are so involved in the process. Carl Rogers (1965), on his famous "Gloria" videotape, stated that he remembered very little of what had happened during the counseling session after it was over, and only later was he was able to recall more of it. By taking a *consulting break,* you are leaving the room to discuss your session with a colleague, but if you simply leave the room to get distance on what has taken place and gather your thoughts to plan your next step, you are taking a *reflecting break.* You then reenter the session in a different state of mind, with your thoughts clarified, and having a more confident sense of what to do.

Leaving the room moves you from the immersion in the process of *doing* to the higher-ground perspective of *reviewing.* By adding reflections to your experiences of engaging with your clients, you can achieve a synergistic whole that is greater than the sum of its two parts (Lipchik, 2002). Moreover, the consulting break has several positive effects on the client. The first and most powerful effect is that your client's attention is heightened, wondering what you are going to say on your return. Your message of empathy and validation then proves to be both reassuring and relieving. The break also offers your clients a breather from what can sometimes be an intense experience—a chance to get their feet back under them. It is a time for the client to consider what has gone on in the session. It can also hold the client in the mood of the session and keep from breaking the spell. Clients often leave a typical counseling session and immediately face the distracting demands of the day, a hurried transition that can rob them of the opportunity to reflect on the counseling experience. Usually, when the counseling session ends, the client must immediately compose a social face and re-enter the everyday world in a more decorous and superficial manner. Giving the client a break during the session can minimize the impact of this disruptive transition.

Studies of memory have suggested that the formation of long-term memories takes some time (Turkington, 1996). *Retroactive inhibition,* the overlayering of a new experience that eclipses a previous experience, can cause new learnings to vanish before they become part of the client's repertoire. Furthermore, we all know that we must go over something several times before we can truly know it by heart. So taking a break and sitting in silence with one's thoughts can be a very useful learning event for the client that may help to consolidate a memory of the session.

Finally, just imagine the power of the dynamics that are set up by the consulting break! Remember the last time you visited your physician with a nonspecific complaint that worried you? You told the doctor your symptoms, which he or she wrote down, and maybe you had a urine analysis and some blood work performed, or perhaps an x-ray. Then the doctor left the room, and you languished in silence, staring at the walls for what seemed like an eternity. You began to perspire as you sat there, semi-nude, with your legs dangling off the examination table, your butt sticking to that paper they use to cover those tables. You went over again the pointed questions that the doctor had asked during the interview, and you wondered what he or she might have been getting at, what diagnosis was being sought. You noted that the doctor was taking an unusually long time to return. "It must be really bad news!" you thought, "The doctor is trying to think of a way to tell me so I won't cause a scene in the office. It's just as I suspected—I have only a short time to live!" But then, the doctor returned with a big smile, looking over your chart and saying, "Well, everything looks okay."

This dynamic of expectation that is set up by such a consulting break brings about an emotional arousal and a focused attention. The client is eager to hear the news. As a brief counselor, you will deliver news of positive differences and perhaps offer a suggestion as to how the client might proceed. Because of the way the conditions have been set by the consulting break, there is an increased likelihood that the client will be open to your suggestion. When you return and offer acknowledgment of the client's concerns—in the client's language—this tends to place the client in a "yes set." "Clients usually respond to this process by nodding their heads or smiling with recognition. This response is referred to as a sign of a 'yes set'" (Lipchik, 2002, p. 101). In such a state, the client becomes more attentive, agreeable, and open to suggestion.

The Suggestion

You may have a negative reaction to the word *suggestion*. In your training to become a counselor or therapist, you were discouraged from giving advice, taking on the role of expert, and attempting to persuade. Therefore, you may recoil at our recommendation to consider offering suggestions to your client. Even worse, the term may also connote to you a disingenuous and manipulative intervention. However, keep in mind that, as you read in Chapter 2, your client must first invite you to help. If you receive a formal invitation to a party, the card often indicates, "RSVP," or as the French say, "répondez, s'il vous plaît." In this section, we discuss one possible RSVP to your client's invitation to engage in the influencing process. That response can be a suggestion.

A successful counselor cannot help but constantly offer suggestions at a nonverbal level. These suggestions are genuine and heartfelt, but nevertheless hint at intriguing possibilities, imply certain ideas, evoke powerful images, spur motivation, and invite change. For example, your punctuality suggests that the client is worthy of respect, your focused listening suggests that the person deserves empathic understanding, and your optimistic manner suggests that there is hope. Coming out and directly stating these messages of respect, empathy, and hope would sound trite and contrived. However, your actions suggest volumes. Any LUVing encounter offers such rich, complex, and powerful suggestions.

In this chapter, we discuss the intentional suggestions that you can offer with your words during a counseling session. We provide some pointers on phrasing and timing your verbal suggestions. However, as we go over such nuances, never forget that suggestions are only successful when they are invitational, personal, and permissive. If a suggestion sounds like a gimmick or smacks of trickery, then it will surely backfire and compromise your relationship with a client.

Suggestions hint rather than define, evoke rather than explain, and propose rather than command. For example, a poem *suggests* by using words gracefully, creating rich imagery and mood, entrancing us with its captivating rhythm, and inviting us into its metaphorical world. Finding your own voice as a counselor is essential to offering successful suggestions. By being authentic, spontaneous, and fully present as you share a suggestion, you invite your client to embrace the change process. In fact, if you are still uncomfortable with the term "suggestion," you may prefer to think of it as an "RSVP" to their invitation. At least, that's our suggestion!

A suggestion takes place when you influence another person in a paraconscious way (Lozanov, 1978). In other words, the influence takes place largely out of the awareness of the person being influenced. Advice or directives, on the other hand, are more explicit and much more easily defied. If people do not wish to follow a direction, they can argue with its feasibility or they can subvert it in ways that they might not even understand. A well-placed suggestion, on the other hand, sticks in a person's experience at a level where it cannot be argued and where it may not even be noticed.

When a client comes to you, he or she will attempt to explain the concerns in reasonable terms. Not to do so would be to complain in an illogical and crazy way—and people do not want to present themselves as "crazy." If you, as the counselor, respond to your clients only at the level of reason and logic, you are missing the level where most of the action takes place. Freud (1915/1959) called it the "primary process" level of thinking.

In primary process thinking, there is no such thing as "no." Therefore, your suggestions should be oriented toward the positive rather than imply that the client should stop doing something. Your suggestions should be embedded within other statements rather than separated in explicit detail. One way to do this is to wonder aloud about possibilities. Another way is to leave the suggestion open enough so that the client can fill in the gaps. This creates the Zeigarnik Effect, which we discuss below. Either way, the technique of suggesting becomes like a Rorschach ink blot onto which the client can project an experience and anticipate a change.

EXPERIENCING THIS IDEA

Read the following correspondence between a son and his father. See how embedded messages add an entirely new dimension of communication between the correspondents.

Dear Dad,
    $chool i$ really great. I am making lot$ of friend$ and $tudying very hard. With all my $tuff, I $imply can't think of anything I need, $o if you would like, you can ju$t $end me a card, a$ I would love to hear from you.
Love,
Your $on

Dear Son,

    I kNOw that astroNOmy, ecoNOmics, and oceaNOgraphy are eNOugh to keep even an hoNOr student busy. Do NOt forget that the pursuit of kNOwledge is a NOble task and that you can never study eNOugh.

Love,

Dad

Why Can't You Just Tell 'Em?

As we mentioned in Chapter 1, advice, no matter how logical and reasonable, rarely leads to lasting or significant change. Other authors of counseling texts, such as Egan (2002, 2006) and Moursund and Kenny (2002), also caution you against giving advice to clients. The word *advice* even fails to show up in the indices of most of the other popular texts on technique.

Many authors suggest that the urge to give advice is probably more of a need for the counselor than the client. Orlinsky and Howard (1986) conducted an extensive review of the use of advice and concluded that it was ineffective. Kleinke (1994) concurred and pointed out the obvious: "Clients can get all the advice they want from acquaintances, friends, and family members. They hardly need to pay a therapist to tell them what to do" (p. 9).

Harry Stack Sullivan (1970), an early contributor to psychoanalytic literature, had this to say about gratuitous advice givers: "There are few things that I think are so harrowing as the occasional psychiatrist who knows a great deal about right and wrong, how things should be done, what is good taste, and so on and so forth" (p. 214).

Now, we recognize that sometimes a piece of advice at just the right moment can be helpful, but these "just right moments" are very rare. Furthermore, even if you happen to pitch some advice at the perfect time, you are still much more likely to miss the target. Intriguingly, Yalom (2002) opined that more often than not, "it is the process of giving advice that helps rather than the specific content of the advice" (p. 153). However, he used recommendation more as a perturbation to disrupt the process rather than as sage advice.

Donald Meichenbaum (1990) said that he was at his best when his clients were "one step ahead of me offering the advice that I would otherwise offer." "And the artfulness of therapy is how to provide the conditions whereby they come up with it" (quoted in Kleinke, 1994, p. 8). It is this "artfulness" that is, at once, most effective and most difficult to capture in a text on counseling. It comes as one of those "you have to be there" moments. However, we will attempt to describe this art as the use of suggestion rather than advice in the Tools section to follow.

The Zeigarnik Effect

Bluma Zeigarnik was a student of Kurt Lewin, the famous Gestalt psychologist. It was Lewin's custom to carry on lengthy discussions with his students in a cafe while drinking coffee and eating snacks (Hergenhahn, 1992). On one occasion, a number of students had been meeting with Lewin, and each had placed an order with the waiter, who kept no written notes of their requests but who had nevertheless delivered each order without error. When the bill was called for, the waiter tallied up in his head what each of them owed, and the proper amount was paid.

Later, Lewin called the waiter over and asked him if he would write out the check for them. To this, the waiter, who had displayed a fantastic memory for each order and its proper price, replied, "I don't know any longer what you people ordered . . . You paid your bill" (p. 418).

From this experience, Lewin hypothesized that, before closure on a situation is reached, a tension system builds up that keeps items in people's memories, but, once closure is achieved, the tension is discharged and the items forgotten. Bluma Zeigarnik tested Lewin's hypothesis by an experiment in which participants were permitted to finish some tasks but not others. She found that participants later remembered many more of the uncompleted tasks than the completed ones. What the Zeigarnik Effect means for counselors is that, if you want your client to "chew" on an idea rather than forget it immediately, you should introduce—but not complete—the idea.

Have you ever had to leave a really good movie before it was over? Chances are you wanted to know how it turned out. If the movie was a suspenseful mystery, your need to know was increased and probably nagged at you. When the authors of this book were young, we often went to Saturday matinees at our local movie house. Besides the double-feature Westerns featuring Roy Rogers or Gene Autry, there was always a "serial." A serial was a short action feature in which the hero typically faced a life-threatening situation at the very end of the episode. Just as the hero was about to be eaten by alligators, crushed by a collapsing building, or hurled over a cliff in an automobile, the movie abruptly stopped, and an announcer exhorted us not to miss the next exciting episode. We were compelled to come back the next Saturday to find out if our hero had escaped, only to be left once more with a cliff-hanger at the end of the new installment.

You can heighten the Zeigarnik Effect with your client by avoiding closure at the end of your sessions. Leaving unresolved issues "up in the air" prompts clients to continue their own work toward resolution. If you allow your clients to leave your session hanging on at least one suspenseful note, they are more likely to keep reflecting on what happened in their sessions and to seek meaningful closure.

EXPERIENCING THIS IDEA

Some story examples of the Zeigarnik Effect include the film *Limbo* by John Sayles, the story *The Lady or the Tiger,* and most television soap operas. What episodes in your own life have been left unresolved, at least for a few days? What have been your reactions at these times?

Implications of These Ideas for the Counselor

- Always seek consultation on your counseling cases. Not only will this action help prevent burnout, but it will also clarify your thinking regarding what is taking place in your sessions.
- A reflecting team can offer observations and comments so as to extend and elaborate the therapeutic power of your counseling.

- Since you are not likely to have colleagues available for a reflecting team during every session, you will find it helpful to schedule a break in order to collect your thoughts and to design an after-the-break response.
- Clients will also use the break to reflect on what they have said and to anticipate what your response might be. When you come back into the room with "good news," your clients are primed to hear it.
- Suggestions are more subtle than advice and may "stick" better with clients.
- You should attempt to create a "cliff-hanger" for your client's so that the Zeigarnik Effect will keep them reflecting on what happened in your session.

TOOLS

Successful Reflecting

When you are a member of a reflecting team, your job is to offer a highly concentrated version of brief counseling techniques. Within the space of a few minutes, you acknowledge the client's concerns, identify exceptions, emphasize strengths and resources, use the client's metaphors, and work to deconstruct the client's stagnant portrayals. Lipchik (2002) pointed out that the idea of having other people watch and then comment on the counseling session will at first seem strange to clients. Therefore, you should bring up the idea without a hint of hesitation and stress the advantages of having other people working on the client's case. "Two heads (or three or more) are better than one."

You can increase your effectiveness as a reflecting team member by following a few simple guidelines (Friedman, 1997). First, keep in mind that a client is more likely to hear news of difference when your reflecting team first *acknowledges the client's complaints,* difficulties, and issues. Like the counselor, as a member of the reflecting team, you must demonstrate that you have listened, understood, and validated the client's concerns and you have been affected by the client's concerns. The client must see that you and the other members of the reflecting team have an empathic feel for the client's pain and concerns.

Second, you should state your observations in a positive manner. To increase your impact as a reflecting team member, be sure to discuss the client's *strengths, resources, and successes.* Avoid "hollow compliments" and hackneyed generalizations by basing your comments only on the client's specific actions that you observed during the session, as well as particular information that the client has shared.

Third, state your remarks concerning the client in a *tentative manner,* rather than authoritatively. Avoid making definite and certain claims regarding the client's personality traits. Instead, begin your remarks with such phrases as "I'm wondering if . . ." or "It may be that . . ." or "Perhaps . . ." Be sure to have your tone of voice, posture, and demeanor reflect your "I'm not from around here" tentative stance, too.

Fourth, as a member of a reflecting team, you can increase your therapeutic impact by *highlighting the exceptions* to problem-saturated talk that you noticed. You want to emphasize the times the client was successful, either completely or partially, in coping with the presenting problems. When you do acknowledge the client's concerns, you can add follow-up "getting-by" questions. For example, during the discussion, you might ask, "How in the world has the client been able to come this far, given the fact that the concern was so much a part of her life?"

Fifth, speak in *metaphors, images, fantasies, and wonderments,* rather than assertions of "reality." Whenever possible, you want to expand on the metaphors that the client already used during the session. If these were "problem" metaphors, you can conjecture about an unexpected twist or positive outcome to the metaphor. You want to use terms, images, themes, or cues that have personal meaning to the client.

You are most effective when you use your own voice rather than attempt to speak as an objective observer. "Situate your questions/comments in your own life experience. Be transparent; use ordinary language rather than psychiatric jargon" (Friedman, 1997, p. 100).

As a member of a reflecting team, you perform several vital functions. By speaking metaphorically, you generate images that can intrigue and alter the client's understanding of the situation. By pointing out strengths and resources, you are offering the client a more productive view of self and others. By creating alternative stories, you are opening space for fresh perspectives. And by highlighting the changes the client has already made, you are authenticating the transformation process.

If you intend to conclude the reflecting team conversation with a suggestion, you should present it as a tentative wonderment directed to one of the other team members, "Since (give the client's first name) said she hoped to (name the goal), I wonder what would happen if she were to (state the suggestion)."

In subsequent sessions, you can focus on your client's report of any change that has taken place since the previous session, how the client is feeling about the change, and any information regarding strengths or the client's increasing sense of resolve.

LISTENING IN ON A SESSION

Review the story at the beginning of the chapter. The two members of the reflecting team that observed this family's session now convene to discuss their impressions while the counselor and family members watch and listen.

Reflector #1: "I'd like to begin with something that struck me right at the start of the session. There seems to be a lot of stress in this family, especially over the last few months. It looks to me like each family member may be facing different challenges and coping differently with this tension, but it appears that there's plenty of strain and pressure to go around here."

Reflector #2: "Yeah, there especially seemed to be some tension and apprehension in the session at the start, as if everyone had a sense of what was at stake here. It looked like even deciding where each of them was going to sit was an important consideration."

Reflector #1: "They seemed to take some care to stake out their territory, but it didn't have the feel of a 'land rush' where people were competing for the prime acreage. It had more of a feel of a tentative minuet. Did you notice that Dario seemed to be acting the gentleman, allowing the women to enter the room first? Then the daughter and mother had this awkward moment when Dulcinea sat in the middle of this sofa and Dolores sat next to her. Dulcinea then gave a little sigh—maybe of exasperation—and then moved over to give herself more space. I would guess that Dolores noticed her daughter's reaction, but she let it pass. It was neat to see Dulcinea carving out her own area and to see Dolores wisely allowing her daughter to have more space."

Reflector #2:   "They all probably felt apprehensive about what was going to happen in this session, but the three of them settled in here with a couple of gestures that suggested that they were at this session to deal with some important issues, however irritated they may be with somebody or awkward they may feel as they work out new ways of relating to each other. The fact that they all came together is evidence that they would like things to be better in their family."

Reflector #1:   "I was impressed by how the Dulcinea and Dario dealt with Dolores's tears. It was pretty apparent that their mom was upset, but neither of them rushed in to rescue her. I guess they must know that Dolores's crying has been an indication of how much she cares about them. I sensed that Dulcinea is committed to becoming who she's meant to be. As she sorts that out, Dulcinea may be making sure that she has the space to do it. And Dario seems to have his emotional antennae up, and he thoughtfully decides not to jump in when his mom and sister are dealing with their issues."

Reflector #2   "What you're saying relates to two questions I have. How did Dolores manage to get two teenagers to come with her to counseling? And where do they all get their determination to cope with the loss of a father and husband, be successful in school and at work, face these arguments with one another, and still forge ahead with their own lives? It's really intriguing to me since we don't usually see that kind of determination around here."

Reflector #1:   "Yeah, I wonder what answers they will have to your question. You know, at one point, Dolores said that she lives in two completely different worlds. In the work world, she feels successful, talented, and confident. It will be really exciting to see how she's going to apply her creativity and managerial skills to deal with these challenges that she now faces in her home world."

REFLECTING QUESTIONS

1. What metaphors did the reflectors use here?
2. How might you respond to Reflector #1's final statement?
3. If you were the counselor, how might you use this material with the family?

USING THIS TOOL

Meet with three other colleagues to experience the impact of a reflecting team. One of you volunteers to share a personal goal you would like to achieve; another volunteers to be the counselor. The other two serve as the reflecting team. If you do not have access to a room with a one-way mirror, then the reflecting team can observe the interaction sitting off to the side. After the client and counselor have interacted for about 15 or 20 minutes, they switch seats with the reflecting team. The counselor and client then observe as the team members discuss the client they have been watching. The reflecting team should acknowledge the client's concerns, offer positive comments, give observations tentatively, present exceptions, and offer metaphors. Afterward, discuss your reactions to this process from your perspectives as client, counselor, or observer.

Taking a Break

In your work setting you may not always have the luxury of a readily available reflecting team or a colleague with whom you can consult during a break in your counseling session. In this case, you will be taking a "reflecting" break. As we indicated above, it is often beneficial for both you and your client to experience these moments away from the intense counseling session. You need to inform your client at the beginning of the session of your intention to take such a break. Again, you want to introduce the break as a routine procedure that will ensure that you will be offering your most thoughtful attention (Lipchik, 2002).

As a way of introducing this practice, you might say either of the following:

> "We will be working together for about 30 to 40 minutes, and then I will take a break to put together my thoughts on what we have discussed. I will return after a couple of minutes so we can talk about where we go from here."

> "I want to let you know that toward the end of the session I will leave the room to think over what we talked about today. I will come back in a few minutes to give you my thoughts and to hear what ideas you have come up with during the break."

On returning from the break, you will be offering a summation message (Lipchik, 2002), presenting a suggestion, and inquiring about your client's thoughts during the break. However, if you ask the client something on the order of, "What thoughts did you have during the break?" you will likely hear the client return to problem-saturated talk. If this happens, it is your signal that the client wishes to make sure you know how troubling the situation is.

In your counseling work, you may have noticed that your clients often bring up new details of their concerns near the end of your sessions. One of the authors of this book (J.E.M.), who regularly comes up with colorful descriptions of counselor and client behaviors, calls this phenomenon "dumping the dragon." Of course, if your client dumps the dragon when you return, you must return to acknowledgment with the LUV Triangle. Otherwise, the client will be left with the Zeigarnik Effect of negative unfinished business. A couple of ways to avoid more problem-saturated talk when you return is to say, "I was wondering what other ideas you had for changes that would move you nearer to the goal you said you wanted," or "What other things came to mind about ways in which you have previously handled problems like this in effective ways?"

Once you have established that the client is ready to hear your thoughts, your summation message should include a listing of what you heard the client say about the concern (the acknowledgment), the times when the problem is not happening (the exception), the strengths and resources the client has displayed in the face of the concern (resilience), and the desired goal the client has stated (the teleonomic path). Following this summation, you then can offer a suggestion.

Preparing for the Suggestion

Sometimes, when you are out of the room reflecting on the session, it is useful to jot down your remembrances of the client's statements during the session. If this technique is something you would want to try, draw a line down the middle of the page and write all the things you can remember that the client has said about the concern on one side of the page, and all the exceptions, statements of resilience, strength, and coping, on the other side. You will be surprised at how much you can recall by using this method. Make sure you write the client's descriptive words and metaphors as accurately as you can.

On returning, the client should be impressed at how much you have thought about the session, and, by sticking to the client's descriptions, you will begin to stimulate a "yes set." You will notice that the client may smile faintly on recognition of some of his or her own words and will perhaps nod affirmatively as you provide this accurate recapitulation of what has been said. Whether you actually produce the paper—after the break—on which you have written these comments depends on your own style and your guess as to how the client will respond. Some clients will be pleased that you have written everything down, while others might experience your reading from the paper as too clinical. If your client seems to be in a "yes set," and you deem the time to be right, you may wish to offer a suggestion after feeding back your acknowledgment of the client's concerns and your punctuation of the client's strengths.

The following checklist will be helpful to you as you design your suggestive feedback to deliver after the break. Ask yourself the following questions:

1. Do I truly feel invited to suggest something to my client?
2. Has my client already come up with a possible remedy? If the client's idea is "more of the same"— a first-order change—is there a way I can modify it?
3. How has my client responded to any other suggestions?
4. How can I incorporate my client's own words in the framing of this suggestion?
5. How can I offer my suggestion in a way that will bridge from the client's goal?
6. How can I offer my suggestion in a tentative and helpful tone?

Tailoring Suggestions

Perhaps it might be helpful to you to think of the after-the-break procedure as specific to what you perceive to be your client's level of motivation. In other words, your responses and suggestions will be tailored according to how you see your relationship with your client. As we discussed in Chapter 4, your clients may be *visiting, complaining, engaging fully,* or *involuntary* in their relationships with you. (We will discuss the involuntary relationship in a later chapter. In such relationships, you will not, as a rule, take a reflecting break. If you do, and you go too far from the counseling room, your client might not be there when you return!) Below, we offer some ideas based on these different relationships.

Clearly, if your client is fully engaged in a counseling relationship with you, your job is going to be easier. You have been able to establish the proper conditions for the client to be ready to move toward a positive change. So your first response on returning from the break might be to acknowledge your client's concerns using "Carl Rogers with a Twist" (O'Hanlon & Beadle, 1994) while remaining sensitive to whether your client is in a "yes set." As you will recall, this means that you place the concerns in the past tense and add a possibility statement, such as, "And so far, you have not yet found a way to . . ."

If the client has a clear picture in response to your use of the miracle question but has not named exceptions you might use the "as if" suggestion (DeJong & Berg, 2002). For example, you could say to your client, "I wonder what it would be like for you if you were to pick one particular day this next week and pretend that this miracle has happened, and live out that day just the way you described it here to me."

When you are dealing with a client who is motivated but has not stated any clear goals or identified any exceptions, you could suggest a different response to the problem. Following de Shazer's (1985) suggestion, you could respond, "Wow! This has certainly been a stubborn situation for you. I just had a crazy thought. What do you think would happen if, when that comes up again, you would just do something completely different— even if it seems totally weird or off-the-wall to you?"

In addition, you can emphasize your client's goal-seeking behaviors if the client has clear goals and self-caused exceptions. In this situation, you might say, "It is amazing to me that you remain so clear as to how you want things to turn out!—that, in spite of some setbacks, you have continued to hang in there, and that you can describe so clearly how these behaviors are getting you closer to your goal. I think I'm hearing you say that you want to do those things that are working even more this week."

If you determine that your counselor–client relationship is a visiting type, as described in Chapter 4, then you must honor the person's reluctance to invest in change. If you remember the admonition from Chapter 2 stating that the ways of the fish are more important than the tools of the fisherman (Young, 1992), then you know that moving in too quickly will only cause the visitor to seek escape. A visitor must be lured by your empathic presence.

When you go into a retail store and the sales clerk comes up to you and asks if he or she can help, and you say, "I'm just looking," you are probably annoyed if the clerk stalks you and keeps asking to help. Similarly, the visitor wishes to "peruse the merchandise" before making a commitment to become fully involved.

As the counselor, you have a number of options for dealing with a visitor, but, whatever you decide to try, you always want to acknowledge the client's reluctance. You could say, "Even so, it was good of you to be here. I can see that you are hoping that this problem will be solved very soon." After offering the LUV Triangle, at some point you may want to reframe the behavior of remaining aloof in the session in positive terms. One possible reframe is to mention, "It's clear that you don't want to make things worse by adding your problems to an already difficult situation and that you are the type of person who likes to work things out on your own." Another option, particularly with a very hesitant client, is to use a bridge and invite him or her back for a later session. For example, you might say, "So, we should work together to get you out of this situation as soon as possible. What would you say to meeting next week and working toward that goal?"

If you judge your counselor–client relationship to be a complaining type, then your client is likely viewing the counseling session as a place to come and emotionally vent his or her troubles, but is not yet to the place of seeking change. You must, of course, acknowledge the client's complaints by including the terms and metaphors that he or she has used to describe the stated problems. Display your concern, but do not emphasize the negative affect. Deconstruct, if you can, but do not dispute what the complainant is saying.

Carl Rogers with a Twist is often useful in such circumstances, so you might say, "It sure sounds like it has been one damned thing after another for you lately. Because of everything that has happened, you're finding it hard to get your feet under you and come up with a way to climb out of this pit you've been in."

Delivering Suggestions

So that suggestions do not sound as if you are implying they will absolutely solve a problem, it is sometimes a better strategy to disclaim them. For example, you can say,

- "This is going to sound strange, but I just had the image of you . . ." Then describe the behavior that might bring about the resolution to the problem in vivid detail.
- "I don't know if I am getting this right, but it seemed to me that you were saying you wanted to (add the suggestion)."
- "I was imagining you in a year, after you have gotten past this trouble. I saw you . . ." Then name a behavior that would help the client transcend the current situation.

The artfully delivered suggestion is subtle. If it results in a change in clients' viewing or doing, they should think it was their own idea, or they should be encouraged to come up with their own interpretation of what you suggested in the session. The bottom line is that all good suggestions should end up being constructed by the client. If you offer suggestions softly, tentatively, and skillfully, they won't be remembered as yours. Your clients will feel certain that it was their own insight that created the new idea, attitude, or behavior. Remember our previous discussion of constructed memory (Cozolino, 2002) in which eyewitness testimony can be altered by the interrogator simply substituting different words during questioning in court. Depending on the nature of the suggestive word, the person's recall of events is changed.

Memory is malleable. The way you inquire into people's recollections will actually alter the neural networks in their brains. Their autobiographical memories are stored as narratives in the brain's neural networks. If your suggestions to clients come in under their radar, you can perturb their neural nets enough to create the chaos in the story that will lead to a positive reorganization.

A great metaphor for an effective suggestion is Milton Erickson's "utilization" story of how he got a stubborn cow into the barn. Instead of pulling it forward or pushing it from behind, he grabbed hold of its tail. The cow attempted to get away, and, as it did, Erickson steered it in the direction of the barn. Seen this way, it was the cow's will to resist that gave the cow the idea that it wanted to go to the barn (Lankton & Lankton, 1985). When you offer suggestions to clients, you should not be pulling or pushing them toward a certain thought or behavior. You are simply following their will to a desired end.

Your suggestions can take many forms. Suggestions can be offered as metaphors, speculations, paradoxes, fantasies and dreams, anecdotes, confusion techniques, oxymorons, and, only occasionally, as direct advice (Lankton & Lankton, 1986). You can offer suggestions in a soft tone of voice, with a shift of emphasis on the part that you wish to punctuate. Be sure that your suggestions are tentative, nonauthoritarian, and fit the "facts," as told by the client. Finally, when you give a suggestion, consider using the Zeigarnik Effect by leaving the idea without closure.

Delivering the Suggestion (A Protocol)

When you return to your client after the break, begin by asking what might have occurred to him or her that would be good for you to know as you two work toward a resolution of the client's concerns. If the client has come up with a way of resolving the situation while you were out, then capitalize on this idea. Marvel—out loud—at the proposed solution using the "encouragement triad," making sure you communicate your enthusiasm for the idea (energy), that the idea seems like something the client can surely do (agency), and elaborate as well as you can your sense of how things will be different once the client has begun this change (imagery). As we mentioned, however, the client will sometimes respond by going back to problem-saturated talk. Of course, if this happens, it will be your signal that you must acknowledge these concerns. In general, you may begin the postbreak interaction by following the protocol below:

1. *Re-acknowledge* your client's stated concerns, but also continue to relabel and deconstruct as you had before. Use your client's metaphors that were descriptions of the concerns. At this point, you are speaking in a kindly, but not energetic, tone of voice. You are communicating your empathy but not your sympathy.

2. *Compliment* your client on having coped with these concerns thus far, restate the exceptions to the problem, and point out your client's strengths and resources as they were indicated in the prebreak conversation. At this point, you are speaking enthusiastically to entrain your client's emotional arousal.

3. Determine whether the client is in a "yes set." See if your client is accepting your feedback as accurate by nodding affirmatively to your acknowledgments and compliments.

If your client does *not* appear to be affirming your compliments, you may wish to use an immediacy designed to turn the client's response toward a "yes set." For example, you could say, "As I am saying these things, I notice that you are looking down, shaking your head, and frowning. I guess that there is something I have said that doesn't ring quite true for you; tell me the part that I'm getting wrong, if you would." The client may then indicate that you seem to feel that he or she is stronger than he is. This response indicates that the client feels pressured to accomplish something but is not quite ready. You might respond by saying, "I guess I misinterpreted what you were saying about your (exceptions, coping, strengths, etc.)." You might then say, "I guess all those things you said are true, but you are not quite ready to unleash that arsenal toward resolving your difficulties."

In this situation, you could scale the client's hope by saying, "I guess you think I'm a little more optimistic than you are right now. On a scale of 1 to 10, with 1 being that you are reluctant to believe that things will get better, and 10 being that you are absolutely convinced, where are you now?" Another possibility is to scale commitment: "On a scale of 1 to 10, with 1 being that you are feeling helpless and needing to just wait for all this to blow over, or your troubles to solve themselves, and 10 being that you are willing to do anything to resolve these issues, where would you say you are right now?" After getting a number on hope or commitment, you can ask the usual, "If you saw yourself on the way to (the next higher number), how would you be different?"

4. If the client is in a "yes set" after your compliments, then you can *bridge* from the client's goal to your suggestion. For example, you might say, "And because you said that what you would like to work on in the future was (name the stated goal), I got the feeling that you meant the first thing you might try is (name a step toward the goal)."

5. See if you can add some suspense or positive uncertainty to the suggestion. By employing the *Zeigarnik Effect,* you ensure that your client will not simply dismiss the suggestion and forget about it. Here's an example: "If you were to do (name a behavior the client has indicated) maybe it could lead to (name a positive consequence) or maybe (name another positive outcome). I wonder which it will be." Another Zeigarnik suggestion is to say something like, "I've noticed something about you that you have not yet discovered for yourself. My guess is that it's really going to help you get past this situation. But I think it would be much better for you to discover this thing yourself, than for me to tell you what I see."

Obviously, this after-the-break protocol is more a rough sketch of the process than a script. Because you can never anticipate exactly how your clients will respond, you should regard this protocol as only a guide. Use your own creativity and what you know of your client to design suggestions that stand a chance of making a difference. If your client follows your suggestion and never gives you credit, you have been a success.

LISTENING IN ON A SESSION

Review the story at the beginning of the chapter and the previous session excerpt.

Before reconvening the session, the counselor thought he would sneak a peak at his schedule for the rest of the afternoon. He was still trying to get used to his PDA that his wife and children had given him for his birthday; their attempt to ease him into the digital world. They teased him constantly about his old-school ways of continuing to use his day planner. He wasn't anti-technology or threatened by the newest electronic marvels; it was just that he felt more comfortable with a big, full-paged calendar showing the whole month at once. That way, he reasoned, he could see the month at a glance without pushing buttons or having to fool with that silly stylus. Also, the PDA was so small, he was afraid he would lose it, even though he could spot the fire engine red calendar cover from across the room. Only when his daughter asked him what a "troglodyte" was did he finally acquiesce.

As he scanned the screen on his PDA, it began flashing a low battery signal. "Damn," he swore softly, "I forgot to charge the ridiculous thing again. One more thing my old calendar never needed!"

He thought he'd better scroll ahead quickly before he ran out of time. He had planned to force himself to sit down that evening and begin reading a colleague's latest book on family therapy activities. He had skimmed through it but hadn't taken the time to peruse the work as he had promised. He thought to himself that if he were going to do it right, he really needed to have a family do some of the suggested activities and give him some feedback. His mind jumped ahead to Dolores, Dulcinea, and Dario waiting for him in the family counseling room. If only they could . . . .

Meanwhile, the PDA began to produce an ominous electronic shrieking announcement: "Warning! Your battery needs recharging! Data will be lost!" In the nick of time, he was able to plug in the charger. However, checking his evening's schedule, he discovered that he had already scheduled a family activity. Well, as his maternal grandmother used to say, "Never bite off more than you can chew, but if you do, puff out your cheeks and go slow; it will all go down somehow."

The family and counselor return to the room and sit in the same places to continue the session. Near the close, the counselor turns and addresses each member of the family.

Counselor: "Before we end the session, I have something I wanted to say."
(He shifts his posture uncomfortably and looks somewhat awkward.)

Dario: "Yeah, man, you look all freaky. What's up?"

Dolores: *"Dario!"*

Counselor: "No, you are right, Dario. I'll try to explain the reason."
(He carefully describes his predicament about the book and makes a request.)

"Since my friend's book has a lot of suggested activities for families, I thought I'd be able to give him better feedback if a family would try them out, say one or two, and give me their honest opinion. Now, like I said, I'm facing a deadline in ten days. It's my fault because I've procrastinated, but who knows, some of the exercises might be fun and helpful, too."

(Noting their lack of response, he tries being even more immediate.)

"Look, I know that timing for this suggestion or favor, if you will, seems suspicious and I could see how you might think it is a ploy on my part to trick you into working together."

(They begin to come alive a little with his last statement and so he continues.)

"I'd be happy to get the email from my colleague if it would help . . ."

Dolores: (Interrupting, and apologetic.)
"Oh, we don't think that at all, it's just that, well, I'm awfully busy at work and I can't imagine that we could be of any help to you. We're not exactly the Brady Bunch as you know." (Pause of several seconds.) "Would we have to write anything?"

Dario: (Groaning, and making a face.)
"Oh man, do we have to? I have enough homework."

> **Dulcinea:**   (Before the counselor can make another pitch for his "suggestion/ favor," Dulcinea interrupts.)
> "Listen to the two of you. Quit being so negative. Sure we'll help you out. Come on. He screwed up and he needs help—just like us."
> (She takes the book from the counselor.)
> "We'll have our assignment by next week; but try not to let it happen too many more times."
> For a second or two there is dead silence, then there are smiles all around as everyone realizes that something quite different had transpired in the session.

REFLECTING QUESTIONS

1. In what ways did this suggestion differ from advice?
2. How was the counselor's immediacy in the session like a suggestion?
3. What do you think transpired in the session that was "quite different?"

Task Proposal

Following the break, you will have to decide whether to simply leave the client with a tentative suggestion or to offer a task that the client might try between the current and next session. Tasks are certainly more intrusive than suggestions. They lie somewhere between suggestions and advice, but they differ from advice in that tasks are designed to move the process along rather than to solve a problem. Tasks are certainly more direct than suggestions, but they do not have to come across as directive (Bertolino & O'Hanlon, 2002; Lipchik, 2002).

Tasks given to clients should maintain the therapeutic momentum of the session and to "carry the work of the therapy session into the client's real life" (Butler & Powers, 1996, p. 238). The best times to offer these tasks are usually after the consulting break and at the end of the session. If you are indeed able to consult with a colleague during your break, you must have informed your client at the beginning of the session that this is what you will be doing. You might say, "Toward the end of our session today, I will take a break and leave the room to consult with a colleague about what we have said. I hope to get this person's ideas as to how you and I can better proceed together."

Offering a task to the client who knows you have consulted with another professional can help maintain your status as the appreciatively inquiring nonexpert who is "not from around here." You can return to the room and say, "While we were consulting, my colleague gave me this idea. Tell me what you think of it." (Then offer the task.) Of course, if you have the lucky circumstance of having a reflecting team behind a one-way mirror, then, when you and your client take a break to hear what the team has to say, the team members will offer the task.

Perhaps the most successful task assignment that the early solution-focused therapy team hit upon is what they called the "Formula First Session Task" (de Shazer in O'Hanlon & Weiner-Davis, 1989). You merely say something like, "Between now and the next time we meet, I would like you to observe what happens that you would want to continue happening."

In a follow-up survey, 50 out of 56 clients returned having noticed things that they wished to continue in their lives, and 46 out of the 50 described at least one of those things as something new. When the client arrives for the next session after you've offered the Formula First Session Task, it is crucial that you *not* ask, "Did you notice anything?" You should always approach the follow-up interview with presumptive language by saying, "What was one thing you noticed happening in your life this week that you would like to see happening more?"

Studies on the Formula First Session Task assignment conducted by Adams, Piercy, and Jurich (1991) found that 60 percent of those clients given this task at the end of the first meeting reported that their situation had improved upon their return. However, this same study revealed that tasks that were tailored to the stated problem were equally successful. In another study of the Formula First Session Task assignment, Jordan and Quinn (1994) found that clients generally reported that their situations had improved, their optimism that these concerns would be resolved had increased, and they saw their first session as having been a positive experience.

A Task Construction Paradigm

Friedman (1997) set up a matrix based upon whether a task would be offered directly or indirectly. This "Task Construction Paradigm," as he called it, would then yield four different types of tasks:

1. *Direct-behavioral.* These tasks involve obliquely suggesting what the client might do: For example, you might say, "[What if you were to] do one good thing for yourself each day" (p. 78), or "How do you think your wife would react if you were to surprise her by doing something unexpected that she would like?"

2. *Direct-nonbehavioral.* These are tasks that involve suggesting a focus for the client's thinking. "How about thinking of something you could do that would be totally different from your usual way of approaching your husband about his drinking, yet might help you worry less?" or *"Notice* when your wife is acting in ways you would like" (p. 78, emphasis added).

3. *Indirect-behavioral.* These tasks are suggestions regarding possible actions the client could do. "I wonder if you visited your father's grave and got his advice about this problem, what he might say" (p. 78).

4. *Indirect-nonbehavioral.* Here is a metaphor delivered to a woman who had lost her house after 50 years: "Losing your house is like a turtle losing its shell. You're all vulnerable and exposed. I wonder how a turtle goes about growing a new shell" (p. 78).

Friedman's task construction ideas might be helpful to you as you attempt your own designs. We have found it especially illuminating to distinguish between direct and indirect tasks. Direct tasks may seem to border on advice but are usually offered tentatively and without the assertion that they will necessarily "fix" anything. You must gauge the quality of your relationship with your client in order to determine whether you want to offer a suggestion or a task after the break. Either way, this sort of intervention will work only if your client's own theory of change is compatible with what is being suggested.

LISTENING IN ON A SESSION

Review the story at the beginning of the chapter and the earlier session excerpts. The second session began much differently as both teenagers sat closer to their mother and to each other. They were all chatting away like old friends at a reunion when the therapist walked into the room.

Counselor: "Hello, everyone, I'm glad to see you back. What would you like to accomplish today with the time we have together?"

Dolores: "Well, we had a pretty good week but we're sorry. We didn't do any of the exercises in that book."

Counselor: (Glances around the circle to see that everyone is smiling and looking expectantly at the counselor.)

"From the smiles on your faces, it looks like you must have had a *very* good week. Gosh, when you left here last week I really didn't know what to expect. I'd really like to learn how the family got together in such a short period of time."

Dolores: (Long pause, as the three of them exchange glances and giggle a little bit. Dolores holds back until both children urge her to "go ahead and start." The counselor notes that their interaction is quite different from last week's session.)

"OK, I'll start. Nobody talked much in the car on the way home and I forgot about the book you gave me until I finally did find some time when a customer stood me up for lunch. As I skimmed through the book I became interested in a case study about how a family turned their lives around by essentially learning to be positive with each other. There were some 'tricky' parts that I wasn't sure of but in spite of my misgivings, I decided to tell these two about it. Allll right, somebody else talk for awhile. I don't want to hog the spotlight."

Dulcinea: (Trying to sound annoyed but not being very convincing.)

"Well, I don't know if Mom drank a magic potion or what, but all of a sudden she wasn't getting on my ass about everything. It was pretty cool."

Dario: "Yeah, Mom fixed this great breakfast for us and—"

Dulcinea: (Interrupts.)

"You better not count on that every morning, Dorko!" (Pauses) ". . . I mean Dario."

Dario: (Bows slightly toward his sister and continues without mentioning the interruption.)

"Anyway Mom goes, 'Hey you two, I was reading that book Dr. Miller gave me to read last weekend. There was this one part about this family that was a lot like us, you know—divorce, and everything—they even had a teenage girl who everybody blamed for the trouble.'"

Counselor: (He grimaces slightly as if anticipating something very unpleasant.)

"Wow! Then what happened?"

Dario: "Dulcinea freaked, what did you expect?"

(Dario continued his explanation by delivering a fair rendition of Dulcinea's reaction to her mother. He demonstrated how Dulcinea's hands flew to her ears and how she warned her mother not to deliver another lecture.)

Counselor: "Well, I have to tell you that I'm really stumped. I mean, no offense, but I haven't heard anything yet that would get you all to come together like you have today."

Dolores: "I don't know what happened to me, but all of a sudden when I read about that family I realized I was so angry at my husband and his drinking that I had been taking it out on the kids. Of course, they were both doing really dumb things, but I didn't understand what was going on until I read that book."

(Looking at Dulcinea and Dario.)

"I realized that you two were trying to keep the family together the only way you knew how. You thought if somehow you could divert all the negative attention to yourselves—kind of like lightning rods—that your dad would quit drinking, we wouldn't get knocked around, he and I wouldn't fight and the family would stay together." (Turning to the counselor.) "They were heroes, I'm so proud."

(Dolores pulls out a tissue and begins to cry. Both children move closer to her and put their hands on her shoulders.)

Dario: "It's, OK, Mom. We'll be fine."

REFLECTING QUESTIONS

1. Point out the ways that the counselor influenced the clients.
2. Identify the client strengths that are emerging.
3. How would you respond to the clients at the end of this segment?

USING THESE TOOLS

Meet again with the three other colleagues who had experienced the reflecting session. Continue with the helping sessions that you had started earlier. This time, the counselor, with the help of the two observers, offers a task at the end of the helping session. Then discuss your observations, reflections, and reactions.

SUMMARY

Whenever possible, you should take advantage of your colleagues to give power to your counseling work. A reflecting team can offer a compelling and transformative experience for your clients. Using a consulting break can also be valuable for both you and your client. When you offer suggestions, you need to tailor them to your client.

SEGUE TO CHAPTER 12

In order to help you synthesize the ideas and tools in the next chapter, we would like you to think of a time when you had been practicing a series of specific and separate competencies that were components of a complex skill that you finally mastered. This process may have involved studying the grammatical elements of a foreign language, practicing the particular steps in a gymnastics routine, learning to drive a car, or learning to play a musical instrument. Whatever the skill, think about how you were able to integrate all these parts into a unified whole. Reflect on how you accomplished that feat of gracefully, naturally, and effortlessly juggling all those individual competencies.

Resource

European Brief Therapy Association
www.ebta.nu

Brief counseling and therapy has garnered an international following. One example is the European Brief Therapy Association. This website offers information about EBTA conferences, a collection of material, and links leading to information about brief counseling and therapy.

CHAPTER 12

The "Brief Attitudes" and Consolidating Change

> "Life is either a daring adventure or nothing. To keep our
> faces toward change and behave like free spirits in the
> presence of fate is strength undefeatable."
> *Helen Keller*

CHAPTER GOALS

Reading and experiencing the ideas in this chapter will help you to understand this:

- Brief therapy is not just a set of techniques—it is an attitude about the nature of reality, people's resilience, the process of change, and the importance of every therapy session.

Reading about and practicing the tools in this chapter will help you to develop skills in using the following techniques:

- Encouraging and consolidating change.
- Using termination as an opportunity for reflecting on lessons learned and resources discovered.
- Writing a follow-up letter to clients.

STORY

Let's go back to Bhavana's story in Chapter 2. As you may recall, she decided to seek the counselor's help after a series of events left her believing that her "whole life was screwed up." Before continuing with Bhavana's story here, you may want to review both her first story and the two Listening in on a Session segments of the first session in Chapter 2. Toward the end of the first session, the counselor made a suggestion that some things in Bhavana's life might change over the next week, and it would be would be good if she kept track of them.

REFLECTING QUESTIONS

1. What changes did you notice in Bhavana?
2. How could you use these changes?
3. How might you begin your next session with Bhavana?

OVERVIEW

In this chapter, we offer a review of the fundamental ideas that form the "brief attitude." Brief therapy is not just a set of techniques to be applied to a "problem." Instead, it is a way of regarding the world and what clients need in order to move from a "stuck" position to one of creative possibilities.

In the Tools section of this chapter, we focus on working with your client to consolidate changes as they are made and how to handle termination so that your client walks away with his or her own tool kit for coping. We discuss techniques for deciding when to terminate with clients, as well as rituals for consolidating changes that the client has made. Clients sometimes have misgivings at the termination of counseling, so we suggest some ways of dealing with these concerns.

IDEAS

Brief Ideas and the "Brief Attitude"

Back in Chapter 1, we explained to you that we had designed this book's format to parallel the process of brief counseling. Because the therapeutic process is goal oriented, we began each chapter with a statement of goals. Since the narrative perspective is central to brief therapy, we offered in each chapter a story in order to give life to the concepts and techniques. Because we emphasize multicultural competence, we presented clients who come from a variety of backgrounds. And to be consistent with our belief that theory and practice are intertwined, we included both concepts and techniques in all chapters. Now that you are well into this book, we invite you to engage in another process that parallels the work of your clients as they near termination: to consolidate the lessons learned, discoveries made, and perspectives developed.

Brief counseling is an attitude that you embrace, and not just a series of influencing tactics that you employ during the session. The "brief attitude" comes from both using the tools described in this volume and also adopting the beliefs, or ideas, that support the tools. Remember that Immanuel Kant said, "Intuitions without concepts are blind." Concepts, attitudes, and beliefs are actually tools to which you can return when things get foggy in your work with clients.

Why Use Brief Approaches to Counseling?

As a counselor, your first responsibility is to your client. Yet, you may hear that the reason the profession is moving toward brief approaches to counseling is that caseloads are growing larger or insurance companies are becoming stingier. Both these statements may be true. More people value counseling as a useful way of working through their concerns. In schools, agencies, and hospitals, where resources remain limited while the demand continues to expand, counselors are asked to do more with less—especially in less time. Third-party payers (insurance companies) are also demanding more results in fewer sessions. With the advent of managed care, a counselor who wishes to be paid through the client's insurance must be able to state an explicit plan. The counselor will then be allotted a limited number of visits in order to accomplish the goals for counseling. Managed care now covers more than 80 percent of people who receive their health care benefits through their employers, and the percentage is increasing (Prochaska & Norcross, 2007).

But neither the supply-and-demand contention nor the managed-care argument can be the primary impetus for adopting brief methods in counseling. Both are external to the needs of clients, the people to whom counselors are primarily responsible. If we use brief methods because of the money, then we are mercenaries. If we sell out to the marketplace, then we are prostitutes. We must always do what we do because we believe it is in the best interest of our clients.

Let us ask a hypothetical question. If all counselors were independently wealthy and there were enough of them to give clients all the time they requested, would we, then, ever consider using brief methods? Likewise, if clients could pay for all the sessions they wanted, and they were willing to devote all their time and energy to complete makeovers, would we still believe that working briefly was a good idea?

O'Hanlon (1995) cited a number of studies that suggested that "brief" is what we do anyway. For example, one study (Garfield, 1978) concluded that, in both private practice and community mental health centers, the average duration of therapy was five to eight sessions, regardless of the theoretical orientation of the therapist. Another study (Lambert, Shapiro, & Bergin, 1986) suggested that 75 percent of the clients who benefit from therapy do so within the first six months, and that the major positive impact of therapy takes place in the first six to eight sessions. Several other studies indicated that the most common length of treatment is a single session. Seventy-eight percent of clients in one study stated that their problem was "better" to "much better" after one session and that they had gotten what they wanted from the counseling (Talmon, 1990). School counselors know that one session is often all they will get to work with a student and that sometimes they have to do their counseling "on the run"—in a vacant classroom, hallway, or cafeteria. If we are going to see clients for such short periods of time anyway, perhaps we should adopt brief methods for dealing with their concerns.

If we could offer our clients unlimited counseling—as many sessions as they wanted—would they benefit more or simply take longer to get better? We don't really have the answer to this question, but it does seem clear that a counselor can ethically adopt a "brief" attitude toward counseling, and that this position can be for the client's benefit rather than for the insurance company, the demands of the marketplace, or for any other external reason.

Efficient Versus Brief Counseling

In 1966, Richard Fisch proposed the establishment of a research project to study the change process in counseling and psychotherapy. For want of a better term, the research group referred to its model as "brief therapy" (Watzlawick, Weakland, &

Fisch, 1974), and the institute they established became known as the Brief Therapy Center of the Mental Research Institute (MRI) in Palo Alto. The term "brief" caught on and came to be regarded by many as the primary emphasis of the work. The MRI researchers, however, were never really comfortable with this emphasis. They stated their discomfort in the following passage: "The name is unsatisfactory because 'brief' therapy often refers to some sort of stopgap, superficial, or first-aid measures undertaken provisionally until 'real' long-term therapy becomes possible" (p. xiv). Nevertheless, it was the term "brief" that stuck. Many traditional therapists opposed the idea of working briefly because they viewed it as merely a truncated version of real counseling.

Rather than wasting time probing the client's background for causes or the "real problem" before initiating treatment, our version of brief counseling focuses on the intention to immediately roll up our sleeves and get to work. The fact that this way of working turns out to be brief, meaning fewer sessions, is a byproduct. The term "efficient" better describes the use of time in this counseling approach. And even though this is an efficient way to work, effectiveness, not efficiency, matters more.

The fact that the idea of "brief" has currency in the marketplace is both a blessing and a curse. Counselors who claim to work briefly seem to have fewer problems dealing with HMOs and other managed care agents. On the other hand, there seems also to have been a counselor backlash to the notion of working briefly, and the term "brief" for many counselors is an anathema. The approach to counseling offered in this book is designed primarily for its effectiveness with most issues brought to the counselor's office. Fundamentally, "brief" is an attitude. The counselor who begins the work intending to be successful, while also being scrupulously efficient in the use of client's time, will likely have fewer sessions with clients. Parkinson's Law, a well-known principle in physics, states that a task will expand to fill the time allotted to it. If you and your client expect that getting better will take a very long time, it will.

EXPERIENCING THIS IDEA

Suppose a salesperson must display her product to potential customers in five cities: Arborville, Bellville, Carterville, Dodgeville, and Elmville. Arborville is the salesperson's hometown; she must travel to the other cities by car. As you can see in Figure 12-1, the distances between cities are indicated on each of the 10 roads that connect them. The salesperson would like your help in planning the itinerary. What would be the *best* route for the salesperson to travel? Once you have planned the trip, read the next paragraph.

We're betting that, as you did this exercise, you attempted to find the shortest route for the traveling salesperson to follow. It makes sense that if time and money are involved, then the shortest route would be the *best* route. However, if sightseeing is your aim, then time is less important. When clients come for counseling, they generally do not have unlimited amounts of time, money, or emotional stamina. They usually would prefer to get to their destination with the least amount of travel. Keeping the goal in mind helps avoid sightseeing.

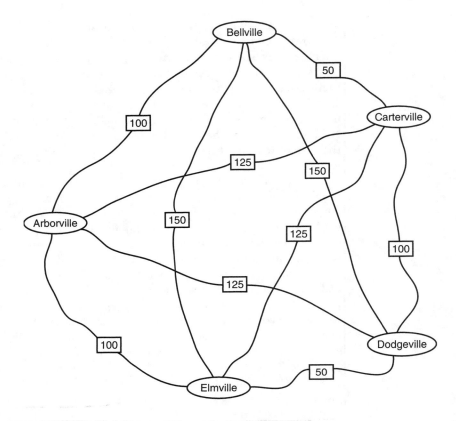

FIGURE 12-1 The traveling salesperson problem.

The Brief Attitudes

What follows is a collection of briefly stated ideas that make up the "brief attitudes." They are culled from the concepts and theories we have described earlier. We offer them as a list for you to ponder as you near the completion of this book:

• **Change is inevitable, except from vending machines.** You do not have to motivate people to change; they are already in the process. Your job is to help your client channel this change process toward the desired end.

• **Small change leads to big change.** Contrary to one of the popular myths in counseling, the amount of time it takes to reach a resolution does not have to equal the amount of time involved in acquiring the problem in the first place. Neither does the strength of your intervention have to surpass the strength of the problem. A gentle nudge may be all that's necessary; it's the Butterfly Effect.

• **Resistance is relational.** What counselors have traditionally called "resistance"—and have believed to reside within the client's "bag of skin"—is actually a quality that exists in the relationship between you and your client. The "resistant," reluctant, or hesitant client is telling you that he or she is not ready to cooperate with your current tactics but might cooperate in some other way.

- **Clients have all they need to resolve concerns.** Clients are the experts on their own lives. Their concerns are usually not the result of ignorance, stupidity, or illness. Given the opportunity, they can resolve their own concerns. Your job is to help them believe in themselves and realize their overlooked resources.

- **Meaning is co-constructed.** Lives are stories that we have constructed. They are made up of meanings. When you work together with your client, you are deconstructing the old life story and co-constructing a new one.

- **Actions and descriptions are recursive.** Nothing in the world has a label that we haven't given it. We define what a problem is in the world. Our reactions to labels and "problems" then validate the labels and problematic nature of the things to which we are reacting. This expectation becomes a vicious cycle. Once we begin to see things as simply the labels we have given them, and problems as we have defined them, then we can change the way we react to these phenomena.

- **If it works, don't fix it.** Even if you would not do it the way your client does, if it isn't a problem for the client, it isn't a problem. Do not seek "underlying" or "deep-seated" issues that the client does not see. Remember that different people have different cultural values. It is not your job to sell your values to your client.

- **Stuck? Do something different.** Do not simplistically adopt the "if at first you don't succeed, try, try again" admonition. If at first you don't succeed, don't try harder, try something else. See if you can come up with a difference that makes a difference.

- **Keep it simple.** Since small perturbations can produce large changes in the system, you really don't have to come up with grandiose strategies for change. Most of the time, something simple will do. Furthermore, clients would rather try something simple that seems easy than to attempt a heroic plan.

- **Approach each session as if it were the last.** Since studies show that most counseling is single-session, your first meeting with your client is likely to be your last. Make hay while the sun shines.

- **There is no failure, only feedback.** So-called "failure" is merely a message that what you have tried isn't working. As it is with cybernetic "smart missiles," feedback will give clues as to the location of the target. The future is teleonomic, so failure is simply a course correction in the general direction of success.

- **Don't go "sightseeing."** As early as possible, you should help clients determine their goals for counseling and then relentlessly help them pursue these goals. Stay away from side issues and lines of inquiry that have stimulated your curiosity but have nothing to do with the therapeutic goals. Clients will "peel their own onions" during their work—meaning that if something else needs examination, the client will bring it up.

- **Your client determines the goal.** Don't unilaterally decide that the client should be working on something else rather than what the two of you have agreed upon. If the client seems to have little energy for the stated goal, you should ask if the goal has changed.

- **Label jars, not people.** Accepting diagnostic labels or pejorative terms as if they are reality only serves to reinforce your client's negative story. You are working to deconstruct such stories, so describe your client in terms that suggest emergence, competence, and uniqueness.

- **Listen for client intrigue.** Pay particularly close attention when your client becomes intrigued or enthused by an idea. Sometimes these differences will emerge or change in the midst of problem-saturated talk. It takes a sensitive ear to pluck them out of the noise.

- **Custom design interventions.** General strategies never apply to an individual; each person is different. Even though we have offered you techniques that can be helpful, you need to tailor all these counseling interventions to fit your individual client.

- **Look for the way out, not the etiology.** Figuring out why the client has the problem rarely helps. You don't need to know very much about the problem to be helpful in resolving it. Don't waste your time—and your client's—worrying over how the client got into this fix. Just look for the way out. Archeology cannot reveal the future.

- **Use what is already being done.** People are always solving problems; your job is to find out how they do it. Clients are more amenable to doing something that fits their style than trying something that seems foreign to them. Keep reminding yourself that it is better to channel a river than to dam it.

- **Work with the client's worldview.** Work with the worldview of the client—not the world "out there." Your role is not to align the client's thinking with "reality." Neither is it your mission to straighten up your client's "crooked thinking." Deconstruct your client's story—don't dispute it.

- **Watch your language.** The way you talk about your client's situation helps to make it "true." If you conspire with the client to use language that implies pathology, absoluteness, and hopelessness, then that is the world you and your client will create together. On the other hand, if you use words that open "problem" descriptions to new interpretations and that indicate that change is inevitable, then you have helped your client to create a different world. Use presumptive language to make exceptions definite.

- **Go for the goal.** If you don't know where you are going, how will you know if you get there? The well-formed goal is focused on change in the client's viewing and doing, and the presence—rather than the absence—of something. Make sure that you and the client are always revisiting the goal. Find out how much of the goal must be accomplished in order to be "good enough." Keep going until you get there—then stop.

- **Seek resolutions, not solutions, to major life concerns.** If you can't decide whether to serve red or white wine at your dinner party, you have a problem. The problem will have a solution, probably based on what food you are serving. However, problems and their solutions are trivial compared to the major life concerns that people bring to counseling. People do not "solve" life concerns. Instead, they achieve some form of resolution by transforming themselves, transcending the issues, or translating chaos into meaning. Rather than being merely solved, life concerns are *dis*-solved, *ab*-solved, or *re*-solved.

• **Understand your client's context.** A behavior takes its meaning from the situation in which it is behaved. For example, wearing a swimming suit at Daytona Beach conveys a quite different meaning than wearing the same swimming suit in London's Saint Paul's Cathedral. Once you understand the psychological and social context of your client's concerns, you have a better chance of helping your client find a resolution. Sometimes, all it takes is for your client to move to a different psychological or physical place that offers a different context.

• **Systems have rules.** "Every transaction is a rule." Once behaved, a transaction may come to be expected as "the way we are supposed to behave with each other." After a time, we may not even be able to say what our rules for behaving with each other are, although we may feel slighted if the rules are not observed. As a brief therapist, part of your job is to deconstruct or expose these rules so that clients can discover that rules need not be so tyrannical in their lives.

• **People punctuate reality.** She says, "I nag you because you drink." He says, "I drink because you nag me." Both believe that they have the better grasp on reality. The way in which we punctuate, or emphasize, aspects of our experience is purely arbitrary. Any event can be punctuated another way. This offers the opportunity for you to look elsewhere for explanations.

• **Solutions become problems.** People try to solve problems by doing what seems to be intuitively obvious. These first-order attempts at solution sometimes only add another level of concern: helplessness in the face of the "problem." If you can assist the client to interrupt the loop that maintains the problem situation, then change is possible. As with the nine-dot problem, you must break the perceived boundaries for a second-order change.

• **Like painting, brief therapy requires detail work.** By encouraging your clients to be detailed and specific in describing their current circumstances and future goals, you are helping to set the stage for therapeutic change. When clients state their concerns in behavioral terms and depict their circumstances with attention to the particulars, they are making it more possible for you to offer a "relabel," or reframe, that addresses the facts of the situation but changes its meaning.

• **Client's metaphors are bridges.** What is not literal in your client's portrayal of the concern is metaphorical. For example, the client may report feeling "down," "dumped on," "slammed," or "blown off." If you employ these terms in your acknowledgments, the client will feel understood, and you will have bridged a connection.

• **All client behaviors make sense.** Before you can communicate respect for the client's position, you must believe that people do the best they can and are making reasonable decisions, given the way they view the situation they are in. If they could see the situation differently, they would do something different. As the TV psychologist Dr. Phil puts it, "People do what they know. When they know better, they do better."

• **All counseling is collaborative.** You must have a relationship with the client in order to do effective work. If you communicate that you are listening, understanding, and validating your clients, if you have a truly empathic feel for what it is like to be your clients, if you are "by the side" of your clients, rather than "on their side," then they will trust you enough to collaborate with you on working toward a resolution.

- **Remember that clients are complex adaptive systems.** If you insert a perturbation into your clients' systems of thought, they will temporarily pass through a chaotic disorganization of their life story but will inevitably self-organize. Confusion can be a useful technique for stimulating the emergence of something new and for moving clients away from fixed or circular attractors that create despair.

- **Be positive, resolution focused, and future oriented.** You don't need to probe for where it hurts. Clients will tell you all you need to know. Instead of focusing on your client's painful recollections, you can move the dialogue to a discussion of goals and emphasize past successes that will be helpful in working toward change.

- **Exceptions are clues.** The times when the problem is not happening involve the behaviors and thoughts that can lead the client to the goal. You will have to search for exceptions, because they usually go unnoticed by the client. The problem is not always happening; exceptions are clues to resolution. Get the client to do more of what is already working.

The Stages of Change as an Integrative Approach

In recent years, the counseling literature has seen a number of attempts to synthesize or integrate the seemingly disparate ideas of various counseling theories. According to Prochaska and Norcross (2007), the three most popular approaches to unification are common factors, technical eclecticism, and theoretical integration. The *common factors approach,* which we discussed in Chapter 2, holds that "a positive therapy relationship, a hopeful and hardworking client, and an empathic therapist probably account for more of treatment success than the particular treatment method" (p. 478). *Technical eclecticism* focuses on techniques and is actuarial rather than theoretical. This approach draws on research that attempts to discover which type of intervention works best for which type of client. *Theoretical integration* is the attempt to merge aspects of apparently dissimilar belief systems into a unified body of knowledge. Rather than choosing techniques from various theoretical approaches, as the technical eclectic might do, the integrationist attempts to blend the theories together.

One such attempt at integration is Prochaska and Norcross's (2007) transtheoretical model that focuses primarily on change. Their assertion is that the major psychotherapeutic approaches "differ on what to change but tend to agree on how to change" (p. 512). A well-known element of the transtheoretical perspective is the *stages-of-change model.* This model identified seven aspects of the change process and attempted to help counselors recognize where, in the process of change, their clients might be. These stages are: precontemplation, contemplation, preparation, action, maintenance, recycling, and termination.

People in *precontemplation* are unaware or underaware of needing help for their concerns. Others may see them as having a problem, but, if they are coerced into therapy, they will likely enter as involuntary. At this stage of change, clients are reluctant (some would say resistant) to engage in a working alliance with a counselor.

We should point out that Bertolino and O'Hanlon (2002) have abandoned the visitor, complainant, and customer nomenclature in favor of the stages-of-change terminology. They worried that these terms from the solution-focused literature came perilously close to the negative labeling of clients. Actually, we find that these colorful terms lend a vivid description to these dynamics of change, so we have decided to preserve them. However, please keep in mind that "visitor," "complainant," and "customer" describe the current relationships that clients have with their counselors rather than someone's personhood.

People in the *contemplation* stage know they could use some help but have not yet made a full commitment to seek it. At this point in the change process, they are considering possibilities and assessing options. The risk at this stage is that contemplators may ruminate and mull over prospects but remain stagnant and unchanging. They are like Scarlet O'Hara in the movie *Gone With the Wind*, who said repeatedly, "I'll think about that tomorrow." Clients at this stage have difficulty conceiving of a goal and are not even sure that changing would be worth the effort (Bertolino & O'Hanlon, 2002). With such ambivalent clients, one approach is to join with their hesitancy and recommend that they do not rush into any drastic transformation.

In the *preparation* stage, people have the intention of changing and may have already taken some steps in the direction of change. Perhaps they have tried to cut down on their angry outbursts or their volume of drinking. They are in the "starting gate," but are still hesitant, caught between that devil they know and the devil they don't.

The *action* stage is when you are most likely to be seeing some change in clients. They will appear ready to commit their time and energy to dealing with their issues. This is the stage at which much of their progress is noted, and they are aware that there may be times when they could backslide and that they need to put in place certain safeguards against this possibility. Their commitment to changing is evident. These people are customers.

As we have previously mentioned, change brings with it uncertainty. Old, more comfortable ways of "viewing" and "doing" will beckon to someone in the *maintenance* stage like Sirens attempting to wreck Odysseus's boat upon the rocks. In this stage, relapse prevention is needed. Good social and environmental support is helpful, and follow-up sessions with the counselor may be required.

As is well known, people trying to change a behavior often need several attempts at it. Especially in cases of trying to overcome habitual behaviors such as smoking or drinking, you can expect that clients may require a number of rehearsals before they overcome these concerns. In other words, they will be *recycling* back though the contemplation, preparation, action, and maintenance stages. About 15 percent of people in the process of recycling regress back to the precontemplation stage (Prochaska & DiClemente, 1984). It is important, during this *recycling*, for you and your client to maintain an expectation for change. According to Lambert (2004), expectation itself accounts for between 10 to 40 percent of success. It is also necessary that you normalize your client's recycling, since it is not an unusual part of the change process.

The *termination* stage occurs when clients have succeeded well enough with their goals that they are "good to go." But, of course, since nobody ever reaches a 10 on that scale of resolution, clients may return occasionally for booster sessions when life throws them a new curve. If you have been successful enough in your work with clients, they will have an effective tool kit from which to draw in the face of new challenges. Perhaps the word *termination* is a misnomer, since it implies an end to problems. Perhaps the best any of us can hope for is long-term maintenance.

Whether you conceive of your clients as visitors, complainants, and customers, or you instead see them as in a certain stage of change, you must accommodate your expectations and your interventions to better fit the level of your client's motivation. According to Bertolino and O'Hanlon (2002), understanding your client's stage of change is a better predictor of outcome "than variables such as age, socioeconomic status, problem severity and duration, goals, expectations, self-efficacy, and social supports" (p. 99).

Implications of These Ideas for the Counselor

The ideas regarding the brief attitudes have important implications for how to work with clients in the second session and beyond.

- Since you have demonstrated these attitudes in the first counseling session, keep the changes going.
- Continue to look for small exceptions in your client's report regarding the past week.
- Build on reports of success by gathering more details.
- Find out what the client considers to be "good enough" success. This information will give you a clue as to when to suggest termination.
- Understand your client's stage of change, and remember that even the most successful clients relapse.

TOOLS

What Next?

Your client returns for a subsequent session. You have used most of the influencing techniques that have been described thus far in this book. So, what do you do *now?* The answer is that you continue to do most of what you have already done with the client but with a slightly different emphasis.

You and your client have created a history together, and it is likely that your client now trusts you more than he or she did during the first visit. If this is the case, you will not have to reinvent the wheel; a relationship is already present, so it is not necessary to begin at the beginning. Another difference is that your client has already "learned the drill"; he or she has more accurate expectations about how the counseling session will go. Therefore, you can capitalize on what has already been done. Begin by asking presumptively, "What did you notice that got *better* since last time?" This question starts the session with the desired emphasis on the positive.

No matter what your client's motivation is for returning, you can assume that you now have some sort of leverage. The leverage may be that your client trusts you, believes that counseling will be helpful, or is simply submitting to the influence of a referring party. You should regard your client's presence as an opportunity to help him or her move closer to a goal. Furthermore, you probably left your client with a suggestion at the end of the last session. The client's response to this suggestion should give you some clues as to how to proceed. However, rather than asking at the beginning of this session whether the client did what you suggested, ask a question that is more oblique. For example, you might say, "Since our last meeting, what have you found yourself doing that is *different* than usual?"

Of course, at some point, you will want to know whether your suggestion was helpful to your client, but it is better to wait and let your client spontaneously mention it. If you do not hear from your client, you can wait until the end of the current session to decide whether to offer something else. You might say something like, "The last time we met, I offered you a suggestion at the end of our session. How *useful* was that for you?"

Another way to discuss the outcome of last session's suggestion is to introduce the subject through the scaling technique we described in Chapter 4. For example, you could ask, "On a scale of 1 to 10, with 1 being that my suggestion was a total flop and 10 being that it greatly improved your situation this week, what number would you give it?" As we discussed earlier, scaling can invite your client to focus on the process of progressing toward a goal. If the client responds with "3," you can then ask, "So, if something could have been *added* to my suggestion that would have made it a 4, what would it have been?" Answering this follow-up query, your client is tailoring the suggestion to best fit his or her needs, and is focusing on improvement, rather than the failure of the suggestion.

Our review of the recent literature suggests that task assignment does not occupy the same central role in brief counseling that it had initially. The emphasis has moved to supporting tasks that the client has designed. So far, you have likely offered indirect suggestions and metaphors in a somewhat indirect and gentle manner. However, some clients will want explicit suggestions in the form of homework. You have to determine your client's expectations, but sometimes you cannot do this accurately until you learn the results of the suggestion you made in the last session. "Textbook" clients do not exist, so you must custom design your interventions to fit each unique client.

How your clients respond to the first session will vary tremendously. Some will experience sudden and dramatic change, while others will proceed more slowly, and still others will show no movement. You must be careful to guard against displaying impatience with your client's progress. If your client reports change for the better, rejoice and attempt to consolidate the change. If your client returns to problem-saturated talk, then you must go back to acknowledging (the LUV Triangle), because this is your signal that the client is not sure you fully understand the painful intensity and gravity of the situation.

Consolidating Change

Very few clients will experience sudden breakthroughs that bring them to an epiphany. Most of the time, you must be satisfied with less dramatic, but steady, progress. Because improvement is often a "two steps forward and one step back" process, continue to encourage your client throughout counseling. Clients can become discouraged easily and tend to focus on the "one step back," taking it as a sign that change is impossible. But this backslide is simply an expected "recycling" as indicated in the stages of change model. Do your best to communicate that such a regression is simply part of the change process.

It is not unusual for a client to return for the second session saying, "I tried what you suggested, but it didn't work." If you gave the Formula First Session Task, the client may report not seeing anything that was happening that would be worth pursuing. If you offered a task, the client may report trying what you suggested with no results or not trying it at all. Looking disappointed at this point will only communicate your acceptance of the client's discouraging view. Instead, look for exceptions to the client's report; once again, deconstruct the story without disconfirming it. You might respond with one of the following examples:

"So things are pretty much the same. Well, what were you doing to keep things from getting even worse?"

"That sounds pretty tough. So, how did you manage to maintain your belief that things can be better?"

"Even with all that, you came back, so I take that to be a strong statement about your determination."

Obviously, if the client is unwilling to accept your assumption that he or she has continued to cope or is still hopeful, the conversation will be reverting to problem-saturated talk. In this case, you are nearly back to square one: Don't forget that you have developed a relationship, and you should repeat the first session's LUV Triangle work to set the stage for positive change.

It is vital that your client feel comfortable reporting failures as well as successes. Clients sometimes try to please their counselors by making only positive reports, but it would be counterproductive for you to evoke or reinforce only the stories of successes. There is a dynamic tension between your client's experience of your unconditional positive regard and your expectation that he or she will carry out a between-session task. In other words, how can you accept the client while pushing for the client to change? You must continue to walk that tightrope between communicating acceptance of the client's position while, at the same time, encouraging change. So long as the client believes that you are working for, rather than against, him or her, your client will continue to experience the therapeutic relationship as collaboration.

Notice Small Changes

As you listen to the details of your client's report, you will often find clues that a change, however slight, is taking place in his or her viewing, doing, or feeling. The Butterfly Effect has begun, even though neither you nor your client can know just what will emerge as a result. If you find that you are feeling annoyed that the client has not realized that a change has indeed happened, then you are running too far ahead. Insight on the client's part may not be necessary for the consolidation of change. You must be careful not to invalidate the client's story by arguing that a change has happened, even though he or she has not noticed.

In order to reassure the client that important changes are often small and imperceptible, you must believe it yourself. If it is crucial to you that the client achieve the kind of change that you think *should* be taking place, then you are likely to find yourself dissatisfied with the way things are going, and you will communicate your disappointment to the client on some level. It's a bit like the mother who reports that she finally got her adolescent son to take out the garbage, but she is still not happy because he won't smile when he does it. Your goal is not for your client to gain a life-changing insight or undergo a sudden metamorphosis. You seek only to perturb some small change in a representational system that has become discouraging for your client. You are trying to create a "safe emergency" to bring about an *emergence* of a new pattern of viewing or doing.

Many clients will report progress following the first session. This progress may be due to a variety of reasons. In fact, simply seeking help can sometimes restore a feeling of agency to a person. As we described in Chapter 2, merely experiencing an authentic and supportive relationship can also be a catalyst for change. Perhaps the progress is due to the relief of having shared a burden or secrets with another human being who has not met this confession with a negative judgment. Whatever the reason, if your client reports progress or success, respond to this report with the encouragement triad. Show your enthusiasm, imply agency on the part of the client, and ask for a complete picture of the events. You might say something like either of the responses below:

"Wow, that couldn't have been easy to do!"

"I'm not sure I would have thought to say that."

When the client returns and you ask, expectantly and presumptively, "What's *better* this week?" whatever the client reports will be grist for your mill. If the client says that things are better, you may find that the improvement had little or nothing to do with the suggestion you offered in the last session. The client has perhaps found a new path toward a resolution, drastically revised your suggestion, or developed a new perspective on the situation. In any case, you follow the client's positive report with that solid-gold question, "How did you get yourself to [do, see, believe] that?!"

If the client reports that things are the same or worse, then you should accept the responsibility for the suggestion that was not useful to the client. "Well, I guess that idea that I offered you was a real dud!" So long as you do not express disappointment with the client, or annoyance when you learn that the client did not really implement the suggestion, you avoid a relationship in which the client feels he or she has failed you. You should be guided by a principle first articulated by William Glasser (1965), in which he said that the client never fails—it is only the plan that fails.

Furthermore, the plan was not truly a failure in that you now know more about what *not* to do. Remember the cybernetic foundations of the work you are doing. A missile that is on target receives little or no feedback, but one that has strayed receives feedback that will correct its course. This is the reason that counselors who work briefly say, "There is no failure—there is only feedback." De Shazer (1982) offered a metaphor that you may find useful to keep in mind: Client feedback is like a red light on the dashboard of your car. It tells you what action needs to be taken in order to get everything running smoothly and optimally again.

LISTENING IN ON A SESSION

Review Bhavana's story in Chapter 2 and the continuation of her story at the beginning of this chapter. Here, the counselor is beginning the second session with Bhavana.

Counselor: (Smiles and speaks with energy)
"Bhavana, tell me what you've found yourself doing that's different since our first meeting."

Bhavana: (Exhales heavily as she shakes her head, arches her eyebrows, and shrugs her shoulders in exasperation)
"Well, everything in my life is still kind of a mess."

Counselor: "So it sounds like there are still some things you want to work on. I'm glad to see that you've decided to come back. With all those things continuing to be in kind of a mess, how were you able to make it through in spite of that?"

Bhavana: "I don't know, I guess it helped that I didn't get into as much trouble this week." (She quickly adds) "Probably because I was out sick one day."

Counselor: "Oh, I'm sorry to hear that you were sick. It looks like you've recovered well from whatever you had. And somehow to me you seem a little different this week—maybe more relaxed—I'm not sure. What do you think?"

Bhavana: (Looks thoughtful and a little more interested)
"Hmm, I don't know, I don't feel much different. At least, I don't think that anybody else has told me that."

Counselor: "If you looked in that mirror over there, I wonder if you would be able to see something that's different about you this week."

Bhavana: (Looks in the mirror, and fusses with her hair and collar)
"Oh god, I look awful, look at that zit."
(She turns quickly away and giggles.)
"I don't think *that* was there last week."

Counselor: (Smiles slightly after a brief pause)
"I guess that's a nice way of telling me that my suggestion wasn't very helpful. Darn, I guess I messed that one up. What could we change about the suggestion that might make it work better?"

Bhavana: "Oh, I don't think it was your fault exactly. It's just that I have so much to do that I didn't have time to think of whether things were good or bad or whatever. I don't know, maybe I chilled out a little more since last time and maybe things don't seem like the end of the world anymore."

Counselor: (Leaning forward slightly more and speaking slowly)
"So the keeping track wasn't important, but you got yourself to chill out when things started getting tough. I wish I would have thought of that—it sounds like a good strategy. I'd really be interested in hearing what you said to yourself when you decided not to let things bother you so much."

REFLECTING QUESTIONS

1. If you were the counselor, how would you respond to Bhavana?
2. What does Bhavana want from you?
3. How is she portraying herself in the session?

When Should You Stop?

Since the research shows that the modal number of sessions for any type of therapy is *one,* there simply may not be a "next time." Obviously, if you are doing crisis work, or if you are a school counselor who may see hundreds of students in an academic year, the probability that you will have only one session with a client is quite high. Whatever the setting in which you see clients, you should always treat each session as though it is your last.

Even if you do see your clients for multiple sessions, your most significant impact will likely take place in the first few meetings. Koss, Kutcher, & Strupp (1986) conducted research that suggested that the maximum benefit in counseling sessions takes place within the first six to eight meetings. The most important criterion that would indicate when it is time to stop is that the client has made sufficient progress to carry on without meeting on a regular basis. If you are uncertain as to whether the client has arrived at this level of resolution, use the scaling technique to gauge progress. You can invite your client to reflect on improvement since the first session by saying, "When we first met, you said that your problem was at a 3. Where would you say you are now, and what number will we have to get to, that will let you know you can carry on without counseling?"

Another approach is to focus on the present by asking, "On a scale of 1 to 10, with 10 being that you are absolutely confident that you can keep these changes going yourself, and 1 being that you are not at all confident, where are you right now?" You can then follow up on your client's answer by asking, "Where will you have to be for your work here in counseling to be a success?"

If your client is reporting being close to the desired level of progress or change, then you might ask, "How many more times do you think we will have to meet in order for you to get to that number?" By responding to this question, your client is predicting success by a certain point in time. This prediction can then become a self-fulfilling prophecy.

Termination and Flight into Health

In the conventional view of treatment, termination comes only after the doctor has cured the patient, at which point the patient is dismissed. Budman (1990) suggested that Sigmund Freud, who saw the therapist as the surgeon who excised malignant issues from the patient's consciousness, promulgated this model of terminating psychotherapy. If the issues have been removed, the patient is cured. Then, if the patient ever has to seek help after termination, this would indicate that the therapy had been a failure, the patient had a new illness, or the individual had previously experienced a deceptive flight into health, causing a premature termination of the therapy in the first place.

A flight into health is a rather sudden—but false—experience of improvement. The conventional wisdom suggests that when such a flight into health occurs, the counselor should persuade the client that the time is not yet right to end the therapy. In fact, some therapists would use the tactic of predicting doom for these clients, leaving the impression that there was a ticking bomb in their psyche that would eventually bring them back to therapy. Conversely, counselors who do brief work expect to terminate with clients as soon as possible. When they suspect that their clients are experiencing a flight into health, they suggest that the treatment of choice is to "keep 'em flying" (Weiner-Davis, 1993).

In mental health settings, 70 percent of all clients come for six or fewer sessions (Taube, Goldman, Burns, & Kessler, 1988). And as we stated previously, the most common number of sessions for all types of counseling is one. Budman (1990) suggested that the conventional notion of termination—taking place only after a cure has been achieved—just does not fit the facts of the situation. In several follow-up studies he reviewed, nearly 60 percent of terminated clients later returned for additional counseling, even though they often felt the original sessions had been successful. Therefore, if clients return to you for counseling, they are doing so not because you failed to "cure" them. Instead, they are now wishing to reconnect with you to address additional concerns that they have encountered.

Termination, then, is simply the occasion when you and your client will no longer have regular appointments. It is the session in which you attempt to "take inventory" and consolidate the work that you have done together so that the client can carry on without counseling. Your job as a counselor is to, as quickly as possible, work yourself out of a job.

Dealing with Client Misgivings

You can end your counseling relationship in a way that ensures the changes your client has made will continue. Of course, termination of counseling should be a cause for celebration. After all, your client has successfully achieved the goals for counseling. However, when the two of you have had several sessions together, your relationship has likely deepened to the point that termination will present some possible relationship problems. For example, when your clients have felt that you have helped them, then they may wonder if they can go it alone. In addition, your clients could have feelings of abandonment—of being set adrift in a sea of trouble.

Endings often can be ambiguous (Teyber, 2006), so you should anticipate and clarify this ambiguity. You have communicated empathy and care for your client, and you must remember that these are scarce commodities in the world "out there." Your client may be reluctant to give up an intimate relationship in which he or she feels unconditionally accepted. Finally, the client will often feel unfinished. He or she may believe that all concerns must have been addressed and resolved before stopping counseling.

The best way to know when to terminate counseling is to regularly communicate, right from the start, the expectation that your work together will end when your client achieves the counseling goals. For example, early on you can ask, "How much of this situation that is so troubling to you would have to clear up to let us know that it is time to stop our work together?" Since no life concerns are ever fully resolved, you are consistently suggesting, from the time your client sets the counseling goals and during times when you review your progress together, that termination will be taking place once the client feels confident to continue addressing these concerns on his or her own.

Sometimes clients will have anxious feelings about stopping their counseling, and they may even feel angry or disappointed when talk of termination becomes the focus. They may, however, keep silent because of their fear that they are not being a "good client" and that you might be disappointed in them for having misgivings. They may believe you think they are stronger than they actually are. Remember that whenever the client experiences feelings of anguish, you must acknowledge them. You might open the subject by saying, "When people have accomplished the goals that they have set for themselves and it is time to stop counseling, even though they feel confident and able to carry on, they might also, at the same time, have some negative feelings about stopping. I wonder if there is any of that going on with you." With such a statement, you can validate these concerns and invite your client to bring them "to the table." Of course, the length of time you and your client have been working together will determine the strength of some of these negative feelings. One of the benefits of working briefly with people is that deep feelings of transference and dependency typically do not develop as much, so the stress of termination is eased for the client.

If your original goal setting with the client included the explicit presence of something that was doable in a brief amount of time, then it should be clear to both parties when that goal has been approximated. You will have also communicated to the client early on that, on a scale of 1 to 10, nobody ever reaches a 10.

Keeping Changes Going

Michele Weiner-Davis (1993) suggested that when positive changes have taken place in people's lives, they are reluctant to "look a gift horse in the mouth." People worry that analyzing success might cause it to vanish. Somehow, you must help your clients overcome this reluctance to talk about these positive changes in analytic detail. You want your clients to tell you how the changes have affected other areas of their lives. How have these changes affected the way the client feels about himself or herself? What would a significant other person say are the changes he or she would want to see continue? What else is needed to keep these changes going? What challenges are still present that may threaten these changes, and what plans does the client have for dealing with these challenges?

You can help your clients to understand that change happens in small steps, and that occasional backsliding is not failure. Clients should not expect too much too soon. Clients must also understand that change must be evaluated in "good enough" terms, rather than expecting that "perfect 10."

Sometimes people do not trust their own successes. Despite tentative hopefulness, they may still secretly suspect that everything will eventually collapse and that they will be thrown back into the same situation that brought them to counseling in the first place. You can inoculate clients against such obsessive thoughts by suggesting these misgivings represent sound reasoning on their part (Weiner-Davis, 1993). Predicting a relapse is occasionally a good way to normalize events that might otherwise signal catastrophe to your client. All our lives involve some good and bad periods, happy and tragic occasions, and any significant progress we make usually includes some setbacks. You may want to follow Weiner-Davis's suggestion of inviting your clients to wonder how long these changes must last for them to say to themselves, "'Something different is going on here. This isn't just another false start. It looks like things are really beginning to change'" (p. 215).

You can also help your clients to avoid taking this change for granted. The reason that change is taking place is because your clients are responding differently to their situations and have new ways of doing and viewing. In order to keep the changes going, your clients must continue to practice these new ways of acting and to maintain the new perspective they have gained.

You will want to watch for notions that might undermine the work that your client has done. If misgivings come up in the conversation, you can deal with them directly. In addition, you could say, "Well, you scale your confidence level that these changes will continue to happen at an 8. I assume that means you still have a few worries. Let's talk about these so we can plan how to handle them if they come up." The trick, of course, is to help clients deal with misgivings at a time when they are also feeling confident enough to continue on their own. You do not want to "throw cold water on their hopefulness." We trust that you are enough of an artist in your counseling work to be able to gently deal with client worries without dashing client hopes.

You may also wish to offer your clients an appointment in 6 months or some other reasonable period of time for a "check-up." This will communicate to them that you are available for support and they will not have to continue these changes "cold turkey." The notion of a "check-up" or "booster session" is usually seen by clients as an opportunity to report further success and to make minor course adjustments. This plan also keeps some leverage on clients—meaning that if they plan to see you in 6 months, they will likely feel the desire to report success and, as a result, actually be successful.

Making Saying Good-bye Work

Based on the goal that you and your client established early on or renegotiated as you went along, the criteria for knowing when you have done enough should be reasonably clear. When you and the client agree that you are nearing termination, it is time to plan to make saying good-bye work.

Some of your clients will experience termination as a loss (Epston & White, 1995). When clients leave therapy, they lose the hand holding of the therapeutic relationship and must then face the world alone. The most productive scenario at termination would be for clients to feel more confident and fully aware of their abilities. You need to do everything you can to promote the notion that termination is an anticipated rite of passage.

Certain therapeutic rituals at termination can help secure the gains your client has made in counseling (Epston & White, 1995). For example, you can conclude counseling relationships by inviting your clients to attend a special meeting so that what they have learned from the counseling can be documented. Clients will have learned more about themselves, others, and relationships and will have developed new strategies for achieving their goals. However, they may have not been fully aware of just how far they have traveled in their short time with you, and they will need to be reminded. In this special meeting, the centerpiece for interviewing clients regarding their successes is the question of presumptive agency: that is, you continue to ask the "How did you get yourself to do that?" question.

You should never address successful events as though they might have happened by accident, were due to the behaviors of someone else, or were caused by some fortuitous alignment of the planets. The purpose of this termination interview is to make clear your client's successful steps toward resolution, call attention to the resources your client possesses, and give your client a third-person view of progress by asking how he or she would advise others. This process confirms that your client has made valuable discoveries that could be shared with other people.

Epston and White have made major contributions to our understanding of the use of termination ritual in counseling. The careful selection of the words and phrases that they use with clients points out how important it is to choose language for its impact. You must strategically design your interventions, right up to the final session, in order to maximize the lasting efficacy of your work. When clients terminate their collaboration with you, you wish for them to carry with them the seeds of future work that they can perform on their own. Making a good good-bye can have great therapeutic value beyond your time with the client.

Get It in Writing

It was Bertha Pappenheim, Freud's "Anna O," who coined the phrase "the talking cure" (Schultz & Schultz, 2000). Now, more than 100 years later, we counselors are still talking to our clients and asking them to talk to us. But, instead of listening for the hidden symbolic meaning in their verbal utterances, as traditional Freudians did, we take their talk at face value and try to understand the stories of their lives.

Clients tell stories, and you enter into these stories. For clients, just being able to tell their stories to someone who is truly an interested listener is a rare and wonderful event. How often do people get this opportunity? But even beyond this oral communication, there is something that may be even more powerful: the written word. The idea that written language may be more influential than spoken language might, at first blush, seem strange to counselors. But consider this: Once a verbal utterance is aired, it vanishes. Our tradition of writing makes words official only when they are down in black and white. In a literate culture, verbal contracts have a much shakier credibility in a court of law than ones that have been written, witnessed, and signed by all parties.

What can be read and reread obviously lasts longer than what can be heard. Written documents have the capability of enduring. Even in a technological age, when sound recordings are possible as a way to archive information, it is the visual event that makes the more lasting impression. White and Epston (1990) suggested that this is because of our "ocularcentrism." People who exhibit a vast amount of knowledge are often called "insightful," "perceptive," and "farsighted," while those who lack this quality are considered to be "blind" or "shortsighted." As a counselor in our ocularcentrist culture, you should consider "getting it in writing," as well as in talking. For example, you might consider developing a written contract with clients regarding the nature of your work together. Especially with young clients, there appears to be enchantment involved in this ritual.

Presenting an award for an accomplishment is a long-standing tradition (White & Epston, 1990). Perhaps you are displaying on your wall some certificate, diploma, or other written proclamation of your own accomplishments. Moreover, school counselors know that they increase the impact of awards by arranging to have a person who is known only by reputation to present them. The principal of the school, dean of the college, and president of the company are all people whose names are known, but students or employees do not regularly consort with them. These people, and those who hold similar positions, constitute what White and Epston called the "exotic audience."

The counselor, too, is an exotic audience for the client. So long as counselors remain somewhat mysterious, there is a desire on the client's part to know what is in the counselor's mind and a desire for the counselor to approve of him or her. It is one thing to receive such approbation in the session but quite another thing to achieve the same validation in a written message. A letter, whether it is sent by the postal service or email, can be a powerful tool you can use to support your client's useful discoveries, positive decisions, and successful changes.

Of course, people enjoy receiving correspondence—both old-fashioned and electronic versions. "You've got mail!" is the favorite greeting our computer can offer us. Words in the written form, even if on the computer screen, offer us a tangible record of someone's thoughts, observations, and reflections. Clients can return to electronic or hard-copy letters whenever necessary. As Friedman (1997) pointed out, "Letter writing makes concrete the ideas discussed with clients, further amplifies and highlights exceptions, and opens the door to action possibilities" (pp. 86–87).

A study conducted by Nyland and Thomas (1994) indicated that the impact of a letter written to a client was equivalent to more than three face-to-face sessions. Some of the participants in the study claimed that one letter was worth 10 sessions, and 50 of those surveyed responded that the letter alone was responsible for their major gains in therapy. Similarly, David Epston (in White, 1995) claimed that one letter was equal to 4.5 sessions of therapy. Especially now that email has resurrected written correspondence as a popular form of communication, writing to your clients is a counseling strategy that should be part of your therapeutic tool kit.

We have found that clients who receive letters from their counselors tend to hang on to them and re-read them on numerous occasions. One caveat, however, is that, once something is in writing, it may not be as confidential as the conversation that has taken place in the safety of the counseling room. Before you send your client a follow-up letter or email, you should find out how secure their "snail mail" or electronic mail is.

You might say, "I would like to send you a note containing my thoughts about our work together. How can I do this to ensure that you are the only person who can read it?" The conspiratorial nature of this question reinforces the fact that you take the client's confidentiality seriously. Of course, if the possibility exists that someone other than the client might read your message, then, if the client is willing, you could ask him or her to come by the office on a certain date and pick it up.

USING THIS TOOL

Gather a small group of your colleagues to participate in this activity. Each of you anonymously composes a note to every other member of the group. Start your note with "The thing I like best about you is . . ." and complete the phrase. Then tell about a particular time when this person showed this trait. Exchange the notes with one another. Each person then reads his or her notes aloud and then shares reactions.

A Protocol for a Follow-Up Letter

In the protocol below, we offer suggestions for what you can include in a letter to your client after a productive relationship. You will want to modify your letter according to the needs of your client. Take the following only as an example:

1. *Thank* the client for coming, and indicate your pleasure in working together.
2. Restate your pledge of *confidentiality* to the client.
3. Reacknowledge your client's *main concerns,* and suggest how the client is coping in spite of these challenges.
4. *Externalize* the problem as an outside force that is attempting to influence or trick your client, and point out *exceptions*—times when the client refused to be influenced.
5. *Compliment* your client on the strengths, resources, and insights that you noticed. As much as possible, use your client's own descriptions and metaphors.
6. Offer a *bridge.* Restate a goal that your client stated in the session and begin your suggestion with something like, "and since what you wanted to work on . . ." or "because what you were hoping for . . ."
7. Before making a suggestion, determine whether your client–counselor relationship could be characterized as *visiting, complaining, engaging,* or *involuntary.*
8. Based on the above estimate, *offer* something you think might encourage the client to think about the concern in a different way. Be careful about suggesting behavioral change.
9. Suggest that you know the client is working hard toward improvement and that he or she has been able to, in spite of occasional setbacks, continue to get better. Offer *encouragement,* not praise.
10. *Close* your message in a friendly, collaborative manner, rather than sounding like a distant expert.

FOLLOW-UP OF THE SESSION: A LETTER TO BHAVANA

Review Bhavana's story at the beginning of Chapter 2 and the excerpt from her counseling session earlier in this chapter. Here is the counselor's follow-up letter to Bhavana:

Dear Bhavana,

I first want to thank you for your willingness to come in, work intensely, and make the most of our two sessions together. Many students don't take the risks that you did, so I was both surprised and glad to see you being so open and honest. I really enjoyed working with you in such productive meetings.

Before I offer you some of my thoughts and impressions, let me just remind you once again that everything that you have shared with me is confidential. The only exceptions are if you give me your permission to share information with somebody else or if you are an imminent danger to yourself or to others. You have my personal guarantee that I will carefully protect your confidentiality.

When you first came to my office, you were feeling really angry and upset—at your boyfriend, your classmates, and even yourself. With all the misunderstandings and frustrations that you had been through, you were feeling pretty discouraged. So one important counseling goal for you was figuring out how you could feel like a winner in your life.

I remember how intensely you were feeling these concerns and how you wanted to be sure that your words captured the strength of these feelings. In fact, one thing you said really stuck with me. You said that you felt like you were in really deep water and couldn't even see the shore.

I'm just wondering about the "Undertow," that force that's been trying to sneak up on you and pull you out into deep water again. It's not satisfied until it pulls your spirits down, too. In spite of the Undertow's efforts, you've been able to keep your head above water and swim back to shore. My guess is that your sense of humor, honesty about yourself, enthusiasm for life, and passion for words have given you the power to swim against that force.

Since your dream is to feel like a winner, I was wondering if you didn't already have most of the pieces of this puzzle—taking good care of yourself, seeking relationships where you feel valued and respected, and staying more relaxed under pressure. As you find out how these pieces fit together in your new life, I wonder what new joys you'll find.

Thanks again, Bhavana, for getting our work together off to such a fine start. I'm looking forward to hearing how you continue this positive momentum!
Sincerely,
Fiona McCoy, Licensed School Counselor

SUMMARY

When you do brief therapy, you cannot merely apply a set of techniques; you also take on an attitude about the nature of reality, people's resilience, inevitability of change, and importance of every therapy session. In this chapter, you examined how change is a process that you can encourage and consolidate. You also explored the important dynamics that termination can arouse and how you can use this event as an opportunity for reflecting on lessons your clients have learned and resources they have discovered. Finally, you learned how to write a follow-up letter that your clients will find meaningful, powerful and helpful as they continue to face life's challenges.

SEGUE TO CHAPTER 13

Think of a time that you were required to meet with someone against your will. Perhaps the meeting was a requirement that you considered to be unreasonable, was a punishment for something you had done, or was seen by others to be "for your own good." What were some of your feelings as you began that meeting? How were you behaving?

Resource

The Institute for the Study of Therapeutic Change
PO Box 578264
Chicago, IL 60657-8264
773-404-5130
www.talkingcure.com

Scott Miller and Barry Duncan are the codirectors of this institute. The topic boxes on this website include such intriguing titles as "What works in therapy?" "What can you do to increase your effectiveness?" and "What's the latest baloney?"

CHAPTER 13

Humanistic Counseling and Working With Involuntary Clients

And the end of all our exploring
Will be to arrive where we started
And to know the place for the first time
T. S. Elliot

CHAPTER GOALS

The goals of this chapter are to help you to understand these ideas and to use these tools:

- Brief and humanistic perspectives have fundamental parallels, share many basic assumptions, and can be integrated in your interventions.
- People's worlds are both socially constructed and individually constructed.
- Brief counseling can have "depth" results that reach all the way into the self of the client.
- Ways of dealing effectively with involuntary clients and their referring third parties.

STORY

ACT I

He sat in the counselor's office slumped in a chair with his arms and legs crossed and a look of studied indifference on his face. The assistant principal had escorted him, holding his arm tightly, and had shoved him through the open door. Exclaiming in a loud voice that betrayed intense frustration, the assistant principal had said, "Here's Zeshaun. You'd better convince him to clean up his act, or he's outta here for good!"

The counselor had seen Zeshaun many times before because of his antics in class, his acts of minor vandalism, and his generally surly attitude that his teachers found intolerable. This time, however, it seemed that Zeshaun had added the "straw that broke the camel's back." He would need to show some dramatic change in behavior, or he would be expelled from school.

The counselor believed that Zeshaun was basically good at heart but had developed a rebellious style as a self-protective façade. "Well," said the counselor, "It looks like we need to work together to find a way out of this scrape. Want to tell me about it?"

"I don't give a damn!" said Zeshaun, trying to look nonchalant and attempting to hide the fact that his eyes were moist. "They can all take a flying leap as far as I'm concerned!"

REFLECTING QUESTIONS

1. How would you be feeling if you were the counselor in this situation?
2. What strengths can you imagine finding behind Zeshaun's facade?
3. How would you attempt to convince both Zeshaun and the assistant principal to give it another try?

OVERVIEW

In this chapter, we discuss the similarities between humanistic and brief approaches to counseling. We wish Carl Rogers and Steve de Shazer had been collaborators, because, while Rogers wrote about the importance of the relationship and de Shazer suggested the techniques for working briefly, their fundamental ideas can be integrated into a resolution-focused approach to counseling. Rather than being a superficial method, brief counseling can reach clients at a deep level and alter more than people's behaviors and thoughts.

In the Tools section, we discuss in greater detail the challenges presented by the hesitant involuntary client and offer hints on helping this person become fully engaged in the counseling process, along with suggestions for dealing with the referring third party.

IDEAS

Returning Home

We had decided to write this book because we were attracted not only to some of the techniques of brief therapists but also to their positive regard for human potential and their optimistic outlook on change. We saw in these approaches an unspoken humanism that appealed to us.

Although some have criticized brief therapies as "selling out" to the managed care establishment, which has demanded short-term work with clients, Wong (2006) pointed out a happy paradox in the relationship between insurance companies and the providers of mental health services. The demand for brief therapy has forced us to focus more on positive human character strengths and to search for a more refined understanding of what works with clients. "Arguably, the culture of managed care practices and the character strengths perspective converge on the notion that humans have the resources to change quickly for the better" (p. 135).

Nearly half a century ago, Abraham Maslow (1968) wrote of the human need to self-actualize. Beginning his professional life as a behaviorist, he later became discouraged by the mechanistic attitudes of psychology, and so he launched into a search for what allows people to become "fully functioning" (Rowan, 2001). From this beginning came the "third force" in psychotherapy, personified by Carl Rogers. Rogers believed in the innate desire of humans to grow, even flourish, if they were given the opportunity to achieve their unique potential. "Because of the faith in human nature expressed in Rogers's theory, it is considered a humanistic approach to counseling" (Welfel & Patterson, 2005, p. 209).

The third force offered an outlook on human nature that stood as distinct from the dark view of the selfish, grasping "bad animal" nature of people promulgated by Freud, and the simple "rat-o-fication" of humans promoted by the animal experiments of the behaviorists. Rowan (2001) declared that most therapies, other than the humanistic ones, aim primarily at adjustment to the environment and relief of symptoms. Such approaches are "simply enabling the person to go on functioning at the old level, in the old way . . . the goal of such therapy is to avoid change rather than to embrace it" (p. 29).

Some psychologists believe that the humanistic movement was merely a passing fad that peaked during the 1960s. Looking back on the influence of humanism in psychology, one observer pronounced it an unsuccessful movement. He opined, "Humanistic psychology was a great experiment, but it is basically a failed experiment in that there is no humanistic school of thought in psychology" (Cunningham, 1985, p. 18). Carl Rogers himself (in Schultz & Schultz, 2000) was quoted as saying, "Humanistic psychology has not had a significant impact on mainstream psychology. We are perceived as having relatively little importance" (p. 466). Schultz and Schultz, in their history of psychology text, displayed a timeline showing the existence of humanistic psychology as beginning at the end of World War II and ending sometime in the 1980s.

However, this disappearance seems to have been a situation similar to that of Mark Twain, who, on reading of his own demise in the newspaper, suggested that rumors of his death had been greatly exaggerated (Presbury, McKee, & Echterling, 2007). A funny thing happened on the way to postmodernism. People began to resurrect some of the notions of the humanistic movement, and in psychotherapy the ideas of Carl Rogers began to be seen as a fresh approach to working with clients.

Wickman (2000), after analyzing the 1965 "Gloria" film (Rogers, 1965) in which Rogers demonstrated his "Client-Centered" approach, determined that Rogers was really a postmodern "constructivist." Lynch (1997) viewed Rogers as a postmodern narrative therapist. According to Becvar and Becvar (2003), most so-called postmodern approaches to therapy have been shaped by the Rogerian attitude. For the postmodernist, "the goal is to deconstruct 'facts' by delineating the assumptions, values, and ideologies on which they are founded" (p. 93). But in order to get permission from the client to attempt such a deconstruction, the counselor must first establish a caring relationship. The therapist can then promote new schemas that enable clients to make the changes they desire.

We think of this approach in terms of Wittgenstein's metaphor of "showing the fly the way out of the fly bottle," which we discussed in Chapter 1. The client (in this case, the metaphoric fly) is responsible for the work of self-liberation from this entrapment, but is assisted in this effort by the interventions and perturbations of the counselor. Hoffman (1985), a postmodern family therapist, predicted that the relationship between counselor and client in the future will be remarkably similar to that proposed by Rogers: a collaborative relationship, rather than a hierarchical structure. Such a relationship will set the context for change, while not prescribing or specifying the change. It will be a "non-pejorative, non-judgmental view" (p. 395). We believe that Hoffman's future is now.

It is not unusual for someone to attend a workshop or conference where people are speaking with great enthusiasm about a new idea or technique that has been developed in their field, only to realize that the content is right out of a Carl Rogers book. Often, without credit to Rogers, the "new" approach will have been given a new name and proudly declared a new discovery—much like Columbus "discovering" America in spite of the fact that people were already living there when he arrived (Presbury, McKee, & Echterling, 2007). "Rogerian values and methods have become part of the therapeutic mainstream and assimilated into cognitive, self-psychology, feminist, experiential, and constructivist therapies" (Prochaska & Norcross, 2003, p. 167). Moursund and Kenny (2002) stated that the ideas of Rogers are ubiquitous. "Some of what must be present in all types of therapy goes back to Carl Rogers's work" (p. 13).

We were originally trained in the Rogerian approach to counseling, and have remained closet humanists through the long "relationship drought" in counseling. Our own journey, like that of the psychotherapeutic establishment in general, has now led us home, back to the place where we started. As T. S. Elliot suggested (earlier), we know that place again, but as if for the first time.

Social Construction and "Strength-Centered Therapy"

Just as we were about to finish up the revision of this book, we came across an article describing a therapeutic model that parallels our own in many ways. It is known as "strength-centered therapy" (Wong, 2006). This model is a synthesis of positive psychology (Seligman & Csikszentmihalyi, 2000; Synder & Lopez, 2002) together with therapeutic ideas from social constructionism (Burr, 2003; Gergen, 1999). The emphasis of this approach is the enhancement of the client's character strengths and virtues, such as courage, humility, and integrity. Character strengths are like traits because they consistently inhere within an individual's style. If clients do not currently possess them, they typically long to develop these strengths. Furthermore, most desired traits are achievable through determination and effort (Peterson & Seligman, 2004; Worthington & Berry, 2005). Wong (2006) listed 24 "universal" character strengths that included integrity, kindness, courage, humility, hope, and love. Looking at this list, we were reminded of Maslow's (1968) similar list of traits possessed by self-actualized people. Most people will admit to being deficient in some of these character traits along with the desire to possess more of them. What character trait do you aspire to strengthen?

Social constructionism emphasizes that cultural forces and institutionalized practices shape the meanings we attribute to our experiences. As we previously discussed in Chapter 6, according to social constructionism, what we desire in life and how we esteem ourselves depends on the environment in which we were raised. One important aspect of this belief that fits well with our own way of working with clients is the notion that language does not merely describe our thoughts and feelings but shapes them. For this reason, we help clients to begin talking about successes and exceptions to their concerns.

There is a certain irony involved in merging personal character strengths with social constructionism. Character is something intrinsic to an individual and is displayed in behavior. Wong's (2006) assertion is that character traits are the result of personal dedication to self-improvement. On the other hand, the social constructionist model asserts that our environment has made us who we are as people. The former seems to be an "inside-out" matter of free will, while the latter would be an "outside-in" type of determinism.

However, if you accept that all our personal meanings are dialectical, rather than dichotomous, then both forces can be considered to be true. Much of who we are, what we think about the world, and how we believe social interaction should take place, has been "poured over us" by our culture like sticky syrup on pancakes. Nevertheless, within the forces of culture, we also construct a world that is uniquely our own and can be modified by putting our minds to the task. Like so many apparent dichotomies, such as nature versus nurture, good versus evil, and so on, if we approach the issue of social constructionism versus individual constructivism with a dialectical spirit, we see that both sides of the argument can easily coexist. As Carl Jung put it, the opposite of truth is also true.

Wong's (2006) strength-centered therapy shares with our approach to brief counseling several fundamental assumptions. First, it is best to focus as much as possible on "harnessing clients' positive resources and not merely alleviating pathology" (p. 137). Second, we elicit character strengths from within our clients, rather than teaching or imposing them on our clients. Third, we participate with clients in the co-construction of new meanings together. Fourth, while remaining sensitive to the fact that meanings vary among cultures, we pay close attention to the ways in which our clients may have introjected negative and self-defeating meanings. Finally, because we can never be the experts on the subjective experiences of our clients, we offer all comments and suggestions tentatively, withdrawing them when our clients do not seem to agree. In addition to the assumptions and interventions mentioned above, Wong suggests the use of empathic listening, scaling techniques, reframing and relabeling, and the management of emotional arousal.

We have inserted this sketch of strength-centered therapy to serve as another example of how various theoretical approaches to counseling, along with their philosophical assumptions, are beginning to integrate into transtheoretical models (Prochaska & Norcross, 2007) and how the approach of working briefly is becoming the norm rather than the exception.

How Deep Does Brief Counseling Go?

Those who do "depth" therapy often criticize the brief approach as being a superficial, Band-Aid method. While brief work focuses on "problems," they say, it remains a "cosmetic" intervention that never really reaches the self of the client. These critics react negatively to the narrative notion that people's lives are stories. They argue that to view the client's lived story as a poetic metaphor that can be deconstructed dehumanizes the client's experience. "Poems don't feel pain, people do" (Prochaska & Norcross, 2007, p. 468). Detractors view the narrative form of brief work as dismissive of the client's real angst and the vulnerability of the human condition (Shaddock, 2000). What is lacking, they claim, is recognition of the inter-subjectivity between counselor and client. Thus, the opponents of the brief approach would have the client say to the counselor, "If you don't have a way of knowing who I am as a real person, then I don't want to know who you are as a pscyhotherapist" (Prochaska & Norcross, 2007, p. 468).

As brief counselors, we are certainly interested in behavior change and the alteration of how people see their situations, that is, changing their "doing and viewing." But we also strive for a modification of a client's self-experience. We hope to change the client's subjective experience of self and the world at a deep level. While we do not directly probe negative self-concepts or ask for detailed accounts of the client's existential terrors, still we believe that our way of working has an indirect "trickle-down" effect that positively influences the client's sense of self and enhances being-in-the-world.

Dan Zahavi (2005) pointed out that, if you were to go to a movie, as you sit there watching, not only are you intentionally directed at the movie, you are additionally aware that you are the one who is watching. "In short, there is an object of experience (the movie), there is an experience (the watching), and there is a subject of experience, myself" (p. 99). When clients come for counseling, they usually tell us a story about the objects of their experience as if these situations and people were in a movie, but they are also protagonists in the plot. In Zahavi's example of movie watching, of the three levels—the movie, the watcher, and the innermost experiencer (the self)—only the first two levels would be obvious to a third-person observer. We agree with the critics mentioned above that it is the innermost level, *the personal experience of the self,* that is often overlooked by many theories of counseling and psychotherapy that have adopted the objective third-person perspective. A "problem-solving" approach to counseling, for example, will attempt to alter the plot of the story by changing the behaviors of the protagonist in response to the storied situations without attempting to fully understand the subjective experience of the protagonist. Such an approach comes from watching the client's movie, not the watcher.

To illustrate this point further, again suppose that you are watching a movie. Someone who might be sitting beside you in the movie theater would have roughly the same experience of the movie. This person beside you would also have an experience of being a person who is watching the movie. However, this person would not have your subjective experience—you are being uniquely affected by the watching. At this innermost level, the movie will likely be quite a different experience for you than for the person sitting beside you. You may have found the movie to be profoundly touching, while the other person may see it as "sappy." You may have been intrigued by the character development, while the other may have found the plot to be boring. In this case, the same event, and a similar experience of viewing the event, brings about a markedly different self-experience.

Of course, the easy explanation is that there are simply "different strokes for different folks." We all know that. But a careful analysis of these three levels of experience suggests that there is no way anyone can objectively know whether the movie was good or bad, life changing, or a waste of time. No degree of consensus by moviegoers or critical interpretation by experts can change the individual's self-experience. We simply cannot be talked out of our innermost meanings.

As counselors, we are like "the other" who sits in the theater next to the innermost self of the person we are trying to help. If we proceed according to our own experience and subsequent interpretation of the "movie," we will overlook the fact that it is the client's inner experience of the event that is crucial, not what we have made of it. Forgetting this, we may come to believe that our experience is the same as the client's experience and be tempted to offer suggestions as to what we would do in the "same" situation.

Getting to the Self

As we have mentioned several times, beginning counselors who believe they have the answers to client problems often ask, "Why can't you just tell 'em?" Our reply is that "telling 'em" rarely works because it is an "outside-in" intervention. It may not reach all the way to the self of the client. Beyond that, when clients offer the narrative of their life, remember that they are the only ones who have truly "seen the movie." We counselors cannot assume we accurately know anything about the characters or the plot. We need the client to tell us what the movie is "really" about in their narrative presentation. When we elicit, rather than instruct, our clients, we are reaching for the self at a deep level. Still, the events we imagine and take from the story being told are never the exact inner experience of the client. We simply do the best we can to empathically understand.

A self is not a static thing. It is an ongoing process, constantly changing and becoming (Zahavi, 2005). A self-concept, on the other hand, can become a fixed or foreclosed idea regarding the self. Often, clients come to us with negative and out-of-date concepts or constructions of who they are. For example, if they are self-deprecating, clients may characterize themselves as "a loser," "a failure," "a slacker," and so on. But the good news is, as Zahavi (2005) put it, "As long as life goes on, there is no final self-understanding" (pp. 104–105).

A self-concept is a construction, while *self* is a process. As Sherry (2007) put it, "Life isn't about finding yourself. Life is about *creating* yourself" (p. 240, emphasis in original). We can deconstruct negative self-concepts by asking about the self-in-process. We might ask what the client is doing that is "slacker" behavior or what events have led the client to the conclusion that he or she is a "loser" or a "failure." Ivey and Ivey (2007) stressed the importance of maintaining a discourse of "concreteness" in our work with clients. "It is important to seek specifics rather than vague generalities" (p. 224). Therefore, one of the most useful open-ended questions is "What would be a specific example?"

Once we know the details that underlie the self-construction, we may be able to find alternative characterizations for the behaviors that have led to these interpretations. In attempting to relabel clients' self-constructions, we are not trying to teach them the correct label but are trying to perturb and loosen their fixed notions of self. When clients speak concretely of their experiences, the conversation is enlivened and the descriptive level of events becomes the focus. The descriptive or concrete level provides you the opportunity to inquire about aspects of the client narrative that might not support the negative construction.

Be warned: It is important that you neither dispute the "facts" of the situation being described nor challenge the self-label that the client has constructed. You are not trying to talk clients out of their reality. That would be an "outside-in" intervention, implying that your interpretation of events is superior to that of your client. You can, however, fully accept the description of the concrete "facts" while feeding back new constructions of the experiences being described.

A "slacker" could be someone who has not yet found activities to which he or she can fully commit. A "loser" might be someone who has suffered repeated misfortune. A "failure" may be someone who is still searching for an opportunity leading to success. White and Epston (1990) called this process of throwing a monkey wrench into the client's story and self-characterization "creative misunderstanding," and Steve de Shazer (1988) termed it the "binocular view." When we creatively misunderstand the client's self-construction, we help relax the connection between the events and the labels in the client's narrative. Likewise, with the binocular view, the client sees the event through one lens, while you see it through a slightly different one. You are both looking at the same situation but with a different interpretation. If your client's old version of the story is deconstructed—but not disputed—by your comments, the possibility exists that a new story, and a new self, can be constructed.

So long as we help the client stay at the level of describing, rather than labeling, with concrete portrayals of what has been going on, we keep open the possibility that both the situation and the self-construction will stay flexible. This allows for an "inside-out" change, meaning that the client provides his or her own reconstruction. The self in the client's narrative can slip out of the rigid constraints that have kept the client stuck in place. We often live our lives held in place by the lock and chain of our beliefs without realizing that we hold the key. "Who we are depends on the story we (and others) tell about ourselves. . . . The narrative self is, consequently, an open-ended construction that is under constant revision" (Zahavi, 2005, p. 105).

Implications of These Ideas for the Counselor

- Brief counseling and humanistic psychology are not mutually exclusive.
- While many of our beliefs are socially constructed, we can still deconstruct and reconstruct them ourselves.
- People can achieve the personal characteristics they desire for themselves by deliberate hard work.
- The term "brief" should not be associated with "superficial." People are changed by this approach at a deep-self level.

TOOLS

Counseling Is Not for Everyone

How many counselors does it take to change a light bulb? (Answer: Only one, but the light bulb has to really want to change.) While we believe that counseling could be helpful for everyone to simply clear away the confusing flotsam and jetsam of everyday life, not all people see counseling as a necessary part of their lives. Indeed, most people go through life quite well without ever seeing a counselor. Even in cases of extreme crisis or trauma, the overwhelming majority of those who have suffered such insult or injury display no clinically significant consequences (Echterling, Presbury, & McKee, 2005; McNally, Bryant, & Ehlers, 2003). People are remarkably resilient!

For those who do seek counseling, this innate resilience tends to validate the "strength" approach that attempts to elicit positive talk and images from clients. Psychological trauma can cause people's awareness of their own strengths and coping ability to be temporarily eclipsed by feelings of helplessness and hopelessness. When you help clients find the way toward transcendence of their psychological injuries and resolution of lingering concerns, first acknowledge the story of pain. Then you can help them see the other face of the Necker cube. As we have pointed out several times in this book, you must go slow and always return to acknowledgment with the LUV Triangle when your clients signal their hesitance to be influenced by your positive agenda.

Despite the fact that you are a talented, empathic, and well-trained helper for people who *do* seek counseling, not all those who arrive at your office will be immediately willing to engage in a working alliance with you. Welfel and Patterson (2005) called these hesitant people the "ambivalent, indifferent, and oppositional clients" (p. 185). Very few people come to counseling as "customers." All clients are at least ambivalent, and you must win their trust before they will commit to going through the process of change. "Indifferent" clients are "visitors" who, while they are physically present, will state that they see no reason for being with you in a counseling relationship. In Prochaska and Norcross's nomenclature, these people are in the "precontemplation" stage of change. "Oppositional" clients are usually those who have been coerced and who feel the need to defend themselves against you. We call these clients "involuntaries." Usually, they have been sent by a third party who wishes some specific change in their behavior but which these clients claim is not in need of changing. So, as you sit there with the involuntary client, trying your best to appear benign and caring while your client glowers back at you, what can you do to be helpful with this person?

Who's the Client?

The resolution approach to counseling is a consumer-oriented model that espouses a philosophy of "The customer is always right." But those who come to counseling because they are mandated or coerced by others are often very reluctant consumers. In fact, they are not "customers" at all: Someone wants them to participate in counseling, and they are not buying it. They would have you believe that they are the light bulb that does not really want to change.

Welfel and Patterson (2005) suggested that trying to impose counseling on someone who does not want your services brings up ethical considerations that must be addressed. What is the justification for trying to counsel someone who has no interest in it? These authors offered several reasons why counseling involuntary clients may be consistent with your ethics, even though you are attempting to foist counseling upon these people. First, you have a moral and ethical obligation to help people live more fully, even if they are not seeking help. Second, as a trained professional, you are able to recognize that so-called "resistant" behaviors are reasonable coping responses to environmental pressures but may be amenable to your attempts to help. Finally, you know that early intervention can "lead to more rapid and more complete resolution. . . ." "This may serve as justification for a counselor to begin working with a client before the client recognizes the need for help" (Welfel & Patterson, 2005, p. 194).

While your client is disclaiming the need for counseling, the referring agent is demanding it. This situation brings up the old "Who's the client?" problem that counselors often face. The person who sits with you in the first session, looking annoyed, indifferent, or frightened, is your primary client. However, in the involuntary scenario, there is a referring agent who is also a client. This person may be the parent, teacher, principal, social worker, judge, probation officer, or someone else who possesses coercive power over your primary client.

Whether you are a counselor in a school, an agency, or in private practice, you will regularly find yourself in the situation of having a primary client mandated by a referring client. Each of these people may appear to have a different agenda, and you can often feel caught in the middle. For example, a teacher may perceive a student as having a "bad attitude" due to a "poor self-concept" and refer this student to you, expecting that you will fix this problem. The primary client—the student—may interpret the situation as "the teacher doesn't like me" and only expresses to you the wish for this teacher to "get off my case." So how do you go about trying to reconcile these opposing views?

Can both of these clients be satisfied? Your counseling work in these situations will feel very much like a high-wire balancing act. You may believe that you will be required to side with one or the other of the clients, because neither person is a customer for the stated goal of the other. At best, they are both complainants, believing that their problems would be solved if the other party simply changed his or her beliefs or behavior. The real art involved in dealing with any involuntary situation is to discover how each party might become a customer. Everyone is a customer for something. If you can help them find a goal that is congruent with the desires of both parties, then it may be possible to have a win-win situation. In order to achieve this arrangement, you must find a way to "cooperate" with both parties (Lipchik, 2002).

Walter and Peller (1992) suggested that there are several roles that may be placed upon you when dealing with involuntary clients. These roles include the investigator, reporter, and manager. Aside from these roles, you are usually most interested in playing a fourth role—that of the helping person.

The *investigator* is someone who tries to find out what is going on in the world of the involuntary client that may be harmful. For example, the referring agent may suspect a child is a victim of sexual abuse and wishes for you to confirm this suspicion. In another case, the referring agent may suspect that the client is a perpetrator who is physically abusive to his wife or is driving while intoxicated. Your investigation is expected to take the form of interviewing collaterals, testing and interviewing the involuntary, or bringing in others who may even exacerbate the problem. Obviously, the involuntary client would be wary in this situation.

The *reporter* is the person who communicates to someone in authority about some wrongdoing. This role follows on that of the *investigator*. The most obvious example would be if you were to learn that the involuntary client, who is a child, has indeed been abused or neglected. In such a case, you are required by law to report this knowledge. The *reporter* role can seriously reduce the candor with which the involuntary client responds in the session. Despite your desire to allow the client to have a confidential talk with you, the law supersedes any pledge of confidentiality you might have made to the abused person. In the case of the child who reports abuse, he or she may fear that this disclosure will send the perpetrator (often a parent) to jail, and you may come to be seen by the client as simply an agent of the legal system.

The *manager* role conforms to the requirements that constitute the achievement of the referring agent's goals. In cases of court referral, the *manager* checks up or attempts to prevent a reoccurrence of problematic behavior. In this role, you may find the referring agent expecting you to bring the involuntary into compliance with the rules of the system. The client will, no doubt, expect you to behave in ways similar to law enforcement and judicial personnel. If you are a school counselor, your client may see you as just another teacher or administrator. As *manager*, you take on the task of discipline, something the client is familiar with and for which he or she has a well-rehearsed defensive tactic.

The *helping person* is the role in which you attempt to facilitate change that the primary client desires but that will also be seen as improvement by the referring client. By our definition, this role is the one you will be playing as you follow the procedures outlined in this book and work for the benefit of the primary client. This does not mean, however, that you ignore the desires of the referring client, who is, after all, part of the primary client's problem. And unless referring parties are satisfied with the change brought about by your counseling, they will continue to see your primary client as their problem and may view you as ineffective.

Performing the roles of *reporter, investigator,* and *manager* can seriously compromise your ability to perform the role of *helper.* If these other roles are necessary, then, ideally, someone else should perform them. Keeping these roles separate and clear would allow you to focus on the challenge of converting an involuntary client into a customer. As Walter and Peller (1992) warned, "When you are both therapist and manager, involuntary clients can have a harder time separating your role as social control agent who may take away their children or put them in jail from your role as . . . therapist" (p. 245). Unfortunately, however, you will have to report back to the referring person or agency or sometimes play the role of *manager* or *investigator.* This will make your job as counselor more difficult, but, if you can create a trusting relationship with your primary client, it is not impossible.

Cooperating With Both Primary and Referring Clients

Tohn and Oshlag (1995) suggested that there are six essential components to working in an involuntary, or mandated, situation. These steps include honoring your clients' worldview, establishing well-formed counseling goals, using the referral sources to further establish these goals, using the referral source to sustain progress, and helping clients move toward their goals.

Little needs to be said here about the first two steps because these have already been covered in Chapters 2, 3, and 4 of this book. We should point out, however, that it is sometimes easy to slip into the assumption that the involuntary client may, or at least should, have the same worldview and goals as the referring agent. Taking this idea for granted is guaranteed to result in a muddle.

Most referring agents are credible people who are sincerely interested in improving the situation for the involuntary client. Since they are often people in authority, it is easy to believe that their version of reality is accurate and can be taken as a good starting point for the counseling work. However, this assumption can lead to a situation in which you believe you must convince the involuntary clients that they have a problem and should see things the same way as the referring parties. If you perceive your clients to be "in denial" in such situations, your clients may be wondering if you have truly listened, understood, and validated their worldview. Of course, any attempts to convince your clients to change will strengthen your alliance with the referral source. However, in doing so, you may have failed to establish rapport with the most important person— your primary client. It is crucial, when speaking to the referring person prior to seeing your primary client, that you get concrete descriptions of both the behaviors that he or she sees as problematic *and* the specific behaviors that would be the goals for the work. Do not accept vague referrals or those that detail only negative behaviors. If you are going to establish goals with your primary client, you must know how closely related they are to those of the referring client.

Involuntary clients often come to counseling believing that you and the referring agents are working together in a conspiracy to make them change against their will. You will have to be careful not to engage in behaviors that strengthen this suspicion. You must always start with a "clean sheet of paper" with involuntary clients, even though you may already possess a great deal of referral information. But don't behave as if you know nothing about what brings this client to you, or your client will see you as a fake.

Opening the session   There are a number of openings you can use with involuntary clients. For example, after introducing yourself, you might simply inquire, "What do you think [the referring person] wants you to be doing differently as a result of our work together?" With this question, you focus on what is expected, rather than what is wrong (Lipchik, 2002). Of course, in response to such a question your client may simply shrug and claim not to know. If you have done your homework with the referral and have obtained stated goals, you might then say, "Well, let me tell you what he/she wants so you can see what he/she hopes you might do differently." Your next step is to check if any part of the referral goal matches with your primary client's goal. You might say, "How about you? How much of [the referring party's] goal would you also want to see happen?" If your client responds that there is some part of this goal that makes sense, then you might proceed as you would with a voluntary client. If not, you can ask, "Well, now that you are here, let's see how we can work together to make this situation better for you. We know what [referring agent] wants, what do you want?"

Our belief is that the task of trying to align goals between the people involved is better done in a conjoint meeting in which the goals of all parties can be clarified. Those attending such a meeting would be, at least, the referring agent, the involuntary client, and you. In such a meeting your primary client can see that you are not on the side of the referring person but are merely trying to get everyone "on the same page." Another possibility would be to ask the referring agent to fill out a Counseling Goals Form (See Chapter 4.) indicating the behaviors the referring party wishes to see increased and which behaviors the client already exhibits. You can then show this checklist to the primary client and inquire as to which behaviors in the list might possibly be strengthened.

What Does an Involuntary Client Want?

If you ask your involuntary clients what they really want, they will likely tell you that they would wish not to participate in counseling. They would rather be just about anywhere but here. This may be a reasonable goal, but it does not fit our criteria for a well-formed goal. Remember that old "instead" question you ask to turn the desire for the absence of something into the presence of something. So, take this opportunity to ask, "If you didn't have to come here anymore, what would you be doing instead?" If your client says he or she would rather be home, at work, or even at a baseball game, then help the client elaborate on this hint of a goal statement. Consider, at this point, that your client could be a customer for being there, rather than here. Then, once your client has clearly created an image of this goal-state, ask, for example, "What do you think it would take to convince the people who referred you that you don't need to come here anymore, so that you could be at home instead?"

The client may be able to state some behaviors that the referring person would wish to see in order to be convinced that he or she no longer needed counseling. If this is the case, then you might ask, "Which of those behaviors that this person wants improved do you think you would like to work on so you can get home?"

The Counselor as Shrink

As previously mentioned, we believe that involuntary client relationships often begin more negatively than visitor relationships. In fact, these clients often view the involuntary relationship as an adversarial one (Lipchik, 2002; Welfel & Patterson, 2005). In the clients' view, you are simply there to complete the punishment by forcing him or her to engage in the procedure of counseling. In everyday conversation, you can often hear people say that someone has "undergone" counseling, as though it were a surgical procedure or a brain-washing technique. The term "shrink," which refers to counselors and other psychological helping professionals, implies that one will be somehow diminished after having been counseled. It is reasonable for clients to seek to escape from such a relationship before great harm comes to them. Obviously, this is where your skill at relationship building comes in to play. You must enchant the clients into believing that, despite the fact that the referring agent is also your client, you are not there to carry out some surgical "character-ectomy" dictated by the referral.

Using the referral source to sustain treatment progress is another important strategy with involuntary clients. At the beginning of your relationship, inform the primary client that you are obligated to keep the referring person informed, but make explicit the limits of what you will be reporting. You should routinely "check in" with the referral person and other involved parties to discuss any progress they have noticed. By checking in frequently, the message you are communicating to referral sources is that they should expect to notice positive change. Sometimes the referring agents are so angry and discouraged that they are not likely to notice any changes or acknowledge the clients' efforts.

Remember that the referring persons are your clients, too. If you do not acknowledge their frustrations and concerns, they will be uncertain as to whether you really understand the seriousness of the problem, and so they might feel the need to continue to notice more problems until you are completely convinced. Furthermore, when the primary client, the involuntary, does show improvement and the referring person fails to notice, the primary client might figure, "What's the use?!" Then you will have two discouraged and hopeless clients on your hands.

By keeping in touch with the referring person, you stand a better chance of being able to influence both clients at the same time. For example, Tohn and Oshlag (1995) show how you can work both ends of the referral at the same time. After your involuntary client has agreed to try something different, you might use a variant of the Formula First Session suggestion by communicating the following to the referring client: "Between now and the next time we meet, my counseling client will be working on some issues. I would like you to notice what this person is doing differently that you would like to see more of."

Even if your primary client does nothing different in the next week, but the referring person notices something different, you are on your way to the iatrogenic resolution of the problem. Studies have found that much of client improvement can be attributed to the placebo effect.

Because your involuntary client has not "self-selected" a relationship with you, it is important to acknowledge the client's reluctance and possible resentment at being ordered to come. State your interest in hearing his or her side of the story. For example, you might say, "I guess if I were in your shoes, I wouldn't have been too happy at being sentenced to counseling either, and I'd have a hard time seeing what good it will do. I've heard from the judge why she thought you should be here, but I'd like to hear your side."

If possible, attempt to refocus the client from being forced to be here to having chosen to be. You can take the client's presence as *prima facie* evidence that he or she is avoiding a worse consequence by showing up for counseling. You might comment, "While coming for counseling would not have been your first choice, the fact that you are here means that you have chosen this over something else. What purpose will coming here serve for you?"

If the client does not name a purpose, ask what the referring party wishes for the client to do differently. If the client can name something that the third party wishes to see changed, you might then seek to shift the focus back to the client. For example, you can state, "So Ms. Thompson thinks you should be doing your homework and staying out of trouble in school. What part of what she wants is something you want, too?"

If the client were to reply, "I just want her to get off my case!" then you might say something like, "How would things be different for you if she got off your case? [Client names a difference.] So maybe you and I could work together on getting [named difference] to happen."

If the client cannot say what the referring party wishes, you might send the client to the referring party to ask. On return, find out if this change is something the client also wishes. If not, explore the consequences of not coming to sessions. If the client wishes to take the consequences, say "good-bye," and express your willingness to meet again should the client have a change of heart. Finally, if sessions are required anyway, state the conditions for further work together in order to gain leverage. For example, you could propose, "Since you have been required to come for eight sessions (that's 8 times 50 minutes), and I am required to report on our work together, any time you are working to change in the session, I will count those minutes toward the total 400 minutes that are required." (Buy a stopwatch, and produce it at this point.)

Obviously, we would want all our relationships with clients to be customer types. Unfortunately, as we have stated, it is rare for any client to enter counseling as a full-fledged customer. Your job is to search for something that clients might be a customer for, while at the same time honoring the hesitant position they have adopted. When people feel that you have listened, understood, and validated their point of view (LUV), they will often move closer toward the customer relationship. If, on the other hand, you challenge them or try to overcome their resistance, they will "circle the wagons" and try to protect themselves from your assaults. Promoting such a siege mentality will only make your work more difficult.

Some cautions: Lipchik (2002) advised that, before you try any of the influencing techniques that she suggested, and that we have outlined here, you must take a longer time to empathically communicate that you wish to be someone different from the others whom the client has been opposing. You should be careful about the use of questions when beginning with the involuntary client. These clients will have a negative reaction to questions because they have previously experienced them as interrogative traps.

What If the Involuntary Client Remains Involuntary?

As you read the past few sections on dealing with the involuntary client and the referral source, you may have found yourself feeling skeptical. You may have had involuntary clients before and found them to be "impossible." In some instances, so have we.

Sometimes, regardless of your best efforts to invite and enchant an involuntary client, you pull your best rabbits out of the hat and not much happens. As you reflect on your sessions with the client, you may notice that you have been working much harder than the client is working. Your time together just doesn't seem to go anywhere. You may even feel burned out. When you are confident that you and your client are wasting each other's time, you can say, "Well, we have been trying to work together for [the number of sessions]. Could we agree that right now we are at a standoff? Perhaps there will be a time when you are more willing to work with me, or maybe you would prefer working with someone else."

If your client indicates his or her belief that to continue trying would be fruitless, express your regret, invite the client to return if at a later date he or she reconsiders, and state that you must report to the referring person that you have mutually agreed to terminate. Any hints of exceptions, possibilities, resources, strengths, positive goals, and so on that the client has revealed during the sessions should be emphatically pointed out to both the involuntary client and the referring person.

LISTENING IN ON A SESSION

Review Zeshaun's story at the beginning of this chapter. The counselor asks Zeshaun if he could wait a few minutes while she makes some preparations to meet with him. Zeshaun mutters his acceptance, and the counselor heads for the vice principal's office. Vice Principal John Von Sant is a young (late 20s), action-oriented, and energetic man who is sometimes uncomfortable in his position around older teachers and staff members.

Act II

Counselor: "John, I wanted to chat a few minutes before I begin my meeting with Zeshaun. Can you spare some time now?"

Vice Principal: (Calmer than earlier and apologetic)
"Yes, sure, come in. I'm sorry about barging in on you like that, but that kid drives me crazy."

Counselor: (Opens a small notebook and begins writing)
"John, I could tell it was an emergency because otherwise you would have scheduled an appointment. Now, I wanted to get a few things down to get me up to speed before I see Zeshaun. OK if I take a few notes?"

Vice Principal: "No problem, what do you want to know?"

Counselor: "Whatever you want to tell me that I might not be able to find in his file. You know, maybe what you would like to see happen with Zeshaun."

Vice Principal: (He telephones the secretary in the main office and asks for the in-school suspension and the afterschool detention files. He checks both files for a few minutes.)
"Well, it turns out that Mrs. O'Connor is Zeshaun's homeroom teacher and his 10th grade English teacher third period. All the in-school suspensions and afterschool detentions were initiated at her request. I'd say those two don't . . . (He stops himself.)
Anyway, Zeshaun has got to learn to get along with everyone, including Mrs. O'Connor. I mean, I know his folks from church and they've had some problems but that's no excuse.
(He speaks louder and with intensity.)
He's such a hothead, he'll get right up in your face if you push him."

Counselor: "You gave me an idea, John. I like to check with referring teachers anyway, so if you don't mind, I'd like to chat with Mrs. O'Connor before I see Zeshaun tomorrow."

Act III

The counselor returns to her office where Zeshaun is moodily staring out the window.

Counselor: "Zeshaun, I'm awfully sorry, I'm not going to be able to talk to you very long today other than to set up another time we could meet."
   (Zeshaun remains silent and detached with no eye contact.)
   "I'll bet it seems to you that you've been sentenced to counseling, huh?"

Zeshaun: (He smiles slightly in spite of himself.)
   "What are you going to do—analyze me? If anybody needs analyzing around here, it's O'Connor."

Counselor: "I'll try not to do too much analyzing. If I do, you can call me on it, OK?"

Act IV

Counselor: "Thanks for agreeing to see me on such short notice, Mrs. O'Connor. I understand that you have referred Zeshaun to us and I thought I'd check with you first and learn what you would like to see Zeshaun accomplish."

Mrs. O'Connor: (Has a condescending attitude toward anything "modern," such as counselors, self-help movements, MTV, and the Internet)
   "First of all, I did not refer anyone to guidance or counseling or whatever you people call yourselves. I was teaching high school before there was such a thing as 'counselors' and we seemed to get along fine."

Counselor: (With intense interest)
   "Mrs. O'Connor, I wasn't aware that you began teaching when teachers pretty much had to 'do it all.' I can't imagine the energy that must have taken."

Mrs. O'Connor: "No one does. Why, I can't tell you how many girls I helped who had 'gotten in trouble.' In 1957 alone, I . . . (She takes about 5 minutes to replay her 1957, and she becomes quite enthusiastic toward the end.)

Counselor: "With all the work you had to do, you still found time to help these young people. I imagine it felt good to help those kids that everyone else had given up on. I guess, in a way, they were kind of like a lot of kids today . . ." (The counselor trails off.)

Mrs. O'Connor: "Well, not exactly, those girls adored me, they didn't wear those stupid baseball hats, sass me, or make fun of me the way that Zeshaun does."

Counselor: (Again, she pulls out her ever-handy small notebook.)
"This has been so helpful, Mrs O'Connor. I want to get some of this down, so Zeshaun and I can begin working on some goals together, OK?"

Mrs. O'Connor: "That would be fine, but what can I do? Kids are a lot different than they used to be even 10 years ago. Sometimes I don't even have a clue about what they are talking about and they laugh at me. I wouldn't know an MP3 or a Blackberry if one came to my house for dinner."

Counselor: "I was wondering how you could help me with Zeshaun. As I work with him, perhaps you could watch for signs that our efforts are successful . . . maybe jot down small positive changes in his attitude. Judging from what you have said about him, you will have to watch carefully to see his small signs of improvement."

Mrs. O'Connor: (Laughing)
"With 32 students, I don't think I have time for a behavior mod program." (She pauses.) "If I happen to notice something, I'll let you know, but don't get your hopes up."

Act V

Counselor: "Thanks for coming back, Zeshaun . . ."

Zeshaun: (Slumping in chair, then interrupts)
"I thought I had to."

Counselor: "Gosh, you had me worried a little bit there. I was afraid you were going to choose afterschool detention instead."

Zeshaun: (Smiling)
"Naw, I was just kidding. I'll stay here."

Counselor: "Zeshaun, how would you like to use the time we have together today?"

Zeshaun: "I'd just like to get these people off my case and quit accusing me of having an attitude problem."

Counselor: "Zeshaun, it sounds like you'd like to find a way to get others to see you the way you really are."

REFLECTING QUESTIONS

1. In what ways did the counselor work with both the primary client and the referring agents?
2. How can the counselor build on this collaborative foundation?
3. Write a possible response to Zeshaun's last statement.

Two Giants of Counseling

We owe much to Steve de Shazer and Carl Rogers. They were seminal thinkers and would have had much to talk about together.

Steve de Shazer

(June 25, 1940–September 11, 2005)

We are sure that Steve de Shazer would appreciate the irony that his life ended on a trip in Vienna, where Freud had started his therapy. De Shazer had reversed the traditional psychotherapy process by shifting the focus of treatment from recalling the origins of problems in the past to envisioning solutions in the future.

Carl Ransom Rogers

(January 8, 1902–February 4, 1987)

Like Steve de Shazer, Carl Rogers transformed the fundamental dynamics of therapy. He equalized the power differential between the patient and therapist by promoting therapy as a collaborative, person-to-person relationship in which the therapist empathically, authentically, and unconditionally works with the client.

SUMMARY

For too long, brief techniques have been portrayed as incompatible with humanistic psychology's concepts and values. However, brief counseling can have "depth" results that reach all the way into the self of the client. The involuntary client presents special challenges to our counseling work. In this chapter, we offered guidelines for helping this person to become engaged more fully in the counseling process and suggestions for dealing with the referring third party.

SEGUE TO CHAPTER 14

Recall a particularly memorable experience you have had with a supervisor that dramatically affected your growth as a counselor or therapist. You may have found yourself "getting it" in a new and powerful way. You may have gotten a handle on some fundamental technique that led to profound changes in the ways that you encountered clients. Whatever the experience, what did you find especially helpful about your supervisor?

Resource

Association for Humanistic Psychology (AHP)
1516 Oak Street, #320A
Alameda, CA 94501-2947
510-769-6495
http://ahpweb.org/index.html

The website for AHP provides an overview of the history of humanistic psychology, a calendar of training events and conferences, bibliographies, and Web resources. AHP is an international, nonprofit organization that promotes human dignity and fosters personal actualization.

CHAPTER 14

Other Brief Approaches and Theory as a Tool

God has put a secret art into the forces of Nature so as to
enable it to fashion itself out of chaos into a perfect
world system.
Immanuel Kant

CHAPTER GOALS

The goals of this chapter are to help you to understand these ideas and to use these tools:

- Motivational Interviewing, brief Gestalt therapy, time-limited existential therapy, brief psychodynamic therapy, brief behavior therapy, and brief cognitive-behavioral therapy are only a few of the theoretical models of brief counseling and therapy.
- Many practitioners are now integrating these different theoretical perspectives.
- Theory is a practical tool in your counseling and therapy work.
- One of the major tasks in your professional development is to develop your personal theory of counseling.

STORY

The faculty supervisor is meeting with Pembrooke, a second-year counseling student, for their second weekly supervison session. Pem is counseling an older married woman with a family, and he has seen her for two counseling sessions.

Supervisor: "Well, Pembrooke, oh, I forgot, you prefer Pem, right?"

Pem: "That's OK, it's easier to say and remember."

Supervisor: "Anyway, we have about 50 minutes, how would you like to make the most of our time together in supervision?"

Pem: "Umm, I've been rushing, trying to catch my breath, so I haven't given it much thought. I'm sorry."

Supervisor: "Well, then, how about telling me about the best thing you did with your client this week."

Pem: (He looks thoughtful and then worried.)
"I'm afraid I won't have much to talk about then."

Supervisor: "How so?"

Pem: "Well, you remember, I only have the one client and I had seen her once before and I mostly just listened and let her tell her story. My on-site supervisor said I should try some intervention strategies because my client tends to ramble. In our second session, she had three or four concrete examples that were straight out of the writings of those cognitive behaviorists—Beck, Michenbaum, Burns—I can't keep them all straight right now, I guess Ellis, too, but he comes across a bit crankier—irrational beliefs, or faulty thinking. Anyway, my client was telling me about how *she just knew* that people were talking about her at work because when she walked in the lunchroom one day last week, no one was talking and *she could just tell* that something bad was going to happen because she had won $50 on a scratch-off lottery ticket. Now she was sure that something was going to happen to one of her children, so she's thinking about keeping them home from school for a few days."
(Pem pauses to catch his breath and shifts in the chair uncomfortably. He looks at the supervisor who just nods her head slowly with encouragement and understanding.)
"I know I shouldn't have referred to these ideas of hers as cognitive errors, but I guess I got kind of excited and I felt like, for the first time, I wasn't stumbling around in an ambiguous fog with a client. I felt like I could give some clear direction."

Supervisor: "That must have felt freeing: to be on your own like that and making your way out of the fog."

Pem: (He pauses, sighs, and continues.)
"Not exactly. This part is painful but I feel like I have to come clean. She didn't know what cognitive errors meant, so when I explained what crooked thinking was, she understood, but she didn't like it one bit. In fact, she said that it made her sound like she was really nutty, but she was quick to point out that she knew lots of people that thought the same way. Then, I remembered Glasser's line: I think it was something like, 'How does keeping those ideas seem to be working for you?' and that got her attention for a little bit but she continued to be defensive. I just kept getting in deeper and deeper, especially when I pointed out her defensiveness. At that point, she clammed up and seemed to withdraw. She must have been

quiet for what seemed to be 2 or 3 minutes when I asked her if she would like to talk about what just happened. And then we sort of ran out of time."

Supervisor: "How did you know to do that?"

Pem: "Oh, you mean the immediacy thing? I'm not sure, I was pretty mixed up about what to do next. I even thought about a two-chair exercise from Gestalt therapy, but then I decided that chasing around from one theory to another was probably what got me into trouble in the first place. So, I just decided to stick with what I knew was working before."

Supervisor: "So you decided to go with what worked before. Tell me more about what you're doing when things are working well."

Pem: "Not so much with her but the previous semester, I had a client in our consulting group who would shut down whenever I failed to be present with her or got ahead of her, and I guess I got pretty good at reading the signs, so then I adjusted accordingly."

Supervisor: "I'm sorry to be so concrete, Pem, but maybe you could give me an example of when the situation you described happened and you 'adjusted accordingly,' as you put it."

Pem: "Well, let's see, I guess one time I was going on a fishing expedition by asking too many goal-directed questions without really being invited and the client began playing 'yes-but' with me, mainly because she wasn't ready to go for goals yet."

Supervisor: "So you recognized the game you were in and decided to change the situation, I guess. Tell me the details; what did you say?"

Pem: "It's been about two months, I'm not sure I remember exactly."
(The supervisor leans forward expectantly, and nods her head patiently.)
"I think I took one for the team and said something like, 'Pam, I don't blame you for not wanting to talk about setting goals yet, you probably feel like I'm on my horse, sword raised, sounding the bugle charge, and you haven't even decided whether you want to fight.'"

Supervisor: "A very vivid picture, I imagine she liked it."

Pem: "She laughed out loud and admitted that sometimes she did feel overwhelmed by my enthusiasm. She decided to tell me in the future when she felt that way and, for my part, I tried to be more aware of her reluctance."

Supervisor: "I think I see how that worked out so well for you, and it was a good example." (She pauses briefly.) "I'm curious though, what will you be doing differently with your present client to get a similar reaction from her?"

Pem: "I'm not really sure. I guess I'll have to think about it; I'm sure I'll be able to come up with something."

Supervisor: "So, it looks like you'll be able to trust your instincts when you read those signs again. I was wondering if there were something else that you . . ."

Pem: (He interrupts.)

"I'm sorry. But, I'm almost 30 years old and I have this awful feeling that I've made a foolish mistake with this client and you're probably thinking that since I'm in my second year of the program, that I should know better than to try theory testing on every client who comes along. I didn't sleep well last night because I kept thinking that maybe I don't belong, that maybe I wasn't cut out to be a counselor."

REFLECTING QUESTIONS

1. If you were the supervisor, what might you say to the counselor?
2. What is meant by the term "imposter syndrome"?
3. In what ways did the supervisor ask the counselor to draw on inner resources and successes in their supervision session?

OVERVIEW

In this final chapter, we explore the exciting developments toward integration in counseling and therapy. We also examine specific brief approaches, such as motivational interviewing, brief Gestalt therapy, time-limited existential therapy, brief psychodynamic therapy, brief behavior therapy, and brief cognitive-behavioral therapy. As you will see, although they have different emphases, these approaches are variations on the fundamental theme of achieving the greatest impact in the least amount of time.

Ultimately, you need to value theory as an essential tool in your counseling and therapy work. In order to help you begin the task of developing your personal theory of counseling, we suggest that there are five main approaches to helping that are emphasized by the existing theories.

IDEAS

"Brief" as an Evolving Paradigm

According to Nugent and Jones (2005), brief counseling and therapy has a long history, dating back to Freudian psychoanalysis. "Freud at first limited his analysis with patients to 6 to 12 sessions . . . [and] psychoanalysts Alfred Adler, Otto Rank, and Sandor Ferenczi objected as analysis became longer" (p. 157). Despite this protest, the conventional notion was that it takes a long time for repressed material in a client's unconscious to emerge and be worked through.

In later years, so-called ego-psychologists and post-Freudians became less interested in recovering material from clients' unconscious minds and more concerned with helping them deal with their immediate concerns. Consequently, the stage was set for brief approaches to counseling and therapy. Already, in the United States, behavioral research was beginning to inform therapists as they attempted to apply scientific findings to therapy that naturally culminated in briefer work with clients. Once practitioners began to think of people and their families as "systems" rather than "mechanisms," new ideas about change and how it could be accomplished briefly began to proliferate.

More recently, approaches to brief counseling and therapy, with their emphasis on pragmatism and flexibility, have spurred the field's movement toward integrative approaches. Also, as you read in Chapter 9, there is a growing recognition that successful counseling has a detectable impact on the brain by creating new synaptic connections and releasing neurotransmitters. Therefore, not only is there greater integration within theories and practices of counseling and psychotherapy, the gap between neuroscience and the mind is narrowing. Moreover, these exciting findings in neuroscience already support the therapeutic effects of positive psychology and its focus on strengths rather than deficits (Peterson & Seligman, 2004; Seligman & Csikzentmihalyi, 2000).

Integrative therapy, with its "stages of change" model; solution-focused therapy, with its emphasis on progress toward the future; and narrative therapy, with its emphasis on the reconstruction of life stories, have all made recent significant contributions to models of working briefly with clients. While divisions among therapeutic approaches still exist, it seems that every theoretical view now has a brief approach to counseling and therapy. Below, we list some of these brief methods that have emerged in recent years.

Motivational Interviewing (MI)

Prochaska and Norcross (2007) suggested that the therapeutic approach known as *Motivational Interviewing* (MI) is a successor to Rogerian theory—"Carl Rogers in new clothes" (p. 154). It is a directive approach designed to enhance clients' intrinsic motivation for change by honoring their ambivalence regarding change (Rollnick & Miller, 1995). This type of work is employed with difficult clients and is growing in popularity.

Miller and Rollnick (2002) identified four central principles of Motivational Interviewing practice. The first, and most important, principle is that the counselor must express empathy and display a caring concern for the client. As you read in Chapter 3, the empathic relationship is fundamental to success. Second, the counselor must help reveal the discrepancy between the client's stated values and behaviors. In Chapter 4, we discussed similar ideas regarding the importance of generating goals. Third, the counselor must honor resistance, rather than confronting it. As you learned in Chapter 1, resistance exists in the interaction between yourself and the client. Finally, the counselor must support the client's experience of self-efficacy by intervening in ways to bring about change and reinforce optimism. Self-efficacy is a term originated by Albert Bandura (1977). People who have a sense of self-efficacy hold the conviction that they are capable of producing needed behaviors for dealing with challenging tasks, whether they actually possess these required skills or not (Ryckman, 2004).

Motivational Interviewing (MI) was originally developed for working with clients who are challenged by substance abuse, but the approach seems to work well for all clients who display reluctance to change (Ivey & Ivey, 2007). Early research into the MI approach suggested that it was the counselor's empathy that made the greatest contribution to the client's success, not the specific treatment (Prochaska & Norcross, 2007).

The centrality of empathy in the counseling relationship seems to be making a comeback as clients tire of the types of therapy dictated by managed care, along with their sometimes sterile techniques (Bohart & Greenberg, 1997). According to Prochaska and Norcross (2007), clients "hunger for a real human relationship that is a genuine meeting of two individuals" (p. 168).

MI counselors waste no time in getting the interview started. Right away, the counselor begins "change talk," by asking for details regarding the client's hopes. In addition, the counselor might scale the client's desire for change by using a scaling method similar to the one we described in Chapter 4.

If the client were to seek change for an alcohol problem, the counselor would take care not to immediately "side" with the change. He or she would ask about aspects of drinking that are enjoyable or useful in some way for the client and then contrast these "benefits" with the problems that drinking behavior is creating in the client's life. This strategy makes it less possible for the client to "resist" change. By remaining nonjudgmental and attempting to empathically understand the client's world, the counselor becomes an ally rather than an adversary.

The standard approach to dealing with substance abuse has generally been to cajole, coerce, or confront the client: "You must quit drinking!" Such direct attempts to control clients have merely escalated their resistance. Instead of attempting to persuade clients to change, the MI counselor elicits from them their own reasons for changing. In this process, the counselor uses a technique known as "motivational discrepancy," during which the actual behaviors of the client are contrasted with those that are desired. We found this technique reminiscent of William Glasser's Reality Therapy (1965), in which clients take inventory of what they are actually doing versus what they wish to be doing, and then commit to some small change in the direction of the desired outcome (Corey, 2005).

Finally, as the process of change continues, the MI counselor takes care to illuminate the client's strengths through a "positive asset search" (Ivey & Ivey, 2007). Focusing on client strengths and applauding each move toward the goal are counselor behaviors that are familiar to anyone who is working for the resolution of client difficulties in ways described in this book.

One of the reasons that Motivational Interviewing has suddenly become popular is that it appears to be a radical departure from the attitudes that many substance abuse counselors have traditionally displayed with their clients. There is also empirical evidence to support the effectiveness of working with clients in this way. Many of the aspects of this type of counseling should now be obvious to you, since the assumptions about the relationship, empathy, honoring client ambivalence, and focusing on the positive fit well with the resolution approach of this book.

EXPERIENCING THIS IDEA

Think about a particular behavior, such as exercising, eating or smoking, that you would like to change. Whatever you choose, carefully consider how your current behaviors are enjoyable or useful. Once you have mulled over these "benefits," think about the problems that this behavior has created in your life.

1. In what ways did this exercise affect your resistance to change?
2. How might you develop a strategy for change that offers comparable joys?

Brief Gestalt Therapy

In the introduction to his book *Brief Gestalt Therapy,* Houston (2003) stated the following: "Gestalt Therapy is integrative in its nature. Of all brand-name therapies, it may be seen as one highly suited in its holism for use in brief counseling" (p. 2). As early as 1951, Fritz Perls, founder of Gestalt therapy, articulated one of the major assumptions of current brief therapies. He asserted that in successful counseling, the client continues on his or her own what the counselor had set in motion. Instead of a cure or finished product, the goal of counseling is to help a client develop the tools to deal with ongoing challenges that life will present.

In keeping with the Butterfly Effect, the first contact between client and therapist is crucial for setting a tone that will influence subsequent sessions. In particular, the client is on the lookout for therapist behaviors that might signal a lack of presence. One awful example takes place in the movie *Happiness,* in which a client shares all the anguish and turmoil in his life while the therapist mentally makes a list of chores to carry out after the session. If you are preoccupied with other issues, somehow and some way you are sending cues that you are not completely present in the counseling relationship. These signals may come across through your disengaged posture, lack of eye contact, or facial expressions that are not in tune with the client's emotional messages. Being fully with your client is crucial to a successful counseling relationship.

Many agencies require that clients fill out an "intake" form at the first meeting. Houston (2003) suggested the use of an awareness-raising questionnaire as a way of befriending clients and setting expectations for the work. In such a questionnaire, clients are asked to state the reason for seeking counseling, what special successes they see in their life, and the nature of the change they are seeking. Querying clients in this way sets the expectation that there have been, and will be, exceptions to their current state and that they should focus on their goals for the work with the counselor. As discussed in Chapter 4, goals should be reasonable, achievable, and positive rather than focused on symptom reduction.

Employing Houston's (2003) model of brief Gestalt therapy, from the start you would share your expectations of working together for up to eight sessions. Although the specific goals would vary from client to client, your ultimate hope would be to help expand personal awareness. Perls originally called his therapeutic approach "Concentration Therapy." By *concentration,* he meant bringing the client into high focus, high attention, and increased excitement or energy so as to mobilize client strengths. In Chapter 9, we referred to this process as bringing the client into "the zone."

The brief Gestalt therapist attempts to form a working alliance with the client and does not impose a therapy plan, but either elicits or negotiates one with the client. In order for the therapy to be brief, the stated goals or foci must continually be kept in mind as the relationship continues, but this must be done by "other than draconian or schoolteacher admonishments" on the part of the therapist (Houston, 2003, p. 57).

There are two aspects of a therapeutic relationship that are simultaneously present between client and counselor. One is the task on which the people are focused, while the other is the affect or emotional substrate—the bond between the people (Bertolino & O'Hanlon, 2002). When working toward the goal, the therapist and client must maintain their focus, but there must also exist a caring, supportive aspect to the relationship. "Caring, however, is not a substitute for coping. Excellent rapport, without . . . task competencies, does not constitute therapy" (p. 59). Many beginning therapists make the mistake of believing that displaying their affection for the client is sufficient for successful therapeutic work. According to Houston, it is certainly necessary, but not sufficient. Brief Gestalt therapists see client issues as a kind of "stuckness." Either by habit or through fear of experimentation, clients repeat unproductive behaviors and become numb to their own experience. They lack "response-ability," and the counselor must try to increase their responsiveness by elevating their emotional arousal.

The famous admonition of Fritz Perls—we should lose our minds and come to our senses—provides the basis for interventions in brief Gestalt therapy. Insight is typically not enough to propel clients toward successful resolution of their difficulties. Sometimes insights into the etiology, or cause, of their problems actually serve as excuses for not getting better. Such alibis constitute the old game of "wooden leg," in which the client says, "I can't do that! Don't you see that I'm handicapped? I have a wooden leg." Of course, the wooden leg may be a deprived childhood or some other excuse for stagnation.

A brief Gestalt therapist often challenges such "mind games" by asking clients to perform experiments, or enactments, having to do with their concerns. One example with which many people are familiar is the Gestalt technique of the two chairs. In this enactment, clients are asked to move from one chair to the other and have a dialogue with themselves representing the two poles of their existence. As we previously mentioned, Perls sometimes referred to these two positions as the "top dog/underdog" polarities. Clients sitting in the top dog chair will admonish the underdog to change, but, after moving to the other chair, clients—as underdogs—will declare helplessness and their piteous inability to alter their circumstances. The top dog then is asked to escalate demands for change by talking louder, pointing fingers, and demeaning the underdog, who then responds by admitting defeat and claiming incompetence to take any steps toward change.

When enacting this internal dialogue, clients do not talk *about* their resistance; they behave it to the point of absurdity. The "two chairs" technique is only one of such enactments that therapists use to break into the client's sensory experience. The top dog/underdog dialogue is an example of the client's attempt at a first-order change, but the experience of acting this out throws the struggle into a different context and may result in a second-order change. Readers who are interested in learning more about the various experiments used in this form of therapy should consult the Gestalt therapy literature (unless your underdog thinks that would be too much trouble).

Time-Limited Existential Therapy

When we think of a therapeutic approach that is designed to deal with profound existential life concerns, it seems almost ludicrous to believe that anyone could consider this type of work to be brief. However, as existential therapists Strasser and Strasser

(1997) declared, "There are certain situations where a time-limited approach is the only option available to the therapist, although we have found that there are also distinct advantages" (p. 45). In fact, setting time limits tends to compress, make more urgent, and increase the efficiency of the work. Moreover, not needing to make a long-term commitment to therapy can be a source of tremendous relief.

Existentialist therapists consider humans to be living in four simultaneous worlds: the Umwelt (physical world), the Mitwelt (public or social world), the Eigenwelt (private world), and the Uberwelt (spiritual world). How clients respond to each of these worlds or dimensions will create their existential condition.

Umwelt is the predetermined physical and biological dimension of life. The features of this world may seem immutable, but the way an individual relates to them is flexible. Geography and biology are not destiny. To be sure, certain constraints are placed on the individual by physical and biological forces in life. Of course, the major issue is death: It comes to us all, and the way in which we anticipate it will color our life. If we live in dread, our outlook will be grim and our energies will be drained away from living here and now.

Mitwelt is our relationship with others. The major issue at this level is how clients are treating and being treated by others, and how much "fellow feeling," or affinity for others, they have for both acquaintances and intimates. Often, they have adopted a problematic existential stance toward others by assuming a position of dominance, submission, or withdrawal. Relationship problems seem to be a crucial part of all concerns that people bring to counseling.

Eigenwelt is the relationship one has with oneself. Ontological "givens" in life include anxiety, isolation, loneliness, and potential meaninglessness. Existentialists state that these are not disorders to be cured but conditions to be coped with. The way in which one regards his or her existential condition and the strategies one develops to deal with fundamental "angst," which never leaves us, ultimately will dictate the person's lifestyle and self-esteem. Being capable of knowing oneself and loving oneself are issues at this level.

Uberwelt is the world of a person's search for meaning. We all ask the following questions concerning existence: What is life for? What values do I live by? How do I find and give love? Where do I belong? The main reason for the popularity of religion is that it provides answers to such issues. Many people discover that these answers offer solace from the vagaries of life, while others continue to seek their own meanings. Clients regularly appear in counseling sessions having experienced a crisis of faith or suffering despair because they have failed to find meaning in their lives.

Given the immensity of such existential concerns, how is it possible that counseling in this mode could be done briefly? The trick is that the goal is never the elimination of anxiety or the arrival at a cure. It is more the provision of a nourishing I–Thou relationship that is focused on a concern the client is experiencing in one of the four areas above. The average number of weekly sessions is 12, with two follow-up meetings. Brief existential therapists structure the interviews so that the focus remains on dealing with the presenting issue. Even though most existentialist therapists would design their process with clients to be more open-ended, Strasser and Strasser believed that structure provides both the "anchor" and "oar" as the client and counselor navigate troubled waters together. It also makes it possible for their work to remain time limited. No problems of living are ever cured, but one can adopt a better philosophy of life that will yield more joy.

EXPERIENCING THIS IDEA

Pick out a current problem that concerns you. Describe how this problem impacts your four simultaneous worlds: the Umwelt (physical world), the Mitwelt (public or social world), the Eigenwelt (private world), and the Uberwelt (spiritual world).

REFLECTING QUESTIONS

1. How do these four facets enrich your understanding of the meaning of this problem?
2. How might you use these four worlds as you seek a resolution to this problem?

Brief Psychodynamic Therapy

Brief psychodynamic therapy is the direct descendent of psychoanalysis, having retained the basic ideas of resistance within the client and the use of interpretation as a basic tool for intervention (Prochaska & Norcross, 2007). Some of the pioneers of this brief approach are Lester Luborsky (1984; Luborsky & Crits-Cristoph, 1990), James Mann (1973; Mann & Goldman, 1982), Peter Sifneos (1992), and Hans Strupp (Strupp & Binder, 1984). "Many psychoanalytically oriented therapists are attempting to creatively meet modern [or postmodern] challenges while retaining their original focus on depth and inner life" (Corey, 2005, p. 85). "Brief" therapy in this psychodynamic approach takes place when clients are seen for between 12 and 40 sessions. The treatment process for this type of work is as follows:

- Creating a strong working alliance
- Targeting an interpersonal problem
- Eliciting the expression of emotions
- Exploring resistance as clients avoid or block discussion of certain content
- Identifying themes or repetitive patterns in the client's life
- Emphasizing past experiences as "templates" for current relationships
- Discussing the client's interpersonal style
- Interpreting the client's wishes, dreams, and fantasies
- Focusing on the therapeutic relationship
- Interpreting resistance and transference as it appears in the therapeutic relationship

In contrast to standard psychoanalytic approaches, in which the therapist allows the treatment process to take its course, the brief psychodynamic practitioner develops a target issue to be the focus of the work. Messer and Warren (2001) created an approach that has a pre-established time limit of 10 to 25 sessions. This therapy concentrates on the current interpersonal issues that originated in early development. By establishing a strong working alliance, brief psychodynamic therapists focus on interpreting the reen-actment of transference in current relationships, including that between the counselor and client.

Edward Teyber (2006), whose brief therapeutic approach is grounded in the work of Harry Stack Sullivan and John Bowlby, emphasized the interpersonal aspect of the therapeutic relationship. Bowlby's attachment theory suggested that problems with early caregiving have prompted the client to develop defensive strategies that are still in use. While these strategies worked to help the client survive a hostile or indifferent early environment, they are now counterproductive. As Gelso and Fretz (1992) ex-plained, "There are countless experiences throughout life that revive repeatedly the sense of loss and anxiety related to separation-individuation phase" (p. 317). Such losses stimulate a person's old self-defense strategies and tend to bring them into the counseling relationship. In the therapy session, the client experiences transference to the therapist and begins to employ these old defenses in the session. The corrective emotional experience takes place when the therapist responds in ways that are different from everyone else, and the client gains insight into his or her own style.

Teyber (2006) asserted that this work can be accomplished in 10 to 16 sessions, but it "requires therapists to 'bring the conflict into the relationship' and to make overt how the therapeutic process may reenact aspects of the client's conflicts with others" (p. 36). Once clients have learned better ways of relating with the counselor, they develop a more pro-ductive interpersonal repertoire so that they can, as we like to say, "take it on the road."

Brief Behavior Therapy

Practitioners of behavior therapy have had a long history of promoting interventions that were time-efficient and evidence based. "They were adherents of brief therapy be-fore it became fashionable" (Porchaska & Norcross, 2007, p. 292). In general, behavior therapists report that they see only 7 percent of their clients for more than a year.

In their work with clients, behavior therapists quickly attempt to identify specific behaviors as the targets of change. They then implement research-supported methods to alter these behaviors. Behavior therapists make no assumption as to the cause of the behaviors and typically do not explore the client's past, except to learn when and where these behaviors occur. As you read in Chapter 1, behaviorists conceptualize a problem as simply the existence of too much or too little of a behavior. If there is too much, then the goal is the reduction or extinction of the behavior. If there is too little, then meth-ods are employed to increase the behavior's frequency. Whether the behavior might be overeating or lack of assertive behavior, therapists who operate with this approach be-lieve they can bring the target behavior into line in a short period of time.

Brief Cognitive and Cognitive-Behavioral Therapy

The three main proponents of therapies within the cognitive and cognitive-behavioral realm are Albert Ellis, Aaron Beck, and Donald Meichenbaum. What these three theorists have in common is the belief that how people think about what happens to them will create their moods and reactions to events. Faulty thinking is the source of emotional upsets and ineffective behavior (Welfel & Patterson, 2005). Obviously, then, the aim of these treatments is to straighten out, or reprogram, erroneous thinking.

The various cognitive approaches to brief treatment claim effective results from a set of structured and directive interventions. For example, Aaron Beck's manualized treatment prescribed no more than 16 sessions (Prochaska & Norcross, 2007). Albert Ellis's Rational Emotive Behavioral Therapy (REBT) offered change in between 1 to 20 sessions that he claimed was "better, deeper, and more enduring" (Prochaska & Norcross, 2007, p. 336).

While each of these therapists varies slightly in his explanation of how people come to grief and the type of relationship to be established with clients, their "constructivist" notion that cognitive schemas create people's worlds unites them. The letters in Ellis's (2001) alphabet soup, REBT and ABCDEF, serve to label his theory and describe the client's process in therapy. Rational Emotive Behavioral Therapy (REBT) sees clients as experiencing an *activating* event (A), which triggers the person's faulty *beliefs* (B) that lead to the *consequence* (C) of negative emotions; however, therapy teaches the client to *dispute* (D) these thoughts and helps the client gain a more *effective* (E) philosophy of life, with more comfortable *feelings* (F) (Corey, 2005). Ellis believed that a forceful debating style with clients tends to dislodge their "crooked" thinking quickly, although many practitioners have expressed concerns regarding his caustic manner and sarcastic style.

Aaron Beck (2005) is known as the father of cognitive therapy. He believed that one's thinking, if it is without foundation, can become "depressogenic." His approach to working with clients was called "collaborative empiricism," and, by its name, you might suspect that he was less argumentative with clients than was Ellis. The cognitive therapist works together with the client to identify the types of thinking that may be problematic and then to check out the validity of these thoughts in a more-or-less scientific manner. Borrowing from Burns (1989), we have adapted a partial list of some of these erroneous ways of construing events that are the work of cognitive therapy. A few of them seem very familiar, don't they?

- *All-or-nothing thinking:* You see things in black and white categories. If your performance falls short of perfect, you tend to see yourself as a total failure.
- *Overgeneralization:* You see a single negative event as a never-ending pattern of defeat. If you fail at one thing, you anticipate failing at everything.
- *Mental filter:* You pick out a single negative detail and dwell on it exclusively. Unlike in our Necker cube example, you cannot see the other face of possibility.
- *Disqualifying the positive:* You reject positive experiences by insisting they "don't count." If, for example, people compliment you on some aspect of your personality, you can't accept the compliment, because they don't know "the real you."
- *Jumping to conclusions:* You make a negative interpretation even though there are no definite facts that convincingly support your conclusion. Two of these conclusion-jumpers are listed below:

Mind reading: You arbitrarily conclude that someone is reacting negatively to you without bothering to check it out.

The Fortune Teller Error: You have some method of knowing that things will turn out negatively, such as, "Bad things always happen in threes."

- *Magnification (catastrophizing) or minimization*: You exaggerate the importance of things (such as a typo on an important paper you have written), or you shrink things until they appear inconsequential (So what if you are 20 pounds overweight? You still don't qualify as morbidly obese!).

- *Emotional reasoning*: You assume that emotions are good indicators of how things really are: "If I feel a sense of dread, that means something bad is going to happen."

Even though we all can identify with some of these cognitive distortions, anyone who constantly makes sense of events this way is just not thinking straight. Beck urges his clients to come up with the evidence for any such beliefs and, in the absence of evidence, proposes that the beliefs must be abandoned.

Donald Meichenbaum has worked from a cognitive-constructivist perspective with clients. He developed a technique, known as "stress inoculation," in which clients worked to develop coping strategies for when anticipated problems might occur (Sharf, 2004). Meichenbaum's approach stressed the quality of the relationship between counselor and client, along with keeping the main focus on the interpersonal style of clients that create difficulties in their relationships.

Meichenbaum also employed what he called the "Columbo" attitude, after a TV detective character who always acted as if he knew nothing until the facts begin to pile up. His style was less confrontive than the other two cognitive therapists, though it also was seen as a brief approach. In a personal communication (2006), Meichenbaum jokingly stated that the secret to becoming an effective brief therapist was to be an expert. He said that the difference between a novice and an expert counselor is that an expert knows how to carefully select the clients who are likely to be successful. Actually, Meichenbaum's "secret" is just another example of his wonderful sense of humor, but, as in any joke, there is an important grain of truth in his words.

Like Columbo, you can know nothing about your clients' worlds in advance of meeting them. However, you do have general knowledge of people and the expertise for knowing how to create the conditions that are most likely to contribute to their success in counseling. In other words, you have a theory that will drive your behaviors and serve to make your approach more efficient.

Implications of These Ideas for the Counselor

These ideas have important implications for your work with clients.

- Your theoretical perspective may emphasize deep psychological dynamics, fundamental issues of human existence, and complex behaviors, but your default option can still be using brief counseling.

- Different brief counseling and therapy approaches may differ in emphasis and nuance, but they share fundamental commonalities.

- There is nothing so practical as a good theory.

TOOLS

Using Theory as a Tool

While we normally think of tools as being *techniques,* some time ago Lambert (1992) found that technique accounts for no more than 15 percent of outcome variance in counseling. So, what is it that makes a difference in counseling? When clients are asked about the factors that have been most helpful to them, they "rarely mention therapeutic interventions or techniques." "Instead, clients typically respond with statements such as 'My therapist listened to me' or 'I felt as though the therapist understood me'" (Bertolino & O'Hanlon, 2002, p. 17).

In this book, we have offered a number of techniques borrowed mostly from other forms of brief counseling. Used in a timely fashion with the right clients, these techniques can prove useful. However, more than anything, it is your guiding theory that will assist you in your work with clients. You cannot capture the heart of successful counseling in a cookbook, flowchart, or protocol. In your encounter with a client, you cannot rely on a recipe, formula, or procedure. Central to your theory should be the relationship you attempt to establish with your clients.

In addition to this I–Thou meeting of two people in relationship, you need to create a map of the territory you will traverse together with your client. As we have stated, the map can never contain an accurate representation of the route you will follow, but the map is a *theory* about how to choose among various paths along the way. As Teyber (2006) pointed out, while personal experience, common sense, good judgment, and intuition are important assets, "in order for the therapist to be effective with a wide range of people and problems, these valuable human qualities need to be wed to a conceptual framework" (p. 4).

Scientists often consider a good theory to be one that allows hypothesis testing. During the process of your work with clients, you are constantly developing hypotheses about clients, yourself, and your therapeutic relationships. You also are hypothesizing possible strategies for achieving your therapeutic goals. These hypotheses allow you to test out behaviors that might prove useful and, if any one of them doesn't work, to quickly come up with a different hypothesis. To paraphrase what Cheshire Cat said to Alice when she visited Wonderland, if you don't have in mind where you want to end up, it doesn't matter much which way you go—you'll get somewhere if only you travel long enough. There are two problems with the Cheshire Cat's advice: First, you don't want to do a lot of unnecessary traveling, since you are attempting to work briefly. Second, ending up just anywhere might not be a good thing for your clients. You should at least have a general direction in mind. And you need a flexibly teleonomic map of this uncertain territory.

Mapmaking, in this sense, is a collaborative effort between you and your client. The client contributes his or her personal experience and the desire to reach a certain goal. You bring your theory and expertise to help refine the direction for travel. Then, together, you head off with a pretty good idea of where you want to end up. In order to possess such a map, you need to develop a theory that will be centered on your answers to two main questions: What is an effective therapeutic relationship? and How does change happen? Below, we will summarize the answers we have offered in this book so you can reflect on how much of it fits your own evolving theory.

The Theory of Relationship

Each client with whom you come in contact is a different person, a walking culture all his or her own. "All individuals are, in some respects, like no other individuals" (Sue & Sue, 2003, p. 12). While we are all humans, we differ in that we have grown up in dissimilar contexts that have socially constructed many of our meanings. We also have had a lifetime of unique personal experiences that have further contributed to our own construction of reality. You connect more easily to those clients whose background and experiences seem familiar than those who have been raised in cultures and meaning systems unlike your own. But even those clients with whom you can easily identify are going to be different enough that you must adopt the "I'm not from around here" stance.

Yalom (2002) asserted that accurate empathy was the most important aspect of being with your client. He called it "looking out the patient's window" (p. 17). Without truly caring for your client and doing your best to empathically understand what it is like to be that client, all your other efforts will fall short of optimal success. Caring, in this sense, as we previously stated, means having regard and respect for the humanity of your client. You do not have to accept everything about this person, but you should, at bottom, positively regard him or her as a person with dignity who possesses inner resources that can be illuminated and utilized to turn his or her life into a better existence.

It is one thing to understand your client's plight, but, if your client never knows that you empathize, then your finely tuned receptive skills are useless. You must communicate to the client that you "get it" and, if you *don't* yet get it, that you truly wish to try. By feeding back what the client has said, by highlighting the client's metaphors, and by communicating your grasp of the client's meanings, you begin to blend the client's world with your own, so that cultural differences are less of an impediment to your work together.

Unless there is an emotional connection between you and your client, and unless the client is emotionally connected to the content being discussed, your relationship will be arid and unrewarding for both parties. When you acknowledge the client's concerns without negative judgment, you will begin to be seen as a safe person. When the client starts to feel understood, you will begin to be trusted with content the client has previously deemed too shameful to divulge. The distance between you and your client will diminish, and you will have developed a working or therapeutic alliance.

No one ever "motivates" another person. Even in the Motivational Interviewing (MI) approach (discussed earlier) you will notice that it is respect for the client's level of motivation that does the trick, rather than some subversive method of instigating motivation in the client. Likewise, no one ever "empowers" another person. You can craft conversations in which clients begin to get a sense of their own latent power, so long as you know that the very best ideas, solutions, and advice come from within the client. Good brief counseling works from the inside out. You elicit, pull for, and call out the resilience and resources that are already in the client. Clients motivate and empower themselves.

Finally, when you are able to be an authentic person with your client rather than hiding behind your role, your client will also begin to emerge from behind a protective façade. The resulting relationship will be unlike any your client has ever experienced and will set the conditions for change.

Theory of Change as a Tool

Briggs and Peat (1989), early writers in the new science of change, asked us to imagine a river in the heat of summer flowing smoothly along. The river is a metaphor representing the inexorable flow and change of life. This river encounters a large rock in its center but flows smoothly past the obstruction, relatively undisturbed. The rock presents no impediment or turmoil in the flow of the river. If we were to put some drops of colored dye in the river above the rock, we would see that the flow lines that are produced will stream past the rock without diverging from each other and without mixing up in any way. *We might consider this situation a metaphor for our optimal psychological comfort.*

But as summer turns to fall, the rains come, at first in a gentle drizzle. Because of the increase of water in the river and the slightly faster current, small vortices (small circles of water) form, just past the obstructing rock, but remain fairly stable for some time. The rock has now become a slight problem for the flow. *Let this condition stand for those times when we are going around in circles, being stressed and nagged by everyday life circumstances.*

As the rain clouds send down more precipitation, the water level elevates, the speed of the current escalates, and the vortices in the river become more rapid and begin to fluctuate periodically around the rock. The river is now becoming seriously disturbed. *We are now metaphorically beginning to experience the tumult that comes with the deterioration of our coping mechanisms in the face of increasing problems.*

With even more rain, the once circular patterns in the water begin to unravel. Now, the rapidly flowing river produces turbulence behind the rock so that the circular patterns have lost all order, and chaos has set in. *We are now in a state of confusion from which we urgently seek a new organization.* We might wish to return to the formerly gentle flowing state, but of course, this is impossible because that was upstream in our experience.

If you have witnessed this sort of phenomenon in rivers, you know that the increase from smooth flow, through circular vortices, to chaos, is a predictable event as energy is added. Scientific investigation of such happenings goes back at least to Leonardo De Vinci, who was fascinated by the process of change that evolves from order to turbulence. This type of change happens because a river is a dynamic, complex system of water molecules.

Another familiar example would be when you heat a pot of water on the stove. At first, seemingly intact bubbles rise from the bottom to the top and burst. But as the temperature rises, the boiling pattern eventually seems to have no order at all to it. Turn off the heat, and after a while there will be no discernable bubbles at all in the water. Likewise, a year of draught might cause our river to run dry. *Our river going dry is an apt metaphor for clients who see their lives heading for a dead end.*

So, what is the main point of the turbulent river metaphor? It is that most theories of change have been based on "classical" science, which tended to view everything as a mechanism—originally a clock. Furthermore, people who attempted to map the process of change thought that it proceeded in a smooth, continuous line, and could be plotted on coordinates of a grid. This flow of change could be placed along a line between

x and y axes representing time and space. All objects were thought to move because some original force had motivated them to do so. And if something seemed to be wrong in the system (the complicated clockworks), a good technician could fix it by discovering the cause of the problem. Isn't this the metaphor for how many people see counseling? But a turbulent river dealing with an obstructive rock and an increase of rainfall is not a mechanism in this sense, nor can its process of change be plotted on an x/y grid. No one can predict where all those turbulent H_2O molecules will end up, nor could their change process be controlled in any way.

Clocks, as well as most other machines, are very complicated, but they are not complex. In order for a system to be complex, each of the parts must interact and each must be affected by all the others.

Think of a family. It is a complex system in which the behavior of any single member is likely to affect everyone in the family. If father loses his job, mother gets cancer, son fails in school, or daughter turns up pregnant, everyone is affected and the order of the entire system might be sent into chaos. But even in the face of such disorder, the system immediately begins the work of reorganizing itself and restoring its order. The river may find a calm pattern of flow again, but that will be downstream from its turbulence, and everything will have changed in the relationship of its constituent molecules. While flowing rivers and boiling pots of water are complex systems, still they are not living systems. Living systems—like people and families—exist in a way that is even more complex and less predictable than lifeless systems. Furthermore, when living systems undergo change, they know it, and their change becomes feedback for further change. We call this psychological "growth," or learning.

As counselors, growth and learning are what we hope to stimulate in our clients. The flowing river can serve as a helpful metaphor as you to begin to think of this process. Your job in promoting change is to perturb the clients' system of thought by adding emotional energy and deconstructing the story they are telling. You create turbulence knowing that this will promote change in the form of new patterns of thought or behavior. Change, like the flow of the river, is always happening, but you can accelerate it with brief methods.

A counselor operating within the change assumptions of the "classical" paradigm may try to dam the river, divert its course, or maybe build some levees to contain it. (We know how useful this was when hurricane Katrina hit New Orleans.) Because of the mechanistic and reductionistic assumptions of classical science, the counselor is cast in the role of "Mr. or Ms. Fix-It," whose job it is to find the problem and, by the use of masterful techniques, solve it. This method is simply inadequate for dealing with complex, living, self-organizing systems like humans. Often, it doesn't even work for nonliving complex systems. Fighting against chaos is a failed strategy. Chaos and order are two sides of the same coin—they are in a dialectical relationship—and human systems exist in perpetual nonequilibrium at the edge of chaos. This is not a bad thing. This principle of change was known long before modern science attempted to turn living systems into mechanisms. "Ancient peoples believed that the forces of chaos and order were part of an uneasy tension, a harmony of sorts. They thought of chaos as something immense and creative" (Briggs & Peat, 1989, p. 19).

We have, no doubt, pushed our river metaphor far beyond its useful limits, but we hope that, by our explaining our change theory this way, you will intuitively grasp how change in living systems cannot be explained by the tenets of classical science. Likewise, the "find the problem and fix it" strategy is ultimately a failed pursuit for helping people change. You cannot really find the offending part and replace it in a living psychological system.

We will leave the discussion of this theory of change with one more metaphorical example. It comes from John Casti (1995). When John was in school at the University of Southern California, he went to a football game between USC and Notre Dame. Arriving at his seat in the student section of the stadium, he found a manila envelope with a number of large colored cards in it. In addition, there were instructions telling him that, when a certain signal was given, he was to hold up the red card, on another signal he was to flash the white card, and so on. He assumed that if everyone in the student section followed the instructions, people on the other side of the stadium, and the TV cameras, would see a gigantic caricature of Tommy Trojan or a Fighting Irishman or whatever image the signaling person was calling for. The entire student section was a system.

At one point during this activity, Casti realized he could never know at any moment which image the system was displaying; he would have had to jump outside the system to be able to do that. He wrote, "Down at the level of the system itself (the level of the individual [card] flashers like me), there was no recognizable pattern but only a seemingly senseless holding up of one colored card after another"(p. 19).

Within a system, there is no discernable pattern. There is only activity. However, if you are a counselor who has a good theory of change, you are, in effect, sitting across from the student section, and its various patterns are obvious to you. Your client can't see them, but you can because you are outside the system. This position gives you the opportunity to call for different patterns. Unlike the capabilities of the student-section system of colored cards, your client's system can self-organize. The client may not at first "get the picture" but will eventually create a new pattern that offers a better image of success.

USING THIS TOOL

Form a group with two colleagues. Describe some current perplexing or confusing situation in which you find yourself involved. The other two members offer you descriptions of the patterns that emerge for them from their more distant perspectives. Once you have completed this process, rotate roles until each person has had an opportunity.

What Kind of Counseling Will You Do?

We view the type of brief counseling that we are promoting in this book as an integrative method that is founded on many of the features of time-limited counseling and on some aspects that are occasionally overlooked. The activity of the brain, the importance of emotions and their arousal, the crucial elements of empathic listening and acknowledgment, the importance of grasping clients' meanings, the idea of attaching emotions to success through encouragement, and the need to perturb client thinking are all ideas that appear in other approaches but are rarely consolidated into a single theory.

Our students often ask us if we believe that a brief approach to counseling such as this one works for all clients and all concerns. Our answer is an emphatic "No!" We begin with all our clients by employing this brief model as our default. However, as one of the previously mentioned brief attitudes states, "If it's not working, do something different." We do believe that good counseling must always include the elements of the relationship described above, but you must modify the techniques depending on what is going on with your clients. You will have to be the judge as to whether this brief approach to counseling continues to be appropriate for your particular client.

Our analysis of the various types of counseling you are likely to engage in, along with the roles you will be asked to fill, suggests that you should be able to perform efficiently so long as you have a good theory and are able to establish a working relationship with clients. As you saw in the Ideas section of this chapter, there are many forms of brief counseling, and, despite their ostensible differences, they have much in common.

In order to help you begin the task of developing your personal theory of counseling, we suggest that there are five main approaches to helping that are emphasized by the theories in the Ideas section of this chapter. Below, we list what we call the "Five Ps" of counseling. We think they represent most of the modalities of counseling and therapy, and we have found ourselves employing all of them at one time or another. No matter which of the roles, indicated by the Five Ps, you will be enacting, your well-considered theories of the relationship and of change will always support you in your work.

THE FIVE "PS" OF COUNSELING

Palliation

Webster's New World Dictionary (1972) defines *palliate* as follows: "1. to lessen the pain or severity of without actually curing; alleviate; ease . . . 2. make appear less serious or offensive; excuse; extenuate . . ."

The role of the **counselor is "beneficent listener."** The palliation notion is that, if people can "get something off their chests" in the process of telling their stories, they will experience a cathartic release and develop greater self-knowledge that will help them to feel better or see more clearly. There is no necessary intention on the part of the counselor to facilitate a change in the client.

Programming

Webster's New World Dictionary (1972) defines *programming* as follows: ". . . 2. to prepare questions and answers for . . . 3. to plan a computer program for (a task, problem, etc.) . . . to furnish with a program . . ."

The role of the **counselor is "knowledge engineer."** The notion is that the counselor is an expert who knows the route to the resolution of a problem. Instruction and advice are thought to improve the client's condition. There is a clear goal-state that is known to the counselor and toward which the client is directed. This teleological approach is usually focused on thought or behavioral change. Techniques can be either explicit or subversive.

Parturition

Webster's New World Dictionary (1972) defines *parturient:* 1. giving birth . . . 3. coming forth with a discovery . . . "The role of the **counselor is "archeologist/midwife."** The notion is that people come needing to make something unconscious conscious. Repressed traumatic events in their past have not come into awareness so that they can be worked through. Patterns of resistance or transference are clues to the location of buried psychological events. A moment of insight or an epiphany may spur the person toward change. Clients give birth to parts of themselves that have previously remained dormant.

Perturbation

Webster's New World Dictionary (1972) defines *perturb* as, "2. to cause disorder or confusion in; unsettle . . . ," and *perturbation* as, "an irregularity in the orbit of a heavenly body caused by the attraction of a body . . . other than the one around which it orbits . . ."

The role of the **counselor is "strategic challenger."** The notion is that people repeat self-defeating behaviors and thoughts, and they need to be prevented from their "repetition compulsions." Once they are knocked off orbit by a perturbing idea, they will create a more productive path for themselves, a better trajectory. The article of faith is that the client's reorganization will contain more possibilities than previous patterns of thought or behavior that had led them around in circles.

Participation

Webster's New World Dictionary (1972) defines *participate:* "to have or take part or share with others (in some activity, enterprise, etc.) . . ."

The role of the **counselor is "fellow traveler."** The notion is that counselors cannot be effective if they stand outside the sphere of the client's concerns. This is the I–Thou relationship in which both participants must journey through "the dark night of the soul" together. Sometimes the journey is just as important as the destination, because enduring tribulation with another person restores one's faith in self and humankind. Both parties are changed by the experience.

SUMMARY

In this final chapter, you read about specific brief approaches, such as Motivational Interviewing, brief Gestalt therapy, time-limited existential therapy, brief psychodynamic therapy, brief behavior therapy, and brief cognitive-behavioral therapy. You also considered some of the exciting developments toward integration of these approaches. Your personal theory is a practical tool that provides a conceptual map for your counseling and therapy work. In order to help you begin the task of developing your personal theory of counseling, we suggested that there are five main approaches to helping that are emphasized by the existing theories.

SEGUE TO YOUR OWN NEXT CHAPTER

As we discussed in Chapter 11, brief counseling is fundamentally an attitude. You may recall a saying that was popularized in the movie *Dead Poets Society*. The slogan was *carpe diem,* or, literally, "seize the day." One of the important themes of this book has been to recognize that you must make the most of whatever limited time you have been allotted to work with a counseling client. Of course, you can apply this perspective to a great deal more than the development of your counseling skills. It's also a great way to view your entire counseling training, career, and perhaps even your passage through life itself. We encourage you to remain resolute in your commitment to not only "seize the day" but to seize your future as you continue your personal and professional journey.

Resource

Association for Counselor Education and Supervision (ACES)
866-815-ACES (2237)
www.acesonline.net

The ACES website offers information on publications, conferences, training opportunities, relevant research, innovative practices, and ethical standards regarding the professional preparation and supervision of counselors.

REFERENCES

Adams, J. F., Piercy, F. P., & Jurich, J. A. (1991). Effects of solution-focused therapy's "Formula First Session Task" on compliance and outcome in family therapy. *Journal of Marital and Family Therapy, 17*, 277–290.

American Psychiatric Association (2000) *Diagnostic and Statistical Manual* (Fourth Edition-Text Revision) Arlington, VA: American Psychiatric Association.

Andersen, T. (1991). *The reflecting team.* New York: W. W. Norton.

Andersen, T. (1997). Researching client–therapist relationships: A collaborative study for informing therapy. *Journal of Systemic Therapies, 16*(2), 125–134.

Anderson, W. T. (1990). *Reality isn't what it used to be: Theatrical politics, ready-to-wear religion, global myths, primitive chic, and other wonders of the postmodern world.* San Francisco: Harper Collins.

Aspinwall, L. G. & Staudinger, U. M. (2003) *A psychology of human strengths: Fundamental questions and future directions for a positive psychology.* Washington, DC: American Psychological Association.

Bak, P. (1996). *How nature works: The science of self-organized criticality.* New York: Springer-Verlag.

Bandura, A. (1977). Self-efficacy: Toward a unifying theory of behavioral change. *Psychological Review, 84*, 191–215.

Bateson, G. (1972). *Steps to an ecology of mind.* New York: Ballantine Books.

Bateson, G. (1979). *Mind and nature: A necessary unity.* Toronto: Bantam Books.

Beck, A. T. (2005). The current state of cognitive therapy: A 40 year perspective. *Archives of General Psychiatry, 62*, 953–959.

Becvar, D. S., & Becvar, R. J. (2003). *Family therapy: A systemic integration* (5th ed.). Boston: Allyn & Bacon.

Becvar, D. S., & Becvar, R. J. (2006). *Family therapy: A systematic integration* (6th ed.). Boston: Pearson.

Becvar, R. J., Canfield, B. S., & Becvar, D. S. (1997). *Group work: Cybernetic, constructivist, and social constructionist perspectives.* Denver: Love Publishing.

Benjamin, A. (1987). *The helping interview: With case illustrations.* Boston: Houghton Mifflin.

Berg, I. K. (1991). *Solution-focused approach to family based services.* Milwaukee: Brief Family Therapy Center.

Berg, I. K. (1994). *Family-based services: A solution-focused approach.* New York: W. W. Norton.

Berg, I. K., & de Shazer, S. (1993). Making numbers talk: Language in therapy. In S. Friedman (Ed.), *The new language of change: Constructive collaboration in psychotherapy* (pp. 5–24). New York: Guilford.

Bergin, A. E., & Garfield, S. L. (1994). *Handbook of psychotherapy and behavior change* (4th ed.). New York: John Wiley & Sons.

Berlyne, D. E. (1960). *Conflict, arousal and curiosity.* New York: McGraw-Hill.

Berne, E. (1964). *Games people play: The psychology of human relationships.* New York: Grove Press.

Berscheid, E. (2003). The human's greatest strength: Other humans. In L. G. Aspinwall & U. M. Staudinger (Eds.), *A psychology of human strengths: Fundamental questions and future directions for a positive psychology* (pp. 37–47). Washington, DC: American Psychological Association.

Bertolino, B., & O'Hanlon, B. (2002). *Collaborative, competency-based counseling and therapy.* Boston: Allyn & Bacon.

Blackmore, S. (2003). Consciousness in meme machines. In O. Holland (Ed.), *Machine consciousness* (pp. 19–30). Charlottesville, VA: Imprint Academic.

Blakeslee, S. (2006). *Cells that read minds. New York Times* online, retrieved January 31, 2006 from http://www.nytimes.com/2006/01/10/science/10mirr.html

Bloom, B. L. (1997). *Planned short-term psychotherapy: A clinical handbook* (2nd ed.). Boston: Allyn & Bacon.

Blume, T. W. (2006). *Becoming a family counselor: A bridge to family therapy and practice.* New York: Wiley.

Bohart, A. C. & Greenberg (1997) Empathy reconsidered: New Directions in Psychotherapy. Washington, D. C. American Psychological Association.

Bornstein, P. H., Krueger, H. K., & Cogswell, K. (1989). Principles and techniques of couples paradoxical therapy. In L. M. Ascher (Ed.), *Therapeutic paradox* (pp. 289–309). New York: Guilford.

Bowlby, J. (1969/1982). *Attachment and loss: Vol. 1. Attachment.* New York: Basic Books.

Briggs, J., & Peat, F. D. (1989). *Turbulent mirror: An illustrated guide to chaos theory and the science of wholeness.* New York: Harper & Row.

Budman, S. H. (1990). The myth of termination in brief therapy: Or, it ain't over till it's over. In J. K. Zeig & S. G. Gilligan (Eds.), *Brief therapy: Myths, methods and metaphors* (pp. 206–218). New York: Brunner/Mazel.

Bulkeley, K., & Bulkeley, P. (2005). *Dreaming beyond death: A guide to pre-death dreams and visions.* Boston: Beacon Press.

Burns, D. D. (1989). *The feeling good handbook.* New York: William Morrow & Company.

Burr, V. (2003). *Social constructionism.* London: Routledge.

Butler, W. R., & Powers, K. V. (1996). Solution-focused grief therapy. In S. D. Miller, M. A. Hubble, & B. L. Duncan (Eds.), *Handbook of solution-focused brief therapy* (pp. 228–247). San Francisco: Jossey-Bass.

Cade, B., & O'Hanlon, W. H. (1993). *A brief guide to brief therapy.* New York: W. W. Norton.

Calhoun, L. G., & Tedeschi, R. G. (Eds.) (2006). *Handbook of posttraumatic growth: Research and practice.* Mahwah, NJ: Erlbaum.

Capra, F. (1996). *The web of life: A new scientific understanding of living systems.* New York: Anchor Books.

Caruth, E., & Ekstein, R. (1966). Interpretation within the metaphor. *Journal of the American Academy of Psychiatry, 5,* 35–45.

Casti, J. L. (1995). *Complexification: Explaining a paradoxical world through the science of surprise.* New York: Harper Perennial.

Chessick, R. D. (1999). *Emotional illness and creativity: A psychoanalytic and phenomenologic study.* Madison, CT: International Universities Press.

Clark, D. J. (2005). A solution-focused brief therapist's perspective on Ruth. In G. Corey (Ed.), *Case approach to counseling and psychotherapy* (6th ed., pp. 251–259). Belmont, CA: Thomson-Brooks/Cole.

Combs, A. W., & Avila, D. L. (1985). *Helping relationships: Basic concept for the helping professions* (3rd ed.). Boston: Allyn & Bacon.

Cooper, T. C. (1998). Teaching idioms. *Foreign Language Annals, 31,* 255–266.

Cooperrider, D. L., Sorensen, P. F. J., Whitney, D., & Yaeger, T. F. (Eds.). (2000). *Appreciative inquiry: Rethinking human organization toward a positive theory of change.* Champaign, IL: Stipes.

Cooperrider, D. L., & Whitney, D. (1999). *Appreciative inquiry.* San Francisco: Berrett-Koehler Communications.

Corey, G. (1991). Invited commentary on macrostrategies for delivery of mental health counseling services. *Journal of Mental Health Counseling, 13,* 51–57.

Corey, G. (2005). *Theory and practice of counseling and psychotherapy* (7th ed.). Belmont, CA: Brooks/Cole—Thompson Learning.

Corey, M. S., & Corey, G. (2007). *Becoming a helper* (5th ed.). Belmont, CA: Thomson-Brooks/Cole.

Cowan, E. W. (2005). *Ariadne's thread: Case studies in the therapeutic relationship.* Boston: Lahaska Press.

Cowan, E. W., & Presbury, J. H. (2000). Meeting client resistance and reactance with reverence. *Journal of Counseling and Development, 78,* 411–419.

Cozolino, L. J. (2002). *The neuroscience of psychotherapy: Building and rebuilding the human brain.* New York: W. W. Norton.

Csikszentmihalyi, M. (1993). *The evolving self: A psychology for the third millennium.* New York: Harper Collins.

Cunningham, S. (1985, May). Humanists celebrate gains, goals. *APA Monitor,* pp. 16, 18.

Curry, M. R. (2000) Wittgenstein and the fabric of everyday life. In M. Crang & N. Thrift (Eds.) *In thinking space.* London: Routledge 89–113.

Damasio, A. (1994). *Descartes' error: Emotion, reason, and the human brain.* New York: G. P. Putnam's Sons.

Damasio, A. (2003). *Looking for Spinoza: Joy, sorrow, and the feeling brain.* London: Heinemann.

Davidson, R. J. (1993). Parsing affective space: Perspectives from neuropsychology and psychophysiology. *Neuropsychology, 7,* 464–475.

Davies, L. (2004). *Education and conflict: Complexity and chaos.* New York: Routledge Falmer.

Davis, M. H. (1994). *Empathy: A social psychological approach.* Madison, WI: Brown & Benchmark.

Dawkins, R. (1976). *The selfish gene.* New York: Oxford University Press.

Day, S. X. (2004). *Theory and design in counseling and psychotherapy.* Boston: Lahaska Press.

Deikman, A. J. (1982). *The observing self: Mysticism and psychotherapy.* Boston: Beacon Press.

DeJong, M. (2004). Metaphor and the mentoring process. *Child & Youth Care Forum, 33,* 3–17.

DeJong, P., & Berg, I. K. (1998). *Interviewing for solutions.* Pacific Grove, CA: Brooks/Cole.

DeJong, P., & Berg, I. K. (2002). *Interviewing for solutions* (2nd ed.). Pacific Grove, CA: Brooks/Cole.

Dembski, W. A., & Ruse, M. (2006). *Debating design: From Darwin to DNA.* New York: Cambridge University Press.

Dennett, D. C. (1991). *Consciousness explained.* Boston: Little, Brown.

de Shazer, S. (1982). *Patterns of brief family therapy: An ecosystemic approach.* New York: Guilford.

de Shazer, S. (1984). The death of resistance. *Family Process, 23,* 11–17.

de Shazer, S. (1985). *Keys to solution in brief therapy.* New York: W. W. Norton.

de Shazer, S. (1988). *Clues: Investigating solutions in brief therapy.* New York: W. W. Norton.

de Shazer, S. (1991). *Putting difference to work.* New York: W. W. Norton.

de Shazer, S. (1998). Personal communication.

Dickinson, E (1960). *Complete poems.* T. H. Johnson (Ed.) Boston: Little, Brown, PSI 541. A1 1960.

Dobbs, D. (2006, April/May). A revealing reflection: Mirror neurons are providing stunning insights into everything from how we learn to walk to how we empathize with others. *Scientific American Mind,* pp. 22–27.

Dobbs, D. (2006, February/March). Mastery of emotions. *Scientific American* Mind, 44–49.

Dolan, Y. M. (1985). *A path with a heart: Ericksonian utilization with resistant and chronic clients.* New York: Brunner/Mazel.

Draganski, B., Gaser, C., Busch, V., Schuierer, G., Bogdahn, U., & May, A. (2004). Neuroplasticity: Changes in grey matter induced by training. *Nature, 427,* 311–312.

Duncan, B. L., Hubble, M. A., & Miller, S. D. (1997, July/August). Stepping off the throne. *The Family Therapy Networker,* 22–33.

Dunlap, K. (1928). A revision of the fundamental law of habit fomation. *Science, 67,* 360–362.

Echterling, L. G., Cowan, E. W., Evans, W. F., Staton, A. R., McKee, J. E., Presbury, J. H., & Stewart, A. L. (2008). *Thriving! A manual for students in the helping professions.* Boston: Lahaska/Houghton Mifflin.

Echterling, L. G., Presbury, J. H., & McKee, J. E. (2005). *Crisis intervention: Promoting resilience and resolution in troubled times.* Upper Saddle River, NJ: Merrill/Prentice Hall.

Egan, G. (2006). *Essentials of skilled helping: Managing problems, developing opportunities.* Belmont, CA: Thomson Higher Education.

Egan, G. (2002). *The skilled helper: A problem-management and opportunity-development approach to effective helping* (7th ed.). Belmont, CA: Brooks/Cole.

Egan, G. (2007). *The skilled helper: A problem-management and opportunity-development approach to effective helping* (8th ed.). Belmont, CA: Brooks/Cole.

Ehrenwald, J. (1986). *Anatomy of genius: Split brains and global minds.* New York: Human Sciences Press.

Ellenberger, H. F. (1958). A clinical introduction to psychiatric phenomenology and existential analysis. In R. May, E. Angel, & H. F. Ellenberger (Eds.), *Existence: A new dimension in psychiatry and psychology* (pp. 92–124). New York: Clarion Books.

Ellis, A. (1982). Psychoneurosis and anxiety problems. In R. Grieger & I. Z. Grieger (Eds.), *Cognition and emotional disturbance* (pp. 17–45). New York: Human Sciences Press.

Ellis, A. (2001). *Feeling better, getting better, and staying better.* Atascadero, CA: Impact.

Emmons, R. A. (1999). *The psychology of ultimate concerns: Motivation and spirituality in personality.* New York: Guilford.

Epston, D., & White, M. (1995). Termination as a rite of passage: Questioning strategies for a therapy of inclusion. In R. A. Neimeyer & M. J. Mahoney (Eds.), *Constructivism in psychotherapy* (pp. 339–354). Washington, DC: American Psychological Association.

Erickson, M. (1954). Pseudo-orientation in time as a hypnotic procedure. *Journal of Clinical and Experimental Hypnosis, 2,* 261–283.

Erickson, M. H. (1967). The confusion technique. In J. Haley (Ed.), *Advanced techniques of hypnosis and therapy.* New York: Grune & Stratton.

Erickson, M. H. (1975). The varieties of double bind. *American Journal of Clinical Hypnosis, 8,* 57–65.

Erickson, M. H., & Rossi, E. L. (1973/1980). A taped dialogue. In E. L. Rossi (Ed.), *The collected papers of Milton H. Erickson* (Vol. 4). New York: Irvington.

Erickson, M. H., Rossi, E. L., & Rossi, S. (1976). *Hypnotic realities.* New York: Irvington.

Erickson, M. H., Rossi, E. L., & Rossi, S. I. (1976). *Hypnotic realities.* New York: John Wiley & Sons.

Erikson, E. H. (1964). *Insight and responsibility.* New York: W. W. Norton.

Fang-Ru, Y., Shuang-Luo, Z., & Wen-Feng, L. (2005). Comparative study of solution-focused brief therapy (SFBT) combines with paroxetine in the treatment of obsessive-compulsive disorder. *Chinese Mental Health Journal, 19,* 288–290.

Fernandez-Ballesteros, R. (2003). Light and dark in the psychology of human strengths: The example of psychogerontology. In L. G. Aspinwall & U. M. Staudinger (Eds.), *A psychology of human strengths: Fundamental questions and future directions for a positive psychology* (pp. 131–147). Washington, DC: American Psychological Association.

Feshbach, N.D. (1978). Studies of empathic behavior in children. In B.A. Maher (Ed.) *Progress in experimental personality research* (Vol. 8, pp. 1–47) New York: Academic Press.

Fichter, L. S., & Baedke, S. J. (2006). *Evolutionary systems.* Harrisonburg, VA: James Madison University.

Fisch, R. (1982). Erickson's impact on brief psychotherapy. In J. K. Zeig (Ed.), *Ericksonian approaches to hypnosis and psychotherapy* (pp. 155–162). New York: Brunner/Mazel.

Fisch, R., & Schlanger, K. (1999). *Brief therapy with intimidating cases: Changing the unchangeable.* San Francisco: Jossey-Bass.

Fiske, D. W., & Maddi, S. R. (1961). *Functions of varied experience.* Homewood, IL: Dorsey Press.

Frank, J. D. (1985). Therapeutic components shared by all psychotherapies. In M. J. Mahoney & A. Freeman (Eds.), *Cognition and psychotherapy* (pp. 49–79). New York: Plenum Press.

Frederickson, B. L. (2002). Positive emotions. In C. R. Snyder & S. J. Lopez (Eds.), *Handbook of positive psychology* (pp. 120–134). New York: Oxford University Press.

Freire, E. S., Koller, S. H., & Piason, A. (2005). Person-centered therapy with impoverished, maltreated, and neglected children and adolescents in Brazil. *Journal of Mental Health Counseling, 27,* 225–237.

Freud, S. (1895/1911). *Project for scientific psychology: New introductory lectures in psychoanalysis:* Standard edition, 22, 3–182.

Freud, S. (1911). Formulations regarding the two principles in mental functioning. In *Collected papers* (Vol. 4). New York: Basic Books.

Freud, S. (1958). The unconscious. In J. Strachey (Ed. and Trans.), *The standard edition of the complete psychological works of Sigmund Freud* (Vol. 14, pp. 159–215). London: Hogarth Press. (Original work published 1915)

Freud, S. (1961). *Beyond the pleasure principle.* J. Strachey, Trans. New York: W. W. Norton. (Original work published 1922)

Friedman, S. (1997). *Time-effective psychotherapy: Maximizing outcomes in an era of minimized resources.* Boston: Allyn & Bacon.

Garfield, S. L. (1978). Research on client variables in psychotherapy. In S. L. Garfield & A. E. Bergin (Eds.), *Handbook of psychotherapy and behavior change.* New York: Wiley.

Gelso, C. J., & Fretz, B. R. (1992). *Counseling psychology.* Fort Worth: Harcourt Brace Javanovich.

Gendlin, E. T. (1996). *Focusing-oriented psychotherapy: A manual for the experiential method.* New York: Guilford.

Gergen, K. J. (1999). *An invitation to social construction.* Thousand Oaks, CA: Sage.

Gharajedaghi, J. (2006). *Systems thinking: Managing chaos and complexity: A platform for designing business architecture* (2nd ed.). Amsterdam: Elsevier.

Gilligan, S. (1997). Living in a post-Ericksonian world. In W. J. Matthews & J. H. Edgett (Eds.), *Current thinking and research in brief therapy: Solutions, strategies, narratives* (Vol. 1, pp. 1–23). New York: Brunner/Mazel.

Gladding, S. T. (2007). *Counseling: A comprehensive profession* (5th ed.). Upper Saddle River, NJ: Pearson/Merrill Prentice Hall.

Glasser, W. (1965). *Reality therapy: A new approach to psychiatry.* New York: Harper & Row.

Goldfried, M. R. (1980) Toward delineation of therapeutic change principles. American Psychologist, 35, 991–999.

Goleman, D. (1995). *Emotional intelligence.* New York: Bantam Books.

Goleman, D. (2005). *Emotional intelligence: Why it can matter more than I. Q.* (10th Anniversary ed.) New York: Bantam Books.

Gribbin, J. (2004). *Deep simplicity: Chaos, complexity and the emergence of life.* New York: Penguin Books.

Grinder, J., DeLozier, J., & Bandler, R. (1977). *Patterns of the hypnotic techniques of Milton H. Erickson, M. D.* (Vol. 2). Cupertino, CA: Meta Publications.

Gross, D. R., & Capuzzi, D. (2007). Developing relationships: From core dimensions to brief approaches. In D. Capuzzi & D. R. Gross (Eds.), *Counseling and psychotherapy: Theories and* interventions (4th ed., pp. 3–25). Upper Saddle River, NJ: Merrill/Prentice Hall.

Gross, J. J. (1998). The emerging field of emotion regulation: An integrative review. *Review of General Psychology, 2,* 271–299.

Haidt, J. (2003). Elevation and the positive psychology of morality. In C. L. M. Keyes & J. Haidt (Eds.), *Flourishing: Positive psychology and the life well-lived* (pp. 275–289). Washington, DC: American Psychological Association.

Haley, J. (1973). *Uncommon therapy: The psychiatric techniques of Milton H. Erickson, M. D.* New York: W. W. Norton.

Hanna, S. M. (2007). *The practice of family therapy: Key elements across models.* Belmont, CA: Thomson-Brooks/Cole.

Hanson, B. G. (1995). *General systems theory beginning with wholes.* New York: Taylor & Francis.

Harvey, J. C., & Katz, C. (1985). *If I'm so successful why do I feel like a fake: The imposter phenomenon.* New York: St. Martin's Press.

Hawkins, J. (with Blakeslee, S.) (2004). *On intelligence.* New York: Times Books/Henry Holt.

Hebb, D. O. (1946). On the nature of fear. *Psychological Review, 53*, 259–276.

Hergenhahn, B. R. (1992). *Introduction to the history of psychology.* Belmont, CA: Wadsworth.

Hoffman, L. (1985). Beyond power and control. *Family Systems Medicine, 4*, 381–396.

Hofstadter, D. (2006, February). Analogy as the core of cognition. Lecture conducted at the Stanford University Presidential Lecture in the Humanities and Arts, Stanford University. Retrieved Feb. 7, 2007 from http://prelectur .stanford.edu/lecturers/hofstadter.

Holland, J. H. (1998). *Emergence: From chaos to order.* Reading, MA: Perseus Books.

Houston, G. (2003). *Brief gestalt therapy.* London: Sage.

Hoyt, M. F. (1994). Characteristics of psychotherapy under managed care. *Behavioral Healthcare Tomorrow, 3*, 59–62.

Hunt, J. M. (1965). Intrinsic motivation and its role in psychological development. In D. Levine (Ed.), *Nebraska symposium on motivation* (Vol. 13). Lincoln: University of Nebraska Press.

Ickes, W. (1997). *Empathic accuracy.* New York: Guilford.

Ivey, A., Ivey, M., Meyers, J., & Sweeney, T. (2005). *Developmental counseling and therapy: Promoting wellness over the lifespan.* Boston: Lahaska/Houghton Mifflin.

Ivey, A. E., & Ivey, M. B. (2007). *Intentional interviewing and counseling: Facilitating client development in a multicultural society* (6th ed.). Pacific Grove, CA: Brooks/ Cole.

James, R. K., & Gilliland, B. E. (2005). *Crisis intervention strategies* (5th ed.). Belmont, CA: Thomson-Brooks/ Cole.

Janoff-Bulman, R. (1992). *Shattered assumptions: Towards a new psychology of trauma.* New York: The Free Press.

Janoff-Bulman, R. (2006). Schema-change perspective on posttraumatic growth. In L. G. Calhoun & R. G. Tedeschi (Eds.) *Handbook of posttraumatic growth: Research and practice* (pp. 81–99). Mahwah, NJ: Lawrence Erlbaum.

Jones, E. E., & Nisbett, R. E. (1971). *The actor and the observer: Divergent perceptions of the causes of behavior.* Morristown, NJ: General Learning Press.

Jordan, K., & Quinn, W. H. (1994). Session two outcome of the Formula First Session Task in problem- and solution-focused approaches. *The American Journal of Family Therapy, 22*, 3–16.

Jourard, S. M. (1971). *The transparent self.* New York: D. Van Nostrand.

Kahn, M. (1991). *Between therapist and client.* New York: W. H. Freeman.

Kauffman, S. (1995). *At home in the universe: The search for laws of self-organization and complexity.* New York: Oxford University Press.

Kemper, T. D. (2000). Social models in the explanation of emotions. In M. Lewis & J. M. Haviland-Jones (Eds.), *Handbook of emotions* (2nd ed., pp. 45–58). New York: Guilford.

Kessler, R. C., Davis, C. G., & Kendler, K. S. (1997). Childhood adversity and adult psychiatric disorder in the U. S. National Comorbidity Survey. *Psychological Medicine, 27*, 1101–1119.

Keyes, C. L. M. & Haidt, J. (2003) *Flourishing: Positive psychology and the life well-lived.* Washington, DC: American Psychological Association.

Kirsch, I. (1990). *Changing expectations: A key to effective psychotherapy.* Pacific Grove, CA: Brooks/Cole.

Kleinke, C. L. (1994). *Common principles of psychotherapy.* Pacific Grove, CA: Brooks/Cole.

Kline, W. B. (2003). *Interactive group counseling and therapy.* Upper Saddle River, NJ: Merrill/Prentice Hall.

Kolb, B., & Wishaw, I. (2003). *Fundamentals of neuropsychology* (5th ed.). New York: Worth.

Kolb, D. A. (1984). *Experiential learning: Experience as the source of learning and development.* Englewood Cliffs, NJ: Prentice Hall.

Kopp, S. (1985). *Even a stone can be a teacher: Learning and growing from the experiences of everyday life.* Los Angeles: Jeremy P. Tarcher.

Koss, M. P., Butcher, J. N., & Strupp, H. H. (1986) Psychotherapy methods in clinical research. *Journal of Consulting and Clinical Psychology, 54*, 60–67.

Kosslyn, S. M., & Koenig, O. (1995). *Wet mind: The new cognitive neuroscience.* New York: The Free Press.

Kral, R. (1986). Indirect therapy in the schools. In S. de Shazer & R. Kral (Eds.), *Indirect approaches in therapy: The family therapy collections* (Vol. 19). Rockville, MD: Aspen Press.

Kuang, M. (2001). *On metaphoring: A cultural hermeneutic.* Boston: Brill Academic Press.

Kurzweil, R. (1999). *The age of the spiritual machine.* New York: Penguin Books.

Lakoff, G. (1987). *Women, fire, and dangerous things: What categories reveal about the mind.* Chicago: The University of Chicago Press.

Lambert, M. J. (1992). Implications of outcome research for psychotherapy integration. In J. C. Norcross & M. R. Goldfried (Eds.), *Handbook of psychotherapy integration* (pp. 449). New York: Basic Books.

Lambert, M. J. (2004). *Handbook of psychotherapy and behavior change* (5th ed.). New York: Wiley.

Lambert, M. J., Shapiro, D. A., & Bergin, A. E. (1986). The effectiveness of psychotherapy. In S. L. Garfield & A. E. Bergin (Eds.), *Handbook of psychotherapy and behavior change* (3rd ed.). New York: Wiley.

Lankton, S. R., & Lankton, C. H. (1986). *Enchantment and intervention in family therapy: Training in Ericksonian approaches.* New York: Brunner/Mazel.

Larsen, J. T., Hemenover, S. H., Norris, C. J., & Cacioppo, J. T. (2003). Turning adversity to advantage: On the virtues of the coactivation of positive and negative emotions. In L. G. Aspinwall & U. M. Staudinger (Eds.), *A psychology of human strengths: Fundamental questions and future directions for a positive psychology* (pp. 211–225). Washington, DC: American Psychological Association.

Lazarus, A., & Fay, A. (2000). *I can if I want to*. New York: FMC Books.

Lazarus, R. S. (1991). *Emotion and adaptation*. New York: Oxford University Press.

Le Doux, J. (1996/1998). *The emotional brain: The mysterious underpinnings of emotional life*. New York: Simon & Schuster.

LeDoux, J. (2002). *The synaptic self: How our brains become who we are*. New York: Viking.

Lee, M. Y., & Mjelde-Mossey, L. A. (2004). Cultural dissonance among generations: A solution-focused approach with East Asian elders and their families. *Journal of Marital and Family Therapy, 30*, 497–513.

Lemley, B. (2006, August). Shiny happy people: Can you reach nirvana with the aid of science? *Discover*, 62–77.

Lemoire, S. J., & Chen, C. P. (2005). Applying person-centered counseling to sexual minority adolescents. *Journal of Counseling and Development, 83*, 146–154.

Levenson, R. & Ruef, A. (1992) Empathy: A physiological substitute. Journal of Personality and Social Psychology, 63, 2 (No page numbers)

Levenson, R. W., Ekman, P., Heider, K., & Friesen, W. V. (1992). Emotion and autonomic nervous system activity in the Minangkabau of West Sumatra. *Journal of Personality and Social Psychology, 62*, 972–988.

Lewin, R. (1999). *Complexity: Life at the edge of chaos*. (2nd ed.). Chicago: The University of Chicago Press.

Lewis, R. (2005). Individual counseling: Brief approaches. In D. Capuzzi & D. R. Gross (Eds.), *Introduction to the counseling profession* (4th ed., pp. 173–193). Boston: Allyn & Bacon.

Lipchik, E. (2002). *Beyond technique in solution-focused therapy: Working with emotions and the therapeutic relationship*. New York: Guilford.

Lipset, D. (1980). *Gregory Bateson: The legacy of a scientist*. Englewood Cliffs, NJ: Prentice Hall.

Loftus E. (1997, September). Creating false memories. *Scientific American*, 51–55.

Lozanov, G. (1978). *Suggestology and outlines of suggestopedy*. New York: Gordon & Breach.

Luborsky, L. (1984). *Principles of psychoanalytic psychotherapy*. New York: Basic Books.

Luborsky, L., & Crits-Cristoph, P. (1990). *Understanding transference*. New York: Basic Books.

Luborsky, L., Rosenthal, R., Deguer, L., Andrusyna, T. P., Berman, J. S., Levitt, J. T., Seligman, D. A., & Krause, E. D. (2002). The Dodo Bird verdict is alive and well—mostly. *Clinical Psychology: Science and Practice, 9*, 2–12.

Luborsky, L., Singer, B., & Luborsky, L. (1975). Comparative studies of psychotherapies: Is it true that "everyone has won and all must have prizes"? *Archives of General Psychiatry, 32*, 995–1008.

Lyddon, W. J., Clay, A. L., & Sparks, C. L. (2001). Metaphor and change in counseling. *Journal of Counseling and Development, 79*, 269–273.

Lynch, A. (1996). *Thought contagion: How belief spreads through society*. New York: Basic Books.

Lynch, G. (1997). The role of community and narrative in the work of the therapist: A post-modern theory of the therapist's engagement in the therapeutic process. *Counselling Psychology Quarterly, 10*, 353–363.

MacCormac, E. R. (1985). *A cognitive theory of metaphor*. Cambridge, MA: The MIT Press.

Magai, C., & Haviland-Jones, J. (2002). *The hidden genius of emotion: Lifespan transformations of personality*. New York: Cambridge University Press.

Mahoney, M. J. (1988). Rationalism and constructivism in clinical judgment. In D. C. Turk & P. Salovey (Eds.), *Reasoning, inference, and judgment in clinical psychology* (pp. 155–181). New York: The Free Press.

Mahoney, M. J. (1995). The modern psychotherapist and the future of psychotherapy. In B. Bonger & L. E. Beutler (Eds.), *Comprehensive textbook of psychotherapy: Theory and practice* (pp. 474–488). New York: Oxford University Press.

Mahoney, M. J., & Moes, A. J. (1997). Complexity and psychotherapy: Promising dialogues and practical issues. In F. Masterpasqua & P. A. Perna (Eds.), *The psychological meaning of chaos: Translating theory into practice* (pp. 177–198). Washington, DC: American Psychological Association.

Mann, J. (1973). *Time-limited psychotherapy*. Cambridge, MA: Harvard University Press.

Mann, J., & Goldman, R. (1982). *A casebook in time-limited psychotherapy*. New York: McGraw-Hill.

Martindale, C. (1981). *Cognition and consciousness*. Homewood, IL: Dorsey Press.

Maruyama, M. (1963). The second cybernetics: Deviation-amplifying mutual causal processes. *American Scientist, 5*, 164–179.

Maslow, A. H. (1968). *Toward a psychology of being*. New York: Van Nostrand.

Masterpasqua, F. (1997). Toward a dynamical developmental understanding of disorder. In F. Masterpasqua & P. A. Perna (Eds.), *The psychological meaning of chaos: Translating theory into practice* (pp. 23–39). Washington, DC: American Psychological Association.

Mayr, E. (1982). *The growth of biological thought: Diversity, evolution and inheritance.* Boston: Harvard University Press.

McAdams, D. P. (1988). *Power, intimacy, and the life story.* New York: Guilford.

McLeod, J. (2003). *An introduction to counselling* (3rd ed.). Buckingham, GB: Open University Press.

McNally, R. J., Bryant, R. A., & Ehlers, A. (2003). Does early psychological intervention promote recovery from posttraumatic stress? *Psychological Science in the Public Interest, 4,* 45–79.

Mearns, D., & Thorne, B. (2000). *Person-centered therapy today: New frontiers in theory and practice.* London: Sage.

Meichenbaum, D. (May 19, 2006). *Treatment of depression and suicide: A life-span perspective.* A workshop presented at James Madison University.

Meichenbaum, D. (Speaker). (1990). *Cognitive-behavior modification* (Cassette Recording C289-9). Phoenix, AZ: The Milton Erickson Foundation.

Merriam Webster's Collegiate Dictionary. (2007) http://www.m-w.com/dictionary/dis. Retrieved Feb. 2.

Messer, S. B., & Warren, C. S. (2001). Brief psychodynamic therapy. In R. J. Corsini (Ed.), *Handbook of innovative therapies.* (2nd ed., pp. 67–85). New York: Wiley.

Miller, G. (1997). *Becoming miracle workers: Language and meaning in brief therapy.* New York: Aldine de Gruyter.

Miller, S. (1996). *Solution-focused brief therapy.* Workshop given for the Virginia Counselors Association Convention, Williamsburg, VA.

Miller, S. D. (1995). *Solution-focused brief therapy: Focusing on "what works" in clinical practice.* Chicago: Miller.

Miller, W. R., & Rollnick, S. (2002). *Motivational interviewing: Preparing people for change* (2nd ed.). New York: Guilford.

Minsky, M. (2003). What comes after minds? In J. Brockman (Ed.), *The new humanists: Science at the edge* (pp. 197–214). New York: Barnes & Noble.

Modell, A. H. (2003). *Imagination and the meaningful brain.* Cambridge, MA: The MIT Press.

Moore, R., & Gillette, D. (1990). *King Warrior Magician Lover: Rediscovering the archetypes of the mature masculine.* San Francisco: Harper Collins.

Moursund, J., & Kenny, M. C. (2002). *The process of counseling and therapy* (4th ed.). Upper Saddle River, NJ: Prentice Hall.

Mozdzierz, F., Macchitelli, F., & Lisiecki, J. (1976). The paradox in psychotherapy: An Adlerian perspective. *Journal of Individual Psychology, 32,* 169–184.

Murphy, B. C., & Dillon, C. (2003). *Interviewing in action: Relationship, process, and change* (2nd ed.). Pacific Grove, CA: Brooks/Cole.

Neimeyer, R. A. (1993). Constructivist approaches to the measurement of meaning. In G. J. Neimeyer (Ed.), *Constructivist assessment: A casebook* (pp. 58–103). Newbury Park, CA: Sage.

Neimeyer, R. A. (2000). Narrative disruptions in the construction of the self. In R. A. Neimeyer & J. Raskin (Eds.), *Constructions of disorder* (pp. 207–242). Washington, DC: American Psychological Association.

Neimeyer, R. A. (2000). Searching for the meaning of meaning: Grief therapy and the process of reconstruction. *Death Studies, 24,* 541–558.

Neimeyer, R. A. (2006). Re-storying loss: Fostering growth in the posttraumatic narrative. In L. G. Calhoun & R. G. Tedeschi (Eds.), *Handbook of posttraumatic growth: Research and practice* (pp. 68–80). Mahwah, NJ: Erlbaum.

Neimeyer, R. A., & Stewart, A. E. (2000). Constructivist and narrative therapies. In C. R. Snyder & R. E. Ingram (Eds.). *Handbook of psychological change* (pp. 337–357). New York: Wiley.

Nichols, M. P., & Schwartz, R. C. (2006). *Essentials of family therapy* (3rd ed.). Boston: Allyn & Bacon.

Niederhoffer, K. G., & Pennebaker, J. W. (2002). Sharing one's story: On the benefits of writing or talking about emotional experience. In C. R. Snyder & S. J. Lopez (Eds.), *Handbook of positive psychology* (pp. 573–583). New York: Oxford University Press.

Nietzche, F. (1888/1968). Twilight of the idols, Harmondsworth, UK: Penguin.

Norcross, J. C., Beutler, L. E., & Levant, R. F. (2005). *Evidence-based practice in mental health: Debate and dialogue on the fundamental questions.* Washington, DC: American Psychological Association.

Norcross, J. C., & Goldfried, M. R. (2005). *Handbook of psychotherapy integration* (2nd ed.). New York: Oxford University Press.

Novaco, R. W., & Chemtob, C. M. (1998). Anger and trauma: Conceptualization, assessment and treatment. In V. M. Follette, J. I. Ruzek, & F. R. Abueg (Eds.), *Cognitive-behavioral therapies for trauma* (pp. 162–190). New York: Guilford.

Nugent, F. A., & Jones, K. D. (2005). *Introduction to the profession of counseling* (4th ed.). Upper Saddle River, NJ: Merrill/Prentice Hall.

Nunn, C. (2005). *De la Mettrie's ghost: The story of decisions.* New York: Macmillan.

Nyland, D., & Thomas, J. (1994, November/December). The economics of narrative. *The Family Therapy Networker,* pp. 38–39.

O'Connell, B. (2003). Introduction to the solution-focused approach. In B. O'Connell & S. Palmer (Eds.), *Handbook of solution-focused therapy* (pp. 1–11). London: Sage.

O'Connell, B., & Palmer, S. (2003). *Handbook of solution-focused therapy.* London: Sage.

O'Grady, R., & Brooks, D. (1988). Teleology and biology. In B. Weber, D. Depew, & J. Smith (Eds.), *Entropy, information, and evolution: New perspectives on physical and biological evolution* (pp. 247–269). Bradford, MA: MIT Press.

O'Hanlon, W., & Beadle, S. (1994). *A field guide to possibility land: Possibility therapy methods.* Omaha, NE: Possibility Press.

O'Hanlon, W. H. (1995, May). *Brief solution-oriented therapy.* Printed material presented at workshop. Front Royal, VA: Garrison House Seminars.

O'Hanlon, W. H., & Weiner-Davis, M. (1989). *In search of solutions: A new direction in psychotherapy.* New York: W. W. Norton.

Oltmanns, T. F., & Emery, R. E. (1998). *Abnormal psychology* (2nd ed.). Upper Saddle River, NJ: Prentice Hall.

Orlinsky, D. E., & Howard, K. I. (1986). Process and outcome in psychotherapy. In S. L. Garfield and A. E. Bergin (Eds.), *Handbook of psychotherapy and behavior change* (3rd ed., pp. 311–381). New York: Wiley.

Palmer, D. (1994). *Looking at philosophy: The unbearable heaviness of philosophy made lighter* (2nd ed.). Mountain View, CA: Mayfield.

Papp, P. (2005). The daughter who said no. In D. Wedding & R. J. Corsini (Eds.), *Case studies in psychotherapy* (4th ed., pp. 188–217). Belmont, CA: Thomson-Brooks/Cole.

Patterson, C. H., & Hidore, S. (1997). *Successful psychotherapy: A caring, loving relationship.* Northvale, NJ: Aronson.

Pedersen, C., & Seligman, M. (2004). *Character, strengths, and virtues: A handbook and classification.* Oxford: Oxford University Press.

Penn, P. (1982). Circular questioning. *Family Process, 21,* 267–279.

Perls, F. S. (1977). *The Gestalt approach: An eye witness to therapy.* Palo Alto: Science & Behavior Books.

Perls, F. S., Hefferline, R., & Goodman, P. (1951). *Gestalt therapy: Excitement and growth in human personality.* New York: Julian Press.

Peterson, C., & Seligman, M. E. P. (2004). *Character strengths and virtues: A classification and handbook.* Washington, DC: American Psychological Association.

Piaget, J. (1954). *The construction of reality in the child.* New York: Basic Books.

Piaget, J. (1970). Piaget's theory. In P. H. Mussen (Ed.), *Carmichael's manual of child psychology* (Vol. 1, pp. 702–732). New York: Wiley.

Pinker, S. (2002). *The blank slate: The modern denial of human nature.* New York: Viking.

Pollio, H. R., Barlow, J. M., Fine, H. J., & Pollio, M. R. (1977). *Psychology and the poetics of growth.* Hillsdale, NJ: Lawrence Erlbaum.

Polster, E., & Polster, M. (1973). *Gestalt therapy integrated: Contours of theory and practice.* New York: Vantage Books.

Posner, M. (2004). *Cognitive neuropsychology of attention.* New York: Guilford.

Presbury, J. H., McKee, J. E., & Echterling, L. G. (2007). Person-centered approaches. In H. T. Prout & D. H. Brown (Eds.), *Counseling and psychotherapy with children and adolescents* (4th ed., pp. 180–240). New York: John Wiley & Sons.

Prochaska, J. O., & DiClemente, C. C. (1984). *The transtheoretical approach: Crossing the traditional boundaries of therapy.* Homewood, IL: Dow Jones-Irwin.

Prochaska, J. O. & Norcross, J. C. (2003) Systems of psychotherapy: A transtheoretical analysis, (5th edition) Pacific Grove, CA Thomson-Brooks/Cole.

Prochaska, J. O., & Norcross, J. C. (2007). *Systems of psychotherapy: A transtheoretical analysis* (6th ed.). Belmont, CA: Thomson-Brooks/Cole.

Pudmenzky, A. (2004). Teleonomic creativity: An etiological analysis. Submitted for publication.

Ramachandran, V. S. (2004). *A brief tour of human consciousness: From imposter poodles to purple numbers.* New York: P. I. Press.

Ramachandran, V. S. (2005). Mirror neurons and imitation learning as the driving force behind "the great leap forward" in human evolution. Retrieved February 1, 2007 from http://www.edge.org/3rd_culture

Ramachandran, V. S., & Blakeslee, S. (1998). *Phantoms in the brain: Probing the mysteries of the human mind.* New York: William Morrow.

Reis, H. T., Collins, W. A., & Berscheid, E. (2000). The relationship context of human behavior and development. *Psychological Bulletin, 126,* 844–872.

Restak, R. (2003). *The new brain.* New York: Rodale.

Rice, F. P. (1995). *Human development: A life-span approach* (2nd ed.). Englewood Cliffs, NJ: Prentice Hall.

Rimé, B. (1995). Mental rumination, social sharing, and the recovery from emotional exposure. In J. W. Pennebaker (Ed.), *Emotion, disclosure, and health* (pp. 271–291). Washington, DC: American Psychological Association.

Rogers, C. R. (1951) Client-centered therapy: Its current practice, implications, and theory. Boston: Houghton Mifflin.

Rogers, C. R. (1961). *On becoming a person.* Boston: Houghton Mifflin.

Rogers, C. R. (1965). *Three approaches to psychotherapy.* [Pt 1, videorecording]/produced and directed by E. L. Shostrom. Corona Del Mar, CA: Psychological Films.

Rogers, C. R. (1969). *Freedom to learn.* Columbus, OH: Charles E. Merrill.

Rogers, C. R. (1980). *A way of being.* Boston: Houghton Mifflin.

Rogers, C. R. (1987). Comments on the issue of equality in psychotherapy. *Person-Centered Review, 1,* 257–259.

Rogers, C. R. (Commentator and Therapist), & Shostrom, E. L. (Producer/Director). (1965). *Three approaches to psychotherapy* [Pt. 1, videorecording]. Corona Del Mar, CA: Psychological Films.

Rollnick, S., & Miller, W. R. (1995). What is motivational interviewing? *Behavioral and Cognitive Psychotherapy, 23,* 325–334.

Rowan, J. (2001). *Ordinary ecstasy: The dialectics of humanistic psychology* (3rd ed.). East Sussex, UK: Brunner-Routledge.

Rychlak, J. F. (1980). Concepts of free will in modern psychological science. *The Journal of Mind and Behavior, 1,* 9–32.

Ryckman, R. M. (2004). *Theories of personality.* Belmont, CA: Wadsworth/Thomson.

Ryff, C. D., & Singer, B. (2003). Flourishing under fire: Resilience as a prototype of challenged thriving. In C. L. M. Keyes & J. Haidt (Eds.), *Flourishing: Positive psychology and the life well-lived* (pp. 15–36). Washington, DC: American Psychological Association.

Saleebey, D. (2001). *Human behavior and social environments: A biopsychological approach.* New York: Columbia University Press.

Salovey, P., Bedell, B. T., Detweiler, J. B., & Mayer, J. D. (2000). Current directions in emotional intelligence research. In M. Lewis & J. M. Haviland-Jones (Eds.), *Handbook of emotions* (2nd ed., pp. 504–520). New York: Guilford.

Schank, R. C. (1995). *Tell me a story: Narrative and intelligence.* Evanston, IL: Northwestern University Press.

Schmidt, J. J. (2002). *Intentional helping: A philosophy for proficient caring relationships.* Upper Saddle River, NJ: Merrill/Prentice Hall.

Schultz, D. P., & Schultz, S. E. (2000). *A history of modern psychology* (7th ed.). Fort Worth, TX: Harcourt Brace College.

Segal, L. (1986). *The dream of reality: Heinz von Foerster's constructivism.* New York: W. W. Norton.

Seligman, L. (2004). *Technical and conceptual skills for mental health professionals.* Upper Saddle River, NJ: Merrill/Prentice Hall.

Seligman, M. E. P. (1974). *Helplessness: On depression, development and death.* San Francisco: W. H. Freeman.

Seligman, M. E. P. (1991). *Learned optimism.* New York: A. A. Knopf.

Seligman, M. E. P. (2000). Positive psychology: An introduction. *American Psychologist, 55,* 5–14.

Seligman, M. E. P. (2002). *Authentic happiness.* New York: The Free Press.

Seligman, M. E. P., & Csikszentmihalyi, M. (2000). Positive psychology: An introduction. *American Psychologist, 55,* 5–14.

Selye, H. (1976). *The stress of life.* New York: McGraw-Hill.

Shaddock, D. (2000). *Contexts and connections: An intersubjective systems approach to couples therapy.* New York: Basic Books.

Sharf, R. S. (2004). *Theories of psychotherapy and counseling: Concepts and cases* (3rd ed.). Pacific Grove, CA: Brooks/Cole-Thomson Learning.

Sherry, A. (2007). Constructivist counseling. In A. B. Welfel, E. R., & Patterson, L. E. (Eds.), *The counseling process: A multitheoretical integrative approach.* Belmont, CA: Thomson-Brooks/Cole.

Siegelman, E. Y. (1990). *Metaphor and meaning in psychotherapy.* New York: Guilford.

Sifneos, P. E. (1992). *Short-term anxiety-provoking psychotherapy: A treatment manual.* New York: Basic Books.

Sklare, G. B. (1997). *Brief counseling that works: A solution-focused approach for school counselors.* Thousand Oaks, CA: Corwin Press.

Snyder, C. R. (2002) Hope theory: Rainbows of the mind, *Psychological Inquiry, 13,* 249–275.

Snyder, C. R., & Lopez, S. (2002). *Handbook of positive psychology.* Oxford: Oxford University Press.

Snyder, M. (2003). The many me's of the self-monitor. In W. A. Lesko (Ed.), *Readings in social psychology* (5th ed., pp. 130–137). Boston: Allyn & Bacon.

Sommers-Flanagan, J., & Sommers-Flanagan, R. (1993). *Foundations of therapeutic interviewing.* Boston: Allyn & Bacon.

Spangenberg, J. J. (2003). The cross-cultural relevance of person-centered counseling in postapartheid South Africa. *Journal of Counseling and Development, 81,* 48–54.

Stacey, R. (1996). *Complexity and creativity in organisations.* San Francisco: Berrett-Koehler.

Stanovich, K. E. (2004). *The robot's rebellion: Finding meaning in the age of Darwin.* Chicago: University of Chicago Press.

Starkey, C. (2006). Meaning and affect. *The Pluralist, 1,* 288–103.

Staton, A. R., Benson, A. J., Briggs, M. K., Cowan, W. E., Echterling, L. E., Evans, W. F., McKee, J. E., Presbury, J. H., & Stewart, A. L. (2007). *Becoming a community counselor: Personal and professional explorations.* Boston: Lahaska/Houghton Mifflin.

Stein, N., Folkman, S., Trabasso, T., & Richards, T. A. (1997). Appraisal and goal processes as predictors of psychological well-being in bereaved caregivers. *Journal of Personality and Social Psychology, 72,* 872–884.

Strasser, F., & Strasser, A. (1997). *Existential time-limited therapy: The wheel of existence.* Chichester: John Wiley & Sons.

Strogatz, S. H. (2003). *Sync: The emerging science of spontaneous order.* New York: Hyperion.

Strupp, H. H., & Binder, J. L. (1984). *Psychotherapy in a new key: A guide to time-limited dynamic psychotherapy.* New York: Basic Books.

Sue, D. W., & Sue, D. (2003). *Counseling the culturally diverse: Theory and practice* (4th ed.). New York: John Wiley & Sons.

Sullivan, H. S. (1970). *The psychiatric interview.* New York: W. W. Norton.

Talmon, M. (1990). *Single session therapy.* San Francisco: Jossey-Bass.

Taube, C. A., Goldman, H. H., Burns, B. J., & Kessler, L. G. (1988). High users of outpatient health service. I: Definition and characteristics. *American Journal of Psychiatry, 145,* 19–24.

Tedeschi, R. G., & Calhoun, L. G. (1995). *Trauma & transformation: Growing in the aftermath of suffering.* Thousand Oaks, CA: Sage.

Tedeschi, R. G., Park, C. L., & Calhoun, L. G. (Eds.). (1998). *Posttraumatic growth: Positive changes in the aftermath of crisis.* Mahwah, NJ: Erlbaum.

Teyber, E. (2006). *Interpersonal process in therapy: An integrative model* (5th ed.). Pacific Grove, CA: Brooks/Cole.

Tohn, S. L., & Oshlag, J. A. (1995). *Crossing the bridge: Integrating solution-focused therapy into clinical practice.* Natick, MA: Solutions Press.

Tohn, S. L., & Oshlag, J. A. (1996). Solution-focused therapy with mandated clients. In S. D. Miller, M. A. Hubble, & B. L. Duncan (Eds.), *Handbook of solution-focused brief therapy* (pp. 152–183). San Francisco: Jossey-Bass.

Toulmin, S. (1982). *The return to cosmology: Postmodern science and the theology of nature.* Chicago: University of Chicago Press.

Turkington, C. (1996). *The brain encyclopedia.* New York: Facts on File.

Vaughan, S. C. (1997). *The talking cure.* New York: Henry Holt & Company.

Walter, J. L., & Peller, J. E. (1992). *Becoming solution-focused in brief therapy.* New York: Brunner/Mazel.

Ward, M. (2001). *Beyond chaos: The underlying theory behind life, the universe, and everything.* New York: Thomas Dunne Books.

Watson, D. (2002). Positive affectivity: The disposition to experience pleasurable emotional states. In C. R. Snyder & S. J. Lopez (Eds.), *Handbook of positive psychology* (pp. 106–119). New York: Oxford University Press.

Watt, D. F. (2005). Social bonds and the nature of empathy. *Journal of Consciousness Studies, 12,* 185–209.

Watzlawick, P., Weakland, J. H., & Fisch, R. (1974). *Change: Principles of problem formation and problem resolution.* New York: W. W. Norton.

Weakland, J. H., & Fisch, R. (1992). Brief therapy—MRI style. In S. H. Budman, M. F. Hoyt, & S. Friedman (Eds.), *The first session in brief therapy* (pp. 306–323). New York: Guilford.

Webster's New World Dictionary of the American Language (1972). (Second college edition). New York, World Pub., D. R. Guralnik, Editor in Chief.

Weiner-Davis, M. (1993). *Divorce busting: A revolutionary and rapid program for staying together.* New York: Summit.

Weingarten, K. (2001). Making sense of illness narratives: Braiding theory, practice and the embodied life. Retrieved from http://www.dulwichcentre.com.au.kaethearticle.html.

Welfel, E. R., & Patterson, L. E. (2005). *The counseling process: A multitheoretical integrative approach.* Belmont, CA: Thomson Brooks/Cole.

Wethington, E. (2003). Turning points as opportunities for psychological growth. In C. L. M. Keyes & J. Haidt (Eds.), *Flourishing: Positive psychology and the life well-lived* (pp. 37–53). Washington, DC: American Psychological Association.

White, M. (1988, Summer). The externalizing of the problem and the reauthoring of lives and relationships. *Dulwich Centre Newsletter,* 3–21.

White, M. (1995). *Re-authoring lives: Interviews and essays.* Adelaide, Australia: Dulwich Centre Publications.

White, M., & Epston, D. (1990). *Narrative means to therapeutic ends.* New York: W. W. Norton.

White, S. P. (2002). *New ideas about new ideas: Insights on creativity from the world's leading Innovators.* New York: Perseus.

Wickman, S. A. (2000, March). Making something of it: An analysis of the conversation and language of Carl Rogers and Gloria. *Dissertation Abstracts International, 60*(8–13, Sect. B), 4260.

Wickman, S. A., & Campbell, C. (2003). The coconstruction of congruency: Investigating the conceptual metaphors of Carl Rogers and Gloria. *Counselor Education and Supervision, 43,* 15–26.

Williams, R., & Williams, V. (1998). *Anger kills: Seventeen strategies for controlling the hostility that can harm your health.* New York: Harper.

Wilson, J. P. (1989). *Trauma, transformation, and healing: An integrative approach to theory, research, and post-traumatic therapy.* New York: Brunner/Mazel.

Wilson, P. (2000). *The Athenian institution of the khoregia: The chorus, the city and the stage.* Cambridge: Cambridge University Press.

Witmer, J. M. (1985). *Pathways to personal growth.* Muncie, IN: Accelerated Development.

Wolfe, T. (1998). *You can't go home again.* New York: Harper Collins. (Original published in 1934)

Wong, Y. J. (2006). Strength-centered therapy: A social constructionist, virtues-based psychotherapy. *Psychotherapy: Theory, Research, Practice, Training, 43,* 133–146.

Worthington, E. L., & Berry, J. W. (2005). Virtues, vices, and character education. In W. R. Miller & H. D. Delaney (Eds.), *Judeo-Christian perspectives on psychology: Human nature, motivation, and change* (pp. 145–164). Washington, DC: American Psychological Association.

Wright, K. J. T. (1976). Metaphor and symptom: A study of integration and its failure. *International Review of Psychoanalysis, 3,* 97–109.

Yalom, I. D. (1980). *Existential psychotherapy.* New York: Basic Books.

Yalom, I. D. (2002). *The gift of therapy: An open letter to a new generation of therapists and their patients.* New York: HarperCollins.

Yerkes, R. M., & Dodson, J. D. (1908). The relation of strength of stimulus to rapidity of habit formation. *Journal of Comparative and Neurological Psychology, 18,* 459–482.

Young, M. E. (1992). *Counseling methods and techniques: An eclectic method.* New York: Merrill/Macmillan.

Young, M. E. (1998). *Learning the art of helping: Building blocks and techniques* (2nd ed.). Upper Saddle River, NJ: Merrill/Prentice Hall.

Young, M. E. (2005). *Learning the art of helping: Building blocks and techniques* (3rd ed.). Upper Saddle River, NJ: Merrill/Prentice Hall.

Zahavi, D. (2005). *Subjectivity and selfhood: Investigating the first-person perspective.* Cambridge, MA: MIT Press.

AUTHOR INDEX

SUBJECT INDEX